Education, Culture and Values

Volume I

The six volumes that comprise the *Education, Culture and Values* series bring together contributions from experts around the world to form, for the first time, a comprehensive treatment of the current concern with values in education. The series seeks to address this concern in the context of cultural and values diversity.

The first three volumes provide a wide-ranging consideration of the diversity of values in education at all levels, and thus represent a framework for the second three volumes which focus more specifically on values education (moral, religious, spiritual and political) *per se*. The six volumes, therefore, bring the fundamental domain of values together with the important issue of pluralism to generate new, fruitful and progressive reflection and exemplars of good practice.

The series will be of huge benefit and interest to educators, policy makers, parents, academics, researchers and student teachers. The six volumes contain:

- diverse and challenging opinions about current educational concerns and reforms in values education
- chapters from more than 120 contributors of international repute from 23 different countries
- conceptual clarification and theoretical analysis
- empirical studies, reports of practical projects and guidance for good practice.

Volumes I–III: Values Diversity in Education

Volume I – Systems of Education: Theories, Policies and Implicit Values is concerned with the theoretical and conceptual framework for reflecting about values, culture and education and thus provides an introduction to the series as a whole. It is concerned with state and policy level analysis across the world.

Volume II – Institutional Issues: Pupils, Schools and Teacher Education considers values and culture at the institutional level. What constitutes a good 'whole school' approach in a particular area? There are discussions of key issues and reports of whole-school initiatives from around the world. Several chapters focus on the vital issue of teacher education.

Volume III – Classroom Issues: Practice, Pedagogy and Curriculum focuses on the classroom: pedagogy, curriculum and pupil experience. Areas of curriculum development include the relatively neglected domains of mathematics and technology, as well as the more familiar literature and drama. There is a useful section on aesthetic education.

Volumes IV–VI: Values Education in Diversity

Volume IV – Moral Education and Pluralism is focused on moral education and development in the context of cultural pluralism. There are highly theoretical discussions of difficult philosophical issues about moral relativism as well as practical ideas about good practice.

Volume V – Spiritual and Religious Education distinguishes religious and spiritual education and takes a multifaith approach to pedagogic, curricular and resource issues. The important issue of collective worship is also addressed.

Volume VI – Politics, Education and Citizenship is concerned with political education and citizenship. Again chapters from several countries lend an international perspective to currently influential concerns and developments, including democratic education, human rights, national identity and education for citizenship.

Education, Culture and Values

Volume I

Systems of Education: Theories, Policies and Implicit Values

Edited by
Mal Leicester, Celia Modgil
and Sohan Modgil

London and New York

First published 2000 by Falmer Press
11 New Fetter Lane, London EC4P 4EE

Simultaneously published in the USA and Canada
by Falmer Press, 19 Union Square West, New York, NY 10003

Falmer Press is an imprint of the Taylor & Francis Group

Typeset in Galliard by RefineCatch Limited, Bungay, Suffolk
Printed and bound in Great Britain by
TJ International Ltd, Padstow, Cornwall

British Library Cataloguing in Publication Data
A catalogue record for this book is available from the British
Library

Library of Congress Cataloging in Publication Data
Systems of education: theories, policies, and implicit values /
    edited by Mal Leicester, Celia Modgil, Sohan Modgil.
      p.   cm. – (Education, culture, and values; v. 1)
    Includes bibliographical references and indexes.
    1. Educational sociology. 2. Values–Study and teaching.
3. Multiculturalism. I. Leicester, Mal. II. Modgil, Celia.
III. Modgil, Sohan. IV. Series.
LC191.S98   1999
306.43–dc21   99–36827
                                              CIP

ISBN 0–7507–1018–7 (6-volume set)
     0–7507–1002–0 (volume I)
     0–7507–1003–9 (volume II)
     0–7507–1004–7 (volume III)
     0–7507–1005–5 (volume IV)
     0–7507–1006–3 (volume V)
     0–7507–1007–1 (volume VI)

Contents

Contributors

Csaba Bánfalvy Head of Department of Social Sciences, Bárczi Gustav College of Special Education, Budapest

Heesoon Bai Assistant Professor of Philosophy of Education, Simon Fraser University, Burnaby, Canada

Donald A. Biggs Professor and Director of Urban Education, University at Albany, New York, USA

Lawrence A. Blum Professor of Educational Psychology, School of Education, University of Massachusetts, USA

Mike Bottery Senior Lecturer in Education, School of Education, University of Hull, UK

Karen Caple Coordinator, Schools Values Project, Association of Independent Schools of Western Australia, Australia

Stephen Chilton Associate Professor in Political Science, Department of Political Science, University of Minnesota, USA

Ann Chinnery Doctoral candidate in the Faculty of Education, Curriculum Theory and Implementation Program, Simon Fraser University, Burnaby, Canada

Robert Colesante Assistant Professor of Education, Seina College, New York, USA

David Crosier Staff member of the Higher Education Section, The Council of Europe at Strasbourg

Karin Franzsen Senior Lecturer in the Department of Secondary School Teacher Training, University of South Africa

Jennie Harré Hindmarsh Associate Director, National Services, Te Papa Tongarewa Museum of New Zealand, Wellington, New Zealand

Elna van Heerden Senior Lecturer in the Department of Education Studies, Rand Afrikaans University, Johannesburg

Terry Hyland Lecturer in Continuing Education, Department of Continuing Education, University of Warwick, UK

Ken Kempner Associate Professor in Education, College of Education, University of Oregon, Eugene, USA

Mal Leicester Senior Lecturer in Continuing Education, Warwick University, UK

Lorraine M. Ling Deputy Head, Graduate School of Education, La Trobe University, Bundoora

Anne Meyer Undergraduate student, University of Minnesota, USA

Celia Modgil Senior Lecturer in Education, Goldsmiths College, London University, UK

Sohan Modgil Reader in Educational Research and Development, University of Brighton, UK

Imanol Ordorika Associate Professor of Social Sciences and Education, Institute for Economic Research, Universidad Nacional Autónoma de México

Josep M. Puig Rovira Senior Lecturer in Theory and History of Education, Faculty of Pedagogy, University of Barcelona, Spain

Peter A. Roberts Reader in Linguistics, Department of Languages and Linguistics, Faculty of Humanities, University of West Indies, West Indies

Clinton D. W. Robinson Director, International Programmes, SIL UK, UK

Basil R. Singh Reader in Education, University of Sunderland, UK

Joshua Smith Advisement Services Center, University of Albany, New York, USA

Paulo Renato Souza Head of Cultural Section, Brazilian Embassy, London, UK

Keith Sullivan Senior Lecturer and Associate Dean of Postgraduate Students in Education, Victoria University of Wellington, New Zealand

Elza Venter Lecturer in the Department of Secondary School Teacher Training, University of South Africa

Maggie Woodrow Executive Director, European Access Network, University of Westminister, UK

Editors' Foreword

This is one volume in a series of six, each concerned with education, culture and values. Educators have long recognized that 'education' is necessarily value laden and, therefore, that value issues are inescapable and fundamental, both in our conceptions of education and in our practice of it. These issues are particularly complex in the context of cultural pluralism. In a sense the collection is a recognition, writ large, of this complexity and of our belief that since values are necessarily part of education, we should be explicit about what they are, and about why we choose those we do and who the 'we' is in relation to the particular conception and practices in question.

The first three volumes in the series deal with values diversity in education – the broader issues of what values ought to inform education in and for a plural society. The second three focus more narrowly on values education as such – what is the nature and scope of moral education, of religious and political education and of political and citizenship education in and for such a society? Thus collectively they consider both **values diversity in education** and **values education in diversity**. Individually they each have a particular level. Thus volumes 1–3 cover the levels of system, institution and classroom. Volumes 4–6 focus respectively on moral education, religious and spiritual education, political and citizenship education. This structure is intended to ensure that the six volumes in the series are individually discrete but complementary.

Given the complexity of the value domain and the sheer diversity of values in culturally plural societies it becomes clear why 120 chapters from 23 countries merely begin to address the wealth of issues relating to 'Education, Culture and Values'.

Mal Leicester, Celia Modgil
and Sohan Modgil

This paper by the late Professor Barry Troyna is published as a memorial to him and as a tribute to his great contribution to antiracist education. Barry had agreed to contribute a paper to this series but died before he could do so. He had, however, provided this previously published article to indicate the area in which he intended to write.

Beyond Reasonable Doubt? Researching 'Race' in Educational Settings[1]

BARRY TROYNA

Introduction

There is now a prodigious literature on the politics, theory and practice of social research. Within this corpus of work, research on 'race' and racism has attracted some of the more fierce debates, linked as it is to issues of theoretical purchase on practical relevance (Bourne, 1980; Cashmore and Troyna, 1981; Centre for Contemporary Cultural Studies, 1982; Gabriel, 1994). Increasingly, these debates have come to be refracted through the lens of educational research. In this context, the longstanding controversy surrounding the relative merits of multicultural and antiracist education continues to figure prominently (see for instance, May, 1994; Troyna, 1993a). But there are other areas of contention. Some of these stem from critics who have demanded a radical reassessment of the status and efficacy of antiracist education (including its 'reification' of bifurcated identities), especially as it was constituted and diffused through local education authorities and school policies in the 1980s (see Gillborn, 1995; Gilroy, 1990; Macdonald *et al.*, 1989; Modood, 1992, 1994; Rattansi, 1992). Another area of dispute crystallizes around the ethics and politics of 'doing research on race related issues in education' (see Leicester and Taylor, 1992; Troyna and Carrington, 1993). Specifically, this debate focuses on the extent to which 'partisanship' – often interpreted purely and simply as 'bias' – might be said to articulate with and inform legitimately, or, conversely, to corrupt and invalidate, the entire process of self-proclaimed antiracist research.

Broadly speaking, this article is intended to highlight some of the main features in the debate about 'race-related' research as it is configured in the 1990s. More particularly, I want to provide a reflexive account of 'doing partisan research', especially as it articulates with antiracist principles. I am not concerned here, then, with the techniques of doing antiracist research – the nuts and bolts of the enterprise – but with its methodology, a term that Alvin Gouldner argues 'is infused with ideologically resonant assumptions about what the social world is, and what the relation between them is' (1971, pp. 50–1).

I will sustain my argument by offering a position statement on partisan research which contrasts with the stance adopted by, what I have called elsewhere, the 'Methodological Purists' (Troyna, 1993b; see also Gillborn, 1995; Hammersley *et al.*, forthcoming). This group of critics would seem to see 'partisanship' and the political nature of social and educational research as anathema to their own conception of this process (see for instance, Hammersley, 1993a, 1994). The rationale for their intervention into the debate about antiracist education is their assertion that the 'partisanship' of some of its more prolific exponents within the research community has contaminated the data 'collected' in their various qualitative and quantitative studies. According to the 'Methodological Purists' this has led to the interpretation and presentation of 'findings' which chime discordantly with the empirical evidence at hand in their respective studies of racial inequality in schools. In short, they accuse antiracist researchers of distorting their data in order to sustain their political convictions.

I will elaborate on and respond to the 'Methodological Purists'' critique in the second section of the article. I want to begin, however, with a closer look at 'partisanship'.

Partisan research: an oxymoron?

It is a truism to say that researching 'race' in educational (and all other) settings is a tricky business. The enterprise intersects with, and provides the context for, some of the most lively debates associated with social scientific research (see Stanfield, 1994, for instance). It seems to be the case that no stone on the 'race' and education research terrain has been left unturned. As a result, it is around race-related research, as a loosely-tied collection of field-based studies, that exchanges between social scientists have been at their most vital, occasionally vitriolic, sometimes even hostile. It is no exaggeration to say that, in relation to education, this debate has often reached 'fever pitch' as synopses of some of the more animated disputes around methodology provided by David Gillborn (1995) and myself (1993a) testify.

Generally, these exchanges have centred on all aspects of the research process, from conception to dissemination. Among the issues that have been put under the spotlight are: the stance and status of the researcher; the rationale for the research; the focus of the researcher's gaze; the way in which key theoretical, conceptual and analytical terms are conceptualized and operationalized; the conduct of the researcher and the nature of the social relations which are established 'in the field'; processes through which the data are produced, interpreted and presented; and the un/intended audiences of the research report. Issues such as these, of course, are neither new in the field of race relations (Myrdal, 1944; Lal, 1986; CCCS, 1982) nor confined to that field of enquiry. Rather, they represent those enduring controversies which go to the very heart of more fundamental questions about epistemology and methodology in the social sciences (Gitlin, 1994; O'Connell *et al.*, 1994). They also articulate with various ideas about the role of 'the intellectual' in the social and political construction of 'social reality' – within which 'race relations' figure prominently.

It is the juxtaposition of the researcher's political and ideological convictions, on the one hand, and the 'detached', 'impartial', 'neutral' and 'objective' perspective associated with traditional ideas about research, on the other, that has made disputes about studies of 'race' and education most heated and difficult to resolve. What is seen to be of utmost concern here is the issue of 'bias'. This is thrown into even sharper relief when researchers make it clear that they are committed to that genre of social scientific inquiry known as 'partisanship'. One of the fullest and most public expressions of this position is to be found in the work of the American sociologist, Howard Becker, which not only focused on the 'underdog' (prostitutes, drug-takers for instance) but which answered his rhetorical question for social researchers, 'whose side are we on?' emphatically in favour of subordinate groups (Becker, 1967). This form of partisan research comprises a range of methodologies of which 'conviction research' (Smith, 1993), 'empowerment' (Troyna, 1994a), 'anti-discriminatory practitioner research' (Broad, 1994) and the 'advocacy position' (Cameron *et al.*, 1992) constitute some of its principal forms. What unites these approaches is the conviction that research takes place in social settings where power relations are stratified by class, 'race', gender, age and other structural characteristics. It is argued that in this 'unequal world', researchers have the potential to exacerbate and reinforce inequalities both *within* and beyond the research process. Indeed, it goes further in arguing that the inherent properties of mainstream research – the avowed concern for 'objectivity' and approval of traditional 'researcher'/'researched' relationships in the field – provide social science's benediction to these inequalities. The researcher's commitment to the academic mode of production helps to consolidate this set of power relations because, as Ruth Frankenberg notes, in this scenario 'the researcher sets the agenda and edits the material, analyses it, publishes it' and advances her or his career as a consequence (Frankenberg, 1993, p. 29). The superordinate status assumed by the researcher within orthodox social and educational research relations is what Joyce Ladner, the African-American sociologist, drew attention to more than a generation ago. In her indictment of what she saw as the imperialist nature of such research Ladner argued that:

> the relationship between the *researcher* and his [sic] *subjects*, by definition, resembles that of the oppressor and the oppressed, because it is the oppressor who defines the problem, the nature of the research and, to some extent, the quality of interaction between him and his subjects. (1973, p. 419, original emphasis)

It would seem, therefore, that the priority for the researcher committed to 'partisan' research, or one of its constituent elements, is to challenge the conventions of orthodox research by contributing towards social change in and through their research activities.[2] Accordingly, the researcher's political commitments and declared values help to shape and direct all aspects of the research act. In the words of Deborah Cameron and her colleagues, the 'advocacy position', an exemplar of 'partisan research', is characterized by 'a commitment on the part of the researcher not just to do research *on* subjects but research *on and for* subjects'. Cameron and her co-authors continue:

> Such a commitment formalises what is actually a rather common development in field situations, where a researcher is asked to use her skills or her authority as an 'expert' to defend subjects' interests, getting involved in their campaigns for healthcare or education, cultural autonomy or political and land rights, and speaking on their behalf. (1992, p. 15)

In the same vein, Bob Broad, advocating 'antidiscriminatory practitioner research', insists that the rationale for this methodology is to be found in its concern to be '*actively working for change against all forms of discrimination and oppression*' (1994, p. 165, original emphasis). Some proponents of partisan research go even further. Lee Harvey (1990), for instance, in his presentation of 'critical social research' is insistent that those working from this perspective must be committed to deploying their social analysis towards an explicit political strategy to overcome oppression. For Harvey, there are two defining characteristics of critical social research. The first is that it

> does not take the apparent social structure, social processes, or accepted history for granted. It tries to dig beneath the surface of appearances. It asks how social systems really work, how ideology or history conceals the processes which oppress and control people. (1990, p. 6)

It could be argued against Harvey's claim here for uniqueness that this imperative does not depart too far from most other understandings of the social research enterprise, especially those which derive from sociological perspectives (Rex, 1974, p. 8). His second criterion, however, is that critical social research should go beyond description and analysis so that:

> Not only does it want to show what is happening, it is also concerned with doing something about it. Critical social research includes an overt political

struggle against oppressive social structures. (1990, p. 20)

Despite some fundamental, perhaps even intractable, problems associated with translating some of these ideals of partisan research into practice (see Troyna, 1994a for discussion), it is a genre which has attracted the support of an increasing number of antiracists, feminists, neo-Marxists and critical theorists. To reiterate: their declared intention is to frame their research in ways which go beyond what is seen as the researcher's traditional task of describing 'what is going on' and explaining 'why'. As 'partisan researchers' their aim is to give centre stage to the notion of praxis: declaring an intention to harness political action to their research activities (see Green, 1993). For them, unmasking oppressive structures and contributing to social and political change, where it is possible and appropriate to do so, is seen as integral to, even the *raison d'être* of research.

There are then different interpretations of how to undertake social inquiry and what its most appropriate goals might be. Against this background, serious questions have been raised about the epistemological criteria by which knowledge derived from research is measured and assessed. As a corollary, doubts have also been expressed about the suitability and efficacy of technical concepts such as 'authenticity', 'validity', 'reliability', 'generalizability', even 'data' in research discourses. It is argued that, because these and cognate terms are based on 'professional' norms and assumptions, they reflect a specific and partial understanding of research and the grounds on which it should be assessed. Put another way, because the vocabulary derives from a particular perspective, or epistemology, the discourse in which these terms figure is ideologically tainted. Dorothy Smith (1987) follows Joyce Ladner's analogy, to which I referred earlier, in arguing that the framework in which 'mainstream' sociological research takes place smacks of 'cultural imperialism'. For Smith, the outcome is 'to impose the concepts and terms in which the world of men is thought as the concepts and terms in which women must think their world' (1987, p. 86).

As already noted, debates around such issues are now in full flow. A careful interrogation of those concepts which were once accepted as the stock-in-trade of the social and educational researcher now forms part of the agenda for those working in 'postpositivist' paradigms. In this context, the imperfections and fallibility of research – and researchers – are openly acknowledged. Those working within these paradigms ensure that the conduct and reporting of their research reflect the understanding that it is 'something carried out by flesh and blood figures who are engaged in real life activities' (Jacubowicz, 1991, p. 5; see also Guba and Lincoln, 1994).

Postpositivist researchers tend to favour qualitative over quantitative techniques and to carry out their inquiries in their subjects' 'natural settings'. They also avoid conducting their research under experimental or laboratory conditions, settings which are *more* highly favoured by positivist modes of enquiry. The rationale for this is clear: qualitative researchers are interested in documenting and interpreting experiences as they are shaped by and within day-to-day experiences. It is for this reason that postpositivist paradigms attract the particular support of feminist scholars (see, Lather, 1991; Lennon and Whitford, 1994; Reinharz, 1992; Skeggs, 1994; Weiner, 1994); those theorizing and researching from postmodernist and post-structuralist perspectives (e.g. Denzin, 1992; Scheurich, 1992); and, of course, scholars who base their inquiries explicitly on the principles of 'partisanship'. Whatever the specific context, the challenges of postpositivism have thrown into disarray the taken-for-granted assumptions and ways of working which, until fairly recently, tended to be sacrosanct to the educational and social researcher. The historian of science, Margaret Jacob, (1992) characterizes the vast changes which now challenge the credo of social scientific research as a 'cognitive revolution'. The sociologist, Norman Denzin, agrees. It is his view that: 'The age of a *putative* value-free social science appears to be over' (1994, p. 501, emphasis added). Well, maybe it is and maybe it isn't.

The term 'putative' is crucial here, of course. Denzin makes clear his belief that social science could never claim to be value-free; he insists that assertions to the contrary amount to no more than 'wishful thinking' and are both illusory and disingenuous. Following Denzin, I want to acknowledge and celebrate, rather than try to conceal, the fact that research and researchers are socially situated (Troyna, 1994b). What we do shapes and constrains what we can know. So in contrast to some educational researchers (e.g. Kelly, 1978; Walford, 1994) I would want to argue that, by its very

nature, the research process, in its entirety, carries the imprimatur of the researcher's political and ethical values. This is how Sandra Harding, the feminist social scientist puts the case:

> Knowledge is grounded in particular historical social situations. In societies where power is organised hierarchically – for example, by class, race or gender – there is no possibility of an Archimedean perspective, one that is disinterested, impartial, value-free or detached from the particular, historical social relations in which everyone participates. (1991, pp. 58–9)

Note: Harding does not suggest that research should be sacrificed entirely on the altar of value-laden and political convictions. Her argument is that those values and political ideals are integral to the way the researcher carries out the activity. They cannot be wished away. In what amounts to a restatement of the sociologist C. Wright Mills's exposition on the relationship between social science and politics (1959, pp. 177–94), Harding goes on to say that researchers should not distort their efforts or contrive interpretations which end up being in accord with their values and politics but which are not supported by their data:

> It is possible to make reasonable judgements that some beliefs are better supported by empirical evidence than others. No one can tell the one, eternally, true, perfect story about the way the world is; but we can tell some stories about ourselves, nature and social life which can be shown with good evidence to be far less partial and distorted – less false – than the dominant ones. (Harding, 1991, pp. 59–60)

As we shall soon see, phrases such as 'reasonable judgements' and 'empirical evidence' are, in themselves, contentious. They draw their vitality and legitimacy from specific intellectual traditions, speak to particular methodological discourses and therefore have the potential to open the floodgates to spirited debate. For instance, Harding's appeal to 'reasonable judgements' and 'empirical evidence' would fail to impress researchers who are committed to postmodern, poststructural theories and the interpretive conditionality of all representations.

A recent debate in the *Journal of Contemporary Ethnography* (1992) exemplifies the relativist position adopted by postmodernists. This issue of *JCE* focuses on an exchange between William Foote Whyte and W.A. Marianne Boelen about the 'reality of Cornerville' as it is represented in Whyte's *Street Corner Society*, published in 1955. Boelen contests Whyte's interpretations of life in 'Cornerville' on the basis of her series of encounters, observations and interviews with some of his original respondents between 1970 and 1989 (Boelen, 1992; Whyte, 1992). The debate in *JCE* is extended by each of the 'combatants' calling upon witnesses from 'Cornerville' in an attempt to strengthen the authenticity of their respective interpretations (Adler *et al.*, 1992).

Norman Denzin is another contributor to this special issue of *JCE*. However, he challenges the basis on which the debate is predicated, insisting that both Whyte and Boelen are constrained by a positivist, social realist epistemology. For Denzin, then, writing from a postmodernist perspective, neither Whyte nor Boelen has 'told it like it is'. Why? Because there is no 'it', no 'obdurate social world'. He elaborates by insisting that there 'are few facts: concrete occurrences with single, shared interpretations. Instead, there are only facticities or concrete social experiences given different meanings by the same and different individuals over the course of time' (Denzin, 1992, p. 125).

It is on these grounds that postmodernism is said to presage a crisis of reason and to represent a challenge to certainties, even truth. It is for this reason, however, that there are dangers associated with postmodernist arguments. Taken to their logical conclusion they could be used to nullify any kind of collective political opposition to inequalities, including those based on perceived racial differences (see Vieux, 1994). Consequently, I think it is important to acknowledge Jorge Larrain's caveat about postmodernist logic as containing the potential to be 'a convenient ideology of the status quo' (1994, p. 312).

I have argued in this section that social and educational research takes place in an 'unequal world'. Whether, and to what extent, this should figure in the way researchers construct their methodological inquiries is a matter which continues to tantalize.

There are those social and educational researchers, for instance, who elaborate the tenets of positivism in a determined effort to protect and remain loyal to the principles of 'objectivity', 'disinterest' and cognate terms as the appropriate criteria by which to assess research. According to this view, the credibility, authenticity, the very legitimacy of their activity would be negated unless these principles were shown to be sacrosanct. Researchers

working from this perspective do not see direct political action or social change as a logical or desirable goal of their activities. This perspective corresponds with the position of the sociologist Max Weber, who in arguing for the principle of value neutrality in research also asserted that the production of knowledge should be the primary goal of researchers (Weber, 1949).

This non-interventionist stance contrasts sharply with partisan researchers who eschew concern with the principle of value neutrality. Rather, they give priority to a conception of research as *praxis*. It follows that the imperative guiding the development, execution and dissemination of their research is that, because they are operating in an 'unequal world', they must not only document what is going on but intervene and challenge any injustices which their inquiries have uncovered. 'Partisanship', then, rejects the discourse of positivism not only as untenable but as exploitative of existing structural inequalities.

Postmodernists share with partisan researchers a healthy scepticism of the epistemological and methodological principles which inform positivist understandings of 'knowledge'. Their belief in the fragmented and localized nature of 'knowledge' leads postmodernists to challenge many of the central tenets of so-called orthodox social and educational research. At the same time, this commitment to indeterminacy and contingency within the postmodernist frame of analysis can be said to lead to political quiescence and deference to the status quo.

The 'methodological purists'

The status of 'evidence' drawn from avowedly 'partisan' research studies of race relations in education has been the subject of a major debate throughout the early-mid 1990s. Represented largely in the pages of the *British Educational Research Journal, New Community, Oxford Review of Education* and *Sociology*, it has centred on how far research has convincingly shown that racism, in both spectacular and insidious forms, constitutes a pervasive feature of life in British schools. The data in favour of the proposition that racism is institutionalized in schools derive from a range of qualitative and quantitative studies of schools up and down the country. But their legitimacy and veracity has been challenged, not only by those explicitly antagonistic to multicultural and antiracist conceptions of educational reform (e.g. Honeyford, 1988; Lewis, 1988), but also by a group of critics, Peter Foster, Roger Gomm and Martyn Hammersley; the 'Methodological Purists'.

The *raison d'être* of the 'Methodological Purists' is based on their belief that the empirical data provided by antiracist researchers are unconvincing. They assert, for instance, that findings adduced from such studies are not conclusive and do not support either the 'teacher ethnocentrism' theory or, more broadly, the contention that racism is an institutionalized and embedded feature of the schools under study. The following represent some of the targets of their criticism.

First, the claim by Bruce Carrington and Edward Wood (1983) that because of the widespread, stereotypical and racist assumption that black people have greater physical than intellectual strengths, teachers in the schools they studied channelled African-Caribbean children into sporting activities at the expense of their academic studies. Second, Cecile Wright's (1986) argument that African-Caribbeans were maltreated in the allocation of students to GCE 'O' level/CSE examination classes because of the teachers' belief that, unlike their white counterparts, they had neither the home background nor resilience to sustain study at the higher level. Third, the argument found in the ethnographies of David Gillborn (1990) and Mairtin Mac an Ghaill (1988) that, because white teachers tend to view African-Caribbean children as representing, inherently, a challenge to their status and authority, they are more likely to use the school's formal and informal rules as a sanction against students from this ethnic background. Fourthly, my interpretation of findings, based on fieldwork carried out by the Commission for Racial Equality (CRE), that students of Bangladeshi origin were, wittingly or otherwise, shortchanged by the routine selective and allocative procedures of a multiracial comprehensive school in England (Troyna, 1991, 1992). This was largely because in a rigidly streamed school, such as the one studied in the CRE research, misallocation on entry to the school – experienced most sharply by the students of Bangladeshi origin because of their relative lack of fluency in English – was likely to have enduring consequences for these students when decisions were taken about who goes where in the allocation of students to high/low credentialling courses.

To repeat: in a series of rejoinders to these studies the 'Methodological Purists' have maintained that the conclusions owe more to the values and ideological convictions of the researchers, their partisanship, in other words, than to the empirical picture provided by the data. For instance, Foster is sceptical of the studies by Carrington and Wood (1983) and Wright (1986) because 'they have serious methodological flaws and fail to provide firm evidence to support the conclusions made by their authors' (Foster, 1990, p. 346). Nor does he accept what Mac an Ghaill and Gillborn say, in their respective studies, about the so-called 'teacher ethnocentrism' theory. Foster counters their arguments by asserting that the studies lack social scientific rigour rendering the 'empirical basis of the claims' made in these studies as 'extremely weak'. Foster also cautions readers against this body of research because the 'teacher ethnocentrism theory is clearly based on a particular value position' and articulates with a model of how 'teachers ought to operate in multi-ethnic schools' (Foster, 1992, p. 95). Gomm's critiques operate along similar lines (1993–1995). In the first of his trenchant responses he points to allegedly 'patchy' and 'confusing' data in my articles which are used 'in an unprincipled way to make a claim [about racial inequality] which they do not warrant' (1993, p. 149). He goes on to propose that the data presented in the 1991 article have been 'obviously massaged into place' and used 'as an excuse for dismissing all the other evidence past, present and future, as junk also' (1993, p. 165). The title of his follow-up critique of this study, entitled 'Strong claims, weak evidence', captures neatly his antagonism towards my interpretation of these research data (Gomm, 1995).

Martyn Hammersley (1993a) has sprung to the defence of Foster and is a major player in the 'Methodological Purists' project (see Hammersley *et al.*, forthcoming). His concerns are less with scrutinizing the intricacies of empirically-based research papers and manuscripts, more with broader epistemological and methodological questions regarding the vexed relationship between politics and research. Thus, his concerns with antiracist educational research complement, to a greater or lesser degree, his reservations about the allegedly distinctive features of feminist methodology. His own position on the relationship between research and politics is clear and unproblematic: 'For me', he writes, 'the point of research is to produce knowledge, not to transform the world, or to achieve any other practical result' (1994, p. 293). It follows from this belief that politics and research can be neatly separated that it is 'an essential requirement of a research community' for researchers to 'operate on the initial assumption that critics are behaving reasonably' (1993b, p. 340). And in his attempt to resolve the disputes between antiracist researchers and the 'Methodological Purists' he suggests that in any research, claims and evidence must be judged on the basis of two considerations: plausibility in relation to knowledge we currently take as beyond reasonable doubt, and credibility in relation to judgements about the likelihood of various sorts of error (Hammersley, 1993b, p. 340).

What is immediately striking about these observations is that they are inherently conservative. For a start, it is doubtful that we can take seriously his appeal to the 'reasonable behaviour' of 'the research community' as a legitimate or real safeguard against bias in the way researchers present and defend 'the truth of their claims' (1993a, p. 438). Why? Because:

> If all or even most social scientists share the same unrecognised biases, as is sometimes the case, then the influences of biased selection of evidence will not be immediately recognized. (Ragin, 1994, p. 68)

Social researchers' blindness to the pervasiveness and institutionalization of racism and sexism in social relations, prior to the emergence of antiracist and feminist perspectives within the social sciences, is testimony to the strength of Ragin's argument and the fragility and conservatism of Hammersley's position.

David Silverman also points to the conservative nature which underscores the criteria by which Hammersley wants to assess the efficacy and status of research. Silverman points out: 'If we only accept as valid those accounts which are plausible and credible we are unable to be surprised and condemned to reproduce existing models of the world' (1993, p. 155). Hammersley's criteria, therefore, imply that researchers should defer to what Becker (1970) called traditional 'hierarchies of credibility' in assessing the status and veracity of research. To paraphrase Becker: the findings tend to be 'plausible' and 'credible' when they confirm what everyone knows. And the 'everyone', in this scenario, are those 'at the top' (Becker, 1970, p. 129). Patricia Hill Collins in her critique of what she terms 'the Eurocentric masculinist knowledge-validation pro-

cess' makes a similar point in relation to the ways in which research and the findings it produces are differentially legitimated in a racialized, gendered and classed context. 'For any particular interpretive context', Hill Collins argues:

> New knowledge claims must be consistent with an existing body of knowledge that the group controlling the interpretive context accepts as true. The methods used to validate knowledge claims must also be acceptable to the group controlling the knowledge-validation process.   (1989, p. 753)

It seems to me that what Becker and Hill Collins have to say about the differential credentialling of research exposes the questionable nature of what Hammersley has to say about research 'claims' and 'evidence' for members of a research community who operate on a terrain where voices are not only differentiated but stratified according to class, 'race' and gender. Yet, what is surprising and worrying about Hammersley's criteria is that they are presented (and accepted by the other 'Methodological Purists') as if they are self-evidently protected from ideological contamination: free-standing, hermetically sealed, objective and, above all, rational. This is disingenuous. What is missing from the 'Methodological Purists' critique is a reflexive appraisal of their theoretical and intellectual assumptions which, in turn, would generate the recognition that all researchers, whether or not they are writing from a self-proclaimed partisan stance, speak from 'within a distinct interpretive community, which configures, in its special way, the multicultural, gendered components of the research act' (Denzin and Lincoln, 1994, p. 11).

Conclusion

In this article I have questioned the claim that the term, 'partisan research', constitutes a contradiction in terms by arguing that all research, from its conception through to the production of data, its interpretation and dissemination, reflects a partisanship which derives from the social identity and values of the researcher. To help sustain my argument I have rebutted the recent interventions of a 'triumvirate' of researchers – the 'Methodological Purists' – who have repeatedly accused self-avowedly antiracist researchers of presenting biased and distorted interpretations of events in education which owe more to their political and ideological convictions than to the data they provide in their work. Simply put, the 'Methodological Purists' draw their vitality from their conviction that some antiracist researchers contaminate their data for political and ideological purposes. Among other things, I have argued that the partial understanding of the research process which the 'Methodological Purists' provide, alongside the unquestioning confidence in the universality of their vision of research, reveals a lack of reflexivity that in and of itself helps to shape and sustain a particular and contrived version of what counts as research.

It follows from this that the most important difference between the epistemological standpoint of the 'Methodological Purists' and other social and educational researchers who stake a claim for objectivity, on the one hand, and that adopted by partisan researchers, on the other, is that the values of the latter are explicit and openly incorporated into the research agenda. The audience for self-proclaimed partisan research does, then, have a clearer vision of the enterprise and can judge the analysis from an informed position. As Virginia Olesen (1994) remarks, the acknowledgement of (so-called) 'bias' also has benefits for the researcher. Olesen argues that 'if the researcher is sufficiently reflexive about her project, she can evoke these as resources to guide data gathering and for understanding her own interpretations and behaviour in the research' (1994, p. 165). It is, then, within and through reflexivity that the partisanship of the researcher, and the values which infuse the research process, are made explicit and accountable to the readership. This was precisely the position adopted by Gunnar Myrdal in his methodological appendix to *An American Dilemma* (1944). Myrdal insisted that only when value 'premises are stated explicitly it is possible to determine how valid the conclusions are' (1944, p. 1058).

Writing from a postmodernist position, Denzin insists that it is impossible to prescribe criteria for assessing research which will satisfy the members of a heterogeneous research community. 'Each social science community', according to Denzin (1994), 'has its own criteria for judging the adequacy of any given interpretive statement'. He continues this relativist argument by asserting that 'It is doubtful that a new set of criteria shared by all points of view will, can, or should be developed' (Denzin, 1994, p. 501).

O'Connell Davidson and Layder (1994), however, are wary about this vision of a fragmented 'research community' and the 'methodological Balkanization' which it is likely to engender. For them, what should unite all researchers, and by definition, distinguish their activities from, say, journalism, political rhetoric and personal anecdote, should be their willingness to be reflexive; their attempts to improve and protect the status of their empirical data by triangulation and cognate procedures, and by adopting an ethical approach to the research practice (1994, p. 59). None of these criteria is incompatible with partisan research.

Notes

1 This research paper started life as a contribution to the Racial Equality in Initial Teacher Education project, funded by the Leverhulme Trust (Reference Number F215A.E). I am grateful to Leverhulme and to colleagues on the project for their support in its initial stages. Thanks also to David Halpin, Derek Layder, Sally Tomlinson, Carol Vincent and, in particular, Martyn Denscombe for acting as 'critical friends' in the later phases.

2 It is here that partisan research departs from action research which is more concerned with situational change (see Troyna, 1994a, pp. 17–18 for a more elaborate account of the distinction between the goals of critical social research and action research).

References

Adler, P.A. *et al.* (1992) *Steet Corner Society* revisited: new questions about old issues. *Journal of Contemporary Ethnography* **21** (1), 3–10.

Becker, H. (1967) Whose side are we on? *Social Problems* **14**, 239–47.

Becker, H. (1970) *Sociological Work: Method and Substance*. Chicago: Aldine.

Boelen, W.A.M (1992) *Steet Corner Society* revisited. *Journal of Contemporary Ethnography* **21** (1), 11–51.

Bourne, J. (1980) Cheerleaders and ombudsmen: the sociology of race relations in Britain. *Race and Class* **21** (4), 331–52.

Broad, B. (1994) Anti-discriminatory practitioner social work research: some basic problems and possible remedies. In B. Humphries and C. Truman (eds), *Re-thinking Social Research*. Aldershot: Avebury.

Cameron, D. *et al.* (1992) *Researching Language: Issues of Power and Method*. London: Routledge.

Carrington, B. and Wood, E. (1983) Body talk: images of sport in a multi-racial school. *Multiracial Education* **11** (2), 29–35.

Cashmore, E. and Troyna, B. (1981) Just for white boys? Elitism, racism and research. *Multiracial Education* **10** (1), 43–8.

Centre for Contemporary Cultural Studies (1982) *The Empire Strikes Back*. London: Hutchinson.

Denzin, N. (1992) Whose Cornerville is it anyway? *Journal of Contemporary Ethnography* **21** (1), 120–32.

Denzin, N. (1994) The art and politics of interpretation. In N. Denzin and Y.S. Lincoln (eds), *Handbook of Qualitative Research*. London: Sage.

Denzin, N. and Lincoln, Y. (1994) Introduction: entering the field of qualitative research. In N.K. Denzin and Y.S. Lincoln (eds), *Handbook of Qualitative Research*. London: Sage.

Foster, P. (1990) Cases not proven: an evaluation of two studies of teacher racism. *British Educational Research Journal* **16** (4), 335–49.

Foster, P. (1992) Equal treatment and cultural differences in multi-ethnic schools: a critique of the teacher ethnocentricism theory. *International Studies in Sociology of Education* **2**, 89–103.

Frankenberg, R. (1993) *The Social Construction of Whiteness: White Women, Race Matters*. London: Routledge.

Gabriel, J. (1994) *Racism, Culture, Markets*. London: Routledge.

Gillborn, D. (1990) *'Race', Ethnicity and Education*. London: Unwin Hyman.

Gillborn, D. (1995) *Racism and Antiracism in Real Schools*. Buckingham: Open University Press.

Gilroy, P. (1990) The end of anti-racism. *New Community* **17** (1), 71–83.

Gitlin, A. (ed.) (1994) *Power and Methods: Political Activism and Educational Research*. London: Routledge.

Gouldner, A. (1971) *The Coming Crisis of Western Sociology*. London: Heinemann.

Gomm, R. (1993) Figuring out ethnic equity. *British Educational Research Journal* **19** (2), 147–63.

Gomm, R. (1995) Strong claims, weak evidence: a response to Troyna's ethnicity and the organisation of learning groups. *Educational Research* **37** (1), 79–88.

Green, P. (1993) Taking sides: partisan research on the 1984–1985 miners' strike. In D. Hobbs and T. May (eds), *Interpreting the Field: Accounts of Ethnography*. Oxford: Oxford University Press.

Guba, E.G. and Lincoln, Y.S. (1994) Competing paradigms in qualitative research. In N.K. Denzin and Y.S. Lincoln (eds), *Handbook of Qualitative Research*. London: Sage.

Hammersley, M. (1993a) Research and 'anti-racism': the case of Peter Foster and his critics. *British Journal of Sociology* **44** (3), 429–48.

Hammersley, M. (1993b) On methodological purism: a response to Barry Troyna. *British Educational Research Journal* **19** (4), 339–42.

Hammersley, M. (1994) On feminist methodology: a response. *Sociology* **28** (1), 293–300.

Hammersley, M., Foster, P. and Gomm., R. (forthcoming) *Social Research and the Problem of Educational Inequalities: A Methodological Assessment*. London: Falmer Press.

Harding, S. (1991) *Whose Science? Whose Knowledge? Thinking from Women's Lives*. Buckingham: Open University Press.

Harris, L. (1993) Postmodernism and utopia: an unholy alliance. In M. Cross and M. Keith (eds), *Racism, the City and the State*. London: Routledge.

Harvey, L (1990) *Critical Social Research*. London: Allen and Unwin.

Hill Collins, P. (1989) The social construction of black feminist thought. *Signs: Journal of Women in Culture and Society* **14** (4), 745–73.

Honeyford, R. (1988) *Integration or Disintegration? Towards a Non-racist Society*. London: Claridge Press.

Jacob, M. (1992) Science and politics in the late twentieth century. *Social Research* **59** (3), 487–503.

Jacubowicz, A. (1991) *Race Research and Ethnic Relations in Pluralist Societies*. Research and Policy Papers 1. Bradford: The Race Relations Unit, University of Bradford.

Kelly, A. (1978) Feminism and research. *Women's Studies International Quarterly* **1**, 225–32.

Ladner, J.A. (1973) Tomorrow's tomorrow: the black woman. In J.A. Ladner (ed.), *The Death of White Sociology*. New York: Vintage Books.

Lal, B.B. (1986) The 'Chicago School' of American sociology, symbolic interaction and race relations theory. In J. Rex and D. Mason (eds), *Theories of Race and Relations*. Cambridge: Cambridge University Press.

Larrain, J. (1994) The postmodern critique of ideology. *Sociological Review* **42** (2), 289–314.

Lather, P. (1991) *Getting Smart*. London: Routledge.

Leicester, M. and Taylor, M. (eds) (1992) *Ethics, Ethnicity and Education*. London: Kogan Page.

Lennon, K. and Whitford, M. (eds) (1994) *Knowing the Difference: Feminist Perspectives in Epistemology*. London: Routledge.

Lewis, R. (1988) *Anti-Racist: A Mania Exposed*. London: Quartet Books.

Mac an Ghaill, M. (1988) *Young, Gifted and Black*. Milton Keynes: Open University Press.

Macdonald, I., Bhavaani, R., Khan, L. and John, G. (1989) *Murder in the Playground*. London: Longsight.

May, S. (1994) Review of Barry Troyna's *Racism and Education*. *British Journal of Sociology of Education* **15** (3), 421–30.

Mills C. Wright (1959) *The Sociological Imagination*. New York: Oxford University Press.

Modood, T. (1992) On not being white in Britain: discrimination, diversity and commonality. In M. Leicester and M. Taylor (eds), *Ethics, Ethnicity and Education*. London: Kogan Page.

Modood, T. (1994) Political blackness and British Asians. *Sociology* **28** (4), 859–76.

Myrdal, G. (1944) *An American Dilemma*. New York: Harper and Brothers.

O'Connell Davidson, J. and Layder, D. (1994) *Methods, Sex and Madness*. London: Routledge.

Olesen, V. (1994) Feminisms and models of qualitative research. In N. Denzin and Y. Lincoln (eds), *Handbook of Qualitative Research*. London: Sage.

Ragin, C.C. (1994) *Constructing Social Research*. London: Pine Forge Press.

Rattansi, A. (1992) Changing the subject? Racism, culture and education. In J. Donald and A. Rattansi (eds), '*Race' Culture and Difference*. London: Sage.

Reinharz, S. (1992) *Feminist Methods in Social Research*. Oxford: Oxford University Press.

Rex, J. (1974) *Sociology and the Demystification of the Modern World*. London: Routledge and Kegan Paul.

Rex, J. and Mason, D. (eds) (1986) *Theories of Race and Ethnic Relations*. Cambridge: Cambridge University Press.

Scheurich, J. (1992) A Postmodernist Review of Interviewing: Dominance, Resistance and Chaos. Paper presented to the AERA Annual Conference, San Francisco.

Silverman, D. (1993) *Interpreting Qualitative Data*. London: Sage.

Skeggs, B. (1994) The constraints of neutrality: the 1988 Education Reform Act and feminist research. In D. Halpin and B. Troyna (eds), *Researching Education Policy*. London: Falmer Press.

Smith, D. (1987) *The Everyday Word as Problematic*. Milton Keynes: Open University Press.

Smith, R. (1993) Potentials for empowerment in critical education research. *The Australian Educational Researcher* **20** (2), 75–94.

Stanfield, J.H. (1994) The nebulous state of American race relations theories: anomalies, paradigmatic erosion and decline. *Research in Race and Ethnic Relations* 7, 3–36.

Troyna, B. (1991) Underachievers or underrated? The experience of pupils of South Asian origin in a secondary school. *British Educational Research Journal* **17** (4), 361–76.

Troyna, B. (1992) Ethnicity and the organisation of learning groups: a case study. *Educational Research* **34** (1), 45–56.

Troyna, B. (1993a) *Racism and Education: Research Perspectives*. Buckingham: Open University Press.

Troyna, B. (1993b) Underachiever or misunderstood? A reply to Roger Gomm. *British Educational Research Journal* **19** (2), 167–74.

Troyna, B. (1994a) Blind faith? Empowerment and educational research *International Studies in Sociology of Education* **4** (1), 3–24.

Troyna, B. (1994b) Reforms, research and being reflexive about being reflective. In D. Halpin and B. Troyna (eds), *Researching Educational Policy: Ethical and Methodological Issues*. London: Falmer Press.

Troyna, B. and Carrington, B. (1993) Whose side are we on? Ethical dilemmas in research on 'race' and education. In B. Troyna, *Racism and Education: Research Perspectives*. Buckingham: Open University Press.

Vieux, S. (1994) In the shadow of neo-liberal racism. *Race and Class* **36** (1), 23–32.

Walford, G. (1994) Political commitment in the study of the City Technology College, Kingshurst. In D. Halpin and B. Troyna (eds), *Researching Education Policy: Ethical and Methodological Issues*. London: Falmer Press.

Weber, M. (1949) *The Methodology of the Social Sciences*. New York: Free Press.

Weiner, G. (1994) *Feminism and Education*. Buckingham: Open University Press.

Whyte, W.F. (1992) In defence of *Street Corner Society*. *Journal of Contemporary Ethnography* **21** (1), 52–68.

Wright, C.Y. (1986) School processes: an ethnographic study. In J. Eggleston, D. Dunn and M. Anjali (eds), *Education for Some: The Educational and Vocational Experiences of 15–18-year-old Members of Minority Ethnic Groups*. Stoke-on-Trent: Trentham Books.

Part One

Theories, Concepts and Implicit Values

1 Value Underpinnings of Antiracist and Multicultural Education

LAWRENCE A. BLUM

Values education and multicultural/antiracist education

In the USA values and values education, and multicultural and antiracist education, are matters of vast public concern; yet each has made very little contact with the other. Since the early 1990s movements for moral, value, or character education have made strong inroads in several school districts and schools throughout the country. Yet the values promoted by such programs have tended to be "traditional" ones, such as honesty, self-control, respect, responsibility, courage, fairness, loyalty, rule-abidingness, compassion. Many of these values are seen by some of their proponents as addressing what they take to be a "crisis of values" among American youth, evidenced in teenage pregnancy, an increase in youth violence, greater willingness to cheat in school and to be disrespectful of school and other authorities, and a lack of social concern.

With some exceptions, such as programs influenced by Lawrence Kohlberg's work, these values education programs have failed to engage issues of cultural pluralism, racial discrimination, legacies of racial oppression, continuing economic and social inequities, and, more generally, the rapidly changing ethnic character of the American population. This lacuna is due in part to the generally conservative or moderate character of the values education movement, and in part to a direct reaction against multiculturalism itself. Sometimes multiculturalism is taken to be part of the problem to which values education in the schools is a solution; for example, education emphasizing national loyalty and national community is seen as a counterweight to multiculturalism's alleged valorizing of particular ethno-racial loyalties.

In fact many of the values touted by this conservative/moderate wing of the values education movement do bear on multicultural and antiracist education, either as core values themselves (for example, respect, forms of which underly both multicultural and antiracist education), or as traits of character (for example, courage and responsibility) necessary for individuals to bring about or engage in action directed toward realizing multicultural or antiracist aims.

For its part, the literature of multicultural and antiracist education has also failed to shed light on these connections. This literature has either failed to distinguish multiculturalism's moral and value goals from other educational aims (such as presenting an accurate picture of American or world history, giving due attention to the role of non-white groups and non-western traditions); failed entirely to recognize that multiculturalism and antiracism presuppose and rest upon certain values; or articulated the values – for example, racial equity, or "inclusion" – but failed to explore, ground, or defend them.

Multiculturalism and antiracism: the US and British contexts

I have been using the language of both "multicultural" and "antiracist" education. Thus dual terminology is much more familiar in the British than the American context. The notions of "antiracism" or "antiracist education" have little presence in American educational literature, and in the common discourse of schools themselves. By contrast "multiculturalism" and "multicultural education" are widely familiar. There is nothing in the American context parallel to the visible British political struggles against the National Front and neo-Nazis, nor to local educational authorities that implement what they took or take to be antiracist policies, to ground the notion of "antiracism" in popular consciousness, or at least to make it a widely shared reference point among theorists of education.[1]

American educationalists have not lacked antiracist concerns – disparities in school success among white vs. non-white students, racial discrimination and harassment in schools, racial prejudice and insensitivity among students and teachers, general social inequities of power and economic well being. Rather, these issues have tended to be taken up as part of multicultural education "rightly understood." Some of the most influential multicultural education theorists have come to contrast superficial vs. robust conceptions of multicultural education by the absence or presence of such concerns, whether they are labeled antiracist or not (and they generally are not).[2]

Because of the generally acceptable or even laudatory connotations of "multicultural" in much of the American education community, and the unfamiliar or slightly scary, confrontational resonance of "antiracism," it may be politically wise of these writers to attempt to subsume the latter concerns under the former rubric. However, doing so makes for conceptual and ultimately educational confusion. British educational discourse recognizes the at least partial distinctness of these two approaches, and I will do the same here.

Yet the particular way that the multicultural/antiracist distinction is drawn in the British context is not entirely satisfactory. In particular, it is little better than the American literature in its articulation of the value bases of the two approaches. Sometimes antiracists see their approach as a more adequate, albeit more radical, means to achieve the same goal sought by multiculturalists – namely educational equity among distinct ethno-racial groups. Sometimes the goals themselves are distinct – ethno-cultural maintenance vs. educational equity, for example – yet their evaluative character or basis is not explored.

Despite the inadequacies of the British educational literature concerning links between values and multicultural and antiracist education, it must be said that discussion of these matters is still substantially in advance of the USA. The existence of the Swann Report in 1985 – the product of two prestigious national commissions – addressing questions of education in a culturally pluralistic society with a view to its values and moral dimension, and the public conversation spurred by the report, has no parallel in the USA. Here the public debate, if it can be so dignified, has been shrill, superficial, and reflective of prior political commitments rather than thoughtful and informed attention to the issues. In my discussion, I will focus primarily on the American context for the value underpinnings of antiracist and multicultural education.

Values and their domains

Value education programs in the USA have, by and large, presumed that the values encompassed in those programs are ones to be taught to students as individuals. This focus on the individual is, in part, simply a reflection of a traditional approach to education as directed solely at an individual learner; but it also reflects the conservative influence on the value education movement, one that downplays the importance of social and especially systemic factors in the production of socially unfortunate behavior, in favor of the view that if students just "possessed the right values," we would not have teenage pregnancy, kids shooting each other, and other antisocial behavior.[3]

However, the value dimension of multicultural education cannot be confined to the individual student, as important as that domain is. At least three other domains are involved – teacher, school, and society. Some values appropriate to one of these levels might not be to another, while some may be appropriate to more than one.

Examples of values at the *individual* level might be respect for persons of other cultures, treating people as equals regardless of race, a disposition to intervene to prevent or mitigate racial injustice. *Teachers* are a second locus of multicultural and antiracist values – values meant to inform their practice and professional ethos, primarily in classes. Examples are treating each student fairly, showing respect for the culture of each child, ensuring that each child is given a form of education appropriate to her particular abilities and life circumstances (taking into account race- and culture-based aspects of their experience, and the like). A third locus is the *school*, to which many of the same values apply as to teachers; but these are to be implemented not only in individual classes but throughout the culture of the school as a whole, in its interaction with parents and the community.

Some but not all versions of multicultural education imply that the *society* itself should attempt to embody certain values as well. Exemplifying values might be equality of opportunity, racial integration, affirmative action. A value like equality of opportunity can be practiced at the teacher, the school, or the society-wide level; but it has a somewhat different significance in each venue. At the teacher level it means that the teacher provides as equal an education as she can, taking individual circumstances into account, to all the children in her class. For a school to implement this value means ensuring equal educational resources across different classes and teachers. However, even if one school succeeded in securing equality of educational opportunity within its own boundaries, this goes almost nowhere toward equality of opportunity in society as a whole, given the tremendous inequities in educational resources, qualifications of teachers, staff–student ratios, and the like, among different schools and districts.

While equality of opportunity[4] can operate at teacher/class, school, and society levels, it is not an individual value in the way that, say, respect for cultural difference, treating others as equals, compassion, and courage are. A school or a society can embody, or strive to embody, this value; but an individual cannot. That is, equality of opportunity is not a character value, one implying a complex mix of understanding, attitude, and behavior. However, equality of opportunity can apply at the individual level in a different way. It can be a value that an individual can come to hold, or to believe in. "Held" values involve a much weaker relationship to behavior than do character values. To say that someone believes in equality of opportunity is to say much less about what she actually does than to say that she treats persons as equals.

Nevertheless, held values at the individual level are a not insignificant dimension of multicultural and antiracist education. Moreover, the line between held values and character values cannot be drawn sharply.

Within the domain of individual character values a distinction between *moral* and *civic* values is useful. Though there is no sharp line between these, civic values engage more directly with the polity (at various levels – local, national, and international). Older traditions of "civic education" connected civics very closely with government and with participation in official political processes (voting, petitioning, and the like). However, the conception of civics employed here extends further to encompass civic life or civil society more generally – associations intermediate between the family and the state, such as churches, clubs, neighborhood associations, unions, that affect the quality of interaction between citizens.[5] My own conception goes even further to include the general quality of civic interaction in public spaces outside formal associations. Thus activity that improves the sense of commitment to quality of life in a neighborhood would count as civic activity, even if it were not organized through an actual "neighborhood association."

Accounts of civic values in the literature on civic education and civic life seldom take up issues of race and ethnicity.[6] Yet everyone increasingly recognizes that relations between ethnic and racial groups are deeply unsatisfactory, and that they take a great toll on the quality of civic life in the USA. So values and qualities of character bearing on issues of race and ethnicity should be seen as quite important to civic education in general.

Civic values related to multiculturalism and antiracism include an ability to communicate with persons of different cultures, and to work with them for common civic ends; a disposition to intervene to interrupt instances of racial bigotry and discrimination; a commitment to fostering ideals of racial justice; a sensitivity to when persons who are seen as racially or ethnically "different" are being, or might feel themselves to be, excluded from a collective activity; a disposition to inform oneself about public (including international) issues related to race and ethnicity, and the like. Such qualities are essential to a program of character and civic education informed by multiculturalism and antiracism.

The second subcategory of *individual* values – *moral* values, such as courage, honesty, integrity, justice – are less involved than civic values in direct engagement with one's society. "Justice" as a moral quality, for example, involves being just in one's own dealings with people. It is distinct from the civic value of commitment to social justice in general (though the latter can be seen as an extension of the former). Moral values are not, however, limited to behavior within the domain of one's domestic or personal life (much less to sexuality or gender relations, as the conception of "morality" promoted by religious conservative groups has tended to imply). They also include the personal treatment of strangers, or those otherwise unknown to oneself.

The distinction between moral values and civic values cuts across the other three domains mentioned – teacher, school, society – as well as individual (though the moral is most closely tied to the individual). For example an attempt to make a class or school a form of democratic community involves a civic value that applies to individuals and schools; the attempt to make schools caring environments for each individual student involves a moral value that applies to both individuals and schools.

Antiracism: its value foundations

Let us turn now to the specific values, or families of values, implicated by antiracism and multiculturalism respectively. Antiracist values revolve around racial equity and racial justice, and the evil and wrong of racial hatred and bigotry.[7] The central antiracist value on the moral character level is treating others as human equals independent of their race. This "non-racism," or absence of racial prejudice, is not the same as "color blindness" – not noticing, or entirely overlooking, someone's physical features taken as "racial." Rather, the non-racist attitude acknowledges the historical, social, and experiential differences that "race" signifies, but sees a *common human worth* independent of those differences.

A *civic* antiracist value is the commitment to and disposition to promote racial justice and equity. This civic value has both a negative and a positive dimension. The negative one is to counter racism, for example, by intervening in racist incidents or by protesting racial injustice. The positive involves the promotion of the ideal of racial justice. (Both of these go beyond merely being "*non*-racist" in one's own personal dealings with persons of other races.) These civic values in turn encompass a set of diverse virtues that students can be taught. For example, antiracist interventions often require courage, for courage is the promotion of a good in the face of risk or danger. Antiracist virtues may require being an attentive listener and negotiator in highly charged (even if not actually dangerous) situations.

Antiracism applies to teachers as well, in part because a teacher who harbors prejudices and racist stereotypes will be greatly hindered in teaching students antiracist values. Yet being free of racial animus and bigotry does not by itself guarantee that the teacher will avoid racial discrimination. For example, mere discomfort with students of certain ethno-racial groups may lead a teacher to make less eye contact and generally to give less attention to children from those groups. Similar ethno-racial discomfort may make such teachers less comfortable communicating with parents from those groups, leading to a diminished quality of parent–teacher contact in those cases. Racial discrimination against the children of that ethno-racial group is the result, though unintended and not motivated by racial animosity or bias.

Equality as the fundamental antiracist value

The value foundations of antiracism lie in familiar and age-old traditions of religious, philosophic, and American civic ideals of human equality and common humanity. The Christian idea that all humans are creatures of God and made in God's image, an idea shared in some form by many religions; the Kantian idea that all humans (rational beings) have equal dignity and infinite worth – these are expressions of and foundations for the idea that, on the most fundamental level, all are equal and are to be treated equal, independent of race (as well as other features).

Of course this noble ideal is somewhat vague as to its specific content, though it remains an important standard against which to assess specific forms of "equal treatment." The American political tradition provides further elaboration and some further support for the idea of equality. The 14th Amendment to the Constitution, for example, providing "equal protection of the laws," was understood to secure political rights for blacks. The *Brown v. Board of Education* Supreme Court decision of 1954 can be and has been taken to prescribe equal educational opportunity independent of race. A vaguer notion of equality permeates American political culture (often expressed popularly by citing the Preamble to the Declaration of Independence's "all men are created equal," they are endowed with an "inalienable right" to "life, liberty, and the pursuit of happiness").

Yet American civic traditions by no means support as robust a conception of equality as one can find in certain philosophical traditions, for example John Rawls's Kantian-inspired *Theory of Justice*. In particular they far from unequivocally support a robust conception of racial (and gender) equality. The heritage of slavery, a racialized naturalization policy, exclusion of women and failure to grant women unequivocal equal constitutional rights – these exclusions and inequities are also part of the American political tradition. Still, a popularly recognizable egalitarian strand can be appealed to as a source to advocate for racial equity, providing a particularistic civic underpinning to supplement other more universal forms of racial egalitarianism.

Yet the notion of "equality," particularly in the area of race, can have more than one meaning. We should distinguish at least three of these that are particularly pertinent to antiracist education. The first is equal educational opportunity, as applied to individuals independent of race. We discussed above how this value is not an individual character value but is to be implemented by teachers, schools, or societies.

Moral asymmetries in racism

A second equality value is fairness in the sense of non-discrimination – not discriminating against persons on the basis of their "race." A black person who discriminates against a white person – for example, by unfairly not selecting her for a job because she is white – violates that value as much as a white person who discriminates against a black. They both make use of an irrelevant characteristic in assigning a benefit. Non-discrimination is thus a *symmetric* value with regard to race. This value can be upheld, or violated by individuals or social entities.

Both these two equality-based values operate *on individuals*. It is individuals who are accorded equality of opportunity (or not), and individuals who are discriminated against (or not). A third equality value concerns groups rather than individuals – racial, or ethno-racial, group equity. This value is difficult to pin down precisely. The intuitive idea is that salient ethno-racial groups in a given society should not be greatly unequal in their material circumstances. The operative equality value does not, however, require strict material or occupational equality among groups.

This value is not merely derivative from the previous one, non-discrimination; the objectionability of group inequity does not require commitment to the view that such inequity was created solely by acts of racial discrimination. The intuition of the wrongness of (some unspecifiable degree of) group inequity is partly dependent on, but partly

independent of, our view as to how that inequity came about. If blacks have inferior schools because the state intentionally accords them fewer resources, this is worse than if the inferior schools are a byproduct of residential patterns of segregation, local funding, and the greater poverty of blacks. However, the racial inequity of schools is wrong in both cases, and is so because of the intrinsic wrongness of group inequality, and not merely the wrongness of individual discrimination, or the lack of individual equality of opportunity.

The equality value of group equity makes for a moral asymmetry between agents of different races that is not present with regard to non-discrimination. In a context in which group A is unfairly disadvantaged with regard to group B – i.e. the group equity value is violated with respect to group A and in favor of group B – a racist act against a member of group A will, or may, serve to reinforce the group-based disadvantage of group A. For example, if a black child is miseducated, not only does this violate the value of racial non-discrimination, but it also reinforces and contributes in some small way to blacks' inferior position, as a group, in education and society more generally.

On the other hand if a black teacher miseducates a white student for racial reasons, this also violates the value of racial non-discrimination; but it does not violate the group equity value, since, in the USA and Britain at least, whites are not a disadvantaged group vis-à-vis blacks.

Thus two of our values – equality of opportunity, and non-discrimination – are morally symmetrical with respect to race; but the third equality value is asymmetrical. It is worse when a member of an advantaged group violates this value with regard to a member of a disadvantaged group than the reverse.

Keeping these symmetries and asymmetries in mind can help us come to terms with one criticism that has been made of British antiracist education, and of the antiracist strand of American multicultural education; and that is that it identifies only whites as the perpetrators of racism. Such an approach stems from focusing entirely on *group* inequities and on the social and historical processes that create and sustain them; whites do not suffer from racial injustice in that sense. However, blacks as well as whites, Mexican-Americans, Asian-Americans, Jews, and any other group can engage in objectionable racist acts of discrimination, hatred, and denial of equal opportunity. They violate norms of equality and respect when they do so, and antiracist education must give those forms of racism their due, teaching students of any group the wrongness of engaging in such acts of racism.

At the same time, antiracist education cannot go to the other extreme of presenting all racism as entirely morally symmetrical. It can do so only by overlooking the group inequity dimension of equality as a value. Because of group inequities in a society, acts of racism have a different meaning when perpetrated by a dominant and by a subordinate group member. They violate an additional value if they contribute to an existing group inequity.

Antiracism as resting on a "sameness-based" value

While the three equality-based values I have noted are importantly distinct from one another – in their domain, their group or individual focus, and their symmetric/asymmetric character with regard to race – they are all "sameness-based" values, grounded in some sense of shared humanity or dignity. This sameness dimension of multicultural education is often lost or masked by the constant focus in much multicultural literature and discourse on the idea of "difference." This sameness–equality dimension is a reflection of multicultural education's roots in the Civil Rights movement, other movements for social and political equality in the USA, and in black Americans' struggle for equal education – all of these in turn drawing on, but also helping to shape and extend, the American civic notion of "equality."

To say that the *value* foundation of antiracism is a human sameness does not mean that antiracist education is blind to differences in historical and social experiences of different groups. On the contrary, on the curricular level, for example, antiracist education requires attention to these differences and to the differing social meanings infusing racial designations ("white," "black"), quasi-racial ones ("Asian-American"[8] and "Native-American"), and partly racialized ones (such as "Latino" or "Hispanic").[9] The study of racist systems and practices, such as segregation, apartheid, Nazism, slavery in the modern world, exclusion of "non-whites" from full citizenship in the USA, and the like – integrated into larger units of study in social studies, history, or literature – would be staples of antiracist education on the curricular level.

However, recognition of differences in historical experience due to racism (and perhaps to cultural differences as well) is not the same as, and does not preclude, advancing the fundamental value of equality, common humanity, and shared dignity as the essential ground of antiracist education. From the point of view of values, the basic value driving the antiracist commitment is that of a fundamental sameness and equality among all human beings. It is the violation of this commonality that constitutes the major evil in the different forms of racism.

Multiculturalism: cultural respect

Multiculturalism contains two primary subvalues, or families of subvalues. The first individual value is "cultural respect" – respecting the cultures and cultural identities of individuals. The second is the valorizing of cultural plurality itself.

Let us begin with the first value. Cultural respect contains two distinct strands. One is respect for the cultural identity of the individual person. This form of respect is simply a consequence of the basic value of respecting individual persons, together with the premise that cultural identity is an important dimension of the individual person's identity. There may be disagreement as to whether cultural identity – in the sense of an ethno-culture – is actually important to every individual. Some people dispute this, while some multiculturalists take it as a matter of faith that everyone's ethno-culture is an important part of her identity, whether she realizes this or not. We can sidestep this issue by saying that for persons whose ethno-cultural identity is important, respecting them means respecting that culture as an important part of their identity.

The second strand is respect for cultures in their own right, independent of their role in the formation of individual members' identities. This respect should not be regarded as a prescription of equal respect for every distinct culture. Such a standard would presume that the various aspects of cultures could be toted up into an overall evaluative measure, and then seen to be equal. But cultures and value are not related in this way. Cultures can embody value without there being an overall sum of such value for an individual culture.

Nor does cultural respect require that every aspect of a given culture be seen as valuable. Some aspects of cultures can be seen from the outside to be repellent, though that judgment should be made with caution, and only after understanding the role of the seemingly repellent practice within the context of the culture as a whole.

Why, then, should we respect cultures in their own right? Charles Taylor articulates this presumption well:

> Merely on a human level, one could argue that it is reasonable to suppose that cultures that have provided the horizon of meaning for large numbers of human beings, of diverse characters and temperaments, over a long period of time – that have, in other words, articulated their sense of the good, the holy, the admirable – are almost certain to have something that deserves our admiration and respect, even if it is accompanied by much that we have to abhor and reject.[10]

Because of the value of culture to the individual, the individual has reason to appreciate her own culture, to have a loyalty to it, to wish to sustain it and have it respected by others. It gives her a reason to know about it, its history and traditions. Everything else being equal, schools have reason to provide this learning and, more generally, to validate the individual's attachment to her own culture. That is, schools have reason to respect the cultural dimension of their students' identity, and to teach other students to do so as part of their values education program. So cultural respect has both an inward-looking and an outward-looking aspect (toward one's own culture, and toward the culture of others), and these two aspects apply to both forms of cultural respect – individual identity and cultures in their own right.

There is perhaps a third type of, or possibly better seen as a ground of, cultural respect – toward ethno-cultures that comprise a given culturally diverse nation. Each ethno-cultural group has its place in the history of its nation, and has contributed to the formation of its national culture and institutions. The national culture of the USA has been formed by influences from African-American, Latino, Chinese, Japanese, Native American and other ethno-cultural groups. It is a hybrid culture, and each of its influencing groups deserves respect for its contributions to that national culture.

Multiculturalism has sometimes been criticized for projecting, or presupposing, a static, internally cohesive and holist, "essentialist" view of ethno-cultures. The critics have rightly pointed out that cultures change over time, that they contain various and sometimes contradictory tendencies within

themselves (e.g. regarding the role and value of women), that the changes stem partly from interaction with other ethno-cultural groups, which often produces "hybrid" forms of ethno-culture.

The value of cultural respect does not, however, deny this dynamic and interactionist view of ethno-cultures. It is neutral with respect to the form that cultures take. The cultural identity of a student that is to be respected by others need not have a static character. To teach other students to respect a Bangladeshi student's culture is not to presuppose any particular understanding of that culture, except that it must take the student's own understanding of it into account (though not exclusively).

While it may be true that many advocates of multiculturalism presuppose a unitary and static view of cultures, such a view is not inherent in multiculturalism itself, and in the values on which it rests. Multiculturalist values are quite capable of embracing a conception of ethno-cultures as dynamic, interactive, and internally complex and contradictory.

Multiculturalism: commitment to cultural diversity and pluralism

The other component of education for cultural diversity, and thus the second multicultural value, is the treasuring of cultural diversity and pluralism itself. We want students not only to respect each particular culture, and its individual members, but to welcome the fact of cultural diversity itself. We want them to be pleased and proud rather than fearful or discomfited by the range of different cultural groups that exist within their society, school, city, neighborhood. We wish students to feel themselves personally enriched by this diversity, and able to derive personal enhancement from their ability to attain some access to those cultures. We want them to see that their own society in particular is enriched in what it is able to accomplish and in what it stands for by the presence of manifold ethno-cultural groups.

Cultural pluralism has a crucial civic dimension. We wish students to appreciate cultural pluralism as a dimension of their political and social system. This appreciation involves recognizing how different groups can have different interests, developing the ability to respect those interests, and learning to deliberate with members of other groups to reach political decisions. The civic aspect reaches beneath political processes strictly defined to encompass all sorts of intermediate institutions, as well as informal social contacts. A commitment to cultural pluralism involves learning to work together with, and communicate across the boundaries of, differing ethno-racial groups, in all these contexts.

This value is outward focused. It does not directly affirm the individual's attachment to her own culture (though it is not inconsistent with that attachment). Like respect for the culture of others, it points the individual beyond her own cultural affiliations toward other groups. But, in contrast to that respect, its object is not each culture in its own particularity, but rather the total set of cultures in one's national society, school, or in the world.

Culture-sensitive teaching, equal opportunity, and cultural pluralism

Sometimes confused with the two values just discussed – cultural respect and commitment to cultural diversity and pluralism – is *culture-sensitive* teaching. The former are values to be taught *to students* (though respect in question should be exemplified by teachers and the school as well). Culture-sensitive teaching, by contrast, is a mode of pedagogy, and thus a value *for teachers*. It recognizes students' cultural background as a potentially significant factor in their learning, and enjoins teachers to become familiar with and knowledgeable about the cultural backgrounds of their students. The culture-sensitive teacher must be willing to tailor her teaching, at least to some extent, to the students' culture. For example, Southeast Asian immigrant children who have been taught to revere teachers, with whom they have had a very formal relationship, are often made uncomfortable by American classrooms in which the teacher is informal and friendly, and the student is expected to speak out and ask questions.[11] The teacher should adjust her expectations of these students' participation, though she need not abandon the goal of finding ways to elicit more participation from them.

The idea of culture-sensitive teaching presumes that too much dissonance between the student's home culture and the expectations of the school harm the student's educational progress. There is room for a range of opinions on this issue. It is virtually an article of faith in some multicultural writings that minimizing this dissonance should be

an overriding educational guideline. A more moderate position is the one stated above, that teachers should be willing to make some adjustments in the direction of accommodating students' cultural characteristics. As Sonia Nieto points out, if the classroom itself is culturally diverse, it is impossible fully to accommodate every child's cultural characteristics.[12]

Culture-sensitive teaching generally encompasses a further principle, which has been most persuasively developed by Lisa Delpit, a leading educational theorist in this area.[13] Delpit enjoins teachers to look for the *strengths* in students' cultures, and to build on them. She writes with great insight about instances of teachers wrongly thinking that a student is stupid, cannot speak English, cannot speak "standard English", or cannot read. As instances of strengths on which teachers can build, Delpit cites (as a broad generalization) the African-American community's valuing of oral style – verbal adroitness, quick wit, facility in rhythm and rhyme – and of a developed storytelling ability in Native American children of certain tribes. In one particularly striking example, Delpit describes a teacher confusing the correcting of a child's dialect with teaching her to read, and missing the fact that the child has actually understood the reading selection.

The injunction to seek out cultural strengths – and not to assume too readily that a particular element of the child's culture is a deficit – takes the cultural accommodation stance one step further. The cultural accommodationist takes "cultural mismatch" to be a prime cause of underachievement in some black, Latino, and Native American children. That view does not place any *value*, either positive or negative, on the cultural differences, but simply invites recognition of their educational impact. (Both views, however, contrast with the "cultural deficit" view, which sees the child's culture as itself the cause of educational failure.) Delpit's view, by contrast, places a *positive* value on those cultural differences, or at least encourages the seeking of value or strength in those differences.

While Delpit's cultural strengths approach should certainly play an important role in pedagogy and teacher training, a final position on the matter of cultural differences must acknowledge that cultures and life situations have both strengths and weaknesses with regard to the educational achievement of its youthful members, and that educators must recognize both in order best to support that achievement.

The basic value engaged by culture-sensitive pedagogy is *equality of opportunity* – a value that operates at the teacher level, but as a general value is, as we have seen, applicable to the school and the society-wide levels as well. Culture-sensitive teaching is a way of recognizing differences in order to shape pedagogy and perhaps curriculum and school culture, in order to give every student an equivalent learning situation, that is, a learning situation that will maximize her opportunity to learn to her particular best abilities. Delpit, Nieto, and others enrich our understanding of equality of opportunity in education by pointing to the myriad ways that cultural differences interface with schooling. They help to establish that treating children "the same" is not necessarily, or even usually, the way to provide them with equivalent learning opportunities, and they expand our conception of the differences relevant to achieving equality of opportunity in education.

This advance in a conception of equality of opportunity is, or should be seen as, a permanent and secure contribution to education theory and value, somewhat analogous to the ways that African-Americans' struggles for equality in the USA have enriched our public conception of what "equality" means. It is an extension of the philosophy underlying the USA Supreme Court's requiring of bilingual education (for non-English-speaking Chinese-American students, in the plaintiff's case) in the 1974 *Lau v. Nichols* case.[14] Different resources and pedagogy are required for students differently situated, in order to provide them with "equal education." By contrast, when we discussed equality of opportunity in the antiracist context, it consisted in not allowing racial difference to prejudice the providing of equal education.

Equality of opportunity is an important value in multicultural and antiracist education. But together with the culture-sensitive pedagogies, it does not engage the range of character and social values involved in either cultural respect or commitment to cultural pluralism. While the former pedagogies do, in a sense, involve a notion of "respect for culture" on the part of the teacher, they do not necessarily or essentially involve teaching students to respect one another's cultures, or to value cultural diversity. Culture-sensitive teaching involves neither moral nor civic values of individual character. For this reason, cultural respect goes substantially beyond culture-sensitive teaching. However, Delpit's notion of looking for strengths in individual cultures does involve a form of positive respect for culture as a moral value on the part of the teacher, even if it is primarily in the service of the purely educational value of equality of opportunity.

Antiracist and multicultural education: the differences

In the USA what is generally referred to as "multicultural education" is seldom clearly distinguished from "antiracist" education. They are either run together or antiracist education is ignored. In the British educational tradition, the two are generally kept distinct, but are sometimes presented, both by adherents or detractors of one or the other, as competing means to the same goal. For example, the Swann Report presents learning about, and learning to have respect for, cultures other than one's own as a means to reduction of racial prejudice, and thereby of racism itself. Antiracists reply that racism cannot be eliminated only or even primarily through prejudice reduction, but through dismantling the structures of institutional racism.

What both sides in this dispute miss is that multiculturalism and antiracism have distinct goals and distinct value underpinnings, even if the practice of one might sometimes serve the goals of the other. The Swann Report is probably correct to say that teaching students to learn about other cultures in an appreciative manner goes some way toward reducing prejudice; doing so probably also supports the sense of worth of the child whose culture is being valued, giving her some psychic resources to resist racism against her. However, whether multicultural education accomplishes these results or not, learning to respect other cultures has value in its own right. While the antiracists are correct to think that learning about other cultures is not the only, or even the best, way to reduce racial prejudice, and also that reducing individual prejudices will not wipe out institutional racism, they miss the importance of cultural respect as an educational value goal distinct from racial equity.[15]

What exactly is the difference between these two families of value? Cultural respect is grounded in a recognition of *difference* at the level at which antiracism is grounded in an appreciation of *sameness*. The student is to be taught to see each culture in its distinctness from her own; to recognize that that which is not-her nevertheless has value; and, ultimately, to treasure the diversity and variety of cultures. By contrast, the root value behind antiracism is seeing others as sharing the same humanity and dignity as ourselves. There is no fundamental conflict between these two values. We are the same as others in (some) ways that warrant valuing, and different from others, in other ways, some of which warrant valuing.

The antiracist perspective sees and seeks equality *independent of* or even *in spite of* difference. Prior to our current multicultural awareness, many committed white antiracists, including some activists, did not really have positive respect for African-American culture as such. They saw blacks as, *humanly*, equals to whites, but either were not aware of a distinct black culture or saw what they regarded as black culture as a degraded or inferior one, though this inferiority was not (seen as) inherent but caused by racism. Nevertheless this lack of cultural respect did not diminish the commitment to social, political, and perhaps economic equality for blacks, nor did it necessarily preclude the whites from seeing blacks – as a group and as individuals – as human equals to whites.

This equality affirming but culture non-respecting attitude is or was not confined to whites. Alexander Crummell, a nineteenth century Afro-American minister and pan-African nationalist, devoted his life to equality between the races; but he unequivocally believed African culture to be inferior to European culture (especially to Christianity and to the English language). He saw almost nothing of value in African culture as it existed, yet he believed that Africans, and all "blacks" (people of African descent) deserved equality with whites/westerners, and were capable of that equality.

With our current focus on, or some might say obsession with, "difference," it may be hard to recognize that someone might truly believe in human equality without respecting the cultures of the groups or individuals who are regarded as equal. In a sense we have come to identify a person's ethno-culture so closely with her full humanity that a non-recognition or devaluing of her culture is taken as equivalent to a devaluing of her humanity.

Still, the antiracist outlook that fails to assure cultural respect and a commitment to cultural pluralism is also limited in its value horizon. A multicultural education program must strive for both values – human equality and cultural respect. Helping students to see the wrong of racial discrimination and bigotry, studying the history of racist practices and resistance to them, understanding the nature of racial injustice and institutional racism, learning to be committed to the civic, religious, and moral norms of human equality – these are directed toward the equality side. Studying different cultures, how they provide meaning and value to their members, giving students direct exposure to different cultural expressions and practices, while helping them to achieve a sense of respect for these cultures – these educational initiatives speak to the cultural respect dimension of multicultural education.

In the American context, it is ironic that antiracism would be seen as a more radical approach than multiculturalism. For the value underpinnings of antiracism have much stronger roots in American political culture than do those of multiculturalism. While there have been movements and intellectual tendencies supporting cultural pluralism, these have been distinctly minor compared to the more powerful drive toward an equality grounded in a sense of human or civic commonality.[16] Yet perhaps this is not so strange after all, since one reason why "racism" as a term of moral criticism does carry such force is that it calls people's attention to their violation of a core American value. Moreover, people's resistance to an educational practice is obviously based not only on its value underpinnings but on the potentiality for challenge to power and privilege involved in that practice. In this regard, the antiracists are correct to see antiracism as a more radical, and thus threatening, approach than multiculturalism.

Conclusion

To summarize: antiracist education is founded on three values, all forms of equality – equality of opportunity, non-discrimination, and group equity. All are grounded on a sense of human commonality. Multicultural education comprises two distinct values – cultural respect, and the valorizing of cultural pluralism. These are grounded on a recognition and valuing of certain kinds of human difference. Thus antiracist and multicultural education are distinct, not merely different ways of arriving at the same goals. A values education program must embody both antiracist and multicultural values.

Notes

According to 1996 Census Bureau counts, the current non-Hispanic white proportion of the population of the USA is only 73.6 percent. "Asians, Hispanics to lead US Growth, Census projects," *Boston Globe*, 14 March 1996, p. 3. Because of the generally younger age of immigrants, and their higher birth rates, the school age population is even less (non-Hispanic) white.

I will retain the familiar adjectival form "American" to correspond with the noun "United States." Yet we must keep in mind that Latin American, Mexico, and Canada are also part of the "Americas," and sometimes resent their apparent exclusion in this usage.

1 See Alistair Bonnett, *Radicalism, Anti-Racism, and Representation* (1993, London: Routledge).

2 See for example James Banks, *Multiethnic Education: Theory and Practice*, 3rd edn (1994, Boston: Allyn and Bacon); Sonia Nieto, *Affirming Diversity*, 2nd edn. (1996, White Plains NY: Longman).

3 Two influential conservative tracts in this movement are William Bennett, *The De-Valuing of American: The Fight for Our Culture and Our Children* (1992, New York: Simon and Schuster), and William Kilpatrick, *Why Johnny Can't Tell Right From Wrong* (1992, Simon and Schuster).

4 I have interpreted "equality of opportunity" to mean "equality of educational opportunity." Of course, the former value can be regarded as applying within other distinct domains, for example, access to employment; and can also, possibly, be understood in some overall, total way, as something like "equality of opportunity with regard to life chances."

5 This broader conception of "civics" draws on a more recent conception of civic life, exemplified for example in the work of Robert Putnam ("The Strange Disappearance of Civic America," *in The American Prospect*, winter 1996), and Jean Elshtain *Democracy on Trial* (1995, New York: Basic Books) but with antecedents in Alexis de Tocqueville's *Democracy in America*, and others.

6 See, for example, the influential document *National Standards for Civics and Government*, put out by the Center for Civic Education in 1994.

7 I am including, as members of the set of groups who are the target of racism, ones that might more naturally be thought of as "*ethnic*" groups. So anti-Semitism, and early twentieth-century forms of anti-ethnic prejudice in the USA, are included under "racism." The criterion is whether the ethnic group in question is viewed in a "racialized" manner, that is, as the inheritors of an inescapable identity carrying with it certain distinctive characteristics. The contrast is to ethnicity conceived of as a changeable and non-essentialist culture. An anti-ethnic prejudice would reveal itself not to be a racialized form if it disappeared or was not directed toward members of the ethnic group who were regarded as having "assimilated" to the mainstream culture; and would reveal itself to be racialized if it survived such apparent cultural changes in the group.

Racism is distinct, however, from "nativism" – prejudice against non-nationals (who can be "white" yet the target of "white" prejudice). However, racism is frequently closely tied to nativism when the groups in question are, or are seen as, different races. Since most of the post-1965 immigration to the USA has been of people of color, prejudice against these groups has often been a mixture of nativism and racism.

8 That "Asian-American" is generally taken as a quasi-racial designation, rather than one of culture or geographical origin, is revealed by the fact that Americans use this word almost solely in relation to *East* Asians. *South* Asians (Indians, Pakistanis, Bangladeshis), by far the more numerous and visible Asians in Great Britain and distinct in physical appearance from East Asians, are not, in the USA, normally thought of as part of the group referred to as "Asian-American."

9 I have sometimes adopted an increasingly familiar convention of using scare quotes for racial terms. This is to indicate that there are no such things as actual *races*, only groups *regarded as* such.

10 Charles Taylor, "The Politics of Recognition," in Amy Gutmann (ed.), *Multiculturalism* (1994, Princeton: Princeton University Press).

11 Nieto, *Affirming Diversity: The Sociopolitical Context of Multicultural Education* (1992, London: Longman), p. 115. (There is a 1996 edition of this book. See footnote 3.)

12 *Ibid.*

13 Lisa Delpit, *Other People's Children: Cultural Conflict in the Classroom* (1995, New Press).

14 See L. Ling-Chi Wang, "*Lau v. Nichols*: History of a Struggle for Equal and Quality Education," in D. Nakanishi and T. Yamano Nishida (eds.), *The Asian American Educational Experience: A Source Book for Teachers and Students*, (1995, New York: Routledge).

15 The criticism of multicultural education as failing to serve the goal of ending racism is sometimes conflated with a different criticism – that the form of multicultural education in question is too superficial (the "saris, samosas, and steel bands" syndrome. See Fazal Rizvi's introduction to Barry Troyna's *Racism and Education: Research Perspectives* (1993, Buckingham: Open University Press). (I do not know if Troyna is the source of this expression.) True multicultural education must portray ethno-cultural groups in depth, understanding their role in national and world history, the links between their characteristic traditions, rituals, forms of artistic expression, and the like. It is true that, in practice, multicultural education sometimes amounts to little more than "multicultural awareness day" in a school. But the appropriate corrective for this is not to abandon

multicultural education for antiracist education, but to do multicultural education right.

16   Probably the first and most influential philosopher of cultural pluralism in the USA was Horace Kallen, in his 1914 essay "Democracy vs. the Melting Pot" (reprinted in Kallen's 1924 *Culture and Democracy in the United States: Studies in the Group Psychology of the American People*). There have also been movements to retain instruction in a group's home language, as well as movements to teach respect for other ethno-cultures, such as the "intercultural education" movement of the 1930s and 1940s. On all these matters, see Thomas LaBelle and Christopher Ward, *Multiculturalism: Diversity and Its Impact on Schools and Society* (1994, Albany: SUNY Press).

2 Markets, Managerialism and the Neglect of Multicultural Education

MIKE BOTTERY

Introduction

This chapter will argue that not only has there been a deliberate marginalization of multicultural issues by UK governments over the last twenty years, but that because of the continued use of markets to organize education, and because of an increased emphasis on global competitiveness, and of the use of a managerialist ideology to administer such a system, this situation has been exacerbated. The combination of these factors has led to a situation where work on multicultural initiatives is hampered by a lack of enthusiasm at the policy level, by a lack of co-ordinated effort at the system-wide level, and is neutered by managerialist agendas at the institutional level. It is argued that this neglect is inherent within the policies of both major UK political parties at the present time, within the logic of the market and within the technical-rational, emasculated logic of managerialism. For a more proactive policy to be adopted, both a change of ideology and a change in market and managerial approaches will need to be adopted.

It is argued that the multicultural debate – and its neglect by government in the UK since the mid-1980s – is symptomatic not only of a response to government views on multicultural education, but also of the change in the way that government itself has been conceptualized in the last couple of decades. This is partly a change from a belief in the possibility of a social engineering approach to societal problems to one where economic competitiveness and the market are seen as the major driving forces. It will be argued that not only are economic imperatives, markets and managerialism used to marginalize multicultural initiatives; they also have an internal logic which necessarily leads to such marginalization. So while there are still excel-

lent, committed and effective strategies for such education at the personal and institutional levels, yet both here and at a system or nationwide level, strategies have been severely hindered by the use of market and managerial approaches to education. The argument of this chapter then requires a broader view of educational and political change than is sometimes encountered when discussing multicultural education, but this is seen as essential if an adequate understanding of the issue is to be gained. This chapter will initially describe changes in government thinking towards multicultural education over the last decade before moving to look at this broader policy canvas.

Policy change towards multicultural education

The early 1980s in the UK seemed to many socialists and social democrats to be a time of great hope for the development of a more just, egalitarian, tolerant and pluralist society. Not only were there a great number of local education authorities (LEAs) formulating multicultural and antiracist policy statements (e.g. Troyna and Williams, 1986), but central government was actively involved in this agenda, as witnessed by the publication of both the Rampton Report (1981) and the Swann Report (1985), which bravely attempted to straddle the gap between multicultural and antiracist approaches, and to argue that 'good education' and the development of a citizenship for all necessarily involved a pluralist perspective on society and educational approaches.

Yet there were at the same time intimations that such movement was not happening unopposed. Across the western world, programmes of government educational intervention did not seem to produce the results expected. The Headstart programme in the USA failed to reap the rewards many thought it would bring. The move from a selective to a comprehensive system in the UK seemed to bring as many problems as plaudits. Furthermore, social democratic intervention in education seemed to conservatives on both sides of the Atlantic to become more extreme, with intervention in education to reduce inequalities in both opportunity and outcome based on class differences moving into areas of racial and gender inequality, and then on to questions of homosexual inequality which, as we have seen, seemed to threaten the fundamental values and very stability of their society. Pearce (1986, pp. 136, 141) described the Swann Report as 'a profoundly dangerous document aimed at re-shaping British Society', which would lead to a 'loss of identity for the native British, who have a right to preserve their way of life, and this means that their culture must predominate in our schools'.

Margaret Thatcher, in her speech at the 1987 Conservative Party conference, linked poor educational standards to antiracist initiatives:

> In the inner cities where youngsters must have a decent education if they are to have a better future, the opportunity is all too often snatched away from them by hard-left education authorities and extremist teachers. Children who need to be able to count and multiply are learning anti-racist mathematics, whatever that is.   (quoted in Ball, 1990, p. 49)

In continuing her speech at the conference, she stated: 'Children who need to be able to express themselves in clear English are being taught political slogans. Children who need to be taught to respect traditional moral values are being taught that they have an inalienable right to be gay' (ibid.).

To these conservatives such movements seemed increasingly to shift from a humanistic concern with the treatment of educational problems that these minorities suffered consequent upon their move to a foreign culture (their problem with which the white majority would be good enough to help them), to a situation where the blame was located with the majority culture in terms of not only educational treatment, but also in structured and systematic discrimination within society as a whole. The problem was now seen as located with the majority rather than the minority culture. The former, it was argued, would have to change, which, to

their eyes, smacked of a Marxist interpretation rather than a liberal democratic one (see, for example, Mullard, 1980). Here then were good reasons for such conservatives wanting to see the government withdraw from these initiatives.

Significantly, the 1988 Education Act, the largest single educational reform of the previous forty years, contained little or no direct reference to multicultural education and in a variety of ways exacerbated the situation. First, by radically reducing the influence of LEAs, which had been the prime movers in multicultural initiatives, the Act seriously weakened support for development in this area. Second, the National Curriculum gave clear prioritization to Core and Foundation subjects and made tremendous demands on teachers' time, thus reducing the time they could give to multicultural issues. Third, by neglecting content in social science areas, the architects of the National Curriculum continued the marginalization of multicultural issues by reducing the use of intellectual tools needed to understand injustice and inequality in society.

Finally, while there was reference to multicultural elements in Curriculum Guidance 3 (NCC, 1990), in which it is argued (p. 3) that the use of such perspectives 'gives pupils the opportunity to view the world from different standpoints, helping them to question prejudice and develop open-mindedness', there was not only a clear downgrading of such issues in comparison with the attention teachers needed to pay to core and foundation subjects, but also a vagueness to the conceptualization, implementation and assessment of such elements which yet again located them at the periphery of educational policy objectives. A task group was set up in July 1989 by the NCC to firm up such resolution. Its report was submitted in April 1990, but no subsequent guidance document was published. The writing was very clearly on the wall: this was not an area to which the government of the day wished to pay attention. If one looks at the evidence marshalled by Blair and Arnott (1993) that funding arrangements for multicultural initiatives were so circumscribed that little headway could be made with new initiatives by interested parties, it is unsurprising that an editorial to the *Times Educational Supplement* of June, 1990 should come to the conclusion that 'There seems to be a definite, though unformulated intent to starve multicultural education of resources, and let it wither on the vine' (p. 23).

Government policy was then concerned with

what Gilborn (1995, p. 17) calls 'the deracialisation of social policy': the capture of a discourse so that such issues cannot be raised. This was done in two ways: first, as Margaret Thatcher attempted, by suggesting that issues of race were really questions of individual educational achievement; second, by suggesting that 'Britishness' consisted of being white and middle class, and all others are outsiders. Thus, as the 1992 Education Act was passing through the Commons, Lady Olga Maitland stated that we should 'not allow non-believers to undermine our traditions . . . It is a tragedy that the teaching of the Christian faith has become woefully neglected in the face of multiculturalism, which is promoting minority faiths at the expense of Christianity' (quoted in Gilborn, 1995, p. 22).

A year later the Prime Minister, John Major (1993, p. 9) continued this theme of Britishness being exclusively white in culture and colour:

> Britain will still be the country of long shadows on county grounds, warm beer, invincible green suburbs, dog lovers and pool fillers, and – as George Orwell said – 'old maids bicycling to holy communion through the morning mist' and – if we get our way – Shakespeare still read even in school.

Multicultural education could now be subsumed under individual underachievement; antiracism issues under the headings of left-wing troublemakers and inner-city problems; little Englanders could bicycle to holy communion with their old maids. However, the advent of New Labour has not changed this picture a great deal. As with Conservative governments, New Labour and education could get on with the far more important business of being a major tool in the development of economic competitiveness on a global stage. It is to these larger issues that we now turn.

Policy change in the western world

If there has been change in multicultural policy in the UK over the last decade, there have been huge changes of economic policy in the whole of the western world over the last twenty years which have exacerbated the problems for pluralist educational initiatives. If the USA was at one end of a liberal–economic spectrum and Britain and Sweden at the other, there was, until twenty five to thirty years ago, still a general consensus that government – and lots of it – was a good thing, for it was seen as

central to the attempt to create a better society. Lyndon Johnson's administration was probably the peak of such interventionist aspirations in the USA. Callaghan's government was the last of this kind in the UK, though even there, with oil crises, balance of payments problems and stagflation, the economic measures adopted by his government after 1976 look in retrospect more like those of the next Conservative government under Margaret Thatcher than of a social democratic Labour government. It was her government, though, which ushered in new concepts in government in the UK and Ronald Reagan's which did the same in the USA. But even nominally left and centre-left governments followed the trend. France under Mitterand, Spain under Gonzalez, Australia under Hawke and New Zealand under Lange all adopted the same policy agenda.

Western economies were no longer so buoyant. Three reasons for this may be pointed out here. First, there was a huge increase in oil prices in the early 1970s, which placed large extra burdens upon the western economies. Second, western economies faced increased competition from areas once thought of as little more than economic jokes. 'Made in Japan' had once been the trademark of the cheap import. Increasingly products from Japan and the other Asian tigers were becoming standards for the international hallmark for quality. A third factor concerned problems ensuing from demography, where an increasing proportion of the population in the western world was elderly. This meant that a lower proportion of the population was capable of contributing taxation to finance a welfare state for an increasing number of non-contributors (see McRae, 1994). Western economies were thus facing crises that had not been confronted since the 1930s. These problems were accompanied by increased concerns about financing governmental projects, in particular the most expensive – the welfare state. The debate became one not of provision within a universal welfare state, but of provision within an affordable welfare state.

While these kinds of changes were taking place, radical right-wing writers like Friedrich Hayek (1944) in Europe and Milton Friedman (1961) in the USA, who had tended to be seen as belonging to the lunatic fringe of politics, now came much more centre stage. Political and moral arguments were added to the economic arguments: the state was no benefactor but a big brother, seducing citizens into a dependency which was dangerous for them personally and for any liberal democracy. As Hayek (1944) suggested big government was 'the Road to Serfdom'. Increasing criticism mounted towards the providers within such services and the moral high ground moved from the social democratic left to the radical liberal right: 'rolling back the state' rather than 'piecemeal social engineering' became the dominant phrase. The political argument no longer ranged between provision of a universal or an affordable welfare state, but between an affordable and a residual welfare state (see George and Miller, 1994). If the first two still indicated an adherence to a communal vision of society, the latter indicated little more than a safety-net approach, set within a vision of self-interested individuals pursuing their personal projects free from the deadening hand of bureaucracy, motivated by the spirits of consumerism and entrepreneurialism.

The rise of the market

The vehicle for such change was understandably seen as the market. If the welfare state produced grateful recipients, it was argued that the market would produce discerning and critical consumers. If the welfare state generated self-serving producers, the market would generate an interest in satisfying the consumer, for only then would the customer return and continue to 'buy' a particular producer's services. If the state was deficient in that it used information too distant from the actual site of production to understand what was really needed, the market, it was argued, supplied more accurate information because it generated and allowed the utilization of information at the site of production. Finally, it was argued that because of peer pressure the state would tend to invest money into ailing schemes that were protected from the realities of competition, which then set up malign circles of inefficiency and further state investment. The market, on the other hand, would prevent this by being the final arbiter in the viability of a project, would be deaf to the cries of vested interests and would therefore necessarily be the best means of promoting a healthy economy. Such were argued to be the benefits of a market approach (for a useful discussion on this, see Gray, 1992).

Importantly for educational projects and multicultural education in particular, the market

approach had other effects as well. The fact that the market was the final arbiter meant that many issues which were on a social democratic platform and seen as the responsibility of policymakers were now considered beyond their remit. What were once seen as political choices could now be described as market decisions. Governments could now argue that there was little they could do about ailing industries and the ensuing unemployment, or fears of the cultural ghettoization of schools consequent upon the unfettered choice of parents through open enrolment. The market had to be the final arbiter. For politicians wanting to avoid difficult decisions, the market could be, and was, an immensely useful excuse for non-interference.

But the market was also far more than an excuse, because for radical right-wingers in the Conservative party it was also a dictator of policy. If a market ideology is adhered to, then it becomes a matter of principle and consistency not to be tampered with, even when the results seem to suggest that such interference is desirable. If adherence to market strategy generated greater inequality in the distribution of wealth, as it certainly has done in the UK (Wilkinson, 1996), then this had to be interpreted as either a necessary evil of the system or a spur to greater achievement by those who do less well. But what could not be done was to intervene to alter market operations.

Further, if institutions like schools were put into the marketplace, then the logic of the market dictates that the market must decide what schools should concentrate on and which schools should be kept open. Market logic dictates that such decisions are dependent upon consumer preferences and upon how much money such institutions bring in. They cannot (must not) be based on external judgements by politicians of their worth in some qualitative or communal sense. On this logic, the judgement that counts is the judgement of the consumer: the role of the state is to set up the market, to ensure fair play ensues between providers, and to adjudicate on abrogations. It is not there to decide who should win and who should lose. That is for the market to decide.

With respect to policy on multicultural education, it was clearly not for the state to decide what the consumer should choose. If a parent wished for a child to go to a particular school, then this again needed to be a market decision. If school A ended up with children from only one ethnic, cultural or religious background and School B ended up with only children from another ethnic, cultural or religious background, then such geographical and cultural segregation was not an issue in which state can be concerned or intervene: it was a reflection of the market, of consumer preferences, and so must be accepted. The fact that this may lead to racial and cultural divides, mutual incomprehension and possible intolerance and hostility may be seen as unfortunate, but inevitable. It will be inevitable given the logic of the market, for to interfere is to challenge this logic, which runs against all that is held dear by the radical right. At the institutional and systematic level, then, multicultural education, or indeed any other educational initiative that depends upon decisions which transcend the level of individual consumer preference, will not happen – unless the market dictates that they should. By so adopting the logic of the market, then, value judgements about what is good for communities, regions, or the country as a whole, are simply ruled out. Educational policy, including multicultural education policy, is neutered at the level where it probably has its greatest effect.

The limits of the market

Of course, we have seen that the reality of policy formation and legislation is and has been very different. Under both Conservative and New Labour governments, the evidence is that there has been and continues to be government intervention. At first this appeared to be little more than the kind of argument underpinning Andrew Gamble's (1988) book: that in order to change the perceptions of both consumers and producers, the state needed to be centrally involved in ensuring that changes to a more market-oriented system were properly implemented. State intervention then is no more than the state ensuring that the framework was put into place. So in the case of, for example, compulsory competitive tendering in the UK, the state would need to make quite sure that those local authority bodies which already held contracts were not favoured in the new round of bidding, or even that those entering the bidding were given substantial encouragement to succeed. Similarly, entry into the grant maintained (GM) sector would only be achieved by means of substantial inducement to wean those habituated to local education authority (LEA) practice and control; if this meant favouritism or extra funding of the GM sector, then

so be it. While the state was heavily interventionist here, the belief was that once a market culture had been created and a more level playing field of competition established, the state could quietly withdraw to its more appropriate role of umpire.

But there is a second form of government intervention used by both Conservative and New Labour which is more interventionist, more permanent, more important for multicultural education. This is the kind of intervention which Smyth (1993) talks about when he describes 'post-Fordist' styles of management. While there have been many different arguments and descriptions of this term (see Burrows and Loader, 1994), the crucial element lies in the fact that increased technological advances allow for decreased involvement in style of implementation by the centre without this meaning a decreased control in policy direction (see Sewell and Wilkinson, 1992). Post-Fordism on this argument amounts to the devolvement of responsibility to peripheral institutions, setting them the task of succeeding within a market system of provision, while still allowing the centre to control the thrust of policy. This gives the centre the best of both worlds; it allows it to reap the benefits of competition, yet retain control of those things it thinks it needs to retain. By so doing, a post-Fordist approach allows the centre to deny responsibility for those areas which others may see as areas of policy rather than implementation, but in which it does not wish to become embroiled. In the UK, the multicultural issue seems to be clearly of this type. By leaving this area as no more than a cross-curricular theme in the densely bureaucratized and prescriptive National Curriculum, it clearly implied that multicultural education lacked the status of other Core and Foundation Curriculum areas, and so was not something in which schools needed to take too much concern. Further, by giving priority to the market as to where parents send their children, governments also clearly state that the question of racial harmony and cultural mix in schools is not an area for government policy. The logic of the market must decide; the principles of individual choice and freedom must have priority over cultural understanding and communal harmony. In so doing, it continues the marginalization of multicultural education, as well as avoiding tricky political and ethical issues that would gain few votes whatever it did, but which sow the seeds of cultural disharmony ever deeper, to flower ever stronger at some later date.

The advent of the new managerialism

It is worth recapitulating at this point upon the economic aims of both Conservative and New Labour governments. First, the government has the problem of dealing with demands for expenditure when it has less and less money to spend on such matters; it needs a way of reducing this demand, or at least reducing the amount spent. Second, it will wish to retain control of general policy direction, for it would be a foolish government indeed which left such matters to the workings of the market alone. How will it deal with these two issues?

With the first of these issues the government will be aware that while it may wish to reduce expenditure by cutting services, education and health are very popular with electorates: to cut them outright is most likely a vote loser. Much more acceptable to an electorate is to point out (or create the impression) that such services are poorly run and could be greatly improved. As Margaret Thatcher's ministers discovered and as David Stockman, Ronald Reagan's first Director of the Office of Management and Budget discovered, it is asking for trouble simply to cut social programmes, but it is eminently more feasible to insist that fewer resources go further; and this is a task of management. From this perspective, as Pollitt (1992, p. 49) points out, ' "better management" sounds sober, neutral, as unopposable as virtue itself'.

And yet, as he continues:

> Better management provides the label under which private-sector disciplines can be introduced to the public services, political control can be strengthened, budgets trimmed, professional autonomy reduced, public service unions weakened, and a quasi-competitive framework erected to flush out the 'natural inefficiencies of bureaucracy. (Pollitt, 1992, p. 49)

Here then we have good reason for the advent of the second of the two factors cited at the beginning of this chapter. But as just noted, government will almost certainly wish to implement policy along market lines, but make sure that it retains control. In schools it will want to ensure that professionals, as Pollitt (1992, p. 171) points out, are 'on tap' rather than 'on top'; that they contribute their services to a vision determined elsewhere. A good example of this is the control of the curriculum and increasingly of teaching methods in the UK. How is it to do this? Part can be done by utilizing the

developments in microtechnology to gain information much more speedily; part can then be gained by dispensing with intermediate layers of control and surveillance and having much more direct control. In the education sector, this at least partly explains the reduction in power of the LEAs and the increased surveillance and control produced by testing and publication of results at the ages of 7, 11, 14 and 16 and the huge influence of OFSTED inspections in schools.

However, there will always be the need for a layer of surveillance and control at the institutional level. What will this look like? It will take the form of the encouragement of a new breed of managers, those who run the institutions. In a seminal article Christopher Hood (1991) suggested that one of the most striking trends throughout the western world in the public sector in the last fifteen to twenty years has been the rise of what he calls the 'New Public Management' (NPM), a new kind of manager who, he suggests (pp. 4–5) is characterized by the following seven elements:

- a hands-on professional approach to management;
- use of explicit standards and measurements of performance;
- greater emphasis than previously on output controls;
- practice of breaking up larger units into smaller more manageable ones;
- embracement of greater competition in the public sector;
- enthusiasm for private-sector styles of management practice;
- acceptance of the need for greater discipline and parsimony in resource use.

Hood pointed out that this new breed of management, while underpinned by the principles of economy, efficiency and effectiveness, nevertheless has at least two different forms: one 'hard' and one 'soft'. The harder and chronologically earlier variant is characterized by neo-Taylorian aims of discipline, hierarchy and control and is suitable for managing costs in an aggressive manner and for imposing change on individuals and groups. This kind of approach was seen in UK government throughout the public sector in the 1980s, but was largely unsuited to education for two good reasons. A first reason was as Pollitt (1992, p. 115) points out:

> The new right's vision of efficient management lacked a coherent model of the highly motivated,

productive public servant. If it had one at all, it was a clockwork model that ran on targets and bonus pay, not a flesh-and-blood figure that needed public recognition and self-respect.

A second reason was that due to a lack of 'professional managers' principals were drawn from the teaching profession, in contrast to the health service where managers have little or no medical expertise, but are a distinct body of individuals. In such a situation, the 'hard' approach had a mixed reaction at best from those managing the school (see Grace, 1995). In many cases it became counter-productive, leading to sagging morale, reduced work effort and a need for the kind of 'punishment-centred bureaucracy' which Gouldner (1954) talked about. Indeed, this kind of approach actually contributed to the problems it was supposed to be solving: 'managerial interventions in support of more disciplined bureaucratic control directly reinforce the perceived problem of commitment and collaboration which they were originally meant to solve' (Reed, 1998, pp. 35–6).

In education, it has therefore tended to be substituted by a twin-pronged attack. The first prong is the introduction of the 'softer' model of management that stems from the business literature which stresses notions of 'culture' and 'quality' (e.g. Peters and Waterman, 1982; Deal and Kennedy, 1988). This kind of management attempts to nurture a spirited commitment from its workers to create a culture dedicated to the selling of a particular product and to the prosecution of their institutions' competitive advantage. The second has been for a government quango, the Teacher Training Agency, to take increased control of the in-service development of teachers through specification of what it will contribute to funding on university courses and, as importantly, its specification of the requirement of deputy-principals to qualify for a National Professional Qualification for Headteachers if they wish to move to a principal's position later in their career. By so doing, government attempts to control not only who manages, but more importantly how they manage.

From a teacher's point of view, these changes may not seem to amount to a great deal, but the following should be noted. First, the change to 'culture' and 'quality' management approaches is a change in form, but not in substance, from neo-Taylorian techniques. While the former seems rather less dedicated to the same ends of economy, efficiency and effectiveness, they both require that

teachers accept uncritically the general structure and rules within which their work takes place; their job is to implement others' directives, not to contribute in any substantive manner to the aims and purposes of such work. To take but one example: Murgatroyd and Morgan (1992, p. 121), on the development of Quality Schools and teachers who will want to contribute to such 'products', suggest that the empowerment of teachers:

> begins when the vision and goals have already been set by the school leaders. What a team or an individual is empowered to do is to turn the vision and strategy into reality through achieving those challenging goals set for them by the leadership of the school. Individuals are being empowered in terms of how they can achieve the goals set, not in terms of what the goals might be.

What is very clear is that a management is not required which questions the paradigm within which it works; which develops a workforce contributing to a vision of education; which sees education as a democratically based good for the whole community. Their picture, then, is a million miles away from the kind of normative public good which Grace (1988, p. 214,) describes:

> Might not education be regarded as a public good because its fundamental aim is to facilitate the development of the personality and artistic, creative and intellectual abilities of all citizens, regardless of their class, race or gender status, and regardless of their regional location? Might not education be regarded as a public good because it seeks to develop in all citizens a moral sense, a sense of social and fraternal responsibility for others and a disposition to act in rational and co-operative ways?

Such a vision implies that part of the mission of the teaching force is to have some overview of what the system should be doing and a commitment to ensuring that the system as a whole is dedicated to its achievement. But a post-Fordist agenda requires a very different workforce; one which concentrates upon the mechanics of implementation, the design and production of products which will satisfy the requirements of consumers. Questions about normative public goods, such as the need for multicultural education, are not part of a workforce agenda. These larger issues will be decided partly at the level of central government and, partly by the market; they are not the concern of the workforce.

Now perhaps this should not come as much of a surprise: the culture and quality initiatives in management evolved a business background. As Hollway (1991) points out, changes in managerial styles and philosophies in the business arena during this century have been devised primarily as a means of implementing managerial decisions, not as a means of facilitating the greater involvement and influence of the workforce. Further, as Leat (1993) suggests, if softer approaches fail to facilitate the implementation of managerial decisions in the business arena, they will be dropped and another strategy instituted. For this is what they are: strategies to achieve managerial ends, not fundamental changes in philosophy about worker participation or the development of a more empowered citizenry. This may be suitable for business, though I personally have considerable reservations. But it seems even more challengeable for education, if it is to be seen as a crucial institution in an open and democratic society where tolerance of difference of opinion and participation in decision-making are considered essential elements in the development of tomorrow's citizens.

Yet clearly such a managerialist approach to the running of educational institutions emasculates these ideals. For if the market has the effect of neutralizing concern about multicultural issues at the system level – or indeed of neutralizing concern about any educational initiative which takes a pro-active approach to the restructuring of education beyond that of the market – the new managerialism has the potential to create the same effect within institutions. This is because management is there to work in a quasi-market invented by government legislation, not to develop ideas beyond this marketplace, or to encourage their development by the workforce. Just as the manager at Marks and Spencer may contribute ideas to the greater effectiveness of the company in the marketplace, but will not question the existence of the company in that marketplace, so the educational principal and teacher (manager and worker) are being asked to contribute to the greater effectiveness of their school in the educational marketplace, but not to question the existence of the school in that marketplace.

The connection between the market and managerialism is now complete: the two function jointly to neuter debate about issues beyond those of institutional competitive advantage, to re-form principals and teachers into managers and workers. The logic of the market takes over, reducing the ability of both to look to anything further. As Nichols (1989, p. 298) says:

Whereas management . . . have a definite interest in recognising more fully that production is social production – i.e. in recognising that men are not simply commodities but thinking, social beings, with potentially valuable contributions to make, and with the potential to work together more productively – they also have an interest in limiting the development of these human potentials. And this is because, though it would suit workers to act as if there were really socialism inside work, managers themselves have to operate in a world in which market forces reign and impede the development of the very unstinted cooperation they wish to bring about.

In such a world, and in spite of the good intentions of individuals, multicultural education is going to have a very hard time of it.

Redressing the balance

Management has a centrality to education that is comparatively new. Before the 1970s it would have been difficult to find many books in the area. Since then, for a variety of reasons (see Bottery, 1992), there has been an explosion of literature and interest which has brought education into line not only with other areas of the public sector, but also with the business world. When in a standard textbook Koontz and O'Donnell (1978, p. 1) argued that 'perhaps there is no more important area of human activity than managing', there would still be many in education who would see this as breathtaking. It is, however, an assertion which is becoming increasingly common in the public sector, certainly with the NPMs. Where professionals are seen as 'on tap' rather than 'on top', then the argument that the framing of vision (by managers), the specification of the degree and manner of involvement by professionals (by managers), the co-ordination of their effort (by managers) and measurement assessment of their work (by managers), does add weight to the argument that managers – and the policies they are employed to implement – are central to undertakings.

Yet while it is still possible to conceptualize education in ways different to this mantra, there are a number of points which need to be examined. The first was made some time ago by Dennis Main Wilson when he said of light entertainment at the BBC: 'Comedy isn't talent-led anymore. It's management led. It used to be management's job to support, now they dictate. More and more produ-cers are just given formats to occupy' (quoted in Sedgwick, 1990, p. 5). This is the cry of the profes-sional, no longer able to exercise professional, autonomous choice in how the job is done. It is the cry of Charles Handy's (1987) 'Dionysian' man-agement gods, believing that the organization is there to facilitate their actions, not for them to fit in with some master plan. Many might say that the Dionysian is dead, or well on the way to extinction; some might consider this to be no bad thing, given the way in which some professionals have in the past used their positions to make life easier for themselves, rather than their clients. But it might also be argued that the situation cannot be healthy where those who understand the minutiae of both theory and practice are given little say in their over-all effects. Indeed, the way forward may not be to have professionals either on tap or on top, but to have them and their professional associations work-ing in co-ordination and participation with man-agers and governments to produce the best service for clients both at institutional and policy levels. If this does not occur, it wastes valuable talent, as well as failing to focus on alternative perspectives as what should be the vision of a particular institution.

This latter point is particularly important, because it is unlikely that neither a government committed to the kinds of post-Fordist policy described above, nor its managerial creation, those imbued with the values of NPM, will see the kinds of problems that ensue from the prosecution of their vision. They are unlikely to see that efficiency, economy and effectiveness may be useful goals, but there is nothing self-evident about them which should make them ends in themselves. They are values like any others and need to be assessed as to their desirability. Concentration upon efficiency, for example, can become so obsessive that it takes on the role of being a universal criterion for intelli-gent conduct. Yet it should be obvious that other values, which do not necessarily co-ordinate with efficiency, may be given higher priority in some cir-cumstances. An obsession with the efficiency, economy and effectiveness produces an inability to see that proponents of other values, like community cohesion, equity, justice and tolerance – all hallmarks of a multicultural approach to education – may provide very strong grounds for greater attention to their inclusion in a managerial over-view.

They are unlikely to see that the basis for the evaluation of anyone or anything is not necessarily what people are prepared to pay for their goods and services. This is the fundamental value of individual consumerism in a marketplace and excludes wider ethical judgements, leaving it to the market to decide between competing visions of the 'good'. Yet evaluation of any person or project needs to be at least partially reframed in terms of the contribu-tion that a person or community can make to the social cohesion, the tolerance, the public good of that society. These values of citizenry, democracy and collectivity are very different from the values of the market, managerialism or economic com-petitiveness and they underpin a thoroughgoing multicultural policy.

Furthermore, the 'rational', self-interested indi-vidual of classical economics can only truly function within the framework of a community of a wider moral vision. This is for two reasons. The first is that the 'economic' man is a fiction, a grotesquely dis-torted and reduced picture of fully social and caring humanity. Any policies (and economic theories) based purely upon the notions of such castrated motivation will inevitably do huge damage to the quality of the society in which they are formulated, for they will neglect, even destroy, all that is most precious in the human endeavour. Economics is the means to these other ends, rather than being but a means to these ends. Indeed, a passion for economic productivity is not even an obviously necessary one, for many of humanity's greatest achievements have been in spite of, or even because of, economic privations. This is something that Adam Smith recognized when writing his seminal works, but which many of his subsequent admirers left behind when plundering his writings (see Ormerod, 1994).

But the rational self-interested individual is also an incomplete picture of societal functioning for more mundane reasons: the unfettered pursuit of market objectives leads to the diminution of those choices upon which free market proponents depend. To take a simple example, in an edu-cational free market of three schools, A, B and C, the opportunity to exercise individual choice may well lead to a situation where one school may be forced out of 'business', thus actually reducing the choices available. Markets of all kinds tend to mono-polies, which lead inevitably to the diminution of choice and the return of the power of the producer. Without a framework determined by extra-market forces which attempts to keep a variety of choice available, the market will probably disappear.

Finally, without some kind of external prompting policymakers and managers are unlikely to see that ideas which might have profound effects upon the development of a richer, more democratic and participative management style have, because of the myopia of the market and NPM, been misinterpreted, subverted and then incorporated into the NPM mantra. Take, for example, the notion of 'culture'. Initially a large and welcome step forward on the positivist, natural science approach to management, it gave weight to the notion that the organization was no mechanistic one-value piece of human engineering, but essentially a social construction of meanings and embodied 'an ordered system of meaning and of symbols, in terms of which social interaction takes place' (Geertz, 1973, p. 144).

In so doing, the way was open for a more pluralistic, democratic and tolerant view of values, understandings and meanings within organizations – one's ideal for the flourishing of multiculturalism and for the development and education of those within organizations towards such understandings. Yet what happened within the management of the private sector – and from thence to the public sector and to education – was a different version based upon the message of Peters and Waterman's *In Search of Excellence* (1982). This suggested that culture was not only changeable, but was manipulable to a managerial and ultimately NPM vision. Instead of shared visions as recognition of diverse meanings within cultures, a visionary leadership would transform the vision and meaning of followers towards the managerial path of excellence. They quote (p. 16) with apparent approval the commentary on 3M's version of teamwork, where seemingly 'the brainwashed members of an extremist political sect are no more conformist in their central beliefs'. The next step for such an approach within the public sector is the intolerance of anything different. This is described in education by Hargreaves (1992) as a 'contrived collegiality' which is imposed on groups in schools by those at the top and beyond, and thence upon the individual, such that the individual meaning is outlawed and all must walk to the same drummer. Those concepts which could have emancipated the school communities and led to a flowering of multicultural and other social and ethical initiatives are transmuted and subverted to fit other agendas.

Yet it will be clear from what has gone before that NPM is the spawn of a larger agenda which is concerned with not only the production of markets in education, but also the tight control of policy, tolerating little or no debate and listening to alternative opinion only when forced to do so. So multicultural initiatives are threatened at the managerial and policy levels and it is unlikely that there will be much alteration in NPM until the level of policy is changed. Such policy change would seem to involve two separate but equally important issues.

The first is a re-examination of the functioning of markets and, crucially, of allowing markets to decide how choices are made. Now, it has to be admitted that this can be political quicksand. One need recall the problems in the USA twenty years ago concerning the bussing of black children into white areas to realize that interventions for socially desirable ends can be rapidly transformed into the actions of Big Brother. Yet it should also be remembered that the operation of a free market in parental choice of school – 'open enrolment' – was put forward in the UK Education Bill of 1988, only one year after DES Circular 3/87, which was very clear in its endorsement of the need for forward planning by authorities in order to deal with falling school rolls and to increase efficiency and cost effectiveness. Indeed, there seems to have been remarkably little objection to such a role for forward planning. In the submission to Kenneth Baker, then Secretary of State for Education, Nottinghamshire County Council pointed out that in 1987, 99.88 per cent of parents in their area were satisfied with the existing system (quoted in Haviland, 1988, p. 179). Similarly the Conservative Association stated that 'the vast majority of LEAs manage to meet the first choice of nearly all parents, with a success rate of over 90 per cent the norm. In many LEAs the figure is well over 90 per cent' (*ibid.* p. 183).

Here is a situation where the free market took a back seat to a managed system and yet there has been remarkably little complaint. Some may argue that all this smacks of paternalism, but the point is one of a balance between individual choice and system functioning. What makes this different from post-Fordist management is first that such managed systems involve intermediate layers of government which allow for a greater participation; second, that it is much more tolerant of contrary views than post-Fordist management appears to be. Together with the multicultural policies it encourages, such a system allows, indeed requires, the beat of different drummers, the reconciliation of their different rhythms.

So the final change must be one which bites the political bullet. This will only come about when two things happen. The first, because of the advent of New Labour, may already be in place. This is when the unidimensional, monocultural view of British society ceases to be the dominant ideology behind government policy on multicultural issues. The second which must happen is not quite so party political. It involves the bravery of a government to make proactive decisions on the racial composition of schools, which will upset some voters. Political cowardice on multicultural issues may drive politicians to abnegate their responsibility in this area and instead to insist on the continued use of markets. But for a multicultural policy to be really effective, it must transcend the classroom and school and have support at system and policy levels. The importance of the centrality of multicultural debate, and the acknowledgement that policy-making rather than the market must once again take centre stage, needs to be endorsed by government of whatever hue. This is no easy task and will be subject to attack from those afraid of big government, as well as those who would rather not get involved in a potential vote loser.

However, the creation of a just, tolerant and caring society is not one which can be left to the market, nor to those who would merely compete in it. Society is more than a sum of its individuals, but creates the conditions within which such individuals live and develop. Citizenship is more than the self-interested pursuit of consumable goods, but involves an awareness and concern for others. This points to an interdependence of citizenship and education and, as importantly, of the possibility of a citizenship which transcends national boundaries:

If the citizenship ideal is to remain strong, then multicultural education for both the host and minority populations is imperative. Multicultural education may well, indeed, be the key to achieving further progress in consolidating citizenship in both its cosmopolitan and national democratic sense. It can strengthen world citizenship by showing that, if people of diverse ethnic and religious backgrounds can live in harmony in a state, then the division of the world into separate states on those same ethnic and religious criteria is not immutable. (Heater, 1990, p. 344)

Multicultural understanding, tolerance and the creation of democratic communities do not happen by themselves; it is the task of governments as well as those within the schools to engineer this. The market and technical-rational management are no answer: they only reinforce their continued neglect.

References

Ball, S. (1990) *Politics and Policy Making in Education: Explorations in Policy Sociology*. London: Routledge.

Blair, M. and Arnott, M. (1993) Black and anti-racist perspectives on the National Curriculum. In A. S. King and M. J. Reiss (eds), *The Multicultural Dimension of the National Curriculum*. London: Falmer, pp. 259–79.

Bottery, M. (1992) *The Ethics of Educational Management*. London: Cassell.

Burrows, R. and Loader, B. (eds) (1994) *Towards a Post-Fordist Welfare State*? London: Routledge.

Deal, T. and Kennedy, A. (1988) *Corporate Cultures*. Harmondsworth: Penguin.

Friedman, M. (1961) *Capitalism and Freedom*. Chicago: Chicago University Press.

Gamble, A. (1988) *The Free Economy and the Strong State*. London: Macmillan.

Geertz, C. (1973) *The Interpretation of Cultures*. London: Hutchinson.

George, V. and Miller, S. (1994) *Social Policy towards 2000*. London: Routledge.

Gillborn, D. (1995) *Racism and Antiracism in Real Schools*. Buckingham: Open University Press.

Gouldner, A. (1954) *Patterns of Industrial Democracy*. Glenco IL: Free Press.

Grace, G. (1988) Education: commodity or public good? *British Journal of Educational Studies* 37, 207–21.

Grace, G. (1995) *School Leadership: Beyond Education Management*. London: Falmer.

Gray, J. (1992) *The Moral Foundations of Market Institutions*. London: IEA Health and Welfare Unit.

Handy, C. (1985) *The Gods of Management*. London: Pan.

Hargreaves, A. (1992) Contrived collegiality: the micropolitics of teacher collaboration. In N. Bennet, M. Crawford and C. Riches (eds), *Managing Change in Education*. London: Paul Chapman.

Haviland, J. (1988) *Take Care, Mr. Baker!* London: Fourth Estate.

Hayek, F. (1944) *The Road to Serfdom*. London: Routledge and Kegan Paul.

Heater, D. (1990) *Citizenship: The Civic Ideal in World History, Politics and Education*. London: Longman.

Hollway, W. (1991) *Work Psychology and Organisational Behavior*. London: Sage.

Hood, C. (1991) A public management for all seasons? *Public* 69, 3–19.

Koontz, H. and O'Donnell, C. (1978) *Essentials of Management, 2nd edn.* New York: McGraw-Hill.

Leat, D. (1993) *Managing across Sectors.* London: City University Press.

McRae, H. (1994) *The World in 2020.* London: HarperCollins.

Major, J. (1993) Extract from a speech to the Conservative Group for Europe. *PAIU News* **188**, 93, 22 April.

Mullard, C. (1980) *Racism in Society and Schools. History and Policy.* London: University of London: Institute of Education.

Murgatroyd, S. and Morgan, C. (1992) *Total Quality Management.* Buckingham: Open University Press.

National Curriculum Council (NCC) (1990) *Curriculum Guidance 3: The Whole.* York: National Curriculum Council.

Nichols, T. (1980) Management, ideology and practice. In G. Esland and Salaman (eds), *The Politics of Work and Occupations.* Milton Keynes: Open University Press, pp. 279–302.

Ormerod, P. (1994) *The Death of Economics.* London: Faber and Faber.

Pearce, S. (1986) Swann and the spirit of the age. In F. Palmer (ed.), *Anti-racism: An Assault on Education and Values.* London: Sherwood Press.

Peters, T. and Waterman, R. (1982) *In Search of Excellence.* New York: Harper and Row.

Pollitt, C. (1992) *Managerialism and the Public Services* 2nd edn. Oxford: Blackwell.

Rampton, A. (1981) *West Indian Children in our Schools.* Cmnd 8273. London: HMSO.

Reed, M. I. (1988) The problem of human agency in organizational analysis. *Organisation Studies* **9** 1, 33–46.

Sedgwick, F. (1990) The management of poetry in education. *Curriculum* **11** (1),

Sewell, G. and Wilkinson, B. (1992) 'Someone to watch over me': surveillance, discipline and the just-in-time labour process. *Sociology* **20** (2), 271–89.

Smyth, J. (ed) (1993) *A Socially Critical View of the 'Self-Managing School'.* Lewes: Falmer.

Swann, Lord (1985) *Education for All: Final Report of the Committee of Inquiry into the Education of Children from Ethnic Minority Groups.* Cmnd 9453. London: HMSO.

Times Educational Supplement (1990) Editorial. June.

Troyna, B. and Williams, J. (1986) *Racism, Education and the State.* London: Croom Helm.

Wilkinson, R. (1996) *Unhealthy Societies.* London: Routledge.

3 "Heritable Intelligence": Real and Important, or an Arbitrary Social Construct?

STEPHEN CHILTON and ANNE MEYER

The planet of Pseudopodia had a society of advanced beings, who called themselves "the people," as beings tend to do in their own language. These people had a wonderful anatomy: each of them was born with a unique collection of different-shaped limbs, which grew over time and were of great use both in helping them with a variety of chores and in amusing themselves. Some limbs were particularly suited for coring fruits, some for doing somersaults, some for climbing their version of trees, some for running fast, and so on through a vast variety of shapes. Some people had limbs with no known function. Such limbs were put to use wherever they could be, although their relative disuse meant that they never developed as fully as the limbs with established uses. Occasionally, however, someone invented a game or task for which the limb appeared perfectly suited, and such invention was always an occasion for great rejoicing, the date of the invention being celebrated for centuries afterwards, particularly by the people endowed with the limb, so that during historical periods of great creativity there were often more holidays than work days. Even without an official holiday as an excuse, people were likely at any moment to show off their talented limbs in some impromptu demonstration. An audience never failed to gather, applaud, and join in as each person "showed her stuff," whether she be master of some rare limb or even an infant growing her first limb, for in Pseudopodia everyone was unselfconscious, having from birth a firm understanding that her talents were entirely admirable.

People had by no means the same set of limbs; in fact, there was an enormous variation in form and function among the limbs. However, everyone seemed to have the same number of limbs (and an extensive and interesting variety of them, too), or if fewer limbs, then a correspondingly greater size and dexterity. In fact, things had been so wonderfully arranged by their beneficent Creator, or maybe just Nature, that taking both number and size into account, everyone had been given the same "quantity" of limb. Recognition of this had given rise long ago to a happy egalitarianism among the people: recognizing the equality evident in their forms, they shared freely among themselves. Those whose limbs had no known function made shift to help as best they could, and far from being stigmatized by their odd limbs, they were encouraged to work in the institutes devoted to inventing and elaborating arts, games, and tasks befitting the limbs.

The genetic makeup of the people was such that their limbs were affected by both heredity and environment, much as our own are. Different limb forms seemed to be associated with different genes, and it was often said that such-and-such a limb "ran in the family." But limbs were also subject to the influences of use and environment. When people relied mainly on only a few of their many limbs, those limbs tended to grow stronger and become more finely controlled, while the other limbs tended to atrophy and stiffen with age. Still, cases had been known where a person took up a new limb late in life, and the newly favored limb inevitably grew, strengthened, and functioned as well as its earlier used mates.

This happy society was disrupted when – o woeful day! – a conquering tribe arrived from afar who had limbs particularly suited to . . . to . . . well, the chroniclers had difficulty expressing it, since no such limbs had been seen before, but we humans know what those long limbs with razor edges and needle tips were good for. In short order, the newcomers – we can call them "Sworders," though the other Pseudopodians had a rude name for them – came to rule the Pseudopodians.

The Sworders themselves honored those with the longest and sharpest limb – honor that could always be prompted and reaffirmed by a few pointed "reminders" if necessary. The longer sworded received not just honor but also food; in their constant competition with each other, Sworders were able to command food in proportion to their limb. Sworder philosophers had long justified this practice as merely a matter of survival of the fittest. It was obvious that those with the longest and sharpest limbs were best able to survive, since those without such limbs tended to die young, either from malnutrition or from the "reminders" administered them by their sharper and longer limbed brethren. The Sworders therefore let nature take its course, accepting malnutrition of the poorly sworded in order to keep them from weakening the race – either immediately, by using up food supplies better devoted to the growth of people with the more useful swords, or in the long run, by passing on their genetic inferiority.

This doctrine was only reinforced by the easy conquest of Pseudopodia, whose former happy situation had ignored Nature's demand for Natural selection, represented in the collective person of the Sworders, and so the conquerors imposed their culture upon Pseudopodia, as Nature had obviously decreed. The Sworders were not racists, however; the Pseudopodians lacked both honor and food not because of their ancestry but rather for their lack of Nature's favored limb.

The Pseudopodians discovered what their simple but adequate diet had not shown them before: that malnutrition made all their limbs weaker – weaker, shorter, clumsier. The older Pseudopodians mourned the deformation of their children, but the children themselves, and their children thereafter, having never seen what their limbs might be, began to see their forms as the natural way of things – indeed, as another reflection of their own disgracefully short swords.

Centuries later, the two populations had blended somewhat, and the terms "Sworders" and "Pseudopodians" had become archaic. Philosophers of the now blended society began to re-examine the nature of limb skill within the population. Their researches were skillfully done, their methods subtle and precise, and their conclusions clear and unsurprising. After examining a wide variety of limb types, and after being sure to study people from a wide variety of genetic backgrounds, they found that every form of limb skill was positively correlated with every other. Looking at the descendants of the Sworders, who had long fed well, they found every variety of limb relatively powerful (though obviously not all equal), while among the descendants of the Pseudopodians they found every variety of limb relatively weak. In consequence of these patterns, limb skills all intercorrelated positively, with the consequence that factor analyses repeatedly yielded a single, unipolar first factor. These results convinced the philosophers that limb skill was unitary; some people had it, and some didn't, but these differences tended to show themselves in all limb types.

Further studies of the data revealed that the best measure of overall limb skill, the test that best divided the skilled from the unskilled, was the "long, sharp limb test," i.e., did this person have a long, sharp limb? Since the differentiation among people had long depended on the length and sharpness of the one particular limb, it was not surprising that the "long, sharp limb test" loaded highly on the first factor. Curiously, however, the philosophers found a different interpretation for this phenomenon. It was common knowledge – obvious to the meanest intelligence – that long, sharp limbs were markers of special talent, and the data were held to validate this lore.

It was soon discovered, and this finding made the philosophers nervous, that limb skill was hereditary. This nervousness peaked when the philosophers observed that people at the bottom of the social heap – the descendants of the original Pseudopodians, though the philosophers had no way of knowing that – simply had less limb skill, on the average, than those on the top – the descendants of the Sworders. This was particularly pronounced in the best test they had – the "long, sharp limb test." Clearly, however unfortunately, genetics had condemned those on the bottom to their position.

These latter-day Sworders were good people, of course; the days of raid and conquest were long gone, and they pitied the poor, crippled people on the bottom. But in the face of this genetic deficiency, all the Sworders could do, and do it they did, was provide the underlings with some basic food and medical care, and some scholarships for the occasional lucky child born with long, sharp limbs. Otherwise, all continued as it had, for they believed the analyses were plain, and one cannot fly in the face of Nature. After all, even in those modern times, one had to keep in mind the survival of the fittest.

Scientists and social critics have long debated the existence, measurement, and heritability of "intelligence," and the policy implications of that heritability.[1] *The Bell Curve* (Herrnstein and Murray, 1994) is only the most recent of the works bringing this debate to a head; two decades and more ago, Arthur Jensen's work prompted a similar debate; there were many other researchers before that.[2]

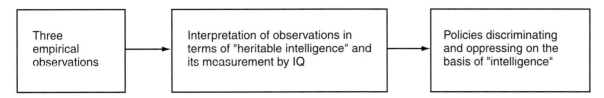

Figure 3.1 The "heritable intelligence" argument

Figure 3.1 shows the basic structure of the argument made by proponents of "heritable intelligence."

We start with three sets of empirical observations: the data on which all subsequent analysis rests:

- *Observation 1*: Quite disparate tests of "intellectual skill" have something in common statistically. In statistical terms, they are all positively intercorrelated and thus – in even more technical language – have some common variance and load positively on the first principal component of their correlation matrix.[3]
- *Observation 2*: IQ tests predict later success in many fields of endeavor. Granted, the prediction is imperfect, but it is present for any number of fields. The highest correlations between tests and success (occupational status and/or salary) occur for those tests that load most highly on the first principal component.[4]
- *Observation 3*: The IQ scores of genetically related people correlate, with the correlation increasing as the genetic relationship becomes closer. Environment is acknowledged to affect IQ scores, but this correlation pattern remains even when controlling for social class, education, race, gender, and the like (Herrnstein and Murray 1994, p. 105).

These three sets of empirical results are then interpreted as reflecting the presence of a unitary, heritable, socially significant mental faculty ("intelligence"), measurable by IQ tests. This interpretation then becomes the justification for various discriminatory, oppressive policies – either against specific groups thought to have less "intelligence" or simply against the "less intelligent" in general.

Opponents of such policies have opposed them through four types of attacks:

1 We should dismiss, ignore, or even suppress the entire discussion before it starts.
2 The empirical data are invalid.

3 We cannot conclude from the data:

(a) the existence of this hypothetical concept called "intelligence";
(b) the validity of "its" measurement by IQ tests;
(c) "its" heritability;
(d) differences in "it" among ethnic or racial groups.

4 The existence of measurable "heritable intelligence", even with differences among groups, does not obviate the normative evil of policies that discriminate or tend to oppress on the basis of "intelligence."

The next section of this work (Section I) presents a variety of these attacks and argues that each is logically invalid, politically counterproductive, and/or normatively weak.

Section II presents a stronger line of attack, based on a prima facie-plausible, alternative hypothesis for the patterns found in the empirical data, namely, that these patterns are the natural result of a society more or less arbitrarily organized to differentially employ and reward one set of skills.[5] In other words, "intelligence" denotes not a "natural" ability but instead a social construct brought into statistical existence in consequence of the oppressive, discriminatory policies embedded in social organization around a particular set of skills. This "arbitrary social construct" hypothesis anticipates and accounts for the statistical patterns found in the data, and reveals that the use of the construct "heritable intelligence" reflects and supports an ethically arbitrary, and therefore oppressive, social organization. The existence of a plausible alternative hypothesis, one with radically different policy implications, undercuts the "hereditary intelligence" position.

Section III explores in a preliminary way the implications of the "arbitrary social construct" hypothesis. It argues that the hypothesis flows out of a prior-to-society perspective, and that this perspective permits, justifies, and points the way toward a society based on an acceptance and appreciation of people's diverse capacities and a politics based on discourse.

Section IV is devoted to a defense and clarification of the "arbitrary social construct" hypothesis to meet the many problems to which it at first blush appears subject.

This chapter will cite little specific empirical research. As mentioned earlier, "heritable intelligence" is an issue of long standing, not one tied to any single work. Today the debate focuses on *The Bell Curve*; yesterday it focused on Arthur Jensen's work; tomorrow it will focus on something else. These works themselves rest on much other work.[6] This chapter takes the position that the empirical claims are most likely correct, on the whole, and thus it is most likely futile to pursue a strategy of refuting this or that bit of research.[7] The attempt to create a discursive politics within a society supporting diversity is served better by this chapter's reinterpretation of the empirical claims than by an heroic, and likely doomed, resistance to them.

I.   The attacks on "heritable intelligence", and problems therewith

This section presents and argues against the four lines of attack mentioned above.

1. We should dismiss, ignore, or even suppress the entire discussion before it starts.

Attack 1
"This research is used to support an oppressive, 'far-right' or 'racist' agenda. Indeed, the Nazis used this sort of thinking to justify racism."[8]

Response
This attack is not an attack on the truth of the claim but rather an appeal to ignore the claim. There are several problems with such a tactic. First, the use to which a truth is put has no bearing on its truth status. One can note that an empirical observation has unfortunate consequences – "Gee, if we didn't have gravity, people wouldn't fall down and bump their heads" – but this is a false trail. If the facts are as represented, proponents of "heritable intelligence" will simply point to the facts over and over again, making such critics as Beardsley and Gould seem blindly oppositional. We may use the prospect of the bad consequences as a motivation to examine

the empirical evidence more closely or to reinterpret their meaning, but bad consequences are not an argument against the facts. Indeed, the charge of racism sometimes seems to be made backwards: the racism of the investigator is judged by the acceptability of his/her results.

Second, our society is divided over (or at least confused about) these issues to such an extent that we have to deal directly with them; there is no elite capable of suppressing this issue; we cannot put the genie back in the bottle. And even if such a hegemonic elite exists, it cannot be taken for granted that it would want to oppose these claims.

Finally, we have to ask if we really want to advocate a politics devoted to the suppression of discourse, particularly when that suppression is organized around what really amounts to name calling ("far right", etc.).[9] Pushing this point to the extreme, do we wish to create or support the existence of an elite capable of suppressing discourse?

Attack 2
"Such empirical research should not be carried out, nor should its implications be discussed, because such research and discussion would exacerbate tensions that could tear society apart."[10]

Response
Certainly tensions will arise from the anger of people who feel that society has discriminated against them. In the face of arguments justifying such discrimination, and in the face of social policy supporting it, such people will conclude that they have no stake in the society. However, there are other sorts of tensions in the society as well: tensions arising from the anger of people who see their well being and their children's threatened. If such people are offered no better explanation for the difficulties they face, then arguments targeting the "hereditarily stupid" will find ready acceptance. The fact is that people are hurting and scared, and if we do not clearly explain the true sources of that pain and fear, then ready-to-hand targets will be found. Politicians say, "You can't defeat someone with no one." In the absence of persuasive explanations and positive policy directions, the effort to suppress discussion will be read by many as simply a dismissal of their concerns.

Attack 3
"Telling people intelligence is innate causes them to

give up trying to use whatever other talents they can bring to bear."[11]

Response
This attack has two problems. First, it acquiesces in the claim that "stupid people's" lack of "intelligence" says something normatively important about them. Certainly in our society this lack says something about their life chances and the oppression they will face, but this is a far cry from acquiescing in the assumption that these lesser life chances and oppressions are objectively determined and therefore normatively acceptable – or at least neutral.

Second, having hypothesized the existence of a "less intelligent" class, this attack adopts a paternalistic attitude toward it. "They may be stupid, but perhaps if we hide it from them, they'll be happier." Such an attitude creates politics predicated on "protecting" each other from unpleasant truths, undercutting the possibility of a politics based on discourse, embodying mutual respect (instead of paternalism) and a clear view of the world (instead of polite fictions). If "intelligence" were innate, by what right would we hide this fact from others? Whose authority have we to decide that others "shouldn't give up"?

2 The empirical data are invalid.

Attack 1
"Since previous research in this field (e.g., Cyril Burt's twin studies) was falsified, we need pay no attention to other research."[12]

Response
Falsification certainly occurs, but it is no guarantee of the invalidity of the theory. For example, the Mendelian theory of inheritance is now firmly established, even though it now appears that Gregor Mendel falsified his results to make his data conform more closely to his theory. Falsification should make us more careful in examining and replicating research, but it does not alter the need to examine evidence.

Attack 2
"Since the researchers or funding agencies have 'far right' or 'racist' political commitments, their interpretations, research methods, or even data will be slanted to reach their predetermined conclusions, and hence may be dismissed without specific examination."[13]

Response
It is surely hard to untangle the web of normative claims, empirical findings, subjective judgments about the validity thereof, and emotional reactions to the complex world. But this argument cuts both ways. To repeat the argument made earlier, do we really want the brutal politics that follows from a rejection of discourse?

Ad hominem arguments are logically invalid, since they attack the claimant but not the claim. They are normatively invalid if one takes as the purpose of politics, as this chapter does, not the defeat of one actor by another but rather the discovery of truth, the reconciliation of disputants, and the re-establishment of mutual understanding. *Ad hominem* attacks are basically arguments that we should pay no attention to the other; do we really desire (or could we even win) the brutal politics that follows from this rejection of discourse? Similar considerations apply to the attempt to suppress discussion on the grounds of its bad policy implications.[14] Finally, *ad hominem* arguments are politically weak, since the proponents of "heritable intelligence" are too strong to be ignored and will not vanish because we speak ill of them.[15]

3 The data do not imply – or at any rate prove – one or more of the following elements of the "heritable intelligence" position:

   (a) the existence of this hypothetical concept called "intelligence";
   (b) the validity of "its" measurement by IQ tests;
   (c) "its" heritability;
   (d) differences in "it" between ethnic or racial groups.

Attack 1
"The data do not prove the existence of heritable intelligence, since correlation does not prove causation. 'Intelligence' therefore might only be the reification of a mere statistical pattern."[16]

Response
Proponents of "heritable intelligence" have provided both data and an explanation of the correlations, an explanation that resonates with widespread ordinary observation. Their explanation will carry the day – deserves to carry the day – unless opponents provide an alternative explanation. The attack as stated above is true only in the narrow sense that further argument is required to

establish causality, not in a sweeping denial that intercorrelations are meaningful. Such a denial could be used to deny examination of any statistical regularity, so its radical application is logically invalid and has a head-in-the-sand quality that makes it politically counterproductive.[17]

Attack 2
"The view of intelligence as a unitary ability is not valid, since factor analysis of the data reveals a multiplicity of factors, not an all-explaining, unitary 'intelligence' factor. This multiplicity is made clearer after the rotation of factors. Therefore intelligence is multifaceted, not a single concept."[18]

Response
Unquestionably people have diverse skills; unquestionably the reduction of "intelligence" to a single number represents a simplification of mental reality. But critics need to explain how, if "intelligence" is in the final analysis multifaceted:

* diverse tests are positively intercorrelated;[19]
* the tests that most clearly focus on "intelligence" (as commonly understood) are most central to what is common among all of the tests;[20]
* this central factor correlates with social success and occupational prestige.[21]

Without some plausible alternative explanation, the "multiple-intelligence" criticism cannot call "heritable intelligence" claims into question.[22] For similar reasons it is irrelevant that several principal components of the correlation matrix can be combined and rotated to reveal the presence of several sub-types of tests; the unipolarity of the first principal component – the positive intercorrelations mentioned above – remains to be explained.

Attack 3
"'Intelligence' is not a valid concept, since several types of evidence contradict the image of 'intelligence' as a fixed, innate capacity. IQ scores can change through life, modified by education and experience. The effect of environment is also shown, albeit indirectly, by the change in IQ scores over recent decades. The test-retest variability of IQ scores also shows that 'intelligence' is not a fixed, innate capacity. Group or even individual differences in 'intelligence' can be attributed to bad teaching, low expectations, differential school fund-

ing, poor social conditions, and many other environmental factors."[23]

Response
This is a straw-man argument, pretending that the oppressive, discriminatory implications of "heritable intelligence" research only apply when "intelligence" is completely resistant to alteration and/or when IQ tests are perfect measures of that "intelligence." Unfortunately, these oppressive, discriminatory implications remain as long as "intelligence" is to some extent resistant to modification and IQ tests measure "intelligence" with some accuracy.

There are few tests for which one cannot train, and there will certainly be practical difficulties in testing for this inherent "intelligence." But the tests of "intelligence" are relatively stable, and so its proponents can fall back on the argument that in the imperfect world of psychological measurement, some variation in scores must be expected and, not being particularly large, do not falsify the theory of an underlying, stable "intelligence." At best, this objection can only argue that the use of IQ scores needs to be toned down in proportion to their inaccuracy.

Attack 4
"IQ is not a valid measure of 'intelligence', since the definition of 'intelligence' is racist and the measures are constructed to favor one race over another. This undercuts the concept of 'intelligence', and certainly undercuts the findings of racial differences in 'intelligence'."[24]

Response
Many IQ tests are likely culturally biased, and any such bias casts into doubt conclusions about inter-racial differences. But the problem posed by the "heritable intelligence" proponents is deeper than the inflammatory issue of racial differences, and we should recognize the full weight of it. If "intelligence" is indeed heritable, then somewhere, sometime, some group will be shown to have a genetically greater or lesser endowment of "intelligence" than some other group. Ultimately, we would have to confront and answer the question of whether the possession of "intelligence" can justify discriminatory policies. The issue we must confront is the meaning and heritability of "intelligence," not racial differences.

This objection is close to the mark, however, in

pointing out that "intelligence" is defined relative to a dominant social group. It goes askew, however, when instead of demonstrating the moral arbitrariness of the concept, it only argues that different races have the same amount of this desirable thing. It is not much of a gain when one oppressed group, claiming it has been incorrectly measured, lets another group be oppressed by a corrected measure.

Attack 5

"The data do not show that IQ is heritable."

Response

The literature is massive on both sides; this chapter will certainly not decide such an extensive, complex issue, or even shed much light on it. The chapter's basic argument, however, is that the heritability of our capacities has, when viewed in the proper light, different and perhaps happier implications than we have been led to believe.

Furthermore, the present authors are persuaded that we humans inherit much of our capacities: not just physical appearance, but also personality and cognitive skills. In our view, stubborn, endless opposition to the possibility of heritability is a blind alley, and if intelligence really is heritable, our stubborn opposition will only weaken us.

4 The existence of measurable "heritable intelligence," even with differences among groups, does not justify policies that discriminate or tend to oppress on the basis of "intelligence."

Attack 1

"There are many skills we value as a society, including determination and hard work, which can make up for many deficiencies of intelligence. Why should we privilege only one set of skills?"[25]

Response

This is where the second empirical observation comes into play. While society certainly recognizes and even rewards a variety of skills, the set most reliably recognized and rewarded is that captured by the concept "intelligence," making this privileging of "intelligence" a natural consequence of social life.[26] Critics cannot subvert this claim of naturalness simply by railing at it. This chapter tries to show how "intelligence" is socially constructed

and rewarded (instead of "natural"), thus providing the necessary subversion.

In addition, this attack accepts the reification of "intelligence" and agrees that its absence is a deficiency, so when the day is done, this attack can only be counter-productive.

Finally, this objection is weak even on its own terms. Since "high-intelligence" people can also have these other strengths, the objection cannot stand against oppressive, discriminatory policies. It argues at best that other strengths should be considered in understanding social success, while admitting that "low-intelligence" folks start with a strike or two against them.

Attack 2

"The genetic variation between races is much less than the genetic variation among individuals within a single race. Applied to 'intelligence' in particular, it is easy to find African-Americans who score higher on IQ tests than some European-Americans, or higher than the European-American average, or higher than most or all European-Americans."[27]

Response

These things may be true, but they have little bearing on the policy debate. The existence of a few exceptional cases proves nothing; the claims buttressing the "heritable intelligence" arguments are about an overall pattern of genetic ability. It is pointless to advance one exception when the other side can advance cases in support.

In addition, this attack accepts that discrimination on the basis of "intelligence" is fine, even though the concept of "intelligence" itself is problematic, as described below, and even though its application will result in racial groups being treated differently from each other on the average. Suppose it were proven that African-Americans had exactly the same average "intelligence" as European-Americans, but our society continued to oppress and discriminate against "low-intelligence" citizens. Would we not still wish to resist such policies as oppression of the diversity of people's capacities? Conversely, suppose it were conclusively demonstrated that African-Americans had substantially below-average "intelligence"; would that justify a continued discrimination against and oppression of them?

The issue of racial differences taps into a deep-seated conflict in American society, and so the debate over "heritable intelligence" tends to get organized around that, even though the existence of such differences is not a logically central issue.[28]

We now turn to a set of three normative attacks on the policies implied by the "heritable intelligence" hypothesis. Since these three attacks each fail in the same way, they are stated together and then replied to *en bloc*.

Attack 3 (the "Rawlsian" attack)
"Since intelligence is an arbitrary asset or since intelligence is a trait that society has chosen to focus on, society has no justification for rewarding or punishing people on the basis of that asset, except insofar as differential rewards make the least fortunate better off."

Attack 4 (the "liberal/compensatorian" attack)
"It is important to give people a stake in society to induce them to buy into the social contract. To put this bluntly, it is more expensive and dangerous to suppress people than to placate them. Compensation for or reversal of environmental or genetic deprivation can be done without much expense. Since IQ is not everything, we should allow people to develop their skills using other means."[29]

Attack 5 (the "communitarian" attack)
"Since a sense of community, a sense that 'we're all in this together', is one of the highest goods available to us, we ought to help the less fortunate members of our community."

Response
We are sympathetic to these lines of attack, but their normative grounds are inadequate. Their problems arise from their common assumption of some "best" skill(s). No matter what skill we choose – "intelligence" is as arbitrary a choice as any other – a society oriented around that skill is subject to the following problems:

- Orienting to and then rewarding "intelligence," we oppress ourselves, in that even if we are highly "intelligent," we are rewarded only for developing that part of ourselves. The richness of our own experience and sense of self is degraded.
- Focusing on and then rewarding "intelligence," we deprive ourselves of the enjoyment of other people's skills.
- Focusing on and then rewarding "intelligence,"

we decrease our sense of social solidarity, which is an important good, as the communitarians have it.
- People not possessing "intelligence" will be inhibited from nurturing their own abilities, the society providing neither money nor a forum for exercising the abilities they do have.
- People not possessing "intelligence" will tend to be viewed and treated with less respect, even under these alternative moral frameworks. "Sure," the attitude is likely to be, "we're all in this together, but jeez I wish we didn't have to drag you along as well." And for the "unfortunates," a shame and social stigma that they do not have what society values.

In short, the myth of "intelligence" oppresses us all.

To summarize the argument so far: the usual attacks made on the "heritable intelligence" thesis are logically fallacious, politically weak, and/or morally suspect. This statement is not meant to advance the theories being attacked but simply to assert that such attacks have failed. This failure makes their continued use counterproductive, opening us up to mockery, encouraging our opponents, and disheartening our allies. Our opponents point to the illogical, discredited arguments and claim, with justification, "We're not being heard" or "You've got your heads in the sand" or "You've made up your minds in advance."

Especially counterproductive are the many arguments that buy into the very oppression we want to oppose. For example, race-oriented arguments that African-Americans are just as intelligent as European-Americans imply, "It's OK to discriminate against genuinely stupid people, but African-Americans aren't, as a class, genuinely stupid." If no stronger lines of attack were available, we might choose to continue such attacks, but given the more fundamental, powerful line of attack advanced later, we should quit making these bad arguments.

II. A better line of attack: the alternative hypothesis of an "arbitrary social construct"

It is for these considerations that we advocate adopting the following perspective as the foundation of a stronger line of attack:

Assumptions about mental and physical characteristics

- Everyone[30] is born with an equal capacity for mental development, where "mental development" includes all brain-related skills, not just "intelligence."
- Physically based characteristics are heritable.
- Physically based characteristics increase their strength and complexity in proportion to their use. This use is increased by rewards given to each characteristic and is diminished by such things as chronic anxiety and malnourishment.
- In the above respects mental characteristics are like other physically based characteristics.

Assumptions about how our existing society treats these characteristics

- Our society is organized to differentially solicit, employ, and reward a certain set of characteristics.
- People possessing these favored characteristics are rewarded, both psychologically (in terms of social prestige) and monetarily (another form of social prestige).
- These characteristics correspond, generally, to the capacities ordinarily understood as "intelligence."[31]

Reinterpretation of the empirical grounds of IQ

- The correlation among different "intelligence" skills reflects not the "reality" and unity of the concept but rather the fact that lack of the favored skills degrades all mental functioning. On the average, people who have the socially rewarded "intelligence" skills are able to support all mental functions at a higher level than people who do not have such skills.
- The association of "intelligence" with social success reflects not the inherent virtue of these skills but rather that society is organized to use and reward them. That is why the tests that load most heavily on the first principal component are also the best predictors of later success.
- The hereditary nature of "intelligence" reflects that all physically based characteristics are heritable. The fact that "intelligence" is affected by

environment as well as heredity reflects that all physically based characteristics are thus jointly affected.[32] The fact that all capacities are affected by both heredity and environment is why controlling for environmental influences does not eliminate the intercorrelation among different aspects of mental functioning.

The following computations for hypothetical data demonstrate how this alternative hypothesis generates the empirical patterns on which the "heritable intelligence" proponents rely.

Index scores on "intelligence" and eleven other "skills" were generated for 400 hypothetical subjects. Each of the twelve skills had a range from 0 (no skill whatsoever) to 10 (complete skill). Using a random number generator, each respondent was given skills in this range subject only to the restriction that the total of all skills was equal to 60, reflecting our first assumption above. The first subject, for example, had skill levels of

6 4 6 5 4 6 5 1 4 6 6 7

with the sum = 60, as required. Each separate skill, therefore, has a roughly normal distribution with a mean of 5 and a standard deviation of 1.58. It was assumed that social success was based primarily on "intelligence"; this was modelled by the equation

Success = 5 × "intelligence" + 1 × sum of 11 other "skills" + error

In other words, it was assumed that in this hypothetical society, "intelligence" was five times as important as any of the other "skills" in determining social success. Given the formula, the "true score" (without the error component) would average 80 – an average contribution of $5 \times 5 = 25$ for "intelligence," plus an average contribution of $1 \times 5 = 5$ for each of the eleven other "skills," for a total of 80. The error term was generated by a random number generator with a uniform distribution over the integers from −40 to +40. The error for the first subject, for example, was −7. Computing Success for this first subject, we get

$$5 \times 6 + 1 \times 4 + 1 \times 6 + 1 \times 5 + 1 \times 4 + 1 \times 6 + 1 \times 5 + 1 \times 1 + 1 \times 4 + 1 \times 6 + 1 \times 6 + 1 \times 7 + -7 = 77$$

as the social success score. Actual Success scores ranged from a low of 27 to a high of 128.

The correlations among the twelve "skills," shown to two decimal places, are as follows:

```
1.00 −.14 −.11 −.07 −.03 −.08 −.07 −.10 −.07 −.09 −.09 −.10
     1.00 −.07 −.20 −.11 −.03 −.03 −.09 −.07 −.03 −.10 −.11
          1.00 −.11 −.05 −.13 −.15 −.15 −.07 −.03 −.12 −.08
               1.00 −.04 −.13 −.07 −.01 −.08 −.01 −.07 −.09
                    1.00 −.18 −.11 −.08 −.12 −.13 −.06 −.12
                         1.00 −.05 −.14 −.13 −.03 −.02 −.07
                              1.00 −.10 −.10 −.09 −.04 −.15
                                   1.00 −.07 −.15 −.10 −.11
                                        1.00 −.02 −.19 −.10
                                             1.00 −.15 −.07
                                                  1.00 −.06
                                                       1.00
```

Notice that all the intercorrelations are slightly negative, as we would expect since the skill scores have a fixed sum: one skill score being high would require that the other skill scores would have to be a little lower, on the average, to maintain the fixed sum of 60.

The first principal component of this matrix has the following loadings for the twelve skills:

```
.19 −.41 −.17  .44  .37 −.34 −.01  .34 −.11 −.14
                                        .13 −.07
```

Notice, as we would expect, that the loadings are bipolar (i.e., both positive and negative). Notice also that loading on "intelligence" – the first loading – is only the fourth highest of the loadings. Since the "intelligence" variable has no special status in these hypothetical data, we would expect this. Finally, notice that these results show none of the patterns employed by the proponents of "heritable intelligence" to buttress their case.

We now introduce a model of oppression: we assume that society fully supports people's level of intelligence, but degrades their other skills in proportion to their "intelligence."[33] This represents the idea that society will permit someone with the highest level of "intelligence" not only the full use of that intelligence but also full enjoyment of all other skills. Someone with no "intelligence" whatsoever will not only have a lack of intelligence but – having no "intelligence" to make h/her way in the world – will have no use of any other skill.

The above hypothetical scores were then transformed using this assumption. The first subject, for example, now has the scores

```
6.0 2.4 3.6 3.0 2.4 3.6 3.0 6.0 2.4 3.6 3.6 4.2
```

Recomputing the intercorrelations using this trans-

formed data, we obtain the matrix shown below, representing the correlations among the twelve "skills," to two decimal places, under the assumption that oppression exists and degrades all non-"intelligence" skills:

```
1.00 .63 .57 .66 .65 .67 .65 .59 .64 .70 .63 .61
     1.00 .29 .30 .35 .42 .37 .32 .46 .41 .35 .31
          1.00 .33 .36 .31 .27 .23 .28 .39 .28 .30
               1.00 .39 .34 .42 .37 .39 .38 .39 .32
                    1.00 .34 .34 .35 .36 .40 .38 .33
                         1.00 .42 .30 .36 .48 .41 .37
                              1.00 .32 .35 .40 .40 .30
                                   1.00 .33 .30 .32 .27
                                        1.00 .43 .28 .33
                                             1.00 .33 .39
                                                  1.00 .34
                                                       1.00
```

Notice that the pattern here is quite different from the previous one. Now, despite the fact that the intercorrelations of the "innate" skills are slightly negative, all the skills as modified by a broad oppression are now positively intercorrelated, just as all the various tests of cognitive skill intercorrelate. We see that this pattern of intercorrelation arises from the application of a broad "oppression" to the "innate skills."[34]

The first principal component of this new matrix has the following loadings:

```
.43 .27 .24 .28 .28 .29 .28 .25 .27 .30 .27 .26
```

Notice now that the first factor is unipolar (i.e., all variables load positively on it). Notice also that the "intelligence" loading – again, the first loading – is now the largest of the loadings by far: .43, while the other loadings range only between .24 and .30. Again, these results show the pattern employed by the proponents of "heritable intelligence" to buttress their case: a unipolar first factor, taken to show that all cognitive skills are connected, and the highest loading being on that skill most taken to be "intelligence."

Now recomputing Success scores based on these new data (and using the same errors as before), we find that Success correlates as follows with the twelve skills:

```
.96 .62 .55 .63 .61 .65 .63 .56 .61 .67 .62 .58
```

Again, we find the pattern taken to validate the concept of "intelligence": all cognitive skills correlate positively with Success, but the skill that correlates best by far is the first, the one thought to most centrally measure "intelligence."

This analysis of hypothetical data proves nothing by itself; rather, it casts doubt upon the "heritable intelligence" theory, because the statistical patterns advanced by the proponents of "heritable intelligence" have more than one explanation.

Of course, theorists need not challenge alternative explanations that have no plausibility – say, that the statistical patterns are really due to invisible Martians fooling with the intelligence tests. As noted earlier, the proponents of "heritable intelligence" have an explanation for the data, an explanation with some face validity. To undercut their explanation requires an alternative hypothesis which itself has some plausibility, which itself has some strength.

It is accordingly important to note here that the alternative hypothesis of an "arbitrary social construct" uses plausible assumptions to obtain its results: that without any oppression, everyone would have the same overall "quantity" of cognitive skill; that cognitive skills are all degraded by oppression; and that our society is organized to differentially recognize and reward one specific skill (or set of skills), thus gauging the level of oppression according to the level of that skill.

Furthermore, this alternative hypothesis undercuts the "heritable intelligence" hypothesis in yet another way: by explaining away its face validity. Even in a society in fact following the assumptions of the "arbitrary social construct" hypothesis, people will nonetheless find "intelligence"-based oppression "natural". Everyday observation will show that "intelligence" is rewarded and that "the intelligent" show this capacity in many areas. Since data appear to show that mental capacities are inherited, books like *The Bell Curve* can appear to bemoan the hereditarily "stupid" with one hand and take away any sense that social inequalities can be remedied, on the other. In other words, the "arbitrary social construct" hypothesis not only explains the data supporting the "hereditary intelligence" position but also explains why it has a superficial face validity. In view of these challenges to its interpretations, the "hereditary intelligence" position must find critical tests that distinguish its predictions from those of this alternative hypothesis.

III. The society and politics following from the "arbitrary social construct" hypothesis

The "arbitrary social construct" perspective implies that since the privileging of any set of skills is arbitrary, society must reorient to support the expression of all such skills. Such a society would be founded on, and its citizens would welcome, a search for the development, exercise, and appreciation of as many skills as may exist.

It may be that Rawlsian-type considerations may persuade us to encourage the development of some set of skills on the grounds that they maximally benefit the worst off in such a society – citizens without those skills, presumably.[35] But even more than that, the differential encouragement of some skills must be justified to all in practice, not just as the conclusion of some metaphysical argument. If society is truly to encourage "the development and exercise of as many skills as possible," the public forum has to hear, fully consider, and make its collective decisions in mutual recognition of each citizen's perspective.

It will be obvious that we are here following Habermas's discourse ethics, based on the universalization principle "(U)":

> *All* affected can accept the consequences and the side effects its *general* observance can be anticipated to have for the satisfaction of *everyone's* interests (and these consequences are preferred to those of known alternative possibilities for regulation). (Habermas 1990, p. 65)

This is not the place to attempt a detailed exposition and justification of discourse ethics; we simply note that in its deliberate demand for consideration of all perspectives and the agreement of all affected, it is consonant with a society seeking the development, exercise, and appreciation of whatever skills may exist.

IV. Objections to this alternative hypothesis

This section attempts to anticipate, acknowledge, and address objections that might be raised to this new line of attack.

Objection
"Regardless of the abstract merits of this

perspective, and however nice the fable of the Pseudopodians is, it is irresponsible to advance an argument (that the set of cognitive skills we call intelligence can be inherited) that will in practice be used by others to support further discrimination against the 'hereditarily stupid'."

Response
This is a legitimate concern. Intellectuals have a responsibility to weigh the consequences of expounding their theories.

A variety of considerations lead us to believe that we are better off making this argument than not. As claimed earlier, we believe the empirical regularities will continue to appear, and we will forever be on the defensive trying to deny them: unable to prevent the consequences we oppose and delegitimizing our concerns by trying. In addition, our current arguments frequently buy into the underlying cause of oppression, thus perpetuating it at one level while trying to fight it at another level. For example, arguments that (e.g.) blacks are as intelligent as whites fail to point out the circular nature of the definition of "intelligence." Failing to subvert the very premises of IQ, we accept the perspective on the world whose consequences (racism, other oppression) we are trying to oppose. Whatever momentary, tactical victories we win in such a discourse, we are shoring up the foundations of the oppression: the legitimacy of the system by which the concept of intelligence has been created and by which people who evidence it get rewarded.

Objection
"This paper seems to support the tracking policies of schools today. It says that there are indeed 'high intelligence' and 'low intelligence' students, that the difference is to some degree heritable and unchangeable, and that we ought to educate them differently. Is that true?"[36]

Response
Before agreeing or disagreeing, we have to note that the very phrasing of this objection buys into the existing view of different tracks as being of different quality and the people in them as being of different value. So our initial response to this question is opposition to a system of tracking that embodies and perpetuates the very view of "intelligence" that this chapter seeks to undermine.

Tracking is a problem not in itself but because our society does not value the diversity of skills. If

we genuinely valued the diversity of human talents, the variety of skills being taught would not be assigned relative value. Magnet schools, for example, embody an attitude that different skills are valued.[37] In contrast to "tracking" systems, magnet schools allow children to develop the skills meaningful to them.[38]

Objection
"Your position seems to support voucher systems for public schools, so that parents can support and even create the variety of schools suitable for their children's diverse needs and talents."

Response
As currently constructed, voucher proposals would increase the funding and quality disparities between schools as wealthy parents supplemented the vouchers to allow their children to attend high-quality, high-tuition schools, while opposing broad-based school taxes. This would severely damage the social equality promoted (however poorly) by the current system of public school financing. Until a voucher system is proposed that fosters an educational system supporting diversity, this perspective argues against vouchers.

Objection
"Your suggestion seems to argue for a return to the 'separate but equal' doctrine, but in their decision in Brown v. Board of Education of Topeka, Kansas, the Supreme Court said that 'Separate is inherently unequal' because of the social opprobrium of one track or the other. Are you disagreeing with that?"

Response
Segregation was based on a forced separation between ascriptively designated groups, not on free associations within a citizenry sharing a common respect for diversity. To rejoice in diversity is the antithesis of unequal treatment.

Objection
"So now it's all right to hold stereotypes such as (say) African-Americans are good athletes and have natural rhythm?"[39]

Response
First, in a society long suffering from extensive oppression and discrimination, we do not know what people's talents are. For example, singing, dancing, and athletics may have been/continue

to be outlets differentially open to African-Americans.

Second, we should not buy into the idea, implicit in the objection, that these other talents are inherently less valuable; it is society that makes them so. Thus social evaluations, not the skills themselves, are responsible for this characterization being regarded as a denigration. This chapter rests on the belief that we would all prefer to live in a society encouraging a multiplicity of talents.

Objection

"This seems to support the elimination of remedial programs, such as Head Start. Are you opposed to remedial programs?"[40]

Response

The most important goal is to resist the fundamental oppression: having society only honor a small range of capacities. By focusing on remediation, we buy into this oppression, leaving unchallenged the claim that the absence of one particular type of capacity is a failure requiring correction. Of course, there are some forms of remediation that may reduce the overall oppression in the society, such as programs ensuring food and medical care for all.

If there is no hope of challenging the oppression at this deep level, there remains the fact that not all ability is inherited, and so to the extent that remedial programs ameliorate the existing oppression, they must be supported.

Objection

"Perspectives like this imply the guidance or even coercion of people with different abilities to go into the fields 'genetically appropriate' for them. True?"

Response

The empirical question of the heritability of abilities bears on, but does not dictate our response to, the normative issue of how we as a society ought to parcel out positions and responsibilities. Even if people's abilities are affected by heredity, there is little reason to violate their right to attempt different fields. Even if society as a whole benefits from people being assigned fields utilizing their strongest skills, such a restriction ignores the role of desire as a component of performance. And even if the hereditary skills were perfectly correlated with performance, the overall social gain does not yield any authorization to so seriously impair people's ability

to pursue their interests and develop their skills as they choose. There may be a point at which such restrictions are useful – the restriction of the presidency to people over 35 springs to mind – but such exceptions are only made rarely and in matters of the greatest moment. An imposed "rational distribution" of career opportunities seems indefensible.[41]

Objection

"You claim that this approach is politically stronger than, say, the Rawlsian approach, but it seems that both approaches depend on the good will of people in the midst of very hard times. What is so special about your approach?"

Response

The approach taken in this chapter has at least three virtues and one great liability. The first virtue is its getting at a root cause of oppression, and doing so through a process of discursive engagement that heals our conflicts instead of exacerbating them. In other words, the political action suggested by this approach is consonant with an overall, supportable vision of politics. We can support this vision of politics regardless of the temper of the times, but in addition the temper of the times makes it particularly appropriate, because the post-Depression cultural hegemony of modern reform liberalism has been broken. There are always two alternatives to resolving political conflict: suppression (silencing one side, whether by death or cultural marginalization) or discursive reconciliation. Suppression is no longer available; and so for both moral and practical reasons, we need to pursue reconciliation.

The second virtue of this chapter's approach is its image of a society that people might actually want to support. People are persuaded by positive images, not by criticisms of their current situation, regardless of those criticisms' accuracy. So in addition to showing the manner in which we are all oppressed, this approach also gives some sense of a different way society might be organized.

Finally, the third virtue of this approach is its recognition that everyone, including both the "intelligent" and whoever else benefits from the current acceptance of the concept, has a personal stake in the success of the change to a different society. The powerful are called upon not to altruistically sacrifice their interests but rather to recognize their truer, deeper interests.

The great liability of this approach is its flying in

the face of society's permeation by the reified concept of "intelligence." Even though this chapter problematizes the concept and reconstructs its origins, it is hard to persuade others (or even to remember oneself) that "intelligence" is only a social construction. At every turn we find "intelligence" taken as reality, treated as a reality, rewarded in reality. How does one convince people the world is round, when everyone can see it's flat? It is cause for hope that we now recognize that the world is round, but we still require a practical strategy for changing our social attitudes.

V. Conclusion

Ad hominem arguments are bad arguments. They work by demonizing people who think differently about "intelligence." While this may serve to rally the troops in a war, it will not end the war, and it certainly will not convince the people on the other side of the issues, who do not see themselves as demons. One of the themes in the debate over "intelligence" has been the protestations of "heritable intelligence" proponents that their arguments have been misunderstood, ignored, and/or distorted. (See, for example, Murray 1994–5.) Our sense of the good society is one in which people listen to each other. From the standpoint of what we are ultimately seeking to accomplish, then, it is counterproductive to deal with people who think differently by ignoring and demonizing them.

Arguments against the empirical foundations of the IQ argument are worth making, as with any other empirical claim. But empirical claims are extremely difficult in practice to prove or disprove. Even direct refutations of certain claims can be overcome by modifications of the underlying theory, leaving the basic implication intact. Scientific discourse is more political than we ordinarily imagine, and we must therefore be careful about the political form in which such discourse is conducted. In particular, we must be careful that we do not devote such intellectual resources to refuting the empirical claims that we are merely neurotically refusing to credit them.[42] In other words, as was said above regarding *ad hominem* arguments, we desire a society where people listen to each other, and it ill befits this goal to mount a suicidal resistance to data just because we dislike its implications. Furthermore, it seems likely that the empirical claims are correct, at least in their general thrust of

showing some heritability of cognitive skills, so that debating the claims eventually becomes mere evidence of a refusal to listen to reason. And finally, we need not mount such a resistance to the empirical claims when they have an interpretation – the "arbitrary social construct" interpretation – that we can support.

Arguments against the empirical claims on the basis of their unfortunate consequences are logically invalid, have no effect on the people who do not see the consequences as terrible or who disagree that these consequences will occur, and, again, are counterproductive to creating a society in which people listen to each other.

Finally, arguments against the policy implications of the empirical claims are problematic because they buy into the institutionalized oppression of people whose mental (or other physical) characteristics do not happen to fit the social structure. It is important to recognize in this connection that we are not proposing a new meritocracy based on diverse talents but rather something different – a society founded on the premise that people's value and worthiness of self-actualization is a birthright rather then something they 'earn' through the exercise of inborn ability.

As the fable of Pseudopodia implies, our release from the common conclusions of these studies lies in advancing a plausible, different interpretation of the empirical findings – an alternative hypothesis. Advancing such an alternative shifts the debate from arguments over facts to arguments over the interpretation of these facts. This shift reverses the "realism vs. idealism" debate: it is the proponents of IQ's existence and importance who are fuzzy-minded. They are fuzzy-minded in assuming without proof that intelligence derives from some innate faculty, when they have failed to previously rule out the possibility that their statistical patterns derive from the effects of oppression. They are fuzzy-minded in assuming that people with different talents can be beaten down with the argument that their capacities – the sources of how they experience their meaning as a person – are really worth less than other, "socially approved" capacities. It is realism, on the other hand, to recognize that a stable, just society must be founded on a firm recognition of people's equal worth, regardless of what skills they may display. So overall, it will be advantageous to shift the ground of debate to the "intelligence"-based oppression within our society and to the way we value and devalue diversity.

To many, the term "diversity" connotes only a banner under which various whining losers try to conceal and reverse their failure.[43] But true diversity is a vision of society under which the enormous spectrum of human capacities is respected, a society in which we honor and appreciate each other in all our facets. It is this appreciation of true diversity that the present authors find absent not just from the proponents of "heritable intelligence" but also from its opponents. In this absence lies no potential for a new freedom but only a perpetuation of the discrimination and oppression that now afflict us all.

Acknowledgments

An earlier version of this chapter was presented by the first author at the panel 'Cultural Conflicts' at the 15th annual 'First Readings' conference, University of Minnesota-Duluth, 28 April 1995. We are indebted to Beth Bartlett, Susan Coultrap-McQuin, Tom Farrell, Sandra Featherman, Harry Hellenbrand, Dick Hudelson, Larry Knopp, Don Kurtz, Mike Linn, Linda Miller-Cleary and the students in her English 5902 ('Composition for Teachers') class, Tom Peacock, Fred Schroeder, Ron Szoke, Eileen Theimer, Graham Tobin, and Janelle Wilson for encouragement and intelligent commentary. We remain, of course, solely responsible for any lapses of judgment.

Notes

1 Throughout this chapter, "intelligence" will be placed in quotation marks to pave the way for the argument that this concept arises from how we organize our society, not from some psycho-physiological reality. Even though the concept is useful in understanding how things work within our existing society, that is, taking our current social arrangements uncritically, the point of the chapter is that the concept has no more fundamental value. The quotation marks remind us not to slip into an uncritical acceptance of existing social arrangements.

   Note that "us" in the previous sentence, and throughout this chapter, refers to opponents of discriminatory, oppressive policies justified by arguments based on "intelligence."

   Quotation marks will not be used when discussing the concept as it appears within the perspective of people who regard it as unproblematic – e.g., Herrnstein and Murray.

   Quotation marks will also not be used around "IQ,"

since IQ is merely a measure. If this chapter were to deal with criticisms of IQ measures (e.g., as culturally biased), then the term would be problematic and would also be enclosed in quotation marks. Such criticisms are not the focus of this chapter, however.

2 See Gould (1981) for a history of research into racial differences, including the origins of "intelligence" research.

3 This first principal component was named "g" by Charles Spearman, for "general intelligence"; it is the foundation of IQ tests. The acknowledged imperfection of the individual measures does not obviate g's claim to meaning.

4 In other words, in the "heritable intelligence" interpretation, the highest correlations are for those tests that most centrally and reliably tap "intelligence." See Eysenck (1971, p. 55).

5 We need to make clear here that our reference to "one set of skills" (i.e., those cognitive skills making up "intelligence") is not the obverse of other cognitive skills but rather of all other skills: cognitive and non-cognitive (reaction time, coordination, leg strength, etc.) alike.

6 *The Bell Curve*'s 280 pages of appendices, notes, and bibliography became a minor story in themselves.

7 We are *not* saying that "heritable intelligence" research is exempt from critical scrutiny, nor that any particular piece of that research is correct.

8 For examples of this line of attack, see Beardsley (1995) and Gould's remarks in Kayzer (1994).

9 The right has long accused the left of such suppression – witness the constant attacks on the "liberal media" – and it is disturbing to find such suppression actually being advocated.

   The suppression one seeks today will be turned against one tomorrow.

   Point not the goal until you plot the course
   For means and ends to man are tangled so
   That different means quite different ends enforce –
   Conceive the means as ends in embryo.
                                    (Bondurant 1971, p. xiii)

10 For an example of this line of attack, see Bell (1995) and Neuhaus (1994).

11 For an example of this line of attack, see Howard and Peterkin (1995).

12 For an example of this line of attack, see Herman (1994).

13 For an example of this line of attack, see Rosen and Lane (1995).

14 Here and elsewhere our reliance on Habermas's "discourse ethics" should be apparent. For one description of discourse ethics, see Habermas (1990, pp. 43–115).

15 "The most profoundly creative way to overcome enemies is to make them our friends. But this involves a series of painful acts. A constant decision never to

achieve our goals by destroying or humiliating others" (Arns, 1994, p. 8). This was an address by Dom Paulo Cardinal Arns, the archbishop of Sao Paulo, Brazil, to a Buddhist lay movement in Tokyo, upon receiving their Niwano Peace Prize. Translated by Florence Anderson.

16 For an example of this line of attack, see Gould (1981, p. 24 and elsewhere).

17 Gould (1981, p. 252) does mention a reasonable alternative explanation – basically the same alternative proposed in this chapter – but never pursues it.

18 For an example of this line of attack, see Kayzer (1994). Gardner (1993) outlines a theory of multiple intelligences. For an example of the "factor rotation" line of attack, see Gould (1981, pp. 252–5).

19 Eysenck (1971, p. 49), citing the original work of Spearman (1904). This observation is more or less equivalent to the observation that all tests load positively on the first principal component.

20 See note 19.

21 See Eysenck (1971, p. 55).

22 A further problem with these explanations is that they can easily be taken to just substitute a slightly more diverse set of mental capacities for the singular "intelligence." And even if we accept the existence of multiple intelligences, there is no good normative argument for rewarding these different intelligences equally, so the oppression continues.

23 For examples of these lines of attack, see Haycock (1995), Rotberg (1995), Weiner and Cooper (1995), Bell (1995), and Moore (1995).

24 We are indebted to Linda Miller-Cleary for mentioning this objection.

25 For an example of this line of attack, see Etzioni (1995).

26 See note 21.

27 This argument appears in Subramanian (1995), a review in *Time Magazine* of a genetic atlas of the world (Cavalli-Sforza *et al.* 1994). See also Sizemore (1995).

28 Such works as *The Bell Curve* make a point not to dwell on this aspect of the debate. Murray and his defenders repeatedly point out that only one chapter of *The Bell Curve* looks at racial differences.

29 For an example of this line of attack, see Slavin (1995), although Slavin would likely reject the genetic tie-in.

30 Barring damage from such physical-developmental injuries as fetal alcohol syndrome, maternal malnourishment, thalidomide, etc., of course.

31 Some people point to the high salaries of (say) sports stars as a refutation of this claim. But the example does not support their argument: comparatively little money is pumped into sports; it is the small number of players that gives them high salaries. But for every Michael Jordan making a jillion dollars a year, and for every dozen ordinary NBA players, there are hundreds of thousands of NBA wannabes who will never see a nickel.

32 The heritability of these properties means that those with "intelligence" and those with other mental faculties can become increasingly differentiated from each other over generations.

33 Mathematically, we assume that people's "intelligence" score remains wherever it is, and that their other scores are altered by the factor of the "intelligence" score divided by ten. In other words, people with the maximum "intelligence" score have their other skills unchanged; people with lesser "intelligence" scores have their other skill levels decreased by the extent to which their "intelligence" is less than its maximum.

34 This pattern of results is not dependent on use of this particular formula to model oppression. Any broad degradation of other skills with a positive relationship to "intelligence" will result in the same positive intercorrelations.

35 The encouragement of such skills could certainly never be used as a basis for the oppression and exclusion of those without them.

36 We are indebted to Dick Hudelson for raising the possibility of this objection.

37 Of course, the curricula constituting the schools are primarily those valued by society, so magnet schools are not yet free of the underlying oppressive system of social valuation.

38 This is not a blanket endorsement of the magnet school concept. The administrative and physical separation of the different schools inhibits a shared sense of appreciation for diverse talents, and we need to ensure that there remains a variety of skills taught and appreciated within each school. There is the potential problem of magnet schools using entrance exams to control who is allowed to enter. And ultimately, we must resolve the problem of how supply and demand are to be matched while supporting a wide variety of magnet programs and the free choice of students among them.

39 See note 36.

40 See note 36. Farrel (1995) raises a related objection by arguing that acceptance by teachers of non-standard English is itself racist in effect, since it implies that (e.g.) minority children cannot learn or, more devilishly racist, should not be taught the standard English necessary for success in society. (For the full flavour of this debate, see Farrell's list of citations.)

41 This view of the situation is obviously strongly influenced by John Rawls's analysis in *A Theory of Justice* (1971).

42 Brad Blanton: "A neurotic is a person for whom the world *has* to be other than it really is."

43 When we allow the concept of diversity to be dragged down into a debate over "goals" vs. "quotas," we have lost, because neither of these honors the core sensibility. The reversal of past discrimination is a worthy goal, but as long as it means only an equal right to participate in an oppressive system, a system rewarding only certain capacities, it loses much of its moral force and certainly loses its force as a movement for true diversity.

Bibliography

Arns, Dom Paulo Cardinal (1994) Develop the habit of peace. *The Catholic Worker*, **61** (4), 8.

Beardsley, T. (1995) Science and the citizen: for whom *The Bell Curve* really tolls. *Scientific American* **272** (1), 14–17.

Bell, L. (1995) Commentary: reacting to *The Bell Curve*. *Education Week* **14** (16), 31.

Bondurant, J.V. (1971) *Conquest of Violence*. Berkeley CA: University of California Press.

Cavalli-Sforza, L.L., Menozzi, P. and Piazza, A. (1994) *The History and Geography of Human Genes*. Princeton, NJ: Princeton University Press.

Covina, W.A. and Jolliffe, D.A., eds. (1995) *Rhetoric: Concepts, Definitions, Boundaries*. Needham Heights, MA: Allyn & Bacon.

Etzioni, A. (1995) Commentary: reacting to *The Bell Curve*. *Education Week* **14** (16), 29.

Eysenck, H.J. (1971) *The IQ Argument: Race, Intelligence and Education*. New York: The Library Press.

Farrell, T.J. (1995) A defense for requiring standard English. In Covino and Jolliffe (1995, pp. 667–78).

Fraser, S. (1995) *The Bell Curve Wars*. New York: Basic Books.

Gardner, H. (1993) *Frames of Mind: The Theory of Multiple Intelligences*. New York: Basic Books.

Gould, S.J. (1981) *The Mismeasure of Man*. New York: W. W. Norton.

Habermas, J. (1990) *Moral Consciousness and Communicative Action*. Cambridge MA: MIT Press.

Haycock, K. (1995) Commentary: reacting to *The Bell Curve*. *Education Week* **14** (16), 31.

Herman, E.S. (1994) The new racist onslaught. *Z Magazine* **8** (12), 24–6.

Herrnstein, R.J. and Murray, C. (1994) *The Bell Curve: Intelligence and Class Structure in American Life*. New York: Free Press.

Howard, J. and Peterkin, R. (1995) Commentary: reacting to *The Bell Curve*. *Education Week* **14** (16), 32.

Kamin, L.J. (1995) Behind the curve. *Scientific American* **272** (2), 99–103.

Kayzer, W. (1994) Stephen Jay Gould. One of eight videos entitled *A Glorious Accident: Understanding Our Place in the Cosmic Puzzle*. Princeton NJ: Films for the Humanities.

Maschinot, B. (1995) Behind the curve. *In These Times* **19** (6), 31–4.

Moore, E.K. (1995) Commentary: reacting to *The Bell Curve*. *Education Week* **14** (16), 31.

Murray, C. (1994–5) [Letter to the editor of *The New Yorker*.] *The New Yorker* **70**, 10.

Neuhaus, R.J. (1994) Going public. *National Review* **64** (23), 40–1.

Rawls, J. (1971) *A Theory of Justice*. Cambridge MA: Harvard University Press.

Reed Jr., A. (1994) Looking backward (Review of *The Bell Curve*). *The Nation* **259**, 654–62.

Rosen, J. and Lane, C. (1995) The sources of *The Bell Curve*. In S. Fraser *The Bell Curve Wars*. New York: Basic Books.

Rotberg, I. C. (1995) Commentary: reacting to *The Bell Curve*. *Education Week* **14**(16), 31–2.

Ryan, A. (1994) Apocalypse now? (Review of *The Bell Curve*). *The New York Review of Books* **41**, 7.

Sizemore, B. (1995) Commentary: reacting to *The Bell Curve*. *Education Week* **14** (16), 29–30.

Slavin, R.E. (1995) Commentary: reacting to *The Bell Curve*. *Education Week* **14** (16), 30–1.

Spearman, C. (1904) 'General intelligence,' objectively determined and measured. *American Journal of Psychology* **15**: 201–93.

Sribala Subramanian (1995) The story of our genes: a landmark study flattens *The Bell Curve*, proving that racial differences are only skin deep. *Time* **145** (2) 54.

Weiner, M. and Cooper, B.S. (1995) Commentary: reacting to *The Bell Curve*. *Education Week* **14** (16), 32.

4   Contested Values and Disputed Cultural Identity in Mexican Higher Education

KEN KEMPNER and IMANOL ORDORIKA

Every nation's educational system is the product of its historical, cultural, social, and geographic circumstances. Historically, the principal educational tasks for a nation have been established in accordance with local needs, traditions, and available resources. Unfortunately, the complexity of modern nations no longer allows the simple luxury of a practically focused and parochial education. Although the people of a nation may still value local educational traditions and customs, contemporary nation states wishing to participate in the global economy must find a place for themselves within the international division of labor. Nations wishing to participate in this global market must then adopt economic, educational, political, and social models considered legitimate at the world level.

Whereas some nations have historically controlled vast amounts of natural resources and have developed large technology systems, other nations have not been so fortunate. Herein, we find the basis for the tension surrounding international conflict, dependency, and the classical distinctions between developed, developing, and underdeveloped countries. The choices for developing and newly industrialized countries are very limited when the resources and technology are controlled by the few developing countries. In the modern world even the possession of valuable natural resources is not enough, however, for economic success. To compete in the global market underdeveloped nations must produce their own commodities, seek a competitive advantage (typically, cheap labor) for their products, modernize their technology base while trying to stay ahead of the other underdeveloped countries seeking the same competitive advantages. To accomplish this developmental task underdeveloped countries require an educational system capable of teaching their citizens the technical skills for production and the knowledge to adopt, create, and manage modern technologies. Whereas simple, agrarian economies necessitated only simple educational systems, complex modern economies now require equally complex educational systems. What a nation values internally may no longer be of external value in the world marketplace.

How a developing nation's internal values clash with the external values of global capitalism and the ways in which these values are disputed internally to shape higher education is the focus of this chapter. We consider here the case of Mexico as an example of a nation struggling to maintain its own cultural identity. Mexico offers an excellent example of a developing country on the periphery of the core, industrial nations – wanting the respect and economic rewards of a developed nation, but seeking this on its own nationalistic terms. In our analysis of how values have shaped Mexican higher education we are especially interested in understanding what is unique about Mexican higher education in comparison to what is unique to Latin America, to other developing nations, and to higher education systems in general.

To understand the unique cultural, historical, and social circumstances of Mexican higher education we are guided by several basic assumptions in our inquiry:

(a) We view education as a site of struggle and confrontation. As we discuss below, higher education, in particular, is the site of confrontation over access to knowledge and social mobility for the middle classes. Mexican higher education has been shaped by this often violent struggle with students who have demanded access, independence, and freedom of expression against the dominant ruling party (the PRI).

(b) Cultural perceptions (values and beliefs) shape and are in turn shaped by university structures and policies. This dialectic of values and beliefs both shaping and being shaped contributes to the unique character of Mexican higher education and national politics.

(c) Cultural perceptions develop as historical and contextualized products and producers. As we have proposed, a nation's educational system reflects its unique historical, cultural, social, and geographic circumstances. Mexico is certainly no exception.

(d) In a peripheral country values and cultural perceptions are also shaped by dominating models. Mexico has been shaped, first, by the historical circumstances of its colonial relationship with Spain and, second, by the geographic circumstances of its proximity and dependent relationship with the USA.

(e) Values are not static. They evolve historically through these processes of confrontation. Not only have external, historical relationships influenced Mexican values, politics, and higher education, but so too have internal relationships and circumstances. From the Mexican Revolution to the Free Trade Agreement (NAFTA) social, political, and nationalistic values are in constant flux.

(f) Historical development of values give form to the contemporary nature of higher education institutions. Given the central role higher education plays in national politics and economic development, the character of higher education institutions are not neutral. Higher education is both the site of political struggle and the exposition of modern global capitalism. Contemporary higher education reflects contemporary values.

Specifically, in our inquiry of Mexican higher education we consider the following basic set of questions:

1 Is Mexico unique compared to other Latin American countries and other developing countries in how its values have shaped its system of higher education?

2 What role does the value of privatization play in restructuring Mexican higher education? Again, is this uniquely Mexican or is it more a reflection of the larger world market of ideas and higher education?

3 How successful is Mexico in its struggle to maintain its national identity and values in the face of global capitalism?

4 What role is higher education playing for a peripheral country such as Mexico in its quest for a place at the table of the core countries who control and maintain global capitalism? Is Mexico's role to be a service country for the core or will it be a knowledge producer itself?

5 What role does the state play in promoting educational reform? How do the values of the modern state contrast with the historical values of Mexico, especially the Mexican Revolution?

In this chapter we will address, first, the effect of the state on higher education. Second, we will review the historical antecedents of contemporary higher education in Mexico and the effect societal values have had on the formation of the National Autonomous University of Mexico (UNAM). In this review we will consider how policies in UNAM have been strongly shaped by intense confrontations over societal and educational values and the strong interrelationship between societal and collegial dynamics. Finally, we address contemporary issues in Mexican higher education with particular focus on the debate over equity and efficiency. We conclude by summarizing the basic questions we pose in this inquiry by distinguishing what is unique about the Mexican experience of higher education.

Higher education and the state

The state, in Gramsci's (1971) view, is the combination of coercion and hegemony. Hegemony is the process of consensual domination through the articulation of a diversity of social groups and interests. It is established through the mediation of ideology (Mouffe, 1979), the terrain "on which [people] move, acquire consciousness of their own position, struggle," it is "a practice producing subjects" (Gramsci, 1971). Hegemony is always an active process. It is not simply a complex of dominant values and beliefs, "it is always a more or less adequate organization and interconnection of otherwise separated and even disparate meanings, values, and practices, which specifically incorporate in a significant culture and an effective social order" (Williams, 1977, p. 115).

Because higher education is part of the state's structure of hegemonic institutions, understanding a nation's system of higher education necessitates an inquiry into the degree the state imposes its economic and ideological control. The state, of course, is an actor in its own right and seeks to gain its ideological hegemony through its "apparatuses" (Althusser, 1971) or institutions (Gramsci, 1971). The state, for example, may choose to distribute education as a commodity to the lower classes to secure their good will to legitimize the state's political control (Weiler, 1983).

Education, as any hegemonic institution, is a site of class struggle through which the state attempts to impose its domination over the subordinate social classes. When the nondominant classes see higher education, in particular, as the path to upward mobility, attempts by the state, in some countries, to limit access are met with swift, and sometimes violent, reactions. The wishes of upward mobility by the lower classes are mediated by the economic realities of how many resources there are to distribute and by the state's interest in maintaining its hegemony. Whereas the state may distribute education to the lower classes as a form of compensatory legitimation to gain their good will (Weiler, 1983), the lower classes may gain no economic advantage if concomitant changes in the economy are not also made. Because "education cannot of itself promote peripheral economic change" (Walters, 1981, p. 95), the state's compensatory use of education may actually create greater dissatisfaction among the lower classes and weaken the state's political control.

The role of the state and its use of the educational apparatus available to it differ, of course, depending upon the social, economic, cultural, and political circumstances of the country under consideration, particularly for dependent countries (Cardoso and Falleto, 1979). Structuralist and class-struggle perspectives must account for the individual conditions of dependency of each country and the constraints under which the state operates in relation to its place in the larger regional and global situation. Nevertheless, reproductive and class struggle theories of the state are critical in understanding the role higher education plays in Mexico and how nationalistic values shape its structure. In particular, the Mexican revolution (1910–17) generated a unique educational philosophy and values that have been transmitted and accepted for generations. In this humanist tradition, higher education was conceived

as a means for national cohesion, for the creation and re-creation of Mexican identity and culture, as a promoter of universal values, as a space to reflect upon, understand and solve the problems of the country, and as an agent to inculcate a scientific spirit among the population. Above all, the Revolution established the idea that public education should respond to the general interest of society because it enhances living standards and the changes for social, economic and cultural improvement of the people (Cueli and Arzac, 1990).

The modernization projects of the former Salinas and current Zedillo governments for public higher education are in open contradiction, however, to the historical traditions of the Mexican Revolution. For the first time in many years the interests and needs of the private sectors prevail in the definition of policies towards higher education institutions and the global economy, as dictated, for example, by the World Bank and International Monetary Fund. Similar to what Slaughter (1990, p. 46) found in the USA, the Mexican state is "socializing the cost of development"; that is, public resources are being used to underwrite private enterprise. Due to the state's financial crisis and pressures from private sector economic groups, support for higher education has been reduced and redistributed to support private sector initiatives. The state, along with the wealthy classes and business interests, has put enormous pressure on higher education to establish new efficiency measures and other forms of privatization to justify the redistribution of resources. While maintaining the myth of the neutrality of the university, the bureaucratic response to this budget crisis has been to focus on business as the basic constituency for the university in order to acquire private funding and support for public institutions.

Within this climate of economic crisis and the privatization of higher education, the university has become the site of confrontation between two broad directions and constituencies for reform:

- the state's imposition of reform through bureaucratic authorities;
- the opposition's alternative proposals for democratizing in the university governance, access, and support for students to enable them to persist to graduation.

In Carnoy and Levin's terms (1985, p. 231), these two constituencies can often be viewed as those interested in greater equality versus those interested in greater efficiency. Within this debate resource allocation is contested in terms of the state's responsibility to finance higher education against the concept of alternative revenue sources and civil society's participation in the support of higher education. The social uses of knowledge and the legitimate function of the university are also central to this debate. From the modernist perspective of the state, higher education must prioritize career preparation and knowledge production in terms of the requirements of the market. Within this perspective applied science and technology research are the most important areas of the institution and social sciences and humanities can be sacrificed because they are not considered productive and efficient.

What will constitute the future of legitimate academic knowledge, academic vocations, and knowledge products for Mexico is currently being contested. How the state legitimates its role in reforming higher education is mediated by the hegemony of the ruling PRI party and private interests, on one side, and the democratizing interests of the nondominant classes, on the other. Ultimately, the question Gumport (1993, p. 6) poses for the development of higher education in the USA is equally appropriate for Mexico to consider: Is the commercialization of knowledge for revenue enhancement a legitimate direction for higher education in the twenty-first century? Because the circumstances in the USA differ dramatically from those in Mexico, however, the question of the state's role in higher education must be posed in terms of the unique cultural values and national history of Mexico. To further understand these cultural values and how they have influenced higher education we present in the next section an overview of the historical determinants of the unique character of Mexican higher education.

Origins of Mexican higher education: between scholastics and science

The origins of higher education in Mexico go back to the sixteenth century in the early colonial period. Only a few years after Cortes defeated the Aztec resistance (1521), the Spanish put together a formidable educational effort in an attempt to Christianize and educate the indigenous population. It was not unusual that education was in the hands of the Catholic Church, given its main objective to bring Christianity to the Indian souls. Furthermore, the Church was the only institution capable of organizing and putting together such a project.

From 1523 to the end of the sixteenth century, many innovative minor and major schools and colleges were founded. These institutions reached a wide variety of ages and groups. They provided instruction in religion, Spanish, fine arts, jobs and crafts (Vazquez, 1981). The first antecedents of colonial higher education were the Colegio de Santa Cruz de Tlatelolco, founded by Bishop Juan de Zumarraga in 1536, and the Colegio de San Nicolas de Hidalgo, founded by Bishop Vasco de Quiroga in 1540. The most important institution of higher education during this period, the Real y Pontificia Universidad de Mexico (Royal and Pontifical University of Mexico), was also promoted by Zumarraga. It was founded by royal decree in 1551 and officially inaugurated in 1553. This period has been called the Mexican renaissance by some scholars (Vazquez, 1981).

The Real y Pontificia Universidad de Mexico was organized in the scholastic tradition of the Universidad de Salamanca in Spain. It was a medieval institution in which preservation of the religious dogma was considered far more important than the discovery of truth (Osborne, 1976). At the end of the century and the early 1600s, European universities started to change as a consequence of the scientific revolution. The Universidad Pontificia and the Colegios were also involved in the polemics between scholastics and the emerging empirical sciences. Both institutions maintained a conservative stance towards the new trends in European higher education.

The Colegios and the University were deeply affected by the Council of Trent (1545–64); the consequences, however, were very different for both institutions. The Universidad Pontificia was weakened by the Trent decision to educate future priests in specialized seminars. As a consequence of this decision, the student population decreased and economic support was reduced. The Colegios, on the other hand, were strengthened with the approval of the Jesuit educational project (Wences, 1984). The Society of Jesus was allowed to found many colegios mayores (major colleges). These institutions would become more open and innovative in pedagogy, methodology and curriculum. Intense critiques against scholastic philosophy and theology generated an academic reform movement in the colegios during the eighteenth century. Jesuits expanded the debate about the scientific revolution, and headed the struggle against scholastics in favor of the modern natural sciences (Wences, 1984).

When the Jesuits were expelled in 1776 a large part of the education system collapsed. The struggle between scholastics and science, however, did not come to an end. The demands of King Carlos III for more concern about the sciences were not met by the Universidad Pontificia (De Gortari, 1980). New secular higher education institutions, parallel to the University, were founded by the Spanish crown in an attempt to develop the arts and sciences. The development of an innovative variety of new institutions, Real Seminario de Mineria (Royal Mining Seminar), The Academia de Bellas Artes de San Carlos (San Carlos Fine Arts Academy), the Real Escuela de Cirugia (Royal School of Surgery), and the Jardin Botanico (Botanical Garden) was not enough, however, to produce a profound transformation of the system.

The colonial period of Mexican higher education coincided with an era of intense debates and transformations of cultural perceptions of the world, knowledge, and education in the presence of events like the Protestant reform and the scientific revolution. Societal values rooted in diverse contexts and historical settings were shaken and transformed in distinct ways and to different degrees. The clash between the Catholic Church and Protestant reform, between religious dogma and science, had a differential impact on southern and northern European universities. The colonies shared many similarities with Spain, but the presence of large Indian and Mestizo populations, the difference of economic roles and political structures, and the mixture of cultural perceptions generated a different set of values which were confronted and reshaped in the arena of higher education.

Scholastic and science-oriented institutions survived the colonial period. The dispute between scholastics and empirical science, between the University, on one hand, and the *colegios* and royal schools, on the other, endured despite the war of independence. This conflict and continuing tension between the national values of scholasticism and science within higher education was never settled and assumed new forms in the modern era of early independent Mexico.

The dispute for the nation: religious versus liberal education

In 1821 Mexico finally acquired its independence from Spain. The early years of independent life (1821–67) were characterized by intense conflicts between liberals and conservatives, by foreign interventions, and reform wars. In the confrontation between liberals and conservatives, struggles about and within education played a major role. One of the main issues in this dispute was about the Church. Liberals argued that the new nation's progress depended on the occupation of the Church's properties, the abolishment of privileges for the Church and the military, the expansion of education to popular sectors of society, and its total independence from the Church (Mora, 1963).

Liberals viewed education as a means to insure the exercise of freedom and, through this, national progress. But it was not the vestiges of colonial education which were to play that role. The liberal project for higher education was founded in the royal seminars and schools established by the Spanish crown in the latter years of the colony. The colegios were transformed into secular Institutos Cientificos y Literarios (scientific and literary institutes). The University retained its conservative stance on the side of the Church and the conservative party. In 1833 the Real y Pontificia Universidad de Mexico was closed by the liberals and characterized as useless, irreformable, and pernicious (Mora, 1963). Detractors labeled the University "useless" because they alleged nothing was taught and nothing was learned. The University was also considered "irreformable," because any reform presupposed the ethical and moral base of the old establishment. Obviously, the University was useless and non conducive towards the ultimate objectives of the establishment. The University was, furthermore, considered "pernicious" because it "gives place to the loss of time and the dissipation of the students." The establishment of the time concluded, that it was necessary to suppress the University (Mora, 1963).

The University was reopened by the conservatives in 1834, closed by the liberals in 1857, reopened in 1858, and closed by Juarez in 1861. During the French invasion Emperor Maximilian restored the University and finally closed it in 1865 to the dismay of his conservative allies. At the root of this confrontation lies the clash between the values of religious dogma and scientific orientations that have continually affected the debate over higher education in Mexico. During this historical period, nonetheless, both parties were clear about the importance of the Church's role in controlling education for the preservation of conservative values and religion.

In the final liberal victory against the French invasion, the conservative party and the Church, the University and the colegios were permanently closed and religious education was banned. In the construction of the new secular educational system (1867–74) the unchallenged liberal government turned its eyes to a modern philosophy imported from France by Gabino Barreda: positivism, the philosophy of order and progress.

Barreda was a disciple of Comte in Paris. Upon his return to Mexico he attempted to spread the ideas of this new philosophy and make a strong effort to show the liberals to be the bearers of the "positive spirit." He argued for the assumption, by the liberals, of the motto *liberty, order* and *progress*: liberty as the means, order as the base, and progress as the end (Barreda, 1973). Barreda founded the Escuela Nacional Preparatoria (National Preparatory School, now a part of UNAM) with its curricula based on the structure of positive science. A few years later Barreda reduced the motto – liberty was dropped as a metaphysical concept. Order and progress was the slogan of the newly created Preparatory School and provided the ideological base for the coming dictatorship (Wences, 1984).

Modernization and order: the adoption of positivism

The adoption of the new philosophy of positivism shaped the entire public education system. At the higher education level Barreda's Escuela Nacional Preparatoria was the principal example. In an attempt to provide general and encyclopedic knowledge the new Preparatory included, among others, courses in arithmetic, logics, algebra, geometry, calculus, cosmography, physics, chemistry, botanics, zoology, universal and Mexican history, German, French, and English (Wences, 1984). It is not surprising that this philosophy of order and modernity constituted an element of continuity in education in the transition from the democratic governments towards the dictatorship and provided essential ideological elements for the survival of the latter until 1910. Positivism permeated the

whole education system and constituted the ideological base for Porfirio Diaz's dictatorship. To promote their guiding value, the ruling political party called themselves los cientificos (the scientists).

Before 1910 and during the dictatorship of Porfirio Diaz, Justo Sierra created the School of Higher Studies within the National University, which was the predecessor of the schools of Philosophy and Sciences. Justo Sierra argued that the National University could not situate itself in an ivory tower, far from the needs and expectations of Mexican society. But a strong reaction against the dictatorship and its ideological foundation was to come with the revolutionary uprising in 1910. At the level of philosophical ideas, a reduced group of notable intellectuals, the Ateneo de la Juventud (Ateneus of Youth), provided a strong critique of positivism from a humanist and religious perspective. At the political and military level, the peasant masses who were to appear in the public arena to promote their own values would completely change the course of Mexican history.

Religious humanism reappeared against the discourse of scientific rationality and order. The Ateneo provided a group of very important intellectuals who would reject some of the values of positivism. One of these intellectuals, Jose Vasconcelos, would play a major role in the new educational projects of the revolution. A complex mixture of the social demands and equality values of the revolutionary armed struggle and some elements of positivism and universalistic humanism would permeate the first educational projects of the populist governments that emerged from the revolution. This mixture would not be exempt from tensions and conflicts that would shape the future of higher education in Mexico.

Populism versus conservatism in higher education in the 1920s

At the end of the armed struggle in Mexico to overthrow the dictatorship between 1910 and 1917 the situation of the National University was extremely unstable. As an institution inherited from the Porfirio years it was branded as "reactionary" and a "product of the dictatorship." After some attempts to eliminate it, in 1921 the Mexican state decided to incorporate the University into the process of social reforms that the state was implementing.

Vasconcelos became the first rector of the

National University after the Revolution. He would later become the Minister of Education of the new Secretaria de Educacíon Publica. Vasconcelos combined a rejection of positivism and its belief that education should be a motor for progress. Instead he argued that beyond any utilitarian objective education should focus on getting rid of the profound cultural deprivation that Mexico had suffered (Vasconcelos, 1981). At the same time he considered himself not a rector of the University but a "delegate of the revolution" and he called the intellectuals and the University to work for the people and abandon the ivory tower (Ilinas Alvarez, 1978). The University would not follow.

It is easy to understand the rejection of the University considering the revolutionary orientation of the new state and the immediate past history of this higher education institution. The National University was inaugurated merely two months before the beginning of the 1910 movement. The revolutionary upheaval was contemplated with strong reservations, not with fear or indifference, by the students and faculty whose vast majority came from the upper income groups in society. Unfortunately, the state's attempts to link the University to the populist education project never succeeded. The University increased its distance from the new educational policies of the state until, finally in 1929, the state agreed to grant the University autonomy. With this action, the institution was able to break completely at the time from the state's process of social transformation.

Two fundamental elements explain the granting of autonomy for the National University. First, the student strike (which did not start with the demand for autonomy) took place in a period of enormous political tensions throughout the country. The recent assassination of a former president and the presidential candidate, Obregon, the armed uprising of General Escobar, the end of the first Mexican guerra cristera (religious war), and the independent presidential candidacy of Jose Vasconcelos were events with very dangerous implications for the populist government. The spreading of the student strike required a fast solution to the University problem. Granting the University autonomy was a concrete measure that could defuse this problem. Second, the University's refusal to be part of the state's education projects can explain autonomy as a decision with the objective of further isolating it from those policies.

This experience is very different from what occurred in most other Latin American countries. In Mexico, political and social change preceded university transformations, whereas in many other countries the universities themselves were responsible for such social change. This situation generated a contradictory process in which the University always trailed or resisted progressive social transformations in Mexico. This contradictory process is even more anomalous when one considers that many liberal Mexican intellectuals are found at the National University. The inherent turmoil both in politics and in internal university relations can be attributed to this unique Mexican clash of values between a modern revolutionary state seeking to legitimate its power and a resistant university seeking academic and social autonomy.

Socialism versus academic freedom from 1930 to 1940

In 1933 the relations between the National University and the state became critical, as this was one of the most difficult moments in the history of this institution. The Primer Congreso de los Universitarios Mexicanos (First Mexican University Congress) took place in Mexico City during the second week of September 1933. The different opinions and clash of social and political values became polarized into two grand blocks. One block was represented by Vicente Lombardo Toledano. He was one of the most important national worker union's leaders and Dean of the Escuela Nacional Preparatoria (National Preparatory School), a part of the National University. The head of the other group was Antonio Caso, a philosophy professor at the University. Caso was also Lombardo's teacher and a well-known intellectual, member of the Ateneo de la Juventud, former Porfirista, and founder of the School of Higher Studies with Justo Sierra.

Lombardo Toledano argued that the Mexican universities had to assume a commitment to the proletariat. Therefore, a materialist scientific approach should prevail in the academic orientation of higher education institutions. Antonio Caso disputed that these institutions should be oriented by a neutral science, with no previous commitment to any theory, due to the ephemeral nature of all such theories (Caso, 1971; Caso and Lombardo, 1975). Lombardo Toledano's position won the debate and the Congress. The Catholic students of the National University, however, commanded by the conservatives Gomez Morin and Brito Foucher, expelled by force Lombardo, Rector Medellin and most of the left wing professors.

The government responded with the approval of a new Organic Law (1933). Full autonomy was granted at this point. The University's right to the title "National" was revoked. After a last grant of 10 million pesos, public funding for the University ceased. The 1933 law sanctioned a democratic organization. A collegial model prevailed. The University Council was its highest authority and it had the faculty elect the rector and school deans. At the level of schools and faculties, faculty and student bodies were very important in the decision-making process. Gomez Morin was the first rector during this period. For him, Brito Foucher, and the conservative activists of the National Catholic Student Union, this decision implied a total victory against the state and the socialist ideas. It was also a triumph for the "free educational enterprise" which created the option of a "neutral institution" with "good manners and creeds." In spite of this attitude the University regained a progressively increasing public funding from the state beginning in 1938. During his presidential period, General Lazaro Cárdenas put forward a radical policy for social reform. As part of this project, a nationalistic and popular educational system was developed. The popular and nationalistic orientation of this project was evident in its objective, as stated by Cárdenas, to: "work together with the union, the cooperative, and the agrarian community to combat all the obstacles that are opposed to the liberating march of workers until these obstacles are destroyed" (Cárdenas, 1978, p. 82).

This new educational policy was popular and uniquely nationalistic in its purpose to immediately benefit students from worker or peasant backgrounds. To make this possible, a support system for poor students was established. This system provided free housing, food and academic materials and extended its coverage to students from primary to higher education levels. During this period the Mexican state's higher education project was based on the newly created Instituto Politecnico Nacional (National Polytechnic Institute). The Politecnico served as the focal point for Cárdenas' educational project by promoting the Mexican value of freedom of access to education for the subordinate classes.

The golden age of the university (1940–60): a developmentalist view of education

The educational policy promoted by Cárdenas came to an end with President Avila Camacho. Similar to the Agrarian Reform and the nationalistic industrialization program promoted by Cárdenas, the popular education system was constrained and in many cases reversed by the dominant ruling party and the state. The new economic model centered its attention on the bourgeoisie and the emerging urban middle sectors. The new policies were able to successfully summon the regime's older opposition. The government's alliance with liberal intellectuals favored a re-encounter between the University and the state. The new government was willing to provide full support to the Autonomous University of Mexico. The Catholic groups within the University, however, kept loyal to their anti-state tradition. They were able to make Brito Foucher the new rector. Eager to maintain control of the University in the hands of the most conservative groups, Foucher imposed deans on several schools and faculties. This generated a student strike. Foucher's violent response generated a new crisis and he was forced to resign. Catholic and liberal groups both named their own rectors.

To resolve the impasse of University leadership, President Avila Camacho suggested that both rectors resign and that an extraordinary council, composed of former rectors, would select a new rector for the University. The new rector would have the faculty convene a University Council specially called to generate a new organic law to be proposed to Congress. Alfonso Caso, Antonio Caso's brother, the newly appointed rector, created the Organic Law for the National Autonomous University of Mexico (UNAM) that was approved by both houses without major modifications. This Organic Law, in place since 1945, established the condition of the University as a decentralized public corporation which would have the autonomy to govern itself (within the limits imposed by this law), administer its resources, and define its academic policies. The University would also be publicly financed.

Within this new governance structure of UNAM many of Brito Foucher's projects to establish control by the rector over the appointment of deans and to establish an indirect elective system for the university council were put in practice. An automatically organized and closed governance body with higher authority than the University Council was created: the Junta de Gobierno (Governing Board). Supporters argued that this body would guarantee the independence of the University from the government and political groups and would ensure the depoliticization of the institution. With the new law, Caso attempted to establish a balance between bureaucratic (rector and directors) and collegiate authorities (university council and technical councils) at two different levels: university (centralized), and faculty or school (decentralized).

The 1945 Organic Law was the consequence of a strategy with the purpose of limiting the university community's participation in the decision-making process and to disarticulate the political initiatives of the different sectors of the University. With the law in place, liberal intellectuals were able to take the reigns of the University and fully implicate this institution in the development project of the new regime. The period from 1945 to 1966 at UNAM was relatively stable and is often referred to as the "golden years" of the University. The institution was a relatively small harmonious community within which a collegiate model prevailed. In 1954, President Miguel Aleman inaugurated the University City. This action symbolically sealed the establishment of a new pact between Mexico's National Autonomous University and the state. At the end of the 1960s this pact would once again be broken.

Humanism vs the global market

The year of 1966 inaugurated an era of intense confrontation within UNAM and between the university community and the government. In the late 1960s the professional expectations of middle-class students clashed with the economic reality. It was the end of the Mexican Miracle. Hundreds of professionals produced by UNAM were underemployed. The economic contradictions and the eroded dreams of the Mexican Revolution generated enormous social struggles within and outside the universities. The lack of democracy and the repressive characteristics of the government were more evident in the light of these events. This clash of cultural values and the appropriate role for UNAM was the context for the student struggles of 1966 and 1968 in most Mexican public universities.

After the repression of the 1968 student movement, where 300 students were massacred, the Luis Echeverria government invested heavily in higher education institutions. This provided an important expansion of student enrollment and, consequently, an increase in faculty. Although the perception of the University as a vehicle for social mobility was restored during this period, a new tradition of democratic opposition against the government, ironically, became embedded within the institution. By the mid-1970s an important fraction of the rebellious students of the 1960s had become permanent members of the UNAM faculty. Because of the state's desire to legitimize and consolidate its power, the Mexican left was free to grow, more or less, within the protected environment of the universities. Faculty and administrative workers' unions were created and new confrontations against the University authorities were generated. In spite of these inherent contradictions, the state continues to be the most important employer of university professionals.

Throughout the 1960s and 1970s enrollment and investment in higher education institutions expanded the world over and Mexico was no exception. Enrollment grew during this period in UNAM from 170,000 students to 275,000 in the wake of student protests in 1968. Following the massacre of students the Mexican government needed to rebuild the legitimacy it had lost within the middle urban class sectors and among intellectuals. During the presidency of Luis Echeverria (1970–76) there were many resources to distribute. The state invested heavily in public higher education with the fundamental purpose of closing the breech between the urban middle sectors and the state, opened by the 1968 student movement. During the Jose Lopez Portillo presidency (1976–82), an economic crisis required a reduction in public expenditures. Investment in public higher education was still large but new requirements were established to rationalize this investment and organize educational institutions along the lines expected by the state. The corresponding official discourse was that of "educational planning."

Planning, of course, was the state's euphemism for imposing its policies on what had recently been an autonomous university. This new policy of "educational planning" exacerbated the already existing tensions and contradictions within the University that are products both of external political intervention and the existing internal dynamics within the University itself. As a principal component of the social, political, and economic system in Mexico, the interaction mechanisms between UNAM and the state are complex and often volatile. As Brunner (1985) notes, such cultural mechanisms between universities and the state are expressed in diverse spheres and frequently produce flagrant contradictions.

Obviously, UNAM is a part of the power structure of Mexican society. In fact, UNAM's rectors meet regularly with the Mexican presidents and many of the latter have commented and written extensively about UNAM. National disputes between public and private interests and the conflictual attempts to redefine the latter, determine and are also determined by the confrontations between the state and the University and within the University. This reality of UNAM's place within the social power structure suggests that the main obstacles to change within UNAM are the product of the lack of legitimacy of the mechanisms used to orchestrate university reform and the incapacity to establish agreements among the diverse political actors in the University (Muñoz, 1990, p. 58). The main impediments to any structural transformation within UNAM are, therefore, political (see Ordorika, 1996). This uniquely Mexican situation between the state and its national university, UNAM, can be attributed to the power relations within the University and the intense and complicated interdependence with the Mexican government. Similarly, these power relations and struggles within UNAM can only be understood when viewed as interwoven with those in the broader Mexican society.

Contemporary trends and current debates

As a consequence of the state's need to gain legitimacy in the 1960s and 1970s investment in higher education grew in real terms until 1982 (Martinez and Ordorika, 1993). During the presidency of Miguel de la Madrid (1982–8) the financial crisis worsened and structural adjustment policies were adopted. Investment in public education was reduced drastically. This retrenchment was paradoxically called "educational revolution." Carlos Salinas, President between 1988 and 1994, focused his discourse on the concept of "modernization" for all Mexico's economic, social, and educational

systems. As in de la Madrid's era, Salinas' principal argument was the quest for quality, even at the expense of reducing educational opportunity for many Mexicans. The "modern" emphasis has been placed on the gaining of administrative efficiency (Martinez and Ordorika, 1993). In this context, public higher education institutions have been severely judged and questioned for not being "efficient." The evaluation and indictment of higher education has, however, been oblivious to the historical contribution of these institutions to national development. Again, we see the contradictions of the cultural values espoused in the founding of the autonomous university, UNAM, and its political fortunes in confronting the hegemony of the state.

From 1982 to the present and in the midst of the economic crisis, there has been an important shift in the hegemonic project within the state. Neoliberal policies have been adopted and the traditional accumulative and distributive role of the Mexican state has been minimized. These changes have produced many struggles in Mexican society and important confrontations within the ruling party and the state itself. In the educational sphere, the state has reduced investment in an attempt to limit its intervention in several levels of the public education system (particularly at the higher education level).

UNAM's hegemonic forces (bureaucracy and faculty elite) agreed with the new state policies and attempted changes to comply with them in 1986 and 1992 to raise tuition, restrict enrollment, standardize testing, and introduce other forms of assessment and evaluation. This situation generated important student and faculty struggles at UNAM from 1986 to 1993. This is not, of course, the only confrontation between the proponents of equity and efficiency (although most of the confrontation is voiced in these terms) in the arena of education (Carnoy and Levin, 1985). The struggles within UNAM are also part of the broader confrontation taking place in society to define the role of the state and the extent of its intervention in the future social, economic, and educational development of Mexico.

In the last twenty years four different university administrations have failed in their intent to transform the development of UNAM. These attempts have been the proposal to change the University's General Statute by Rector Guillermo Soberon in 1979, Rector Octavio Rivero Serrano's University Reform in 1983, modification of the regulations for registration, exams and tuition by Rector Jorge Carpizo in 1986–7, and the unsuccessful venture to raise tuition by Rector Jose Sarukhan in 1992.

The contradictions and failure to institute either the reforms that the state or the opposition wish within higher education are expressed in conflicts around the issues of access, social uses of knowledge (career preparation, and research and service), governance, and allocation of resources. In Carnoy and Levin's (1985) terms, these are the inherent contradictions within any educational system and, therefore, not particularly unique to Mexico. These confrontations are the result of multiple determinants among the present economic conditions of students and faculty and their views about the role of the state.

The conflicting national views and values are what define the controversy over higher education in Mexico and provide its uniqueness among other countries in Latin America, developing countries, and higher education in general. These perspectives are based on unique historical linkages between the urban middle class and the welfare state. The 1968 student movement, the process of faculty and staff unionization, and the quest for a democratic reform at UNAM generated a conservative reaction and the articulation of a new social formation which has since ruled UNAM. This bureaucracy has hoarded political participation and decision making by subordinating the collegial to the bureaucratic governing bodies.

Although the official discourse has condemned politics and has stressed the technical and academic nature of the University, this process has developed into a subordination of the academy to the political interests and performance of the bureaucracy. Any perceived problems in the higher education system are, therefore, attributed to bureaucratic inefficiencies in need of further administrative or state intervention. From this perspective of modernization theory student rights and faculty academic freedom are argued as the impediments and causes of poor performance. If the educational system has not, in fact been functioning on behalf of the collective citizenry, then modernists see the problem as an inefficiency of the system, rather than a defect in the system itself (Fägherlind and Saha, 1989, p. 273).

The legitimating aspect of public higher education becomes secondary to the efficiency-oriented policies of the state-controlled modernists. This policy of the Mexican state towards public higher education was recently expressed, essentially, in

three measures (Programa para la Modernizacion Educativa 1988–94):

1 An aggressive financial policy with severe budget cuts and an extreme reduction in faculty's salaries.
2 Strong support to private higher education institutions.
3 New objectives for higher education:

- implement an evaluation system for public higher education to be run by the state and private sectors;
- reorient the universities toward the new requirements of labor markets;
- determine through evaluation the levels of productivity, performance, efficiency, and quality of institutions, departments and faculty;
- strengthen and create linkages between universities and private enterprises.

The implementation of this Modernization Program for higher education confronts both the historical circumstances of higher education in Mexico and the inherent political conflict between two factions struggling to control the universities. On one side there is the vague and heterogeneous idea of broad groups of faculty and students guided by a set of proposals for democratizing governance and expanding access. On the other side is the government's attempts to impose efficiency on the University through bureaucratic authorities, suggesting policies guided by privatization and modernization. This is the classic conflict between equality and efficiency.

Conclusion

Because the shaping of Mexican higher education is an evolving process we cannot offer a definitive conclusion on what the final product of Mexican higher education will be. As we have shown in this chapter, however, we can offer a glimpse into the future of which values and policies will continue to shape Mexican higher education. The conflicting values and unsettled disputes we have reviewed have combined and juxtaposed to generate a unique culture of higher education in Mexico. Briefly, we review here the principal characteristics responsible for the unique circumstances of Mexican higher education in the past and for the future.

1 *Scholasticism vs science*: the growing trend towards empirical research and technological development has been mediated by the strong tradition of scholarship and academic activity that focuses on producing a synthesis and reformulation of previous knowledge and theories. Historically, Mexican intellectuals have disputed the balance over positivistic and humanistic traditions. Each tradition, in turn, has served to support liberal and conservative stands against and for revolution and academic freedom. It is not a consistent or easy argument to understand without identifying the historical context and the traditions being contested. The character of this debate is truly a contextual one, unique to the times and circumstances of Mexican political, social, and intellectual history.

2 *The market vs social mobility*: currently, even with the strong market orientation of the dominant political party (PRI), arguments in favor of promoting such policies have to be considered in terms of maintaining and increasing the functions of social mobility. Market-oriented policies must account for and compromise with the historical traditions of supporting the public good and promoting equitable national development. The strength of these values is founded in the Mexican Revolution, which forces market-oriented perspectives to adapt to these powerful traditions. For example, an increase in higher education tuition is argued in terms of making the upper classes provide resources for lower class students and expanding their opportunities to access higher education.

3 *Academic freedom vs the state*: once a conservative stance against the revolutionary government's policies, academic freedom has become one of the main arguments against market-driven strategies proposed to guide academic programs and research. Academic freedom coexists with an almost indisputable view that establishes the University's commitment to work for independent development, to improve the living conditions of the lower classes, and to work toward the solution of specific social problems. The value and historical tradition of the interconnection between academic freedom and social commitment is very evident in the case of the Zapatista uprising. Faculty and students have been one of the most important sources of urban support for the Zapatista rebels. Many faculties have reoriented their research projects to look at the situation in the state of Chiapas from a multi-disciplinary perspective. Some faculties have also become advisors for the Zapatista organization (EZLN). Students have also been the most important source of solidarity throughout the country. Even the institution itself, UNAM, officially assumed the need to increase its understanding of ethnic groups, marginalization, and health and social conditions. UNAM reactivated and created new centers and committees related to studies in Chiapas. In 1994 the UNAM University Council called for a peaceful solution between the rebels and the state.

4 *Societal transformations vs university transformations*: Mexico differs from other Latin American countries, as we have noted, in that societal transformations have generally preceded university transformations. The Mexican Revolution offers a typical case of how higher education has not transformed itself prior to societal changes brought about by the state. In contrast, university reform in Argentina preceded broader social transformations in the early 1930s. More recently, however, student activism has changed the historical precedent of the University lagging behind social reform. The struggles and student massacre in 1968 played a major role in promoting democratization of Mexican society at the time. Similarly, in the mid-1980s, the student movement again preceded the broad Cárdenista movement during the election of 1988.

5 *Autonomy vs dependence: internally and externally*: the contested liberal and conservative nature of UNAM, as revealed in the Caso-Lombardo debates, provides yet a further example of the unique interrelationship which Mexican higher education has with the state, the Church, and private enterprise. Because UNAM is so large its politics take on the character of a small nation or medium-sized city, as disputing factions of conservatives and liberals vie for control of this state apparatus. Although other nations have highly centralized systems of higher education, UNAM is unparalleled in size and scope of one institution. For example, whereas the University of Tokyo is the undisputed top of the higher education pyramid in Japan, it does vie with a few other prestigious federal universities and private institutions for exclusive access to business and government power (see

Kempner and Makino, 1996). UNAM, however, is as prestigious as the most exclusive public and private institutions combined in most other countries. UNAM also has only minor rivals in Mexico for its exclusive status (i.e., Universidad Autonoma Metropolitana, Institutio Tecnològico de Estudios Superiores de Monterrey, and Collegio de Mèxico). The internal and external disputes within and between UNAM and the state indicate how central the institution is to the broader Mexican society and the unique interrelationship it has with the Mexican state.

In our inquiry of how values affect Mexican higher education we have raised a number of questions, none of which have definitive answers. First, we considered how unique are Mexico's circumstances of higher education compared to other Latin American countries and to other developing countries. As we have noted, the extreme degree of centralization of UNAM gives it a distinct character unlike most other institutions in the world. As Mexico City has become the largest city in the world, it is not surprising that its national university would also have the largest campus and university. Whereas many other developing countries have a similar, hyper-urbanized central city (Bangkok, Taipei, Seoul, etc.), UNAM is unique in its size, centralization, and interrelationship with the state. These circumstances are not universally positive, however, as they have created the contested situation at UNAM that pits warring factions against each other for political dominance. Certainly, disputes and struggles among intellectuals occur in other countries' national institutions of higher education, but few single institutions have the access, power, and impact of UNAM on the national climate.

Next, we questioned the value privatization plays in restructuring Mexican higher education. Related to this question, we also considered how successful Mexico has been in maintaining its national identity within this global market competition. The contemporary policies of modernization of the Mexican government indicate the central role that privatization is now playing in restructuring higher education. Calls for efficiency and stronger relationships with business and industry are at the forefront in the policies to modernize. Reform, however, is not merely a process of becoming modern. The strong traditions of scholarship, academic freedom, and autonomy mediate attempts by the

state to modernize higher education. UNAM's reticence to reform has at times been a liberal stance against the dominance of a repressive state and at times a conservative reaction to a revolutionary government. As state policies change with new governments, it does not always appear dysfunctional for UNAM to only slowly adapt to these changing political circumstances. This too provides the reluctance to embrace the new policies of modernization. Socializing the costs of development, as Slaughter (1990) terms it, favors the interests of business and industry over the dreams of social mobility of the underclasses. The unanswered question, of course, is whether Mexico can maintain its national values and identity in the global competition for goods, services, and ideas. Will Mexico advance beyond its status as a developing nation on the periphery or will it continue to be a service nation for the core?

In this chapter we have questioned further what role higher education and the state itself will play in maintaining the balance between global development and the preservation of the national values and ideals of the Mexican Revolution. On one hand the sheer size of UNAM and its inability to reform rapidly preserves many of its historical values. On the other hand, however, Mexico may continue to be at a disadvantage on the world market as a producer of knowledge when the historical traditions of UNAM favor synthesis and reinterpretation.

The current policies of modernization are an attempt to move Mexico from the periphery to the core through reallocation of resources from public to private interests in education, research, and economic development. What role UNAM will play and should play as Mexico seeks to produce knowledge, services, and commodities for the world market is not yet clear in the state's quest to modernize. What is clear from the state's efforts is that problems in modernizing UNAM are perceived due to "bureaucratic inefficiencies," as opposed to a greater awareness of the historical traditions the state is wishing to modernize. Rather than understand the historical basis and political reality of the problems, the state has embarked on a process of administrative intervention to root out inefficiency. What is certain is that bureaucratic intervention will continue to be contested between the proponents of the state's modernistic interests in efficiency and the social advocates for equity and freedom at the National Autonomous University of Mexico – UNAM.

References

Althusser, L. (1971) *Lenin and Philosophy and Other Essays*. New York: Monthly Review Press.

Barreda, G. (1973) Oración Cívica. In *Estudios: Selección y prólogo de José Fuentes Mares*. México DF: UNAM.

Brunner, J.J. (1985) *Universidad y Sociedad en America Latina*. Caracas: CRESALC.

Cárdenas, L. (1978) *Palabras y Documentos Publicos de Lázaro Cárdenas. 1. ed.* México DF: Siglo Veintinuno Editores.

Cardoso, F.H. and Falletto, E. (1979) *Dependency and Development in Latin America*. Berkeley: University of California Press.

Carnoy, M. and Levin, H. (1985) *Schooling and Work in the Democratic State*. Stanford: Stanford University Press.

Caso, A. (1944). *Anteproyecto de Ley Orgánica de la UNAM que el rector presenta a la consideración del Consejo Constituyente Universitario*. México DF: Imprenta Universitaria, UNAM.

Caso, A. (1971) *Obras Completas. Vol. I*. Nueva Biblioteca Mexicana, México DF: Dirección General de Publicaciones, UNAM.

Caso, A. and Lombardo Toledano, V. (1975). *Idealismo vs. Materialismo Dialéctico (polémica)*, 3rd edn., México DF: Universidad Obrera de México.

Cueli, J. and Arzac, M. (1990) *Valores y metas de la educación en México*. México DF: Secretaría de Educación Pública y Ediciones La Jornada.

De Gortari, E. (1980) *La Ciencia en la Historia de México*. México DF: Grijalbo.

Fägherlind, I. and Saha, L.J. (1989) *Education and National Development: A Comparative Perspective*. Oxford: Pergamon.

Gramsci, A. (1971) *Selections from the Prison Notebooks*. London: Lawrence and Wishart.

Gumport, P. J. (1993) The contested terrain of academic program reduction. *Journal of Higher Education* **64** (3), 283–311.

Ilínas Álvarez, E. (1978) *Revolución, Educación y Mexicanidad*. México DF: UNAM.

Kempner, K. and Makino, M. (1996) The modernistic traditions of Japanese higher education. In K. Kempner and W.G. Tierney (eds), *Comparative Perspectives on the Social Role of Higher Education*. New York: Garland Press.

Levy, D.C. (1980) *University and Government in Mexico*. New York: Praeger.

Martínez, S. and Ordorika, I. (1993) *UNAM: Espejo del Mejor de México Posible*. México DF: Editorial ERA.

Mora, J.M.L. (1963) *Obras Sueltas*. México DF: Porrua.

Mouffe, C. (1979) Hegemony and ideology in Gramsci. In C. Mouffe (ed.), *Gramsci and Marxist Theory*. London: Routledge and Kegan Paul.

Muñoz García, H. (1989) *Política y Universidad*. México DF: Instituto de Investigaciones Sociales, UNAM.

Ordorika, I. (1996) Reform at Mexico's national autonomous university: hegemony or bureaucracy. *Higher Education* **31**, 403–27.

Osborne, T.N. (1976) *Higher Education in Mexico*. El Paso: Texas Western Press.

Programa para la Modernización Educativa 1988–1994. (1988) México DF: Secretaría de Educación Pública.

Slaughter, S. (1990) *The Higher Learning and High Technology: Dynamics of Higher Education Policy Formation*. Albany: SUNY Press.

Vasconcelos, J. (1981). Discurso con motivo de la toma de posesión como rector, 9 de junio de 1920. In *Textos Sobre Educacíon SEP/80*. Mexico DF: Fondo de Cultura Económica.

Vazquez, J. (1981) El Pensamiento Renacentista Español y los Origenes de la Educacíon Novohispana. In *Ensayos sobre Historia de la Educacíon en México*. México DF: El Colegio de México.

Walters, P.B. (1981) Educational change and national economic development. *Harvard Educational Review* **51** (1), 94–106.

Weiler, H. (1983) Legalization, expertise and participation: strategies of compensatory legitimation in educational policy. *Comparative Education Review* **27**, 259–77.

Wences, R. (1984) *La Universidad en la Historia de México*. México DF: Editorial Linea.

Williams, R. (1977) *Marxism and Literature*. New York: Basic Books.

World Bank (1991) *World Development Report 1991: The Challenge of Development*. Oxford: Oxford University Press.

5 Cultural Pluralism as an Educational Ideal

BASIL R. SINGH

> If we value a society in which diverse ideals of life (and education) may be freely held, we must also be prepared to accept the common ground of meanings, beliefs, values, practices (and education) that enables the society both to cohere and to respect diversity.
>
> Crittenden, 1982, p. 89

Introduction

For the purpose of this chapter cultural pluralism implies both unity and diversity: the one nation existing in multicultural forms or parts. The emphasis here is not on how society is divided into ethnic, social, or religious groupings, but on pluralism of value systems distinguishable from mere diversity in customs, languages, foods, dress, etc.

Our main educational concerns, therefore, are seen as transmitting shared values as well as the core values of all groups within a social matrix that is dynamic and capable of change (Smolicz, 1981, p. 21). Smolicz calls this type of transmission of core values of groups a viable and developing pluralism which, according to him, would remain a sterile notion unless it is seen to permeate the lives of individuals from all groups in society.

The chapter argues the case that cultural identification need not be at the expense of social cohesion or social acculturation. For cultural pluralism and social identification within a democratic framework are seen as complementary, especially when individuals within a cultural pluralist society are allowed the freedom to choose from the available cultural options. The emphasis here is on dynamic cultural pluralism to be described below, which allows individuals the freedom to form or join interest groups for their mutual benefit. This kind of dynamic cul-

tural pluralism avoids the worst conflict that may arise between individual autonomy and group solidarity. For although most members would support the survival of their groups, those who find their groups oppressive must be allowed to leave and form others. The rights of the individual to do so must be protected by the state.

The long-term educational goal of cultural pluralism is seen as bicultural or bicognitive development. The chapter discusses how this goal could be achieved while at the same time protecting ethnic minority cultures and encouraging social cohesion and a commitment to society.

The chapter argues that in order for education to prepare individuals to function autonomously in society, it must assist them to acquire basic forms of knowledge, relevant skills and appropriate moral dispositions. It must aim to prepare individuals to make rational choices between alternative ways of life and should endeavour to free them from the imprisonment of strict socialization and cultural practices. Attempts have been made to show how this could be done in ways that would avoid discriminating against ethnic minority cultures. The chapter recognizes the importance of cultures in the socialization of individuals. The value implications of taking the perspective of ethnic minority cultures into account in teaching and in planning the curriculum will be briefly touched upon. The thesis of the chapter is that an education system must teach the value of diversity and the importance of individual commitment to shared values of society.

In a cultural pluralist society there will be value conflicts. Discussion has been emphasized as a method of resolving value conflicts, and as a method of equipping students to answer moral or value questions. The chapter outlines the procedures that discussion should follow in order to achieve these objectives. Recognition is taken of the fact that some moral or value problems are not susceptible to rational resolution. In this case, discussion is seen as a method that should predispose students toward achieving value compromise.

Cultural pluralism

The significance and meaning of cultural pluralism continue to excite interest and, much debate as well as much confusion. In this chapter we wish to draw a distinction between two types of cultural pluralism: the *descriptive* and the *prescriptive* or *evaluative*. The first type of cultural pluralism is often conceptualized (see Smolicz, 1981) as the co-existence of distinct cultures within the same society with very little interaction occurring between the separate elements. Each element would be interested in maintaining its own language and culture to perpetuate its own heritage into the future generations. One could imagine such separate elements having separate school systems, each emphasizing maximum immersion in their home culture with little consideration given to interaction with other children from other ethnic groups. Thus, in accordance with this view, even if such society as a whole would be pluralistic, the members of the various dominant and minority groups would remain largely within the confines of their own cultures. Individuals would become involved in the culture of other groups only insofar as it was necessary for economic and political co-existence. This type of cultural pluralism assumes that society is culturally pluralistic but individuals are not. Each individual inherits one culture and is monolingual (Smolicz, 1981, p. 133).

Thus the descriptive use of the term cultural pluralism implies the co-existence of many political, racial, religious, ethnic and other groupings living together in such a way to allow each social group to function and maintain itself. It describes a situation in which any number of subgroups in society retain their cultural identity or culture while functioning broadly with each other. In this sense the term cultural pluralism is often used interchangeably with cultural diversity (see Pratte, 1972).

The first type of cultural pluralism could result in the limitation of individual rights and personal autonomy in the cause of perpetuating the cultural group or increasing its viability as a political lobby.

As independent, isolated units this kind of cultural pluralism could encourage a kind of enculturation that relies in part on indoctrination, conditioning and manipulation (Appleton, 1983, p. 141), and one that permits groups to develop habits of mind and character inimical to democratic values of open-mindedness, freedom of choice and rational autonomy of the individual. For these values could be seen as antithetical to group survival. Thus, the freedom and rights of groups to preserve their culture could, in this case, be antithetical to the freedom and rights of individuals to pursue their own interests. Although there is a value element in this description, the emphasis is on the existence of various groups as units that pursue their own ends and have control over their own members' outlook.

Cultural pluralism in the second evaluative sense could be conceptualized as a characteristic not only of society as a whole, but of its individual members. In a society where one group predominates, members of minority groups would come to acquire those aspects of the dominant culture appropriate to their personal needs and aptitudes. In such a system minorities would be allowed or even encouraged to maintain and develop their languages and cultures alongside the dominant one. Individuals within such a society could become bilingual and bicultural. Some members of the majority group could acquire aspects of minority cultures and internalize them for their own purposes, and members of minority cultures could do the same in relation to majority culture. Individuals from both minority and majority groups would have the opportunity to make use of more than one culture in their everyday lives. Smolicz (1981, p. 134) describes this form of cultural pluralism as 'internalized cultural pluralism', since the various cultures concerned are internalized within one and the same person.

In the second, prescriptive or evaluative sense, cultural pluralism carries what Pratte (1972, p. 68) describes as a 'positive of "hurrah" connotation'. In this sense 'cultural pluralism and democracy are equivalent'. Thus, for Pratte cultural pluralism connotes a mixed usage – a theoretical construct and a programmatic position. In this chapter we are mostly concerned with the latter sense of cultural pluralism which is more sharply defined by Klein (1974, p. 684) as: 'one in which there is *value* pluralism [and] . . . in which people have a variety of values and can express these values through the institutions of society' (emphasis added).

Since cultural pluralism is defined in terms of value differences, the units of a culturally pluralistic society would be cultural communities. Such communities represent a plurality of values as well as a plurality of moral values. Thus, as Klein (1974, p. 685) argues: 'Within each cultural community [there] would be a unique set of values, including a unique set of moral values.' We wish to accept this evaluative notion of cultural pluralism which stresses freedom of association for groups and for individuals. This notion, which is shared by both Pratte (1972) and Green (1966), implies a number of important assumptions or beliefs:

1 There is no single way of life which can without question claim to be best.
2 It implies the belief that a humane society must afford room for many competing ways of life.
3 It implies it is a value to have such ways of life in competition and in contact and that the differences between them will not be endangered but enhanced by the contact between them (Green, 1966, p. 11).

Thus, from an evaluative sense cultural pluralism assumes that members of the constituent groups ought to possess roughly equal legal status and to enjoy some minimum of equality of educational and economic opportunity. Minimum equality here means that the range of opportunity and the distribution within that range should be about the same for each group (Pratte, 1972, p. 70). The term as used in an evaluative sense implies that no group should be discriminated against or politically, economically or educationally disadvantaged. Society as a whole would strive towards what can be described as 'internalized cultural pluralism' for everyone.

Our main focus here will be on value pluralism as defined above. We shall not be concerned with superficial differences among groups in terms of how they dress, what food they eat, what music they listen to, how they pray, or in differences in their dance forms, but rather on value and other differences which are fundamental in their lives and which form the core of their culture and their ethnic identity.

Cultural pluralism and social harmony

Although some governments in liberal democratic nation states such as Norway, France and the Netherlands emphasize their interests in the cultural survival of the nation, i.e. in their language, history, literature and the mores of the majority, at the same time they vindicate their democratic liberalism by tolerating and respecting ethnic and religious differences and by allowing all minorities an equal freedom to organize their members, express their cultural values and foster their way of life in civil society and in the family (Walzer, 1992, p. 101). If a liberal society is to be judged by the way it treats its minorities, including those who do not completely accept its definition of the good life, then the societies mentioned above as well as some others could well be classified as liberal democratic societies. Indeed, it is difficult to see how a society could be called liberal or democratic unless it allows its minorities to express their cultural values that do not conflict with the core values of the state. Where the expression of cultural values leads to conflict then some compromise will have to be worked out between the contending groups. How this is to be done will be touched upon briefly below. But first it is worth justifying the existence of the culture of ethnic minorities or cultural pluralism within a democratic framework.

Ethnic separation, ethnic co-operation and social harmony

There is some evidence to show that a support for and an identification with one's own ethnic group is not incompatible with a commitment to the society, indeed, quite the opposite. A failure to provide support for individuals to maintain and develop their own cultural heritage does not result in their increased identification with the state. Instead it leads to a dangerous discontinuity in the social fabric that manifests itself in frustration and eventual demands for structural separatism. The study reported by Richmond (1974) indicates that, contrary to popular expectations, heightened identification with one's own ethnic group is reflected in increased identity with Canada as a permanent homeland. Similarly, the study of Taylor *et al.* (1979, p. 19), shows that security in one's own group creates a climate of acceptance towards others. The results were based on assessments of cultural security of the subjects, as well as their attitudes towards their own group and other cultural groups. Thus it would be seen that: 'Conflict and division arise not out of difference, but rather out of denial of the right and the opportunity to be different' (Smolicz, 1981, p. 137).

A feeling of rejection and discontentment could in time lead to rejection of shared values with a demand for radical transformation of the social order. The American experience is a clear case in point where the belated and inadequate response of the majority group has tried to diffuse an explosive situation and pacify members of the minority group which has retained its identity but was denied the opportunity to develop and express it (Smolicz, 1981, p. 137).

The continued retention of ethnic identity, accompanied by the denial of the means for its cultural expression, represents a potential threat to social cohesion. This is very potent in the case of young people who hold a positive attitude to their mother tongue but are unable to activate it in practice because of neglect of the language at school level (Smolicz, 1981, p. 136).

> Failure to provide support for individuals to maintain and develop their own cultural heritage does not result in their increased identification with the state. Instead, it leads to a dangerous discontinuity in the social fabric that manifests itself in frustration and eventual demands for structural separatism. (Smolicz, 1981, p. 136)

For an identity which has its origins in a language-centred culture, the displacement of the core value of that culture undermines its integrity and subjects the individual to stress. Young people may feel ethnic, but cannot express it in terms of the culture that they hold dear. This could produce a perception of inadequacy, failure and being cut off from the mainsprings of their culture and literary tradition and can cause very serious resentment and anger.

There is some evidence to show that a positive attitude towards bilingualism and cultural pluralism increases the possibility of members of ethnic minority identifying themselves in terms of their own culture while at the same time developing a commitment to the receiving society which is perceived as their permanent home (Richmond, 1974, p. 181).

In his research on 'Language Ethnicity and the Problem of Identity in a Canadian Metropolis', Richmond (1974) found that:

> Immigrants of Jewish religion exhibited a strong commitment to Canadian society as measured by the Canadian identification index. Evidently, in the case of Jewish immigrants the tendency to become naturalised Canadian citizens, to settle permanently and to feel they belong in Canada was not incompatible with the retention of their religion and distinctiveness. (Richmond, 1974, p. 187)

Other studies carried out in the USA by Herberg (1960) also show that although Jewish identification is a multidimensional phenomenon with various components relating to the religious, cultural and social aspects of membership in the Jewish community, strong Jewish identification has not been at the expense of their rapid acculturation into the American way of life or their political integration.

According to Richmond (1974, p. 189) the evidence suggests that the experience of Jews in Canada has been very similar to those in the USA: 'Despite a marked degree of residential segregation in Toronto, and strong attachments to religious institutions, Canadian Jews have become economically and socially well integrated into Canadian society.' Thus, Richmond maintains that a high residential concentration and a relative lack of structural assimilation are not incompatible with a high level of identification. Orthodox Jews, for instance, tended to score higher than other Jews on the Canadian score. According to Richmond, this is partly due to the effect of length of residence. The Orthodox Jews had been resident in Canada longer than others (Richmond, 1974, p. 189). Richmond emphasizes this 'confirms that strong religious identification in the case of Jewish population is not incompatible with an equally strong sense of national loyalty and commitment' (Richmond 1974, p. 189).

Richmond notes that among the immigrants who belonged to one of the Eastern Orthodox churches there is also a tendency similar to that found among the Jewish immigrants. Thus Richmond (1974, p. 190) concludes that 'the maintenance of religious identification is quite compatible with a strong sense of commitment to Canadian society'. On the other hand: 'Members of racial religious and linguistic minorities who felt that they, or their group were subject to discrimination, were unlikely to identify closely with Canada' (Richmond 1974, p. 205).

There is a lesson to learn from Richmond's research in relation to biculturalism and bilingualism. There is a cumulative effect of increased satisfaction leading to greater acculturation and eventual social integration into the receiving society. Retention by members of ethnic minorities of a self-definition in terms of their own cultural, religious, language or national origin seems to be quite compatible with a strong commitment to receiving society as a place of permanent residence and where members feel they belong and plan to stay. So it would seem that there is no inherent conflict between cultural pluralism and the democratic ideal. For cultural pluralism is quite compatible with a democracy which allows cultural pluralism to survive.

Democracy and cultural pluralism

Several theorists writing in support of cultural pluralism treat pluralism and democracy as complements. Villemain (1976, p. 45) for instance, in describing the norms and values which ought to govern the social relationships in and among cultural groups, argues that: 'what is of ultimate worth is the fullest possible development of each person – the realisation of whatever potentiality there may be for excellence'. It is this principle, according to Villemain, that justifies a pluralistic arrangement and should govern the types of groups that are allowed to exist and how they should interact with each other. Were such an arrangement to take place and be governed by this notion of cultural pluralism, then cultural diversity becomes a potential resource, providing an alternative frame of references, value structures and life styles in which individuals may choose their identities.

Pluralism and freedom to choose

Klein (1974) shares the views of Villemain (1976) and Appleton (1983). For Klein the basic conditions of an ideal culturally pluralistic society can be viewed as a model for what an ideal democratic society would be like: 'the value of freedom of choice would be clearly central. . . the individual freedom to choose his [sic] own values, including freedom of association with other cultural group would be emphasised' (Klein, 1974, p. 152).

This freedom to choose cultural or interest grouping is referred to by Pratte (1979) as dynamic pluralism. Dynamic pluralism, as Pratte (1979) points out, assumes that individuals would be free to form communities of interests – special interest

groups – as a result of mutual concern for a problematic situation.

Ideal cultural pluralism

The concept of cultural pluralism postulated by Pratte (1979) would avoid a conflict between the ideals of democracy and the ideals of cultural pluralism. Such a conception emphasizes:

- achievement rather than race or ethnicity as a means of establishing one's position in society;
- a diversity of ethnic, cultural and interest groups;
- a high level of interaction among members of different ethnic groups;
- shared values based on the democratic ideal as well as particular values based on ethnic culture and beliefs, each of these sets of values interacting with each other in a process of development and for the benefit of the individual.

Such a conception of cultural pluralism avoids barring individuals from full participation in the benefits of society on the basis of ethnic or racial backgrounds.

The idea of cultural pluralism we are working with would avoid a possible conflict between individual autonomy and group solidarity. It does not allow the exclusion of one group from another. The stress is not on preservation or maintenance of any group per se but on the functional socio-economic value of ethnic group formation for the purpose of gaining power or influence for social, political and economic advancement. Members of ethnic groups would be given the choice as well as the opportunity to remain within them or to venture out into the wider society and partake in its cultural offerings or adopt other cultural ways (Appleton, 1983, p. 63). The long-term goal of cultural pluralism as envisaged here is bicultural, bicognitive development and group fluidity based on interests rather than merely on culture. Thus, in the long run, interest group membership is voluntary and individuals are free to associate themselves or not to associate themselves with interest groups or communities as they see fit (Appleton, 1983, p. 88). Individuals will interact with one another to meet personal and common needs. It is through these interest group associations that the individual's personal needs could be met. Although the individual could take up many role identities, it is to be recognized that ethnic association is the starting point for establishing group associations. Group association is important in the early socialization of the child and as an identity point from which to launch one's social commitments (Appleton, 1983, p. 88).

The assumption here is that cultural pluralism, by promoting individual membership in and attachment to primary or cultural group life and the socially encouraged involvement in it, should also promote those characteristics in a person usually associated with a healthy personality type – self-esteem, sense of belonging, respect for others, purposefulness and critical thinking (Kallen, 1956, p. 25). Of course many of these characteristics would develop only if individuals are given the freedom or opportunity to encounter and interact with a variety of culturally different others. As Kallen (1956) argues, the more groups an individual can encounter, join or leave and, the more varied their character and function, the more civilized the individual and society as a whole are likely to be. Thus, inter-group fluidity protects against what could otherwise be negative consequences following socially encouraged group membership, especially if that membership means parochialism, is not open to change and/or does not allow contact with other groups. The essence of the system postulated here is dynamic cultural pluralism (see Pratte, 1972). Dynamic cultural pluralism avoids the negative consequences of group solidarity upon individual autonomy.

The essence of dynamic cultural pluralism is for individuals to move beyond their initial subgroups to the formation of communities of interest group formation. On the basis of some common concern or commitment, individuals or minority subgroups could form a social collective with other groups to pursue their mutual interests. Hence, interest group formation would be dynamic – forming and dissolving as interests dictate or when social, economic and political conditions change. In this process individuals would be able to assess the relative advantages and disadvantages, and organize into communities of interest in pursuit of their perception of the common good (Appleton, 1983, p. 87). Granting such fluidity in group formation, then it will follow that there is no contradiction in assuming that loyalty to a society is compatible with socially sanctioned loyalties rooted in a multiplicity of diverse ethnic and cultural groups. There is no contradiction in assuming that a healthy society must be based on a mosaic of autonomous group-

ings reflecting the underlying differences of the population (Torney and Tesconi, 1977, p. 108).

However, one does not wish to deny the dangers to individual autonomy that could be brought about by group solidarity. Nor does one wish to deny that there is potential conflict between the interests of the individual and those of the group. The dilemma this poses is that when individuals are able to exercise free ethnic choice, a threat to the stability of ethnic and cultural groups could result. Conversely, when group interests are allowed to prevail the autonomy of the individual is threatened.

External constraints upon free choice

It should not be forgotten that even when individuals are allowed free choice within a group their freedom could still be curtailed by external constraints which block them from exercising their options or force the adoption of one position over another. Thus, as Appleton (1983) argues, if a qualified individual is forced or channelled into a certain occupation, is treated in a socially inferior manner because of his or her ethnic background or denied the opportunity to practise the ways of his or her native culture by the dominant group, we are justified in claiming that free choice has been denied (Appleton, 1983, p. 140). Such discrimination could be seen as the foundation for inter-group hostility and the basis for the call for group separatism and group solidarity.

Hence, free ethnic choice may be constrained by social barriers that have traditionally restricted the mobility of certain individuals in society on the basis of ethnic criteria. Moreover, the potential conflict between group solidarity and individual autonomy should not divert us from reflecting on the importance or value of cultural pluralism which, as defined here, would allow individual autonomy without destroying the significance of ethnic heritage. There are recognizable advantages to group solidarity and cohesiveness, especially in political and economic struggles. In these struggles strong, cohesive group identity may be the only way to influence those in power and to provide the individual with the foundation and esteem upon which personal autonomy is based (Appleton, p. 64). Thus the cultural pluralist would value and encourage ethnic and cultural group affiliation and insist upon fluidity within and between groups. Hence, although primary and ethnic group memberships are important, individuals must also be free to move in and out of groups, engaging in open communion with others to achieve common goals or ends. According to democratic ideals, cultural pluralism emphasizes openness and fluidity between groups and allows the individual to choose from the available options.

The options open to an individual need not involve the individual having to choose whether to remain more narrowly ethnic or to acculturate. Many children growing up in this society are bicultural. For example, many white groups within this society, while maintaining their ethnic communities, clubs, churches, etc., enjoy a high degree of social mobility and cross-cultural interaction. Individuals enjoy the advantages of their ethnic heritage without becoming trapped or confined by it. The same case could be made for members of ethnic minorities. Although the group and the ethnic community are very important in the socialization of individuals, these same individuals are also strongly influenced by the common culture during their early socialization, even if they never leave the ethnic community or enclave (Banks, 1977). The common culture influences everyone through the schools, the law, the arts, sport, the mass media, science and technology. Thus, although ethnic groups have some unique cultural characteristics, all groups in Britain share many cultural traits. Social mobility precipitates the move towards the common culture, but never destroys the group culture. Many ethnic group members who are culturally assimilated still maintain separate ethnic institutions and symbols (Banks, 1977, p. 237). Thus, individual autonomy and group survival is maintained simultaneously. Individuals need not select between mutually exclusively cultural alternatives, but can enjoy the benefits of both worlds (Ramirez and Castaneda, 1974, p. 28). It could be argued that ethnic communities which pose no threat to the general welfare of society should be allowed to maintain their cultural heritage and group autonomy and to transmit this heritage from one generation to the next. At the same time, individuals who find the cultural community too limiting or who are unable to meet their own needs within those boundaries should be free to venture beyond them. In order to make this possible, individuals within the ethnic community need to acquire basic skills, knowledge and aptitudes to cope within the larger society. The acquisition of these skills is the task of education, to which we now turn our attention.

Education

In order to function as an autonomous person in a democratic society one needs the knowledge and skills to act democratically. Education can assist individuals in making rational choices between alternative ways of life and free them from the restraints of strict socialization and cultural practices (Appleton, 1983, p. 64). However, although the enculturation of some groups in society may involve beliefs and practices that are incompatible with the ideals of cultural pluralism postulated above, education at classroom level can do much to free individuals from potentially limiting life styles, thereby providing a means of cultural mobility that encourages them to go beyond their own culture. This applies to individuals within a minority culture as well as to members of the majority culture.

Education for cultural diversity

Appleton (1983, p. 206) argues that in addition to enhancing the development of basic academic skills, a multicultural programme 'should help students to develop a better understanding of their own backgrounds and those of other groups that compose our society'. He envisions a programme that will help students to respect and appreciate cultural diversity, to overcome ethnocentric and prejudicial attitudes and to understand the sociohistorical factors which have produced the contemporary conditions of ethnic polarization, inequality and alienation.

Appleton argues that the school's programme should help students to analyse critically and make intelligent decisions about life problems and issues through a process of democratic, dialogical enquiry:

> [The programme] should help students conceptualise and aspire toward a vision of a better society and acquire the necessary knowledge, understanding and skills to enable them to move the society toward greater equality and freedom, the eradication of degrading poverty and dehumanising dependency, and the development of meaningful identity for all people. (Appleton, 1983, p. 206)

Teachers should help children develop positive attitudes and feelings about their ethnic identities and heritages. Educational systems in the past have emphasized the dominant culture's values, customs and beliefs while minimizing and disparaging those of other cultures (Appleton, 1983, p. 209). This raises an important question for education: what values, customs and beliefs are educationally relevant and should be taught? If we are to allow that some beliefs could be educationally unimportant or inaccurate, then it may follow that they should not be taught. According to Varga (1984, p. 134), 'if we allow a student to go on believing something that is false, we do the student a disservice'.

Nevertheless, in deciding what should be taught, Appleton (1983, p. 209), argues that we should take account of the fact that 'unless people feel good about their ethnic backgrounds, they can hardly relate positively to those of others'. Feeling good about one's ethnic background should not preclude being critical about one's customs, beliefs and values. However, such questioning should not involve discredit or wholesale rejection of everything that characterizes one's heritage. Perhaps we would all feel good about the results of a critical evaluation of our own heritages, if such evaluation is permitted by the fundamental tenets of our beliefs or values.

Although we admit to cultural differences, we must make some decisions about what is worthwhile to teach when we are trying to educate. Decisions about what to teach will lead us to consider the relative merits of cultural customs, beliefs and values. It is no good just to say that everything should be taught as equally worthwhile, as though it makes no difference what we do, believe and value (Varga, 1984, p. 395).

While pupils should feel proud of their ethnic background and not ashamed of their culture, this does not mean that they should not question some of their ethnic customs, beliefs and values. Each pupil should be helped to make a critical evaluation of his or her heritage. However, we are reminded by Zec (1980) that the criteria for critical evaluation of cultures might be culturally loaded in favour of a particular culture, namely the dominant one. Hence the criteria selected by the teacher should be open to discussion and related ultimately to the basic issues of what ought to be taught in schools and what learning is worthwhile. The school can attempt to provide pupils with the appropriate critical tools to make rational and morally acceptable choices. Schools have the potential to play an important role in maximizing the autonomy and free choice of the individual in a number of ways. First, through curriculum content, teaching methods, teacher–pupil relationships and by example, teachers can foster a sense of self-esteem and the ideology of equality. Stereotyping and racial or cultural discrimination will therefore be discouraged. Second, the school should teach that there are alternative identities and cultural styles and some of these are within the realms of choice for any individual. The school should help individuals, by their own choice, to determine who or what they will be. Pupils should learn to exercise options and how to participate and perhaps succeed in a multiracial, multicultural setting. Ramirez and Castaneda (1974) refer to this as bicognitive development. Students should learn how to function in their own native culture and within the dominant culture without being forced to choose one over the other.

The reality of bicognitive development will demand that the child from, say, an ethnic minority group must learn (a) to function effectively in the mainstream 'European cultural community'; (b) continue to function effectively in and contribute to his/her ethnic cultural community. According to Ramirez and Casteneda (1974, p. 29) a single view of acculturation in education has accepted only one of these realities: to function effectively in and contribute to his/her cultural world. They emphasize a bicultural reality of the child's world which has as its primary educational goal:

> the ability to function effectively in and the responsibility to contribute to developments in both cultural worlds. Under the concept of cultural democracy in education, the term 'equal educational opportunity' can be interpreted to mean that the school is obliged to create programmes of such a nature that the child acquires the skills that are necessary to his [sic] functioning and contributing to both worlds. This perspective for education assumes bicultural educational methodologies. (Ramirez and Castaneda, 1974, p. 30)

At the time when many children enter school, they are the products of the socio-cultural system characteristic of their homes and communities. At school they will be required to acquire the characteristics inherent in the socio-cultural system of the school which would be more compatible with the white, middle-class socio-cultural system. Hence for Ramirez and Castaneda (1974, p. 28) the pressing requirement is the provision of educational experiences necessary to enhance the right of children to be able to function in both cultural worlds – the cultural world of the children as well as the cultural world of the Anglo-Saxon or European white middle class.

Thus, to be effective in developing educational programmes one must take the child's cognitive style and stage of development into account. Group differences must be recognized and differences relating to ethnicity, race and religion must be considered within a democratic framework. Of course, what group differences would be relevant for consideration is a problem for the teacher. However, while skin colour would not be relevant in most considerations, religious differences may be.

Methods and strategies at school level

Measures at the school level will include the reform of the curriculum content and methods of teaching to reflect the principles appropriate to a multicultural, multiracial classroom and society. The school will actively strive to involve parents and the community. The programme should help pupils to analyse critically and make intelligent decisions about life problems and issues through a process of demographic, dialogical enquiry. More specifically, the curriculum would include ethnic studies designed to advance a positive sense of ethnic identity. Pupils would learn about their common history, ancestry and cultures and gain a sense of being a common people. Bilingual education would perhaps be the common currency in most schools. In structure and organization, schools would tend towards community schools. Neighbourhood schools would emerge and be staffed by individuals reflecting the different ethnic populations. The essence of education would be bicultural, bicognitive development. The goal will be the enhancement of the autonomy (intellectual, social, moral) of the individual and the well being of the society in which he or she lives.

Methods and strategies at teacher training level

Most teacher training courses should include modules which combine theoretical, legal and pedagogic considerations relating to human rights. History and the social science subjects could easily include cultural pluralist perspectives in their syllabus. Both initial and in-service forms of training could include cultural pluralist perspectives and could complement each other in a teacher training plan under the heading 'intercultural education' (Best, 1992). According to Paul Hirst (1990), if education has to do with the development of knowledge and understanding and to prepare people to live by reason, then the education system must support genuine diversity and alternative ways of living and should enable students to live in a multicultural, multiracial society. Where there are alternative perspectives on life, religion, the environment and human relationships, then an education system will be effective which takes them into account (Hirst, 1990, p. 45). Education will prepare students to make rational choices from alternative perspectives on life available in society.

Hirst (1990) reminds us that, according to the Kantian view, one cannot be rational about human beings unless one is prepared to start from a platform of treating all as equal. People, as rational agents, should be free to pursue their own ends and fulfilment as they understand them, provided they do not thereby interfere with others. Hirst points out that there are many areas where there is a diversity of beliefs, including our understanding of the economy, the world and ourselves and about how we should live our lives; questions relating to such matters are genuinely open ended. There is no pattern or set of golden rules applicable to every aspect of human life. There is no one kind of institution that will satisfy every aspect of the good life for all (Hirst, 1990, p. 46).

If the concept of a democratic society assumes genuine diversity, alternative views and lifestyles and if inherent in the concept of democracy is the idea of freedom, then the implication must be that as rational agents people are equal because they are fundamentally free to decide and choose alternative ends. Hence the idea of social justice or equality seems to be presupposed by the idea of democracy.

On the notion of democracy, according to Hirst, there could be no rational grounds on which a just society could practise an assimilationist policy. In areas that are genuinely open in human life – religion, art, music, the family, abortion, etc. – there is no case that one perspective is the most rational and acceptable (Hirst, 1990, p. 48); for these reasons 'any rationalist society must be pluralist in this respect'. Thus, 'to live rationally is to live multiculturally' and 'diversity is the nature of rational beings. Part of the enrichment of human life is the recognition of that great diversity' (Hirst, 1990, p. 49).

Any curriculum must endeavour to prepare people to live a rational and moral life in a society which in principle practises rationality and social justice. The curriculum must encourage understanding of the society and its principles, but also what such a society could be like in the interests of social justice. According to Hirst (1990, p. 49): 'The search of what is universal in education necessarily commits you, if you are really true to the real cannons of the discipline, to pluralism'.

Choosing from available cultural options

As long as ethnic cultural variation continues to exist, individuals will be able to draw upon more than one cultural model in the construction of their personal worlds. In this way the cultural and social life of the country will be enriched, as individuals can choose from a number of cultural options. Cultural co-existence could produce a dual system of values. In other forms of interaction some 'blend' or in-between position may be achieved in personal life styles as individuals draw upon family traditions and extended networks of primary relations on the one hand and on the Anglo-Saxon ideals of individualism, self-reliance, independence and personal autonomy on the other (Smolicz, 1984, p. 13).

So in a pluralist, liberal democratic society children should be allowed to make an informed choice between alternative activities and ways of life. This would demand that they be introduced to a range of possibilities (Halstead, 1988, p. 225). A public education or common schooling seems to offer the best possibility that a range of competing conceptions of the good life will be offered to all children. If children's interests are best served by introduction to a range of possibilities of the good life, if children need to become aware of the diversity of beliefs and lifestyles that exist in the world and to develop a capacity to make rational informed

choices between alternatives (Halstead, 1988, p. 225), then the fundamental questions are: What kind of (education) curriculum should the child be exposed to? What principles should guide the construction of such a curriculum? The International Covenant on Civil and Political Rights (1966) offers some guidance on these questions. Article 27 acknowledges the right to the development of one's culture. This includes the right to an equal education, the right to participate in the cultural life of the society and the right of minorities to enjoy their own culture, to profess and practise their own religion or to use their own language.

Ethnic culture, the school culture and curriculum planning

Difficult questions regarding the relationship between the school and the child's ethnic culture are inherent in any curriculum planning and teaching. Although the school should reflect both the child's ethnic culture and the common societal culture, the following questions will still have to be answered:

1 How does the individual function within two cultures that sometimes have contradictory and conflicting norms, values and expectations?
2 What happens when the ethnic cultures of the students seriously conflict with the goals and norms of public institutions such as the school?
3 Do the institutions change their goals? If so, what goals do they embrace?   (Banks, 1977, p. 238)

These are difficult questions to answer. Within the scope of this chapter, I want to provide an introductory discussion on some of the issues thrown up by them.

If the concept of cultural pluralism is to be meaningful in any sense we must assume that important cultural differences will exist; differences in life styles and values will co-exist in society. We must further expect that some of these differences, especially those starting from different value premises, will be incompatible with others and at times will clash to produce cultural conflict not just between two identifiably different cultural (i.e. ethnic or racial) groups, but between the ways of life of a given group (Appleton, 1983, p. 167). Indeed, in a cultural pluralist society there could be conflicts between meeting the socialization requirement of society and the cultural transmission requirement of one's family and community. However, one should not despair about the possibility of culture clash, nor about the plurality of values. As Popper (1945) points out, there is a healthy awareness of the existence of other cultures which prevents our own from becoming a prison. In his defence of an open pluralistic society, Popper argues:

> If we dream of a return to our childhood, if we are tempted to rely on others and so be happy, if we shrink from the task of humanness, of reason, of responsibility, if we lose courage and flinch from the strain, then we must try to fortify ourselves with a clear understanding of the simple decision before us. We can return to the beast. But if we wish to remain human, then there is only one way, the way into the open society. We must go on into the unknown, the uncertain, the insecure, using what reason we may have to plan as well as we can for both, security and freedom.   (Popper, 1945, p. 201)

Thus, given the value conflicts that cultural pluralism throw up, the stress of educational diversity would be on the acceptance and tolerance of different value perspectives on contemporary issues. Pupils would be taught critical thinking skills and to take justifiable stands on social issues. With regard to individual commitment and achievement, schools would work to eliminate sexual, racial, ethnic and cultural prejudice and discrimination. Pupils would learn to appraise an individual's achievements and not his or her cultural or racial background. In addition, schools should seek to have pupils engage in educational transactions that will make them concerned for and effective in their efforts to realize their most valued potentials both as individuals, as members of groups and as citizens of a democratic society.

The thesis of this chapter, as indicated above, is that more opportunities will be offered to students to choose from competing ways of life if they attend a common school. The task of education is to provide students with a knowledge of competing conceptions of the good life and to develop their capacity to choose freely and rationally between them (Bridges, 1984, p. 56). But how should students be prepared to develop their capacity – to choose freely and rationally between alternative value perspectives? One answer to this question is through a process of dialogical enquiry, that is, through a process of (moral) discussion. What follows is an attempt to spell out the implications of such dialogical enquiries, the procedures they should follow. An attempt will also be made to evaluate:

- Their strengths and weaknesses in fostering the capacity to choose rationally;
- Their potential for equipping students for tolerance and harmony in a culturally pluralist society.

Discussion as a method of resolving value conflict

Classroom discussion should equip pupils now and later in life to answer moral or value questions for themselves. For such discussions to succeed, however, according to Hare (1976, p. 13), they have to proceed in accordance with certain methodological principles or rules – the logic of the argument. The substantive views or values of participants concerning the questions at issue should be considered. There may not be disagreement about important substantive questions, but, as Hare puts it, teachers and students 'may yet agree about the methodology and the logic, and the best way to help children to answer the substantive questions is to teach them a method of arguing fairly, clearly and logically about them' (p. 13).

Thus, according to Hare, in such discussions, the disputants would be expected to be careful to understand the question under debate, the evidence adduced in support of assertions and the views of each other. Although individuals could reach their own decisions about values, the method for reaching and discussing them would be determined by certain procedures and the nature of the subject matter. It is not to be assumed, however, that procedures and clarification of terms and the examination of evidence determine what the conclusions will be. For people may still differ for all sorts of reasons, based on their culture, religion, world views or interests.

However, granting all this, and if our purpose is to work towards achieving an objective moral compromise or consensus, then participants must abide by certain rules and procedures. For example, every participant in a discussion or dialogical inquiry must take into account the perspective of the other participants: each must follow the rules of argumentation, of coherence, consistency and validity. Being able to enter into legitimate moral dialogue may in fact presuppose a deliberate adherence to the imperative of 'respect for persons'. A moral judgement evolving from such a dialogue, i.e. from a collaborative endeavour, would be justified if it generates agreement by everyone party to the decision-making group. According to Kohlberg, (1986, p. 497), this process will require, 'equal consideration of the claim or points of view of each person affected by the moral decision'. Kohlberg refers to this collaborative endeavour as 'prescriptive role-taking [which] is governed by procedures designed to ensure fairness, impartiality or reversibility in role-taking' (p. 497).

Following Habermas, Kohlberg, argues that disputants will take the 'performative attitude' in actual moral dialogue, an attitude that is characterized as the active attempt to understand the points of view of others, and co-ordinate this understanding with one's own reasons in such a way that disputants will yield to convincing arguments. Dialogue will be grounded by a number of presuppositions including mutual respect, freedom and rationality of each disputant.

In such a collaborative endeavour within a free society each person's moral views would be submitted to the marketplace of ideas in group discussion. Thus, in engaging in discussion under these circumstances, one hopes to increase the likelihood that just a solution will be found for hard case dilemmas; solutions that will compel agreement because of their evident rationality and fairness. The whole process of dialogical inquiry and communication will therefore proceed towards finding solutions or coming to some agreement (Lapsley, 1992, p. 172). Active attempts should be made to understand the points of view of others and to co-ordinate this understanding with one's own reasons in such a way that disputants will yield to convincing arguments. Dialogue of this sort would be grounded by a number of presuppositions, including mutual respect, freedom from coercion and rationality (Lapsley, 1992). Participants would be expected to strive to give moral discussion a chance to succeed. Such discussion or communication would require some equality of position for the purpose of putting forward solutions and participating in their discursive redemption. In such a dialogical, communicative atmosphere, no one will assume a privileged position by virtue of his or her religion, culture, race or ethnicity. The aim would be seen in terms of a search 'for the best means of regulating overlapping and competing needs and interests for the purpose of a *mutual* "redemption" of . . . [the] validity [of their claims]' (Boyd, 1992, p. 159). What warrants those claims as better or worse can be found only through the quality of the

dialogic activity among the persons concerned (Boyd, 1992).

The aim of such a dialogical enquiry, based on the principles outlined above, would be to bring about a commitment among members to 'talk through our cultural diversity about how we should make sense of it together . . . also for the next generation to talk to us and to each other in the continual activity of making this sense' (Boyd, 1992, p. 158). This requires that we keep open minds, not only for our own sake, but also for those to come.

If the question is to be kept open as to what constitutes the good life for all members of a cultural pluralist society, then it must follow that no static truth claims about morals will be given a privileged position. All claims will be looked upon as means of regulating overlapping and competing needs and interests. The quality of the dialogue could determine the aim or path to be chosen, the decision to be made, the compromise that is to be reached for social harmony and social or moral progress. Dialogical enquiry is therefore directly related to a policy of compromise or tolerance and non-violent persuasion (Crittenden 1982, p. 39). For ultimately social harmony may well depend on it.

Insufficiency of rational procedures

There are those such as Walsh (1976) who question the sufficiency of decisions arising from following rational, objective methods. For Walsh, we still need to ask: 'Do the methods lead to choices that can ultimately be described as "right", "good", "best", "adequate", etc., or as "wrong", "bad", "second-rate", "inadequate"?' (p. 31).

Walsh rejects the idea that a knowledge of the relevant procedures or facts and a knowledge of the meaning of moral words inevitably generates a right answer to moral questions. Why should 'a knowledge of method plus data . . . magically and infallibly produce answers in the moral sphere, or in any other sphere?' (Walsh, 1976, pp. 31–2). But he concedes that 'the concept of a method which could never be used to produce good answers, given the facts, would be an exceedingly odd one' (Walsh, 1976, p. 32).

Value of rationality

Yet in spite of the shortcomings of critical methods indicated by Walsh, others such as Crittenden

(1982) maintain that: 'it cannot be seriously doubted that the practice of critical, reflective rationality is preferable to any that relies largely on the unquestioning acceptance of received beliefs and the pronouncements of established authority' (Crittenden, 1982, p. 42). For, Crittenden adds: 'critical rationality requires a willingness to face the evidence of experience that may count against one's beliefs or ways of thinking and to review them when it does' (p. 42).

Such a policy or disposition to review one's decisions or beliefs, calls for an open mind. Such a review is premised on the presuppositions of rationality, critical evaluation of evidence and argument.

Conclusion

In the foregoing discussion attempts have been made to define cultural pluralism in a descriptive as well as a prescriptive sense, and we have accepted the prescriptive or evaluative sense with its positive or "hurrah connotations" (Pratte, 1972, p. 68). In this sense cultural pluralism and democracy are seen to be equivalent. It follows that members of constituent groups ought to possess equal status and enjoy some minimum of equality of educational, social and economic opportunity.

The concept of cultural pluralism that we have discussed could be seen as an ideal type by which a society could be judged to be liberal and democratic. Such a society will be an open society allowing different cultural groups to flourish. Such a cultural pluralist open society will be characterized by a high degree of interaction among the individuals and groups that compose it and by substantial freedom of movement in and out of groups. In an open pluralist society there will be extensive interaction in secondary associations and at least some in primary associations (Crittenden, 1982, p. 36). The aim of such a society would be to encourage social cohesion of the whole society as well as protecting the cultural diversity within it.

All groups within a democratic society would be expected to uphold the general values of democracy and its basic procedures for political decision-making. The central values are those of freedom and equality. A high value will be placed on the freedom of choice of individuals. Freedom of speech and assembly will be similarly protected by the state. All members of society will be entitled to develop and use their human capacities and in the political sphere to exercise their equal right to vote and to seek election. Decision-making within a democratic system should be in terms of majority decision, sought by non-violent means such as rational persuasion, following rational procedures as described above (Crittenden, 1982, p. 21).

It was not the intention of this chapter to suggest that rational procedures are alone sufficient for generating right answers to moral questions. For given the facts and the rational procedures outlined in the chapter, people may still disagree. Each party to a discussion could be arguing from his or her customary practices and value stance, thereby declaring that his or her preferred beliefs are true and based on rational grounds. Each party to the dispute could also accept that his or her argument, like everyone else's, is culturally context bound. Nevertheless, although we have argued that certain moral premises are incommensurable, it should be stressed that there is a great deal of consensus among people from all ethnic backgrounds about what counts as right or wrong, good or bad, true or false. Thus, there is reason to believe that value compromise could be reached on a variety of moral issues.

Nothing we have said in the chapter should suggest that the idea of cultural pluralism implies a commitment to cultural relativism. We reject the view that nothing is valuable or good unless it is sanctioned by a particular culture. As a closed system, cultural relativism assumes that normative questions of truth, validity and rationality cannot be settled except by reference to standards that are particular to each cultural system. Thus if relativism is true, one would be hard pressed to provide a rational argument against racial discrimination, apartheid or Nazi morality. Although cultural groups should be given certain rights as described in the chapter, members within a group cannot do as they please even within their own groups. They have rights, but also social and moral responsibility to ensure that no one is badly treated and that individual rights or autonomy are not violated.

We have argued that the culture of one's primary socialization has an inherent stabilizing, identifying, forming effect for the individuals within it. But the existence of cultural groups does not provide justification for all social practices within that group. There are (morals or) values such as human rights, individual autonomy, justice, equality and respect for persons that cut across ethnic cultural boundaries. Thus, while educational institutions should aim to transmit the core elements – elements identified by ethnic groups as their core values – or ethnic cultures, they should also transmit the shared values of society. There are times when these values will conflict and in such cases education should equip individuals to talk through value problems and reach compromise.

If our aim is to teach students to think through (moral) value problems, then we should promote discussion and familiarize them with the rules of reasoning in this field. We should strive to get them to understand value questions and to reach agreement in careful, fair, clear and respectful discussion with those with whom they are likely to disagree. But even when all the above requirements are met, disagreements may still remain. People may differ for all sorts of reasons, based either on religion, world views or merely their interests.

Cultural pluralism as discussed above requires that students should be taught that 'there are alternative ways of behaving and viewing the universe' (Banks, 1974, p. 166). They should be helped to view the world beyond their cultural perspectives and provided with the necessary knowledge, skills and attitudes to enable them effectively to participate and transform the social system for the benefit of everyone. For merely to perpetuate a status quo that fits students into existing moulds would not only perpetuate ethnocentrism and discrimination, but also deprive them of their autonomy to freely choose from available cultural options or ways of life.

Education for cultural pluralism must be seen therefore as a process of dialogical enquiry. Through moral discourse students would be working together to resolve problems and towards constructing a truly cultural pluralist society. Boyd (1992) sees this whole process of dialogue as providing the foundation for dealing with value or cultural differences. The principle governing such a process of dialogical enquiry would be respect for evidence and logic and, above all, respect for people. Teachers should make sure that these principled requirements feature in every discussion. According to Hare (1976, p. 21): 'It is this power of coherent thought, rather than explosions of sentiments arising from prejudice, that teachers ought to be trying to bring about.'

Thus, if we value a society in which diverse ideals of life may be freely held, we must also, as Crittenden (1982) argues, be prepared to accept the common ground of meaning, beliefs, values, practices and education that enables the society both to cohere and to respect diversity. Education can play its part in the development of a common ground and a respect for diversity. Thus an open, democratic society essentially depends on the nature of education that children from all ethnic backgrounds receive in schools and colleges.

References

I am indebted to the following authors whose works I have drawn upon for this chapter.

Appleton, N. (1983) *Cultural Pluralism in Education. Theoretical Foundations.* New York: Longman.

Banks, J.A. (1974) Curricular models for an open society. In D. Della-Dora and J.E. House (eds), *Education For An Open Society.* Washington DC: Association for Supervision and Curriculum Development, pp. 43–63.

Banks, J.A. (1977) Cultural pluralism: implications for curriculum reform. In M.M. Tuminn and W. Plotch (eds), *Pluralism in a Democratic Society*, pp. 226–48.

Best, F. (1992) *Human Rights Education.* Summary essay on the work of the Council of Europe. Strasbourg: Council For Cultural Cooperation (CDCC) School and Out-of-School Education Section.

Boyd, D. (1992) The moral part of pluralism as the plural part of moral education. In F.C. Power and D.K. Lapsley (eds), *Education, Politics and Values. The Challenge of Pluralism.* Notre Dame IN: University of Notre Dame Press.

Bridges, D. (1984) Non-paternalistic arguments in support of parents' rights. *Journal of Philosophy of Education*, **18**, 55–61.

Coombs, J. (1983) Essay review: cultural pluralism in education. *Journal of Educational Equity and Leadership* **3** (4), 363–5.

Crittenden, B. (1982) *Cultural Pluralism and Common Curriculum.* Melbourne: Melbourne University Press.

Green, T.H. (1966) *Education and Pluralism: Ideal and Reality.* Syracuse NY: Syracuse University.

Habermas, J. (1982) A universal ethic of communication and problems of ethical relativity and scepticism. Paper presented at the International Symposium on Moral Education. Fribourg University, Switzerland.

Halstead, M. (1988) *Education, Justice and Cultural Diversity.* Lewes: Falmer.

Hare, R.M. (1976) Value education in a pluralist society. *Proceedings of the Philosophy of Education Society of Great Britain* **10**, 7–23.

Herberg, W. (1960) *Protestant, Catholic, Jew.* New York: Doubleday.

Hirst, P. (1990) A curriculum for social justice. *Australian Educational Researcher* **17** (2), 45–52.

International Covenant on Civil And Political Rights (1966) Strasbourg: UNESCO.

Kallen, H. (1956) Individuality, individualism and John Dewey. *Antioch Review* **19**, 299–314.

Klein, J.T. (1974) Cultural pluralism and moral education. *Monist* **58** (4), 683–93.

Kohlberg, L. (1986) A current statement on some theoretical issues. In L. Kohlberg, *Consensus and Controversy*, S. Modgil and C. Modgil (eds). Philadelphia: Falmer.

Lapsley, D.K. (1992) Pluralism, virtues and the post-Kohlbergian era in modern psychology. In F.C. Power and D.K. Lapsley (eds), *Education, Politics and Virtues. The Challenge of Pluralism*. Notre Dame IN. University of Notre Dame Press.

Popper, K.R. (1945) *The Open Society and its Enemies*, vol. 1. London: Routledge and Kegan Paul.

Power, F.C. and Lapsley, D.K. (eds) (1992) *Education, Politics and Values. The Challenge of Pluralism*. Notre Dame, IN. University of Notre Dame Press.

Pratte, R. (1972) The concept of cultural pluralism. In R. Pratte, *Philosophy of Education*. USA Southern University, pp. 61–77.

Pratte, R. (1979) *Pluralism in Education*. Springfield: Charles C. Thomas.

Ramirez, M. and Castaneda, A. (1974) *Cultural Democracy, Bicognitive Development and Education*. New York: Academic Press.

Richmond, A. (1974) Language, ethnicity and the problem of identity in a Canadian metropolis. *Ethnicity* **1**, 175–206.

Smolicz, J. (1981) Cultural pluralism and educational policy. In search of stable multiculturalism. *Australian Journal of Education* **25** (2), 121–45.

Smolicz, J. (1984) Multiculturalism and an overarching framework of values: some educational responses for ethnically plural societies. *European Journal of Education* **19** (1), 11–23.

Smolicz, J. (1989) Types of language activation and evaluation in an ethnically plural society. In W. Ammon (ed), *Status and Function of Languages and Language Varieties*. Berlin and New York: Walter de Gruyter, pp. 478–514.

Taylor, D.M., McKirnan, D.J., Christian, J. and La Marche, L. (1979) Cultural insecurity and attitudes towards multiculturalism and ethnic groups in Canada. *Canadian Ethnic Studies* **1** (2), 19–30.

Torney, J.V. and Tesconi, C.A. (1977) Political socialization, research and respect for ethnic diversity. In M.M. Tuminn and W. Plotch (eds), *Pluralism in a Democratic Society*, pp. 95–129.

Varga, K. (1984) Review article – cultural pluralism and human liberty: a review of cultural pluralism in education. *Educational Theory* **34** (4), 389–96.

Villemain, F.T. (1976) The significance of the democratic ethic for cultural alternatives and American civilization. *Educational Theory* **26** (1), 40–52.

Walsh, P.D. (1976) Value education in a pluralist society. A reply to R.M. Hare. *Proceedings of The Philosophy of Education Society of Great Britain* **10**, pp. 24–33.

Walzer, M. (1992) Comment. In A. Gutmann (ed), *Multiculturalism and the Politics of Recognition*. Princeton NJ: Princeton University Press, pp. 99–103.

Zec, P. (1980) Multicultural education: what kind of relativism is possible. *Journal of Philosophy of Education* **14** (1), 77–86.

6 Diversity and Universal Values in Multicultural Education

JOSEP M. PUIG ROVIRA

Origin of ethnic and cultural diversity

As has occurred so often with other educational questions, the pedagogical reflection which we make here concerning the idea of multicultural education comes about as a response to facts which, in principle, bear no direct relation to education.

Concern about cultural and ethnic plurality arose, and continues to grow, as a consequence of political processes of a highly varied nature. As we shall see, political factors are not the only cause of ethno-cultural plurality, but in many cases they have become in themselves or along with other reasons a key aspect in explaining the appearance of diversity as a socially relevant fact. However, despite political decisions inevitably being entwined with other factors, the direct political causes of ethno-cultural diversity are more pronounced in cases such as political–cultural vindication by minorities, ethnic groups or nations, which have remained hidden for some time, as well as in the efforts that some states make towards economic, political and military integration. Other political motivations, equally explicit but in this case negative, are to be found in the violent explosion of ethnic and nationalistic conflicts that had previously seemed forgotten. The former give rise to the recognition or creation of culturally plural, geopolitical entities, while the others may lead to terrible processes of annihilation of difference. Both situations reveal, in one way or another, the ever-increasing importance of ethno-cultural diversity.

Migration is another of the phenomena which, in the past, most contributed to the growth of cultural diversity and which, according to all current forecasts, will continue to play a preponderant role in the formation of pluricultural societies in the future. The demand for manual workers, the abso-lute lack of possibilities of subsistence for huge masses of populations in their countries of origin, the outbreak of wars and the exercise of political oppression are some of the principal causes of migratory waves. They have also contributed enormously to the introduction of plurality into the ethno-cultural composition of many societies. Such phenomena have, at some time or another, affected the majority of industrialized nations, as well as others, whose populations have grown and become more diversified as a result of the arrival of groups of people from varying cultural backgrounds. When this phenomenon of sudden creation of plurality due to migratory processes occurs in a society, it becomes both convenient, as well as obligatory, to apply political and educational measures that satisfy the cultural needs of the new arrivals. Nonetheless, advantages obtained from the cultural diversity which migration brings about are, on many occasions, accompanied by serious problems. The non-participation, or at best limited involvement, on the part of many immigrant collectives in the political life of the country in which they find themselves, together with the situations of socio-economic margination that they endure, and the often ethnocentric, racist and xenophobic be-haviour of the indigenous population all tend to obscure the positive elements of contact and co-existence between cultures.

Having considered some of the processes leading to the creation of cultural plurality in a defined geopolitical area, we shall now examine factors of a different nature, but which also support proposals for multicultural education. It is no longer a ques-tion of explaining multiculturalism as a result of cultural diversity in a particular area, nor as one of the appearance of new cultural vindications within a dominating majority culture. On the contrary, it is a question of indicating the presence of all the differing human groups and cultures that exist at any point on the planet. The increasing interconnection of societies is enabling us to embrace the entire geographical, cultural and human space of the world. We are exhaustively pluricultural. The efficiency, not always positive, of the means of both communication and action has so reduced the size of the world that we all feel, or could feel, deeply implicated and responsible regarding any act, wherever it occurs. It has become necessary for us to understand what is happening at any given point in the world, to comprehend the reasons that each of the implicated parties has for their action and interpret the position of each and every one of the groups involved. Our horizon has suddenly become pluricultural. Never again will our eyes rest on a monocultural landscape. The diversity of cultures and ways of life will forever be the setting in which we exist.

Cultural diversity as an evolutionary challenge

The actions that we have described up to this point have created a situation which we may consider as new. While it is true that we know of societies in which differing ethno-cultural groups exist and have always co-existed, it is equally true to say that cultural plurality is greater today than it has ever been anywhere. We are confronted by a situation that poses challenges never before encountered by humankind and for which we possess no tried and tested solutions. The co-existence of different ethno-cultural groups in the same geopolitical space, together with the human diversity and difficulties which are evident to any group or individual, have so modified means of human development and harmonious co-existence, that it could be said that we must now learn how to live in a reality different from any we have known to date.

Viewed from another perspective, however, the triumph of difference, liberty and plurality in the heart of a particular cultural tradition has deepened even further the mutation of human means of formation and co-existence. Opinions, beliefs, customs and habits have become enormously varied, even within spaces that were previously considered homogeneous. Uniformity seems, to a certain extent, to be giving way to life styles that are more open and respectful of differences. All of which

does nothing more than contribute to the creation of growing diversity in an ever-increasing number of fields.

Thus, diversity is brought about in areas of life where, until recently, ethnic and cultural homogeneity had been the rule. We find diversity in spaces where previously, ethnic, cultural, religious and life style homogeneity was almost absolute. But here lies the new problem. New because we have no antecedents of such events and problem because we must now carry out new experiments of learning. By this we mean the necessity to build an education which protects both personal identity and social integration in socio-cultural environments which are no longer uniform. Formerly, personal identity, like social integration, was attained thanks to the application of cultural patterns that established the forms and even the criteria of socialization and co-existence. While each individual or group of people lived in environments in which there was only one way of life, the problem was, if we may put it this way, exclusively one of transmission of information and inculcation of beliefs. However, when individuals or groups find themselves in environments which are impossible to define by means of a single mode of co-existence or identification, the problem to which we refer is then raised. This may be summarized in the following questions:

- How can we achieve social integration in geopolitical spaces in which groups from different ethnic and cultural origins, and even possibly with differing traditions of co-existence, are living?
- How can we build personal identity in educational environments in which different understandings of how properly to lead one's life co-exist?
- What, in fact, happens when social integration and personal identity cannot be built by means of repetition of the same, but rather must be brought about starting from the 'different'?

In response to this situation, certain options aimed at solving the evolutionary problem are beginning to take shape. These advocate the combination of two principles which, while seeming contradictory are, in fact, complementary. We refer to the recognition and respect of difference ('difference') and the establishment of universal principles which allow the procedural regulation of co-existence ('universalism'), as well as orientation in the general aspects of building personal identity.

'Difference' and 'universalism' are criteria which, duly combined, may sustain a new mode of orientation in real-life situations and in the formation of enormous ethnic-cultural diversity (Giner and Scartezzini, 1996). 'Difference' covers the ways of being individuals and groups of people, as well as the way they are presented. 'Universalism' first protects differences and prevents the annihilation of ways of life which are characteristic of each group of human beings (as, for example, proposed in the Universal Declaration of Human Rights) and, second, shares the responsibility for co-operating in the solution of the mutual and urgent problems that arise in the immediate environment of co-existence, as well as in the more extensive areas of humanity (as dialogical ethics propose, for example, in the form of discourse procedures). Universality is thus represented by procedural criteria of an abstract and formal nature which need not necessarily enter into conflict with the diverse cultural forms. Put another way, universality is expressed in values which we do not like to recognize as universal, but which, fortunately, we have learnt to observe and demand be put into practice. It seems, however, that we are confronted with the possibility of building personal identity that will forever be rooted in particular and differentiated ways of life, but which, simultaneously, may achieve the formation of an autonomous moral conscience, constituted by procedural criteria shared by the rest of the population.

Towards a system of values and policy of difference and universalism

We shall now briefly examine how this complementary coupling of 'difference' and 'universality' is presented and has been developed in the field of ethics and politics. We shall then go on to consider it in the area of education. An extensive development of neo-Kantian postures has taken place in the ambits of ethics discussion which have determined the sense that we can give to 'universality'. There has usually been less concern over what we have here called 'difference', and what, in the area of moral discussion, we could qualify as personal ways of being and behaving. Despite this, neo-Kantian postures need not necessarily be incompatible with a complementary concern for historical subjects, contextual situations or ethical traditions. It is precisely in the interior of personal realities where the

necessity for universal criteria is detected and where successive formulations arise.

In the area of psychology, the work of Kohlberg (1984) has detected and described a sequence of states of development of moral judgement which he considers universal and which culminate in the acquisition of principles of a post-conventional nature; principles that permit judgement of conflicts from the basis of criteria which go beyond what the same community considers as correct. These principles are useful for the judgement of problems in which distinct moral postures are involved and are thus principles that everyone could eventually recognize.

From philosophical positions, Habermas (1983), as well as others, has also developed a set of universalist ethics which, nonetheless, do not deny respect for the different options of personal ways of being and behaving that would be proper, nor the difficulty in applying moral principles to specific situations. However, they do advocate the necessity to rely on some common criteria that, parallel to differences of values and culture, confer on all people certain minimal guidelines which permit a dignified and fair life for all, and which commit everyone to the task of better guaranteeing the survival of humanity. They have established these criteria on the basis of a pragmatic consideration of language: that is, recognizing a procedural criterion of ethical correctness in human communication. Plainly speaking, we understand that the individual acts correctly who, in a conflictive situation and for the best motives, involves herself in a process of dialogue with all affected parties; these parties being, obviously, everyone, whatever their culture or ethnic origin.

In the field of morals, it is possible to recognize not only the diversity of ways of living, but also the universality of certain procedural principles of values. In the field of political reflection on the nature of democratic states, something similar seems to be occurring. First and foremost, it should be pointed out that, with very few exceptions, the democratic organization of states has been founded on the identification of 'demos' and 'ethnos'. That is to say, the limits of democratic states have tended to coincide with ethnic groups, or they have done everything in their power to consider that they coincide. Democracy has attempted to support itself on a pre-existing ethno-cultural identity. This situation was not real before, as it obscured, often violently, obvious differences; nor is it tenable now, due to the reasons we have outlined at the beginning. We are thus confronted with the necessity to construct democratic forms which are not based on prior identification and integration of an ethnic, cultural, religious or historical nature. We must build the democracy of the difference: a system in which the universalist values of democracy prevail but, at the same time, the values of difference are fully recognized and respected; a system in which civilization is embodied in universal juridical principles that bestow upon all individuals their rights as citizens, but also respect the right of each citizen to live according to his or her own cultural references, within a framework of minimum common juridical principles. With this approach, the universal will avoid affecting sensitivity towards diversity and the different ways of life which co-exist in multicultural societies. In short, we must build a system of personal identification based on democratic citizenship, without this implying the renunciation of individual cultural heritage, or its embodiment in particular historical-national traditions (Apel, 1990).

Criteria for inter-cultural education

The field of educational reflection is also experiencing the tension between 'difference' and 'universality'. There is now general acceptance in pedagogy of the understanding of education as a process of adaptation, of critical and creative adaptation if you will, to the socio-cultural environment in which each individual finds themselves immersed. Only very recently did we begin to realize that this type of reasoning counted, immutably, on the existence of a socially and culturally homogenized educational environment. It was clear that each person easily recognized his or her own culture and adapted to it. It was obvious that this culture was offered without interference and that with the passage of time it would not undergo major changes. All of these certainties are now untenable. The socio-cultural environment has been radically transformed and different cultures have flourished and diversified. But at the same time, as has already become evident, society is becoming less and less monocultural, and our cultural horizon today embraces almost all of the planet. Consequently, the educational environment in which we are living is now infinitely more complex and multiple, with different cultures co-existing or developing within

it in such a way that it is no longer possible to think of adaptation to a homogeneous and perfectly coherent environment. The condensation of cultures in a limited geopolitical space, along with almost infinite extension of the space implicated and related with our most immediate reality, have shattered the image of a non-contradictory and culturally unitary educational environment. In our opinion, this reality is an important mutation and one which educational reflection should not forget. Education is no longer a question of adaptation to a monocultural environment, but is rather a matter of adaptation to one which is pluricultural, highly complex, and almost limitless.

This being the new situation, what should be done? The answer is evidently a question of consolidating a new type of learning that is able to respond to an almost endless socio-cultural complexity. This same need to respond to an incessant increase of complexity has, in fact, already been produced in the area of acquisition of technical-scientific academic knowledge. The interminable growth of such knowledge has extended into the very heart of each field of study, with the result that it is now impossible to dominate one particular area of research and less possible still to consider that this area will not undergo changes within a very short period of time. Thus, the only way to fight the obsolescence of knowledge is either by acquiring methods which enable its rapid renewal (learning to learn), or by using methods which involve working as closely as possibly to the places where knowledge is produced (learning to reflect and investigate from a strong theoretical position). We have before us an approach to education which doubles its tasks: to teach knowledge (the different), but at the same time and above all to teach meta-learning or procedures (the universal).

The same occurs, in our opinion, in the rest of education. Not only has the technical-scientific become impossibly complex, but social-cultural disputes now also defy simple solutions. Democratic and pluralist societies cannot and must not generate single answers to their problems of relations and organization. Furthermore, in democratic and clearly pluricultural societies, different responses and criteria for responses may co-exist in relation to the confrontation of similar problems. Finally, the very extension of the cultural horizon, to the extent that it becomes confused with the planetary horizon, denies with even greater clarity still the possibility of confronting the diverse, disposing solely of the criteria and knowledge characteristic of one's own, essentially local, culture. Thus, it is necessary to come up with new ways of learning which allow individuals better to situate themselves when confronted by this socio-cultural complexity. In a certain way the solution would seem to be orientated in the same direction as previously mentioned with regard to technical-scientific knowledge, that is, to superimpose over the learning of specific cultural traditions that of learning meta-cultural and universal criteria and procedures.

The aim of education can no longer be solely one of socialization in a particular culture. This should be just another phase, running parallel to other efforts, orientated towards the learning of meta-cultural criteria. In this way it would perhaps be possible to direct oneself towards a type of personality that knows how to combine what has been inherited, but is critical of the eternal local tradition, with that constructed with criteria of justice and solidarity with the universal human community. Inter-cultural education has, in this aspect, one of its widest and most ambitious objectives.

In the following pages we shall outline this proposal in three lines of reflection and action:

- guide lines for dialogue and understanding between cultures;
- control of the prejudice caused by difference;
- an approach to universal, ethical criteria.

We hope, in this way, to establish elements which may make possible a more complementary nature of the relationship between difference and universality.

Dialogue and understanding between cultures

When an educational proposal intends to confront a situation of cultural plurality, it seems evident that precisely the way this cultural contact should work must be considered. The inter-culturalism approach would, we consider, involve making a conscious and willing effort towards dialogue and understanding between the individual's own culture and those with which he or she is most directly in contact, while being at the limits of all cultures, to the extent that they may inform us of something (Gadamer, 1951).

Our intention to direct contact between cultures in the direction of dialogue and mutual understanding is due to the fact that it seems insufficient to approach cultural plurality by means of merely informative proposals. It is necessary to count on certain information about the other cultural traditions, but not to the extent that such information is limited to describing their peculiarities, nor to that of their being treated in accordance with the criteria typical of cultural relativism. It is not enough that their existence be accepted, though it be on an equal basis with the individual's own culture, and that they are even given the right to consideration and the possibility of expression. There is no doubt that all of this is done in informative proposals with the greatest respect, but with the coldness and lack of dialogical commitment of one who considers that any cultural proposal can only refer to and be significant in its own context.

These considerations lead towards a form of 'TV documentary pedagogy' which demonstrates and recognizes 'the other', but which very often increases the distance between cultures. We consider this option to be insufficient. Contact between cultures requires a type of pedagogical intervention, probably both scholastic and non-scholastic, which pursues a warm, conscientiously directed dialogue and which aims to guide us towards progressively greater cultural comprehension. It is thus a question of separating ourselves from an image of the school as an auditorium of cultures, and directing ourselves towards school as a cultural forum. In the following section we shall examine some elements which outline this pedagogy of inter-cultural dialogue.

If we aim to exceed the mere co-existence of cultures and build positive forms of cultural harmony, and if we consider that this should be done through dialogue, it is because we assume that there is something important to talk about, though there will probably not be entire coincidence in points of view. The inter-cultural perspective assumes recognition of the more than probable conflict between prospects and options of the different cultures. Cultural contact usually produces problems and perturbations which we neither can nor should hide because, among other reasons, it is thanks to them that the processes of change will be produced. In other words, it is necessary to talk and try to understand one another when some problem comes between us. This is precisely what happens in pluricultural situations and in the progressive globalization of human problems. We must implicate ourselves in a process of dialogue between cultures, for no other reason than because we have problems in common. These include problems of co-existence normally provoked by contact between distinct ethnic groups which, for various reasons, fail to evolve forms of co-operation, tending instead to generate reactions of racism and margination.

In addition, there are problems of collective survival, such as those concerning the distance between north and south, demographic regulation, the lack of respect towards nature, and doubtless many others. While their origin is not to be found in cultural pluralism, their solution demands, among other things, agreement between groups of highly varied cultural backgrounds. Finally, there are the problems brought about by the calls that cultures make on each other regarding the form and sense that the most difficult aspects of civilization itself entail. Thus, we are not dealing with a mere pedagogy of TV documentary information, nor an unspecific and general dialogue, but rather the fact that inter-cultural education implies a dialogue on subjects which have become controversial as a result of cultural contact. Dialogue and the will to understand are brought about because there is no agreement on a subject which is considered to be of some importance.

Dialogue between cultures about common problems, however, does not in any way mean putting one's own opinion and points of view to one side, nor the attempting to shed previously held opinions from which we view the other party. It is impossible to seek an absolute objectivity that would enable us to see others with ostensible clarity. Our view of others, our understanding of their positions and entry into dialogue with them is always attained from an individual framework of references, beliefs, attitudes, values and knowledge which are not always entirely clear to our conscience. The desire to abandon our own points of view in consideration of other cultural positions is bound to end up in absolute failure to understand these positions in any way and, worse still, in the deep-down depreciation of them, as what really matters to us does so in relation to our prejudices. In synthesis, diverse cultural positions only manage to get through to us when we interpret them from the point of view of our own prejudices. Reality only speaks to those who have prejudices from which to ask and view.

We can consider neither the controversial subject itself, nor the positions from which the problem is perceived and appreciated, as the last word in a process of inter-cultural understanding. It will be necessary for all of the participants to truly involve themselves in dialogue, that is, for all the parties to strive to consider the reasons that lead each of them to assume that their position with respect to the problem is the best, the most adequate and, perhaps, the most rational. In a certain way it is a matter of putting oneself in the position of the other parties, in order to understand, and possibly even reinforce, the logic and reasoning of their points of view. Insofar as this concerns dialogue and understanding between cultures, inter-cultural education should seek to create conditions in which everybody can see problems from their own point of view and recognize the perspectives of others, in the way that their cultural tradition allows. But they must, in addition, make the effort to recognize when other cultural positions are right. It is thanks to this effort in recognizing that the other party may have a point with regard to a particular problem that one's own position may initiate a process of change, the result of which will be a certain approximation of cultures.

Considering the reasons of the other party, however, does not signify the non-adoption of positions or critical attitudes. Making an effort to understand the points of view which different cultures hold about particular problems does not mean abstaining from judgement. We learn from others, but others may also learn from us. We may then exercise the right to criticize. We can ask ourselves to what extent contributions of the other cultural positions should be acceptable to all of the parties involved in the problem. At the same time as criticism is directed at others, it should also be used to examine our own prejudices. The consideration of other interpretations will widen the scope of awareness of inappropriate and unjust positions. In short, understanding means to reinforce the other side's reasons, but also to evaluate them and, equally, to evaluate one's own prejudices.

Finally, in practice, dialogue and understanding cannot be separated. Quite the contrary, they must be directed towards reflection on how to behave properly in relation to the situation in which the problem was defined. Understanding clarifies the values that come into play in the situation being analysed, while at the same time applying them and specifying well-defined and determined realities: it criticizes them, verifies their limitations, and redefines them. We have, in understanding, a space in which to seek inter-cultural agreement on values, to recognize and contextually define values which encourage universal comprehension. But understanding also analyses all aspects of the controversial situation, indicates its limits and injustices and points the way to possible futures. It suggests a transformation project in the measure that it supplies us with moral knowledge. It is thus a programme which will enable us to update values criteria acceptable to all the cultural positions involved.

Control of one's own prejudices

Although the primary aim of inter-cultural education is to propitiate mutual knowledge and understanding between cultures, probably even more urgent, given the present situation, would be concentration on the subject of prejudice control and, above all, the control of behaviour based in prejudices.

Contact between different cultural and ethnic groups tends to produce discriminatory, xenophobic and racist behaviour, especially in moments of crisis. These days we have more than enough examples of this. Faced with such tendencies, inter-cultural education must prevent the apparition of this kind of behaviour and, if it is already among us, must contribute to its elimination. It must not, however, limit itself to a task of prevention and cure, but must also be committed to the construction of tolerant means of co-existence and frank openness with others.

While not pretending to examine the subject in detail, we shall now revise the psycho-social elements that come into play in the apparition of negative behaviour in situations of ethnic contact. We shall then investigate what possibilities we have of intervening educationally in such situations. We may begin by assuming that, in a certain way, all behaviour is induced by an attitude that precedes it. Attitudes are, thus, the first concept that we must look into. We understand attitudes to be those predispositions that are learnt and relatively fixed, that orientate the behaviour which, in all probability, will be produced in a given situation, or before a certain object. They have, therefore, positive and negative directions in relation to the situation or object which is polarizing them. They are of a complex nature, as their constitution is made up of

cognitive, affective and, of course, behavioural elements. Insofar as concerns our subject, it seems clear that all ethnic and cultural groups, as well as many of their particular customs, are objects that forge attitudes in persons belonging to other cultural groups with which they come into contact. Such attitudes may be positive or negative but, as we know, it is relatively common that they are negative.

In situations of ethnic contact we very often find ourselves holding negative attitudes based in prejudice; that is to say, attitudes based in imperfect and inflexible generalizations that provoke hostility in the interpersonal relations with members of the group suffering the prejudice. Prejudices are also difficult to reverse, even when confronted by information which refutes them. Prejudicial attitudes towards different ethnic or cultural groups are the first condition for the apparition of discriminatory, xenophobic and racist behaviour. However, as we know, there is no immediate relation between attitude and behaviour. Thus negative attitudes toward other groups will not always be converted into aggressive behaviour.

The distance between attitude and behaviour is important, because it is not always easy totally to eliminate negative attitudes. We must recognize that it is usual to find discriminatory or racist attitudes in any individual. This is probably truer than we would like to think. However, as we have already mentioned, there is a distance between attitude and behaviour, as there is also between racial prejudice and racist behaviour. For an attitude to be converted into negative behaviour, certain inhibiting controls which impede such undesirable conduct must become paralyzed. We normally encounter two kinds of behaviour inhibiting controls: the first, personal, composed of certain regulatory ideas such as values (equality, or justice); the second, social, made up of group pressure and the duty of law. The former may inhibit conduct in order not to break group conformity. The latter may do so by invoking fear of the consequences that presumably would occur when breaking the law. Discriminatory and racist behaviour appears when, in addition to the existence of prejudicial attitudes towards ethnic groups, personal or social inhibiting controls are immobilized.

If we accept this analysis as good, what should inter-cultural education be doing? There is probably no single solution, but the answer would rather be found in the initiation of a range of educational action of a diverse and combined nature, some elements of which we shall now outline. First, an inter-cultural curriculum should create adequate conditions for pupils to become aware of the difficulty of totally shaking off prejudicial attitudes. Recognizing one's own discriminatory, xenophobic or racist predisposition is a necessary condition for their modification. There are at least two ways of achieving this: valorative self-knowledge with regard to this aspect of one's own personality; the knowledge of social psychology studies that inform us about the nature and mechanisms which are set in operation when this type of personal or collective phenomena appears. Thus it seems as appropriate to use exercises of introspection as it does to study and discuss some theories and details of social psychology, conveniently adapted to the age of the pupils with whom one is working. The use of 'docu-dramas' may also be equally beneficial, as they tend to show the precarious situation in which minority cultural ethnic groups are usually found and the responsibility that other groups have for this. They also permit easy identification and reveal personal attitudes.

Second, inter-cultural education should contribute to the formation of second level controls, that is, the ideas of values and respect for both the law and the positive traditions of the group. We should never depreciate the teaching of certain values or moral principles which, though perhaps not always sufficiently rooted in the social fabric and possibly even contradictory to more deeply held personal attitudes, are nonetheless effective at the moment of controlling and inhibiting the passing from negative attitude to unjust behaviour. Knowledge and appreciation of, for example, the Declaration of Human Rights, or criteria of values such as equality and justice are factors which contribute to the appearance of positive behaviour, even in those cases in which personal attitudes do not coincide with that prescribed by such values. Identification with social groups in which the criteria of respect and acceptance of other cultures prevail is probably one of the most efficient factors in behaviour control. Finally, mere knowledge of the law is now in itself an element which will usually contribute to the manifestation of just conduct. This is largely due to its coercive content, but also, in part, to its enormous educational possibilities. The law is a cultural support which society affords itself to regulate collective conduct. It is, in a certain way, a form of collective apprenticeship, which each individual must later re-learn and convert into personal attitudes and convictions. Thus it is important to transmit the value of legislation as a collective effort to optimize life, in accordance with the criteria of justice.

Third, curricular proposals with a multicultural approach should also intervene to try to modify negative attitudes and prejudices. We shall therefore put forward a framework in which different pedagogical proposals may be considered. By this we refer to normative conflict (Roux *et al.*, 1991). We set out from the assumption that behaviour is developed in accordance with two distinct regulating criteria: attitudes, and ideas. In this way it is possible to verify that there is often little relation between one criterion and another. It is quite usual to hold more or less intensely racist attitudes, while at the same time having humanitarian ideas. In cases of discord between attitudes and ideas, one way of modifying the former is to provide the means of enabling the individual to become aware of the conflict in which he or she is living. By this we refer to the conflict between his or her humanitarian ideas and the negative attitudes that result in a kind of behaviour contradictory to his or her beliefs. Once the individual manages to realize that he or she has, deep down, a racist attitude, the process of modification has already begun. Not until the discord is recognized between what he or she thinks and what he or she feels bound to do, will it be possible to commence work on reducing that distance and modifying attitudes.

We therefore propose the carrying out of educational action aimed at revealing and making each individual aware of the existence of normative conflicts in the field which presently concerns us. This task will be extended to include a study of the affective, cognitive and behavioural components of attitudes, and of the relationship between these and more general ideas about values. Among the most adequate pedagogical means available to carry out this type of intervention may be the programmes of activities aimed at working on prejudices from the basis of strategies, such as the discussion of dilemmas, role plays or clarification of values exercises. The formation of school communities made up of individuals from a variety of cultural and ethnic backgrounds, the organization of which is regulated by criteria of participation and dialogue, is another useful resource (Puig, 1995, 1966).

Recognition of universal principles and values

Any project of inter-cultural education that attempts to establish true dialogue between cultures and which also intends to forge a type of co-existence unaffected by discrimination and racism must, inevitably, ask whether any values criteria exist to orientate such tasks. Indeed, it would seem difficult to undertake them at all without relying, either explicitly or implicitly, on certain values which bestow consistence on an inter-cultural project of this nature. Without these values, in our opinion, true inter-culturalism would, in fact, be impossible. This, in turn, would call into question the very possibility of universal understanding and harmony.

It is not by chance that we have reserved this subject for last. In addition to explicitly expressing, from the very start, the principles or values that orientate the development of an inter-cultural education project, the project should also strive to find common values while engaged in the task of cultural dialogue and elimination of prejudices. It is here where their true, internal need will be discovered, far more than in formulations, which may perhaps seem precipitated when explained too soon.

Dialogue and understanding between cultures must never evade criticism or self-criticism aimed at those aspects which diminish human dignity. Dialogical confrontation between distinct cultural points of view will gradually shape the values content that all involved may eventually recognize as criteria for criticism. In other words, it will proceed towards a definition of the minimum values content which is shared by all involved, whatever their cultural tradition. Perhaps along this route values such as freedom, justice or solidarity will appear and we will be able to fill them with content in the context of each individual culture while, at the same time, preserving their essentiality.

This is possibly more clearly the case with tasks aimed at combating negative attitudes and discriminatory and racist behaviour. In these cases, values which we use to criticize a range of unjust behaviour, as well as to guide inter-cultural co-existence in a direction acceptable to all, are already in operation. We may thus assume that, by contextually criticizing reality and by envisaging desirable forms of co-existence, universally acceptable minimum criteria will gradually develop.

Finally, inter-cultural understanding and the forming of ways of co-existence require the use of dialogue as a means of comprehension. Dialogue is not, however, a neutral procedure without values. Dialogue is in itself a criterion and a useful practice. Furthermore, when exercised with the will to understand, it implies values such as justice and solidarity.

If the project for inter-cultural education that we have proposed really requires universal values, then the last issue to address would be that of assuring that such educational intervention brings about their recognition, contextual definition and acquisition, as much in concepts as in attitudes. The range of possibilities available to achieve this is both wide and diffuse. Whether such values can ever really be taught is debatable, though it may indeed be possible to arrange for experiences which would tend to produce them in the individuals involved. We should add that, together with the special tasks that we have outlined for inter-cultural education, which should contribute to the acquisition of such values, any moral education programme will, to a large extent, attempt to generate these kinds of values. Thus, thanks to the enormous transfer capacity that these values have, moral education is also, in a way, a species of inter-cultural education.

References

Apel, K.O. (1990) Una ètica de la corresponsabilitat a Europa i el món. *Actes del Seminari Europa a la fi del segle XX*. Barcelona: Fundació Acta, pp. 101–48.

Gadamer, H.G. (1951) *Wahrheit und Methode*. Tubingen: Mohr.

Giner, S. and Scartezzini, R. (eds) (1966) *Universalidad y diferencia*. Madrid: Alianza Editorial.

Habermas, J. (1983) *Moralbewrsstein und Kommunikatives Handels*. Frankfurt: Suhrkamp Verlag.

Kohlberg, L. (1984) *Essays in Moral Development: Vol II. The Psychology of Moral Development*. San Francisco: Harper and Row.

Puig, J. (1995) *La educación moral en la enseñanza obligatoria*. Barcelona: Horsori/ICE.

Puig, J. (1996) *La construcción de la personalidad moral*. Barcelona: Paidós.

Roux, P., Mugny, G., Sanchez Mazas, M. and Perez, J.A. (1991) Influencia minoritaria y mecanismos psicosociales de la discriminación. In J.A. Perez and G. Mugny (eds), *El conflicto estructurante*. Barcelona: Anthropos, pp. 169–77.

7 Attitudes towards the Mentally Handicapped and Counter Selection in the Educational System

CSABA BÁNFALVY

The way in which people are labelled who are unable to fulfil the normal primary school educational requirements and certain IQ tests has differed very much over the course of time. Traditionally, they used to be called 'debils', 'imbeciles' and 'idiots' depending on the medical, pedagogical and psychological seriousness of their condition. Nowadays these terms are not only considered to be out of date but many people think that they are negative and pejorative terms for defining the learning capacities of a group of people. As a sociologist I am concerned with the meaning of these terms only as far as the general attitude of the public towards the labelled population is expressed through certain terms. The phrases 'handicapped' or 'retarded' are used here in a descriptive and neutral way or as quotations and we will always refer to a certain group in the population *labelled* with these terms by *others*.

The general attitude

Any handicap is not only a biological condition but it is also a social relationship. One who is 'handicapped' not only belongs to the handicapped population but he or she is also outside the 'normal' society. The social integration and general chances in life of the handicapped very much depend on the characteristics of the relationship between the handicapped and the non-handicapped groups of the society.

This relationship is reflected by the expressions people use for describing handicapped people. Some of the originally purely descriptive medical expressions like 'stupid' or 'idiot' have become negative and offending. Some others like 'blind' or 'deaf' still preserve the original neutral meanings

and connotations. So the connotations that certain expressions have gained depend very much on which subgroup of handicapped people they describe. In the Hungarian language, for example, there are thirty-one synonyms describing the mentally handicapped, most of them showing the negative attitude of ordinary people. At the same time there are only six synonyms for the blind and eight for the deaf. Most of these are neutral and descriptive (see Bass and Torda, 1988; Mesterházi, 1985).

The efforts that some of us make to change the expressions used for the 'mentally retarded' from negative to objective, value free and 'scientific' are in vain. As time passes the general social attitude will be expressed in the new negative connotations of the originally neutral expressions. Social values cannot be neutralized through linguistic changes. These social values and attitudes are only partially based on information and sometimes they are clearly non-rational.

For example, in their research in Hungary Illyés and Erdõsi (1986) found an interesting relationship between the knowledge people have about the handicapped and the intensity with which they would like to know something about them (Table 7.1).

The findings in Table 7.1 demonstrate that the less people know about certain handicapped groups, the less they are interested in the TV programmes about them. The mentally retarded are the least known by the public and people are the least interested in TV programmes about them (Illyés and Erdõsi, 1986, p. 24). This lack of information does not prevent people from forming an opinion about and having certain attitudes towards other people, in this case towards the handicapped.

In Hungary, according to Stollár:

Educated people think that the mentally handi-

Table 7.1 Would you watch a TV programme about certain groups of handicapped people?

Would you watch a TV programme about . . . ?	Those who could talk about them %	Those who could not talk about them %	Difference %
The blind	83	69	14
The deaf	75	56	19
The physically handicapped	74	54	20
The slightly mentally retarded	72	50	22
The severely mentally retarded	76	45	31

capped are mentally ill and should be kept in hospitals. Less educated people think that the mentally retarded are dangerous and they treat the mentally retarded as if they were animals (they give them the food that is left).   (Stollár 1985, pp. 137–8)

The negative labelling of the mentally retarded not only means that when somebody is considered mentally retarded he or she is also treated in an inhuman way, it also means that the negative attitude of ordinary people towards other social groups can be expressed through labelling the members of that group as mentally retarded. This legitimizes the negative prejudices towards the members of those social groups too.

The handicapped and labelling in primary education

This process is clearly demonstrated in the way pupils are evaluated in primary schools. Research has shown that many of the children labelled as slightly mentally retarded and transferred to special schools or classes for slightly mentally handicapped pupils have no mental deficiency (in the medical, psychological or educational sense), but are simply living in certain social groups and in social circumstances disadvantageous for their educational progress. Segregated schooling of the handicapped (still a dominant form in Hungary) also serves as a method of social segregation.

Official statistics show that in the early 1990s about 90 per cent of the pupils in schools for the handicapped were classified as mentally retarded and 90 per cent of the mentally retarded were in special schools for the slightly mentally retarded. But while the number of blind and deaf children has not changed during the last decades, the number of those classified as slightly mentally retarded has fluctuated substantially. Between 1954 and 1955 and 1974 and 1975 their number has grown

more then four times (Czeizel *et al.*, 1978, pp. 35–6). In 1989 there were about 32,500 pupils in the special primary schools, but this number had declined to 18,500 by 1993 (Educational Statistics of the Ministry of Education). Although 90 per cent of the handicapped stay in special schools for the slightly mentally retarded, official statistics state that only about 8 per cent of the handicapped adults are mentally retarded (*State of Health of the Population*, Central Statistical Office, 1989). The difference between two figures for school age and adult age shows that the majority of those classified as slightly mentally retarded at primary school age are able to live a normal life (which, by definition, they are not supposed to be able to do) and there is no sign of any handicap at adult age.

One of the early research projects about the situation of the slightly mentally retarded was the 'Budapest survey' (Czeizel *et al.*, 1978). The authors found that a large proportion of pupils in special schools were not mentally retarded. They also found that these children were not able to fulfil the requirements of the normal primary school because they lived in a disadvantageous social environment. The research found that 51 per cent of special school children had never attended nursery school or kindergarten, which is a very high rate compared to the 30 per cent rate of normal primary school children. It was also demonstrated that special school children had less educated parents and lower income families than normal school pupils.

Later research (Csanádi *et al.*, 1978; Illyés, 1984–90; Bánfalvy, 1996) also demonstrated that lower class and/or gypsy origin children have a much higher chance of failure in normal schools and get transferred to special schools through being labelled as slightly mentally retarded. It could also be demonstrated through empirical data that the maximum schooling of the special school kids was in correlation with the education of their parents (Table 7.2).

Table 7.2   The maximum schooling of special school educated adults and level of education of their father

Maximum schooling of ex-special school pupils	Father's maximum schooling			
	7 classes %	8 classes %	12 classes %	Higher education %
10 classes vocational	4.6	11.4	30.8	4.5
11 classes vocational	5.3	3.6	0.0	9.1
12 classes vocational	0.7	0.7	0.0	0.0
12 classes secondary grammar	0.7	2.1	0.0	4.5

Gyenes and Pajor (1993) found that 21 per cent of ex-special school pupils were married at adult age, 25 per cent of them had children and 43 per cent lived without any state assistance in the 1980s. These data were also confirmed by Gayerné *et al.*, (1985) and Stollár (1985). My own research showed that one-third of these adults had drivers' licences and 7.5 per cent of the men had served in the army (Bánfalvy, 1996).

The obvious question has been raised: what is the explanation for the fact that many of the children who are unable to fulfil the normal primary school requirements, though provably non-handicapped, are being transferred to special schools? Some of the explanations are related to the socio-cultural characteristics of the teachers who play a key role in the evaluation of pupils' performance in the normal and special primary schools.

The socio-cultural incongruencies in primary schools

It would be a simplification to say that the background of labelling and pedagogical counter selection in primary schools is only the personal and subjective opinions of the teachers. In fact the individual values, attitudes and behaviour expressed by the teachers' opinions are based on their general socio-cultural characteristics.

In Hungary special educators and primary school teachers are typically coming from the cities where teacher training colleges are sited. The typical primary school teacher is not only a city dweller but also a woman. She has female-type expectations and values based on the general social position of women in the society. As a woman she would differ much more from a man if she had a lower class and/or gypsy origin where the roles, values and behaviour of the sexes are greatly different. But she is typically a middle-class woman whose parents worked as teachers, special educators, in the caring professions or in public administration. These typical urban, female, middle-class values of primary school teachers are substantially different from those of some of the primary school children.

The greatest incongruence between the teachers' and pupils' subculture is demonstrated when the typical special school pupils face the typical primary school teacher and special educator in school circumstances. The classroom looks like an orderly housewife's living room, well kept and well polished with flowers and embroideries and paintings and drawings on the walls. This is an alien environment for most of the poor gypsy boys who populate the typical special school. The meaning of orderly behaviour is different at school from what they experience at home. The language is different too, especially concerning the use of four-letter words and loudness of speech. Gestures and meta-communicative codes have different meanings within their families compared to the schools. The male norms that dominate the pupils' family life (and in fact social life in general) are not those of the female-ruled classroom.

When teachers in normal primary schools form their unconscious expectations of their pupils they use their urban middle-class female values as the basis. There is no question that these values are valid or that they are useful in everyday middle-class life. But there is also no doubt that the typical pupils' lower class, gypsy-male values are as valid as anyone else's. The problem is the incongruence between the two value systems. When the representatives of the two systems face one another they are not in the same 'power situation'. In the school situation pupils are subordinated to their teachers who control them, make the rules and are able to punish rule breakers and troublemakers. In fact, many of the pupils transferred to special schools are characterized by their teachers as having behavioural problems (Csanádi *et al.*, 1978). The conflict is further sharpened by the fact that, in many cases, pupils or their families have no chance to select a school. Sometimes the parents are not even aware of what kind of school their children are attending or being transferred to.

References

Bánfalvy, C. (1996) The paradox of the quality of life of adults with learning difficulties. *Disability and Society* **11** (4), 569–77.

Bánfalvy, C. (1995) *Gyógypedagógiai szociológia.* [Sociology of special education]. Budapest: BGGYTF.

Bass, L. and Torda, A. (1988) 'Õk' és 'Mi'. A fogyatékosság témája a magyar sajtóban. ['Them' and 'we'. About the handicapped in the press]. *Gyógypedagógiai Szemle* **3**, 101–7.

Csanádi G., Ladányi, J. and Gerõ, Z. (1978) *Az általános iskolai rendszer belsõ rétegzõdése és a kisegítõ iskolák.* [The internal stratification of elementary schools and the special schools]. *Valóság* **21** (6), 30–44.

Czeizel, E., Lányiné, E. A. and Rátay, C. (1978) *Az értelmi fogyatékosságok kóreredete a 'Budapest-vizsgálat' tükrében.* [The causes of mental retardation. Budapest – survey]. Budapest: Medicina.

Gayer, G., Krausz, E. and Hatos, G. (1985) Az 1961–64 között született középsúlyos értelmi fogyatékos fiatal felnõttek helyzetének vizsgálata. [The characteristics of life of the mentally handicapped adults born between 1961–64]. In *Középsúlyos értelmi fogyatékos felnõttekrõl.* Budapest: MTA Szociológiai Kutató Intézete, Szociálpolitikai Értesítõ, pp. 15–90.

Gyenes, S. and Pajor, B. (1993) Utóvizsgálatok kisegítõ iskolát végzett fiatalok körében. [The life of ex-special school pupils]. *Gyógypedagógiai Szemle* **21** (3), 197–201.

Illyés, S. (ed.) (1984–90) Nevelhetõség és általános iskola. [Educability and elementary education]. 4 vols. Budapest: OKI.

Illyés, S. and Erdõsi, S. (1986) Az épek fogyatékosképe és a fogyatékosokhoz való viszonya. [The picture people have about the handicapped and their attitudes towards them]. In B. Kolozsi and I. Münich (eds); *Társadalmi beilleszkedési zavarok.* [Social deviancies]. Budapest: TBZ–TTI, Bulletin 6, 3–57.

KSH (1989) *A népesség egészégi állapota.* [The state of health of the population]. Budapest: KSH.

Kuczi, T. (1986) A pedagógusszerep néhány szociológiai jellemzõje. [Some characteristics of the role of educators]. In T. Huszár (ed.), *A magyar értelmiség a 80-as években.* [Intellectuals in Hungary during the 1980s]. Budapest: Kossuth Könyvkiadó, pp. 220–40.

Ladányi, J. and Csanádi, G. (1983) *Szelekció az általános iskolában.* [Selection in primary schools]. Budapest: Magvetõ.

Ladányi, J., Csanádi, G. and Gerõ, Z. (1996) A 'megszüntetve megõrzött' gyogyó. A kisegítõ iskola egy nyomonkövetéses vizsgálat tükrében. [Special school graduates in a longitudinal research]. *Kritika* July, 8–11.

Mesterházi Z. (1984–90) Az értelmi fogyatékosság változó meghatározásainak elõfordulása gyógypedagógiai nevelési dokumentumokban. [Definitions of mental retardation in professional publications]. In S. Illyés (ed.), vol. 2, pp. 185–241.

Stollár, J. (1985) A fogyatékosok (különösen az értelmi fogyatékosok) társadalmi beilleszkedésének lehetõségei. [The social adjustment of the mentally retarded]. In *Középsúlyos értelmi fogyatékos felnõttekrõl.* MTA Szociológiai Kutatóintézete. Szociálpolitikai Értesítõ.

8 Altering Conceptions of Subjectivity
A Prelude to the more Generous Effluence of Empathy

ANN CHINNERY and HEESOON BAI

Introduction

"Is there not a growing conviction," Lingis asks, "clearer today among innumerable people, that the dying of people with whom we have nothing in common – no racial kinship, no language, no religion, no economic interests – concerns us? We obscurely feel," he observes, "that our generation is being judged, ultimately, by the abandon of the Cambodians, and Somalians, and the social outcasts in the streets of our own cities" (1994, p. x). We share this conviction and its underlying suggestion that our moral failure is directly related to a widespread paucity of empathy. To this end, we propose to investigate the ontic and epistemic conditions of empathy. For, inasmuch as our intellect can tell us why we should care about the lot of suffering others – whether in our own families, neighbourhood, or thousands of miles away – after all, it is the heart's empathy which inexorably and generously compels us to act towards alleviating others' suffering.

Several moral theorists have argued that empathy is the primary precondition for moral performance.[1] This view has also been taken up in moral education, particularly in terms of attempts to map and cultivate the capacity for empathy and the other-regarding emotions in children.[2] In this chapter we advance the view that the prevailing conception of modern subjectivity, with its prioritization and privileging of the autonomous self, is an obstacle to the generous effluence of empathy, and that a more robust conception and practice of empathy might be afforded by a reframing of the traditional self–other binary. While the resistance to modern subjectivity has become somewhat of a hallmark of postmodern philosophical discourse, there is not much sign that this change has significantly affected our everyday reality: the world is still

by and large entrapped in modernist individualism. This is not surprising if we consider how deeply the historical roots of autonomous, egoic agency have infiltrated the modern psyche; and it is evident in the fact that we usually assume a biological and psychological necessity to this conception of selfhood. But such a sense of necessity is dispelled when we realize that there are other possible forms of subjectivity and moral agency. The example that Dissanayake gives of a Sinhalese Buddhist village in Sri Lanka illustrates our point:

> Rather than conceiving of human agency as solely individual-based and person-centered, the villagers in Sri Lanka whom I studied made me realize that agency can and does manifest itself in and through networks of interaction . . . Human agency, so far from being the product of atomistic and isolated persons, can be the outcome of a group-centered ethos and orientation. (Dissanayake, 1996, p. xiv)

We propose here to explore two alternative forms of subjectivity: Emmanuel Levinas's prioritization of the Other and the Buddhist deconstruction of the egoic self.[3] Though coming from two very different cultural and intellectual traditions, they nonetheless stand on common ground – the rejection of autonomous, egoic agency in favour of a more mutual, relational conception of agency. In this chapter, which is the fruit of our initial discovery of each other's moral paradigm, our exploration will focus more on this common ground than on the differences between the two. However, it is not our intent here to suggest that we replace the modernist conception of subjectivity with the Levinassian or Buddhist conceptions. Rather, we offer these models as tools to be taken up in the ongoing inquiry into possibilities for moral agency.

But, first, let us problematize modernist subjectivity, by which we mean both to complicate it historically, so as to make us see that it is not a simple, solid fact of our psyche or biology (it is far more unstable than that, as we shall see), and, also, to indicate that there are moral difficulties with the notion. To this end, in the next section, we shall present a brief genealogical account[4] of the modern conception of the subject as it has evolved over the last 400 years.[5]

An account of the modernist subject

On the heels of the Renaissance, the Reformation, and what have been called the European "voyages of discovery" (West, 1996, p. 10), the beginning of the sixteenth century marked a dramatic turn in the western world view. The authority of traditional Christian beliefs and doctrine, characteristic of the Middle Ages, was being called into question and the Roman Church was losing its hold on the construction of knowledge, art, culture, and politics. In its place there was a growing interest in other cultures and civilizations, and a revival of the ancient arts and sciences which favoured human interests, capacities, and concerns over the spiritual or divine (West, 1996). However, while the move to cultural humanism was also paralleled in philosophy and science, a continued appeal to the role of God tempered the possibility of a shift to exclusive secularism.

In stark contrast to the theocentric and animistic world view of the medieval era in the mid seventeenth century, Descartes (typically credited as the "great initiator of the modern age") posited a mechanistic model of the world within which mind and matter are irreducibly separate (Megill, 1985, p. 138; Scruton, 1995). His then radical position necessitated a concurrent reconceptualization of the human subject. For Descartes, the self or subject is disembodied; it is fundamentally a thinking being whose physical attributes are merely contingent and accidental; hence *cogito ergo sum*. As such, the self must find its own purpose; it must be self-defining (that is, autonomous), rather than seeking its place in an ordered cosmos (West, 1996, p. 13). The pivotal aspect of Descartes' conception is that, while consistent in many respects with the theoretical consciousness present in Platonic and Aristotelian thought, and with St Augustine's claim to the self as subject (the one who experiences), the

Cartesian subject marks the first time man was placed at the relational center of all that is – that is, human beings as the only real subjects and the world a passive object viewed solely from the perspective of a human center (Megill, 1985, pp. 138–9). Thus, with Descartes, we have firmly established anthropocentrism and egocentrism.

Following on Descartes' pursuit of the foundation of knowledge in the knowing subject, but rejecting outright the appeal to rational principles and innate ideas, John Locke ushered in British Empiricism with the claim that all knowledge comes from experience. His most important contribution to modern conceptions of the subject is the notion of identity (that is, self-sameness maintained over time) as the defining characteristic of the rational agent (Scruton, 1995, p. 93; Paranjpe, 1995). Locke's claim to the centrality of self-sameness was challenged and, some would say, refuted by David Hume, but then taken up again in Kant's conception of the "transcendental ego." More on this later.

Hume's ultimate rejection of the notion of a unitary and unchanging self marks not just a departure from Locke's position, but a kind of philosophical revolt in western conceptions of subjectivity. Hume's radical scepticism, marked by a claim to contingent connection between distinct "existences" in the world of objects, carried through to his conception of the self (Scruton, 1995, p. 123). After looking into his own mind, he found only separate ideas, impressions, and activities, but no particular entity that corresponds to the "I". There is nothing for one to be identical with, thus the notion of continuous identity cannot hold (Scruton, 1995, p. 124).[6]

Writing in part in response to Hume's scepticism, Immanuel Kant, often cited as the prime exemplar of Enlightenment thought, posited a conception of sovereign, autonomous subjectivity that is virtually indistinguishable from the commonsense understanding of self still in evidence today. Consistent with Locke's pre-Humean emphasis on continuity of the self, a key aspect of Kant's conception is permanence. That is, in order for the self, as rational agent, to know anything, it must "continue to exist at least as long as it takes to make multiple observations, and to analyze, compare, categorize, or synthesize them, and thereby draw some meaningful conclusions" (Paranjpe, 1995, p. 17). Thus, Kant argued, to deny continuity of self is to deny the possibility of knowledge of any kind, which – to the rationalist at least – is absurd (Paranjpe, 1995, p. 17).[7]

Kant's next step, after establishing transcendental ego, is to show how it operates in the moral space. Kant argued that for moral judgment and moral performance to be possible, human beings must be capable of freedom and responsibility. However, rejecting the Cartesian and empiricist priority of the first person, and influenced instead by Rousseau's *Social Contract* (1762), Kant conceived of freedom as the subjection of will to the rational moral law (Baynes, 1995; Louden, 1986; Scruton, 1995; West, 1996). Autonomy, on this view, is exercised by action in obedience to the moral law, and heteronomy seen as a forfeiture of moral agency. To see oneself as free, then, is to see oneself as an agent or, in Scruton's words, under the aspect of agency: "That entails seeing myself not as an object in a world of objects, obedient to causal laws, but as a subject, creator of my world, whose stance is active, and whose laws are the laws of freedom, knowable to reason alone" (1995, p. 151).

While Hegel prized the Enlightenment conceptions of individual freedom and the centrality of reason, he rejected Kant's adherence to a notion of the unitary, monadic subject, and offered instead an historical rather than transcendental account of human subjectivity (Baynes, 1995, p. 290; West, 1996). Most significant for our purposes here is Hegel's understanding of the individual as socially constituted. That is, in contrast to Kant's emphasis on individual autonomy, Hegel insists that the individual exists only in a community which, in turn, reflects a tradition of moral values, duties, and social practices (West, 1996, p. 36; Scruton, 1995). Likewise, the kind of subjectivity Hegel describes in *Phenomenology of Mind* (1807) is markedly different from both the definitive immediacy of Descartes' first-person standpoint (Scruton, 1995, p. 174) and from Kant's unity of the self (Scruton, 1995, p. 138).[8] For Hegel, the individual "I" is but a metaphor, for, in the act of self-cognizance the "individual" is subsumed under the a priori (and therefore, in a sense, universal) concept "I" (Scruton, 1995, p. 173). In terms of morality, then, subjectivity "becomes" moral agency at the moment of resolution of the dialectic relation between oneself and the other. A viable conception of morality on Hegel's view must therefore be based on a reconciliation of individual autonomy and the concrete particularity of communal life.

Hegel's ideas met strong criticism from both Schopenhauer and Kierkegaard and, following them, from Nietzsche and Sartre. However, the complexities of those lines of thought warrant a far more detailed account than can be afforded in this brief inquiry. But, given postmodernism's lineage to Nietzsche, it would be insightful to consider his major criticisms of the modern subject and his valorization of radical individualism.

The next major thinker we shall consider here is Nietzsche. Not unreasonably called the first postmodernist, his philosophy was ahead of its time, anticipating things to come. The theocentric world view that had been crumbling steadily over the centuries received a death blow, as it were, in Nietzsche's pronouncement that "God is dead." Rejecting in a single sweep all trappings of transcendence, Nietzsche sought to revitalize humanity by retapping into the creative energy and love of life inherent in the natural conditions of humanity prior to its enthrallment by the ideals of transcendence. The importance of Nietzsche to our critique of modernist subjectivity is his unreserved valorization of individualism based on creativity, self-mastery, and heroism. He identified the natural condition of human beings to be " 'will to power', driven by the desire to keep expanding our [egoic] vitality and strength" (Solomon and Higgins, 1996, p. 234). Concomitantly, he saw many of the traditional other-regarding moral virtues to be a sign of weakened, in fact, decadent humanity.

Heidegger's primary contribution to western thought is his phenomenology of being, in which he, like Nietzsche before him, attempted to address the apparently irreconcilable subject–object dichotomy of Cartesian metaphysics (Megill, 1985, pp. 10–11; Solomon and Higgins, 1996, p. 271). In Heidegger's seminal work *Being and Time* (1927),[9] he sought an understanding of human existence in the term "*Dasein*" (literally, "being there," but more appropriately taken as "being-in-the-world"), prioritizing neither the knowing subject (being) nor the object (world), but, rather, focusing on the inseparable relationality or unity of the two. Before one is a knowing subject, confronting the objective world "out there," one is always, already intimately engaged with the world in the manner a craftsman is engaged in his craft: it is matter of knowing how, and not so much knowing that. We use the language of consciousness (that is, the grammar of subject–object) to describe our knowing that, but as for knowing how, we can only show it by doing. Significantly, even though *Dasein* is conceived of as fundamentally relational, Heidegger's critics – notably the later Ricoeur and Levinas – contend that Heidegger's continued preoccupation with one's own Being finally reveals his inability to break away from the modernist tradition of self-interested subjectivity he denounces.[10]

The subject reconsidered: a Levinassian perspective

After working for more than 20 years on Husserlian and Heideggerian phenomenology, a critical turn in Levinas's own thought came in 1951 with the publication of his essay "Is Ontology Fundamental?". In that piece, Levinas critiqued Heidegger, and ultimately rejected the traditional appeal to ontology as first philosophy. Levinas's argument rested primarily on the charge that western ontology, and Heidegger's ontology in particular, is ultimately and inescapably egoistic in its conception of the subject as a being whose main concern is its own Being. Levinas countered with an argument for ethics as first philosophy, a position which grounds all of his later work (Peperzak, 1995, p. xi). By prioritizing ethics, Levinas rejects the prevailing metaphysics which privileges Being and autonomous, individual subjectivity.

In order to get a rough sense here of Levinas's radical and controversial position regarding subjectivity, most fully developed in *Otherwise than Being, or Beyond Essence* (1981), we shall frame our discussion around part of a dialogue he had with Richard Kearney in 1986. In that conversation, Kearney asks whether Levinas's ethical thought is an attempt to preserve some form of subjectivity in light of the recent structuralist and poststructuralist debates in continental thought, which are marked by much talk of the disappearance or demise of the subject (Levinas and Kearney, 1986, p. 27).

Levinas responds by first rejecting "the idea of a subject who would be a substantial or mastering center of meaning, an idealist, self-sufficient *cogito*" (1986, p. 27). In contrast to the emphasis on presence and Being that characterizes western metaphysics, Levinas sets out a conception of subjectivity wherein agency is seen to be a radical kind of receptivity. One is "subject to" the other in an ethical relationship that precedes the ontological constitution of subjectivity in its more familiar sense (Ciaramelli, 1991, p. 86). From the standpoint of traditional western metaphysics, however, such a

position cannot hold, for it posits subjectivity as an apparently negative construct – that is, as a break with, or deliverance from, Being itself (Ciaramelli, 1991). In essence, Levinas inverts the traditional "no other-than-self without a self" for a claim to "no self without another who summons it to responsibility" (Ricoeur, cited in Kemp, 1996, p. 46).

Admittedly scandalous by traditional western standards, this inversion of subjectivity parallels Derrida's project of deconstructing the metaphysics of presence by calling attention to the absences and gaps – to what philosophy has historically concealed, forbidden, or repressed in order to remain a philosophy of presence (Bass, in Derrida, 1978, p. x). That is, just as deconstruction can reveal every totality (thing, concept, etc.) to be founded on that which it excludes (Bass, in Derrida, 1978, p. xvi), so too, for Levinas, the other is the very bedrock of selfhood (Davis, 1996, p. 80): the other (or what would be "excess" by reductive standards) is a precondition for subjectivity (or presence), and not derivative of it.

Connected to this emphasis on alterity, Levinas's ethical subjectivity "dispenses with the idealizing subjectivity of ontology, which reduces everything to itself" (Levinas and Kearney, 1986, p. 27). In stark contrast to the ontological relation that ultimately reduces the other to the same, Levinas claims that the ethical is characterized by an event of non-subsumptive relation with the other (Critchley, in Peperzak *et al.*, 1996, pp. 1–2; Peperzak, 1993). A significant point here, in terms of empathy, is that Levinas's ethics would seem to resist any appeal to sameness, even in its thinnest (hence most inclusive) sense, such as the notion of a common humanity, cited in prominent studies of altruistic motivation.[11] According to Levinas, the other cannot be known by the usual categories of perception; rather, one has to find "another kinship than that which ties [us] to being, one that will perhaps enable us to conceive of this difference between me and the other" in a way outside oppression of any kind (Levinas, 1981, p. 177). Whether the two positions are finally incompatible, however, is an inquiry that warrants further study. For his part, Levinas clearly resists a conception of altruism as supererogatory, or as the result of moral commitment or free will: one is responsible for the other, he claims, without having taken on that responsibility – "whether accepted or refused, whether knowing or not knowing how to assume it, whether able or unable to do something concrete for the Other" (1985, pp. 96–7). On his view, subjectivity, as the ethical relation of one for-the-other already signifies "total altruism" (in Peperzak *et al.*, 1996, p. 18).

> Levinas then pushes his inversion of the western subject even further, stating: The ethical 'I' is subjectivity precisely insofar as it kneels before the other, sacrificing its own liberty to the more primordial call of the other. For me, the freedom of the subject is not the highest or primary value. The heteronomy of our response to the human other, or to God as the absolutely other, precedes the autonomy of our subjective freedom. (Levinas and Kearney, 1986, p. 27)

At first blush, it might seem here that Levinas has reframed subjectivity as a forfeiture of subjectivity and agency: he has already rejected the sovereignty of self over other, and he now rejects autonomy in favour of heteronomy. One is defined as a subject – a singular person, an "I" – precisely because one is exposed to the other and abdicates one's position of centrality in favour of the other (Levinas and Kearney, 1986, pp. 26–7; Peperzak, 1993). However, we contend that such a position – that is, a rejection of the traditional privilege granted to individual freedom and autonomy – is not synonymous with a forfeiture of subjectivity. On the contrary, Levinas's argument for "heteronomous freedom" points to the metaphysical violence and unjustness of an ethics which maintains the priority of self over other and insists on subsuming the other into the same. When subjectivity is viewed as heteronomous responsibility, one becomes an ethical "I" – a responsible agent – only to the extent that one agrees to depose or dethrone oneself in favour of the other (Levinas and Kearney, 1986, p. 27): "I am I in the sole measure that I am responsible" (Levinas, 1985, p. 101).

Levinas's conception of subjectivity thus holds profound implications for conceptions of moral agency. However, even his more sympathetic reviewers typically point to his call to unconditional responsibility for the other[12] as naive and utopian. Obviously, the possibility always remains of responding to the appeal of the other by way of violence and hatred; and human lives are filled with moral agonies and ethically intractable situations. Yet, having lost most of his family members in the Holocaust, Levinas is in no way naive as to the potential for human violence and destruction: rather, that experience only strengthened his commitment to the urgent need for a reconceptualization of ethics and subjectivity. And, interestingly, Levinas does not reject the charge of his ethics as utopian. Instead, he says:

> Its being utopian does not prevent it from investing our everyday actions of generosity or goodwill towards the other: even the smallest and most commonplace gestures, such as saying 'after you' as we sit at the dinner table or walk through a door, bear witness to the ethical. This concern for the other remains utopian in the sense that it is always 'out of place' (*u-topos*) in this world, always other than the 'ways of the world'; but there are many examples of it in the world. I remember meeting once with a group of Latin American students, well versed in the terminology of Marxist liberation and terribly concerned by the suffering and unhappiness of their people in Argentina. They asked me rather impatiently if I had ever actually witnessed the utopian rapport with the other that my ethical philosophy speaks of. I replied, 'Yes indeed – here in this room.' (Levinas and Kearney, 1986, pp. 32–3)

Consistent with Levinas, then, we prefer to see the "end" of the metaphysics of presence not as a crisis, but rather as a "golden opportunity for western philosophy to open itself to the dimension of otherness and transcendence beyond being" (Levinas and Kearney, 1986, p. 28).

The subject reconsidered: a Buddhist perspective

The next paradigm of moral agency for empathy that we will examine is that of Buddhism which, in our interpretation, contrasts and complements the Levinassian conception of agency. Though coming out of two different cultural and spiritual traditions, they are united in the critique of the centrality of the egoic self and the effort to supplant it by a relational and emergent subjectivity that binds self and other as one inseparable moral unit. In the vocabulary of Buddhism and other Asian spiritual and philosophical traditions, this realization that self and other are not separate, ontologically and psychologically, is called "enlightenment."

Conversely, the absence of such realization, which characterizes our ordinary understanding and action, is called "delusion" (*avijja*). Delusion means lack of coherence or consonance with reality. When in reality there is not an entity in the phenomenal world which has a self-defining nature and is independent of other entities in the way of how it has come to be and how it exists, to think and behave as if one is such a self-defining autonomous being is a delusion. This delusion is not morally benign since it usually is the source of uncaring and even exploitive relationships we have with the world. Unless and until we "wake up" to the realization of the truth of total and radical interdependence (*paticca-samuppada*, meaning Dependent Co-arising) we perpetuate prioritization of the egoic self, putting the self before the other and pitting the self against the other, driven by the psychic need to fulfill the egoic self.

The above Buddhist view of enlightenment is not utopian because it is supported by carefully and rigorously laid out practices aiming at actually overcoming the egoic conception of the self, which is what is meant by enlightenment. While complete enlightenment may be an ideal that is unachievable for most people, because it is difficult, achievement of the goal here is not a matter of all or nothing. To the degree to which one is not inclined to see and treat the world as an other categorically separate from the self, to that degree one is closer to being enlightened. But what are these practices helpful with ego-deconstruction?

Foremost, there is the mindfulness practice (*satipatthana* – "establishment in mindfulness"), popularly known as meditation. In the form known as *vipassana* or insight meditation, what is aimed at is "seeing" through the constructed nature of the egoic self and reaching the state of self–other nonduality. In the Zen terminology, such a state is metaphorically described as the "original face,"[13] meaning the unconditioned, nondualistic, ground consciousness. Now, there is a method to the recovering of the "original face". First of all, one has to develop a sufficient degree of calm, steady, and focused attention (*samatha* – "concentration") that allows one to undertake the minute observation of one's stream of consciousness. Then one must analyze or "unpack" it into its constituent components, known as "the five aggregates" (*pancakkhandha*): material form, sensation, perception, mental activities, and consciousness.[14] The point of this analysis is to ascertain empirically for oneself the unfoundedness of the substantive ego-self. In *Samyutta-Nikaya*, the Buddha explains: "All formations are transient (*anicca*); all formations are subject to suffering (*dukkha*); all things are without an Ego-entity (*anatta*)" (Goddard, 1966, p. 27).

The "discovery" of absence of the ego-self in the micro-analysis of experience is understandably disturbing from the egoic perspective. Yet, we would like to propose that this loss is really a tremendous gain. For, the loss of the egoic self is like breaking down the ancient walls that have been keeping out the world: now the world floods in, and the self finds itself, not standing apart from the world as before, but in the midst of the world, co-emerging and co-evolving with it. As Varela *et al.* put it (1995, p. 122), "the point of mindfulness/awareness is not to disengage the mind from the phenomenal world; it is to enable the mind to be fully present in the world." The self and the world are transfused. This notion of ego-deconstruction for achieving a radically expanded agency of self-world nonduality is tersely expressed by Dogen (1200–1253 AD): "Studying the Buddha Way is studying oneself. Studying oneself is forgetting oneself. Forgetting oneself is being enlightened by all things. Being enlightened by all things is causing the body-mind of oneself and the body-mind of others to be shed" (Cleary, 1996, p. 32).

The ultimate reality for the Buddhist is not substantialistic: that is, the world does not consist of atomistic, autonomous entities, be they humans or non-humans. The "logic" of non-substantialism is non-identity where A does not equal A. In the vocabulary of postmodernism, the metaphysics of presence and autonomy is denied by this logic. A does not equal A because what A is, how it came to be and maintains itself, implicates everything else that is not A, that is formerly excluded by A. Hence the notion, mentioned earlier, of Dependent Co-arising.

The Buddhist conception of empathy and compassion follows directly from the above view of non-substantialism. For, to hold non-substantialism is to be free of the obstructing conditions that block empathic resonance between beings. If views, values, ways of being and doing do not belong to, or inhere in, a substance called a self – because there is no self as such – then they would not act as reasons and causes for preventing people from freely resonating and communing with each other. Empathy can flow through any difference of bodies, views, and values, provided that these differences are not made into (private) properties of individuals, and in turn individuals are not separated on account of the differences of these properties. The Buddhist doctrine of No-self (*anatta*) is a rallying cry against our tendency to reify non-substantialistic phenomena, such as bodies, views, and values, into substantialistic entities and their properties.

Conclusion

We return now to the point of departure for this chapter – our shared concern about conditions of suffering around the world, and the urgent need for empathic moral response. While the two frameworks for ethical subjectivity we have explored here might, on the surface, seem quite disparate, it is our contention that they hold significant features in common – primarily the fundamental rejection of autonomous subjectivity, and the simultaneous cultivation of non-egoic agency. As social beings already inducted into the ways of egoic agency, and surrounded by other egoically socialized beings, cultivation of a Levinassian or Buddhist moral agency is a very demanding task indeed. What is demanded is not, however, altruism in the traditional understanding of the term; for altruism implies forfeiture of subjectivity, which no traditional morality calls for as one's moral duty. Altruistic acts are therefore supererogatory. As such, they call for moral heroism: they ask us to set aside or even go against our own interests and inclinations, which can paralyze one's moral agency. As indicated earlier, Levinassian and Buddhist conceptions of moral agency have little to do with this kind of altruism. The demanding part of the moral effort goes not into performing altruistic acts against self-interest, but into reconceptualizing subjectivity so that we apprehend ourselves not as self-interested, self-preserving, egoic agents, but as dialogic agents whose beingness is constituted by relationality.

Notes

1   See, e.g., Blum (1980, 1994); Deigh (1995); Eisenberg and Strayer (1987); various works by Martin Hoffman; Monroe (1991, 1996); Monroe *et al.* (1990); Noddings (1984); Nussbaum (1990, 1995).

2   See, e.g., Gilligan and Wiggins (1987); Eisenberg and Strayer (1987); Hoffman (1987); various works on character education, such as Delattre and Russell (1993); Lickona (1991).

3   This chapter, which is a revised version of a paper we presented at the 1998 AME conference, reflects but the first steps toward a comparative exploration of Levinassian and Buddhist thought.

4   We have deliberately chosen the term "genealogical account" over "history" to echo Nietzsche's rejection of history as a continuous, progressive, and teleological movement (Foucault, 1977), favouring instead a view of history as discontinuous and marked by difference, rupture and transformation. Therefore, while our presentation here is roughly chronological, it in no way appeals to a logical progression and continuity of thought.

5   Obviously, any attempt to trace a genealogy as complex as that of the modern subject in these few pages will be superficial and marked both by intended gaps and errors of omission. Likewise, given constraints of space, we are relying here mainly on secondary encapsulations, but will recommend original sources for consultation where appropriate.

6   The Buddhist doctrine of No-self is based on a similar, albeit much more rigorous conceptual and psychological analysis. More on this later.

7   It is worth noting here that Kant established the existence of ego self by way of transcendental argument. A thoroughgoing empiricist like Hume would not accept Kant's argument. Also, in anticipation of the Buddhist theory later, we should note that for the Buddhist the ontological status of Kant's transcendental ego would only be conceptual, not "real."

8   By "unity" here, Kant means that the subject has "an immediate and intuitive apprehension of its own unity: I know immediately of my present mental states that they are mine" (Scruton, 1995, p. 137).

9   See especially M. Heidegger, *Being and Time*. (J. Macquarrie and F. Robinson, eds) (1962, New York: Harper and Row); M. Heidegger, *Identity and Difference* (J. Stambaugh, ed.) (1969, New York: Harper and Row).

10 We shall return to Levinas's critique of Heidegger's ontology below. Referring to Heidegger's collaboration with the Nazis, Ricoeur suggests that Heidegger's insistence on the primacy of Being "did not permit him to have moral and political criteria" to judge his own time. See *Le Monde*, 27 June 1987 (cited in Kemp, 1996, p. 58, n.4).

11 See Monroe (1991, 1996) and Monroe *et al.* (1990) for a comprehensive analysis of altruistic motivation among Gentiles who harboured and rescued Jews during the Nazi Holocaust. Monroe found that the only common determining motivational characteristic was a recognition of the essential sameness of all human beings, and a self-perception as part of a common humanity with all the attendant rights and responsibilities obtaining thereto. See also L. Blum, *Moral Perception and Particularity* (1994 Cambridge: Cambridge University Press); and E. Fogelman, *Conscience and Courage: Rescuers of Jews During the Holocaust* (1994, New York: Doubleday).

12 See Levinas's *Otherwise than Being* (1981) for a full explication of the "ethic of unconditional responsibility

for the other." For insightful interpretations and critiques, see especially Robert Bernasconi, Richard Cohen, Simon Critchley, Alphonso Lingis, Adriaan Peperzak, Michael Smith, or David Wood.

13 The famous koan by Eno (Ch: Hui-neng 638–713 AD) runs: "Not thinking of good, not thinking of evil, just this moment, what is your original face before your mother and father were born?" (quoted by Kasulis, 1981, p. 52).

14 See Kalupahana (1987) for an extended discussion. *The Sakyamuni*, Buddha's own discourse on the aggregates, is found in many scriptures but especially in *Majjhima-Nikaya*.

References

Baynes, K. (1995) Modernity as autonomy. *Inquiry* **38**, 289–303.

Blum, L. (1980) *Friendship, Altruism and Morality*. London: Routledge and Kegan Paul.

Blum, L. (1994) *Moral Perception and Particularity*. Cambridge: Cambridge University Press.

Ciaramelli, F. (1991) Levinas's ethical discourse between individuation and universality. In R. Bernasconi and S. Critchley (eds), *Re-reading Levinas*. Bloomington: Indiana University Press.

Cleary, T. (trans.) (1996) *Shobogenzo: Zen essays by Dogen*. Honolulu: University of Hawaii Press.

Davis, C. (1996) *Levinas: An Introduction*. Cambridge: Polity Press.

Deigh, J. (1995) Empathy and universalizability. *Ethics* **105** (4), 743–63.

Delattre, E. J. and Russell, W. E. (1993) Schooling, moral principles, and the formation of character. *Journal of Education* **175** (2), 23–44.

Derrida, J. (1978) *Writing and Difference*, (trans. A. Bass). Chicago: University of Chicago Press.

Dissanayake, W. (ed.) (1996) *Narratives of Agency: Self-making in China, India, and Japan*. Minneapolis: University of Minnesota Press.

Eisenberg, N. and Strayer, J. (eds) (1987) Empathy and its Development. New York: Cambridge University Press.

Foucault, M. (1977) Nietzsche, genealogy, history. In M. Foucault, *Language, Counter-memory, Practice*, D. F. Bouchard and S. Simon, trans. Ithaca: Cornell University Press.

Gilligan, C. and Wiggins, G. (1987) The origins of morality in early childhood relationships. In J. Kagan and S. Lamb (eds), *The Emergence of Morality in Young Children*. Chicago: University of Chicago Press, pp. 277–305.

Goddard, D. (trans.) (1966) *A Buddhist Bible*. Boston: Beacon Press.

Hegel, G. W. F. (1967) *Phenomenology of Mind*, trans. J. B. Baillie. New York: Harper and Row. (Original work published 1807.)

Hoffman, M. (1987) The contribution of empathy to justice and moral judgment. In N. Eisenberg and J. Strayer (eds), *Empathy and its Development*. New York: Cambridge University Press, pp. 47–80).

Hume, D. (1978) *A Treatise of Human Nature*, P. H. Nidditch, ed. Oxford: Clarendon Press. (Original work published 1739.)

Kalupahana, D. (1987) *The Principles of Buddhist Psychology*. Albany: State University of New York Press.

Kasulis, T. P. (1981) *Zen Action, Zen Person*. Honolulu: University of Hawaii Press.

Kemp, P. (1996) Ricoeur between Heidegger and Levinas: original affirmation between ontological attestation and ethical injunction. In R. Kearney (ed.), *Paul Ricoeur: The Hermeneutics of Action*. London: Sage, pp. 41–61.

Levinas, E. (1981) *Otherwise than Being or Beyond Essence*, A. Lingis, trans. The Hague: Martinus Nijhoff.

Levinas, E. (1985) *Ethics and Infinity*, R Cohen, trans. Pittsburgh: Duquesne University Press.

Levinas, E. (1993) *Outside the Subject*, M. Smith, trans. Stanford University Press.

Levinas, E. (1996) Is ontology fundamental: In A. T. Peperzak, S. Critchley and R. Bernasconi (eds), *Emmanuel Levinas: Basic Philosophical Writings*. Bloomington: Indiana University Press.

Levinas E. and Kearney, R. (1986) Dialogue with Emmanuel Levinas. In R. A. Cohen (ed.), *Face to Face with Levinas*. Albany: State University of New York Press, pp. 13–33.

Lickona, T. (1991) *Educating for Character: How Our Schools Can Teach Respect and Responsibility*. New York: Bantam.

Lingis, A. (1994) *The Community of Those Who Have Nothing in Common*. Bloomington: Indiana University Press.

Llewelyn, J. (1988) Levinas, Derrida and Others *vis-à-vis*. In R. Bernasconi and D. Wood (eds), *The Provocation of Levinas: Rethinking the Other*. London: Routledge, pp. 136–55.

Locke, J. (1959) *An Essay Concerning Human Understanding*, A. C. Fraser, ed. New York: Dover. (Original work published 1689.)

Louden, R. B. (1986) Kant's virtue ethics. *Philosophy* **61** 238, 473–89.

Megill, A. (1985) *Prophets of Extremity: Nietzsche, Heidegger, Foucault, Derrida*. Berkeley: University of California Press.

Monroe, K. R. (1991) John Donne's people: explaining differences between rational actors and altruists through cognitive frameworks. *Journal of Politics* **55** (2), 394–33.

Monroe, K. R. (1996) *The, Heart of Altruism: Perceptions of a Common Humanity*. Princeton NJ: Princeton University Press.

Monroe, K. R., Barton, M. C. and Klingemann, U. (1990) Altruism and the theory of rational action: rescuers of Jews in Nazi Europe. *Ethics* **101** (1), 103–22.

Nietzsche, F. (1966) *Beyond Good and Evil: Prelude to*

Philosophy of the Future. W. Kaufmann, trans. New York: Vintage Books.

Noddings, N. (1984) *Caring: A Feminine Approach to Ethics and Moral Education*. Berkeley: University of California Press.

Nussbaum, M. (1990) *Love's Knowledge: Essays on Philosophy and Literature*. Oxford: Oxford University Press.

Nussbaum, M. (1995) *Poetic Justice: The Literary Imagination and Public Life*. Boston: Beacon Press.

Paranjpe, A. (1995) The denial and affirmation of self: the complementary legacies of east and west. *World Psychology* **1** (3): 9–46.

Peperzak, A. (1993) *To the Other: An Introduction to the Philosophy of Emmanuel Levinas*. West Lafayette, IN: Purdue University Press.

Peperzak, A. T. (ed.) (1995) *Ethics as First Philosophy: The Significance of Emmanuel Levinas for Philosophy, Literature and Religion*. New York: Routledge.

Peperzak, A., Critchley, T. and Bernasconi, R. (eds) (1996) *Emmanuel Levinas: Basic Philosophical Writings*. Bloomington: Indiana University Press.

Schneewind, J. B. (1998) *The Invention of Autonomy: A History of Modern Moral Philosophy*. Cambridge: Cambridge University Press.

Scruton, R. (1995) *A Short History of Modern Philosophy: From Descartes to Wittgenstein*, 2nd ed. London: Routledge.

Solomon, R. C., and Higgins, K. M. (1996) *A Short History of Philosophy*. Oxford: Oxford University Press.

Strike, K. A. and Soltis, J. F. (1992) *The Ethics of Teaching*. New York: Teachers College Press.

Varela, F. *et al.* (1995) *The Embodied Mind: Cognitive Science and Human Mind*. Cambridge MA: MIT Press.

Vetlesen, A. J. (1994) *Perception, Empathy, and Judgment: An Enquiry into the Preconditions of Moral Performance*. University Park, PA: Pennsylvania State University Press.

West, D. (1996) *An Introduction to Continental Philosophy*. Cambridge: Polity Press.

Wright, T., Hughes, P. and Ainley, A. (1988) The paradox of morality: an interview with Emmanual Levinas. In R. Bernasconi and D. Wood (eds), *The Provocation of Levinas: Rethinking the Other*. London: Routledge, pp. 168–80.

Part Two

Systems, Policies and Projects across the World

9 Values in European Higher Education
The Ethnicity Test

MAGGIE WOODROW and DAVID CROSIER

This chapter reviews values in European higher education by investigating its attitudes towards ethnicity, and in particular towards minority ethnic groups. Two questions are of particular concern: two sides of the same coin. First, how far do higher education systems and institutions in Europe themselves recognize, represent and promote cultural diversity? Second, in respect of society in general, is higher education a force for stimulating the social integration, or for perpetuating the social exclusion, of minority ethnic groups?

To answer these questions, this chapter draws extensively, but not exclusively, on recent studies undertaken by the Council of Europe's Access to Higher Education in Europe Project, including surveys by the authors, of under-represented groups, in sixteen countries in both central and eastern and western Europe (Woodrow and Crosier, 1996).

Higher education: a crisis of identity

Higher education, it can be claimed, is a European idea and the university a European invention. Its status and authority as the highest form of institutionalized learning, and as the guardian of cultural and intellectual development is now, with the decline of the role of the Church, virtually unchallenged. Yet it becomes increasingly clear as the century draws to a close, that higher education in Europe is facing something of a crisis of identity.

First, there is a tension between its national and international roles. Higher education has always recognized universalist obligations, encompassing its contribution to world science, its service to an increasingly interdependent economy, and its role in the development of greater international under-standing. Today, these obligations are being extended through a greater mobility, not only of students and staff, but of ideas, research and academic activity, facilitated to a wholly unprecedented degree by the technological revolution. Yet, at the same time, the trend is towards increasing the responsiveness of higher education systems and institutions to national values, national interests and national policies. In central and eastern Europe, instability resulting from the break-up of the communist system and the redrawing of boundaries, has encouraged new and often insecure governments to utilize higher education as a vehicle to strengthen national identities; in the west, unemployment, budget crises and the long recession have encouraged pressures towards a state-serving higher education, as a tool for economic recovery.

Second, there is a consequent tension between the university as a resource for the development and protection of multicultural (and international) values and as a vehicle for the protection of mono-cultural (and national) values. In central and eastern Europe, where recent boundary changes have increased friction between populations ethnically mixed for centuries, higher education offers a means of reinforcing the cultural norms of dominant groups and disadvantaging those in a minority. In the west, conditioned not by changing boundaries, but by the inheritance of a colonial white supremacist past, there are similar pressures on higher education, as familiar scapegoat theories, revived by the long recession, contribute to stricter immigration laws and the resurrection of extremist national parties.

Third, there is an associated tension between higher education as an instrument of social conformity, reflecting and hence reinforcing divisions in society through the maintenance of privilege for a self-perpetuating elite, and as a dynamic for social change, affording mobility for less established groups in society, and distinguished by equity rather than elitism. Nowadays governments and universities alike would say that of course there should be equality of opportunity to participate in higher education, and the recent huge expansion in student numbers is often cited as evidence of a shift towards greater equality. Yet this new 'mass' system has involved an increase rather than a widening of the student intake, and despite some notable gains, mainly in the participation of women, those that were under-represented before are under-represented still (Woodrow, 1996).

In respect of each of the above aspects, attitudes towards ethnicity provide a useful indicator for measuring whether European higher education represents predominantly national, monocultural and elitist values, or whether it is progressing towards more international, multicultural and egalitarian qualities.

Interpretations of ethnicity

The relationship between ethnicity and higher education in Europe is characterized by:

- the lack of a common understanding of 'ethnicity' and hence of the term 'minority ethnic group';
- political sensitivity, and in particular the relationship between ethnicity and nationality;
- the scarcity and incompatibility of data on participation in higher education by ethnic group.

Since interpretations of ethnicity vary and the categorization of the term is problematic, a brief examination of its usage is given here. 'Ethnic group' is not a fixed category in the same way as, say, gender: rather it is historically contingent, and perceptions of ethnicity differ widely not only between different countries, but also within them. It is useful therefore, considering the multiplicity of possible interpretations of the concept, to begin by looking at the origins of the word. Derived from the Greek *ethnikos*, it was originally applied to 'heathens, cultural strangers and outsiders; it excluded the dominant group' (Woodrow and Crosier, 1996).

In certain ways little has changed. 'Ethnic group' is a phrase still generally used to denote 'others', while the dominant group considers itself somehow

to transcend ethnicity. Today, for example, in the Netherlands and the Dutch-speaking part of Belgium, 'the esoteric word "allochtoon", previously non-existent, has gained popularity in political and everyday discourse'. The word has a political function. 'It separates "those who belong" from "those who do not (really) belong"', and is used to refer to non-Europeans, the 'visible minorities: populations of Turkish, Moroccan, Surinamese, Chinese or Antillan background and to refugees from developing countries' (Essed, 1997).

Although the 'allochtoon' can easily be recognized as the 'visible minorities', explanations of ethnicity more often focus not on physical characteristics, but on the importance of a common history and tradition. Schermerhorn describes an ethnic group as 'a collectivity within a larger society, having real or putative ancestry, memories of a shared historical past, and a cultural focus on one or more symbolic elements defined as the epitome of their peoplehood'. To the notion of a common origin is added that of a common culture, including such distinctive characteristics as language, religion and lifestyle so that overall, according to Verma, 'the basic, distinctive attribute of an ethnic group is not physical appearance, but cultural values'.

This interpretation does not help in the identification of ethnicity among those who may for several generations have rejected the common culture and the shared activities of the group, including the religion, language and lifestyle, to embrace quite a different culture. Culture, however, may be a matter of choice; ethnicity may rather be a matter of labelling. More recent studies, for example, by Martiniello, acknowledge the importance of perceptions and recognize that: 'Ethnicity is one aspect of social relations between social actors . . . While there are certainly cultural differences, they are not written on stone, but are reconstructed by the actors', so that 'ethnicity is not defined absolutely by a mix of physical, psychological and cultural characteristics. Rather it is the perception of their importance that matters' (Martiniello, 1996).

This interpretation of ethnicity is particularly significant for its relationship with higher education. Instead of simply reacting to groups already distinguishable by a shared culture, language and lifestyle, higher education is itself one of the actors contributing to the formulation or reinforcement of an ethnic identity. Martiniello also distinguishes between the importance of perceptions at individual level, where they may be 'largely subjective', and at group and society level, where 'ethnicity is about the cultural, social, economic and political constraints, which assign individuals a social position', and it is here that the contribution of higher education can be crucial.

Nationality and ethnicity

It is in their relationship with nationality and hence with nationalism, that interpretations of ethnicity become particularly problematic. Here the situation varies not only between countries, but also between universities, against a background level of tension that may range from a faint memory of historical grievances to armed conflict. In the 1990s, the conflict over ethnicity and nationality in the former Yugoslavia, and the cynical use of the term 'ethnic cleansing' as a synonym for genocide, have added a new and sinister association to the whole vocabulary of ethnicity. At the same time, in both western and eastern Europe, attitudes to minority ethnic groups are being hardened by fears of religious fundamentalism, as an allegiance transcending national frontiers. Overall in these circumstances, the danger is that the term ethnicity, where it is used, will be almost exclusively associated with conflict and social fragmentation.

In Belgium, France, Finland and Sweden there is no legal recognition of an individual's ethnic status or origin. In Belgium and France there are only two categories, those with the status of nationals and those who are classified as immigrants, and stricter immigration laws make movement from one category to another increasingly problematic. Belgium presents an interesting case of a country which recognizes its two 'cultural communities' of French and Flemish origin, with a separate ministry of education for each, but then allows its other minority cultural groups to remain wholly invisible in national statistics. In Finland, under the Personal Data File Act of 1987, ethnic or race origin cannot be used as a background variable and the only legitimate relevant indicator is mother tongue language (Valimaa, 1996).

In Switzerland the large migrant population (approximately one-sixth of the total) is ineligible for national status, while in Germany members of the large Turkish community may still fall into the underprivileged category of 'guest worker', despite many years' residence and although they may be second or third generation immigrants. Similar

examples may be found in central and eastern Europe, particularly in countries seeking to reverse former russification policies. In Estonia, for example, the Law on Aliens (1993) defines most of the Soviet period immigrants as aliens, who are ineligible for citizenship and must apply for residence and work permits (Aarna, 1995).

Elsewhere, the formal recognition of nationality may not be enough as, for example, among the black British, where it was found that: 'Despite a strong sense of social and cultural commonality with the white British, most Caribbeans found it difficult to lay claim to be British. The difficulty was almost entirely based on the knowledge that the majority of white British people did not acknowledge the commonality and really believed that only white people could be called British' – a classic example of the strength of perceptions, as against legislation (PSI, 1993).

Ethnic monitoring

The study of ethnicity and higher education is made problematic by the scarcity of data, at either national or institutional level. The absence of data is curious, since in other respects higher education is awash with statistics whether at institutional, regional, European or global level. In fact, the sheer quantity of data has a smokescreen effect, obscuring its selectivity, its restricted usage and the inconsistency of its format. While the purpose of seeking information is presumably to help to determine policy, it is nevertheless clear that policy has already determined the nature of the information that is to be sought. As measured by the availability of relevant data, the priority given to ethnic issues is generally minimal. As the Council of Europe's Access to Higher Education Project emphasizes, data essential to the formulation and implementation of any serious policy for equal opportunity is missing. Monitoring is part of the normal cycle of rational planning in any field and its absence not only looks discriminatory in itself, but also inhibits the identification and rectification of other inequitable policies. Nevertheless, throughout Europe most higher education institutions would claim, with no academic qualms about inconsistency, both that they are ethnically neutral and that they have absolutely no statistics to prove it.

Monitoring to identify under-represented

groups is additionally problematic in central and eastern Europe, as both the notion of 'under-representation' and the idea of 'groups' are alien constructions. Theoretically education was and is available to all – and this belief/perception remains unquestioned in everyday reality. The concept of 'social groups' was anathema to the former ruling party and it is clear that this is still a construct not considered relevant to the social reality. Individuals rather than groups are the object of study in research and statistics. In this context it is difficult to grasp the idea of monitoring 'under-representation' as individuals cannot be under-represented (Woodrow and Crosier, 1996).

Of the countries involved in the Council of Europe survey, the Russian Federation was alone in central and eastern Europe in undertaking ethnic monitoring on a national scale. Elsewhere, staff interviewed in universities and ministries often expressed surprise and occasionally indignation that questions about ethnicity should be asked at all. In some ways, a rejection of ethnic categorization can be regarded as being positive – especially if it could be achieved in people's everyday perceptions. However, there is no evidence that this non-categorization is not concealing patterns of disadvantage perpetuated from previous regimes. Moreover a denial of the existence of cultural diversity cannot produce a multicultural higher education with a curriculum that responds to a diversity of needs. In this sense there is certainly evidence of under-representation.

The perceived threat in the notion of ethnic monitoring is understandable. Classification by ethnic group has seldom in the past been undertaken in the interests of those who find themselves in a minority. For several countries in central and eastern Europe, the proximity of both 'ethnic cleansing' and religious fundamentalism is effective in reinforcing the view that the possession or even the process of gathering such information could be utilized in ways which might be damaging to social peace and stability. Nevertheless, there is a strong case for saying that 'the ghost of ethnic labelling **for** discrimination must be put to rest' (Wimberley, 1995), if patterns of disadvantage and under-representation are to be eradicated.

In the west, monitoring on a national scale is undertaken only in the Netherlands and the UK. Both systems are new and not compatible with each other. In the UK, where since 1995 ethnic monitoring in higher education has been co-ordinated and controlled by the new Higher Education Statistics Agency (HESA), data collection involves a voluntary process of self-identification from a list of ethnic categories which are consistent with those used in the national population census, thus making possible broad comparisons between the level of higher education participation and the incidence in the population as a whole of each ethnic group. Concerns have been expressed about the choice of ethnic categories provided, particularly in respect of the 'black British', i.e. British-born black people from second or third generation immigrant families. Despite these problems, there is a widely held conviction in the UK that some form of ethnic monitoring is essential if racism in higher education is to be eradicated. Although it was feared that response levels would be low, the first HESA survey achieved a 77 per cent return, providing more data than ever before obtained on participation by ethnic origin (HESA, 1996).

In the Netherlands ethnic monitoring has only very recently been extended to higher education, where it is now a legal requirement, as it has been in the schools sector for some time. The process of data collection is not dependent on self-identification, but on the registration of the country of birth of the student and parents. If either is a country other than the Netherlands, the student will be classified as belonging to a minority ethnic group. This system provides a less subjective means of recognizing ethnicity than the British system, but fails to distinguish the ethnic origin of longer term immigrants.

In other European countries in the meantime, the extent of participation by minority ethnic groups will remain for the most part a matter of speculation and wishful thinking, enlightened only by some monitoring at institutional level, by case studies and research surveys. The rarity of ethnic monitoring in European higher education facilitates the maintenance of the status quo and itself categorizes higher education as a form of social exclusion, while at the same time contributing to the perpetuation of other cultural barriers to participation, of which language is one of the most significant.

Language barriers

From the perspective of many minority ethnic groups, the language of higher education is 'both symbolically and practically of vital importance' (Valimaa, 1996). Those whose mother tongue is not the same as the language of higher education are disadvantaged either directly or by perceptions of their unsuitability. The language issue, as Valimaa explains, is not just about 'the access of minorities to higher education, but the question of what the status of minorities is in society and in its cultural institutions'. Whereas in the case of foreign students language barriers may be seen as the responsibility of the individual, in the case of home students the responsibility is that of the education system, the policies of which can both create and overcome such barriers.

The range of language disadvantage is in a continuum, including those who do not speak the main state language, those for whom it is a second language and who speak it with varying degrees of perfection, and those for whom it is their first language, but not that of their families. In each case, the fundamental question is whether higher education institutions should be monolingual, bilingual or multilingual. The determining factors here are the extent to which language is used by governments to reinforce the ruling group identity; the size and geographic concentration of minority groups; the additional costs of bilingual or multilingual higher education; and language policy at secondary education level.

In central and eastern Europe, language barriers are increasing, for example, in Romania where 'the history of the Hungarian minority is the history of the gradual erosion of their social and cultural position' (Valimaa, 1996). The Education Law of 1994 made Roumanian the compulsory language for all levels of education and for all citizens irrespective of their ethnic origin – a policy which disadvantages the Hungarians in particular as the largest minority group (7.1 per cent of the population). Some countries have sought to reduce barriers through bilateral agreements on mother tongue education, but with limited success. The Lithuanians for example, report bitterly that 'this problem would be less difficult if only all the populations concerned knew about the principles of democracy and human rights' (Smilgevicius, 1994).

Where the language of higher education is only the second language for individuals or for their families, a situation as common in western as in eastern Europe, limitations or variations in language usage may be mistakenly interpreted as being indicative of a generally inferior academic performance and potential, and thus associated with lowering standards in higher education. In the Netherlands, for example, the title of 'allochtoon' widely given to 'racial-ethnic' minority people from a non-European background, 'has become synonymous with language deficit and learning problems . . . Many teachers and professors have low expectations about racial-ethnic minority students and they grade them accordingly'. Evidence that 80 per cent of higher education entrants in this category complete their courses successfully tends to be ignored. Instead, 'the over-emphasis on insufficient control of the Dutch language tends to overshadow other problems, notably those resulting from eurocentrism and racism', which many people 'cannot believe can exist at all in the Netherlands' (Essed, 1997).

Admissions barriers

The actual and perceived language problems discussed above become either directly or indirectly discriminatory when applied to admissions criteria and procedures, and the absence of ethnic monitoring in most European countries makes detection of this discrimination difficult. In the two western European countries where such monitoring is undertaken, the Netherlands and the UK, representation from minority ethnic groups has increased in recent years. In the UK, data from HESA shows that non-white ethnic groups are well represented in higher education, irrespective of age, while those over 21 are better represented than might be expected from the census figures showing their distribution in the population as a whole. Female Pakistani students are, however, an exception to this, forming a smaller than expected percentage, especially among students over the age of 21 (HESA, 1996).

However, both in the UK and the Netherlands there is evidence of 'vertical segregation'. In the UK, research by the Commission for Racial Equality (CRE) shows the over-representation of students from minority ethnic groups in the least prestigious higher education institutions, especially the 'new' universities in inner city areas (CRE, 1994). In particular, black Caribbean and Pakistani applicants were the groups most severely under-represented in securing admission to the 'old' universities. In the Netherlands, while 'racial-ethnic minority' students are under-represented in the higher education system as a whole, under-representation is greater in the universities than in the higher professional schools. Essed (1997) suggests three reasons for this under-representation:

- individual or cultural deficiency;
- racism, discrimination and eurocentrism;
- pragmatic choice.

Of these three, the first, which she castigates as 'blaming the victim', has widespread acceptance. The second is generally rejected as being an affront 'to national honour'. The third, student choice, is inevitably affected by students' own perceptions of the realities of the situation, in terms of discrimination by both universities and employers (Essed, 1997).

In other western European countries, for example, Germany and Switzerland, citizenship laws prevent the consideration of applications from minority ethnic groups as nationals. Elsewhere, the concentration of minority ethnic group populations in particular geographic areas, often in the poorer quarters of large cities, tends to lead also to their concentration, with implications of ghettoization, in local higher education institutions as, for example, the University of Paris 8 in the area of St Denys, where 21.7 per cent of the population is of migrant origin.

Over Europe as a whole though, the greatest admissions barrier, and nowhere greater than in central and eastern European countries, is the criteria for entry. These are broadly the same throughout Europe, being based largely on performance in national 18+ examinations. Dependence on these criteria makes the process of admissions a fairly mechanical one, though institutions may vary this marginally; some to achieve greater participation, others greater selectivity. For example in the UK, 96 of 111 applicants from one school – Eton – gained admission to Oxford University in 1993 (Woodrow and Crosier, 1997). Overall, however, admission by examination grade is widely perceived as fair and sometimes upheld as evidence of the implementation of access policies. It is strongly defended as a more equitable system than those which give preference to applicants who can pay, or who have particular political contacts or affiliations, and this is indisputable. However, such systems, which represented unequal rules for entry, have largely been replaced by rules which are apparently equal (i.e. in that they make the same requirement from everyone), but which systematic-

ally produce unequal effects because they take no account of differing circumstances. The illusion remains that success at 18+ provides neutral evidence of the achievements of a meritocracy unrelated to cultural differences, socio-economic status, or earlier educational opportunity.

Financial barriers

Those from minority ethnic groups often find themselves disadvantaged by the failure of entry systems to take into account not only their different cultural background, but also their socio-economic status and their earlier educational experience. The Romanies, who are in practice almost excluded from higher education in all European countries, provide a classic example of the effects of a combination of these factors.

In western Europe in particular, the funding of higher education is regressive and socio-economic status determines access to higher education. A common pattern is for 70 to 80 per cent of students to be drawn from social classes one and two, professional and managerial groups, and less than 10 per cent from families of unskilled workers. In the east, the widening of socio-economic divisions accompanying the shift to a market economy presages the emergence of a similar pattern. Throughout Europe, recent sharp reductions in higher education budgets have raised the financial barriers considerably, as funding is increasingly shifted on to students and their families. Low income is increasingly both a deterrent factor for participation and a significant cause of non-completion, as students seek to combine study with part-time work, where low rates of pay require a considerable time input.

Evidence of low socio-economic status caused by and contributory to ethnic disadvantage is not hard to find and not only among recent immigrants. In the USA poverty is seen as the main barrier to participation for minority ethnic groups. In western Europe especially, the non-white ethnic groups are most likely to be over-represented at the lowest income levels: for example, in the Netherlands those from the former Dutch colonies of Indonesia, Surinam and the Dutch East Indies; in Spain those from Morocco, the Dominican Republic, Colombia and the Philippines; in France from North Africa; in Germany from Turkey. A system where access is dependent on ability to pay is thus a major factor in impeding the social mobility of minority ethnic groups, who are trapped in a cycle of under-qualification, low incomes and inability to meet the costs of higher education.

The cultural reproduction barrier

Recent evidence, for example, Mora's (1995) study in Spain, suggests that there is a more significant variable than income determining participation and that is parental (especially father's) experience of higher education (Mora, 1995). This also affects progress at earlier stages in the educational system, having a cumulative effect at later levels. Higher education thus tends towards a self-perpetuating elite, postponing the process of change and presenting a major barrier to those from minority ethnic groups, many of whom will be first generation applicants.

Their difficulty in accessing such a system is often compounded by inadequate schooling, where expectations of higher education are 'conditionallyingly' low, and by inadequate advice, guidance and counselling, affecting both entry and performance. In a culturally reproductive system, there is a general subconscious assumption that limited information and guidance will suffice. Even here it is clear that 'guidance is more easily accessible to those who need it least' and that services, where they are available, fail to take into account different cultural backgrounds (Bimrose, 1995). Applicants and students from families, schools or communities where higher education is a rarity must thus educate themselves and their families in the complexities of an alien system, while at the same time trying to promote their future within it.

The cultural reproductive nature of European higher education is evidenced not only by the profile of its student population, but also by that of its staff, where role models for students from minority ethnic groups are often a rarity. This staff profile contributes to the survival of an ethno-centric curriculum in which students from minority ethnic groups find the academic achievements and values of their own cultures neither recognized nor acknowledged. These students, having little choice but to conform to the cultural norm, may find themselves isolated in the process, both from their fellow students and from their own cultural community.

Towards social inclusion

The barriers identified above to the participation of those from minority ethnic groups invoke a discouraging response to the two questions posed at the start of this chapter. On this evidence it seems that European higher education systems and institutions represent national, monocultural and elitist values and that they play a significant part in preserving, if not extending, existing divisions in society in the interests of the dominant culture. Indications in particular countries of a greater, rather than a lesser, commitment to these values are not hard to find, while the effects of reductions in higher education budgets are generally regressive. But are there any signs of a change towards a more inclusive and egalitarian system?

This is a difficult question to answer because specific policies to widen access for members of minority ethnic groups can be interpreted in two ways: first, on their face value as genuine attempts to modify the system to benefit those who are excluded from it; second, as a means of perpetuating an inequitable system by a few symbolic concessions, which in practice simply marginalize those from minority ethnic groups. For example, limited numbers of 'outsiders' may be enabled to enter within the system, not by changing the rules but by making some 'special' arrangements – access courses, for example, or special initiative projects. The encouragement of these 'non-traditional' students may be seen either as a step on the road to a system which is more equitable overall, or as a move (however well intentioned) which in practice provides a safety valve facilitating the survival of an exclusive higher education, by casting over it an unmerited aura of social equity and mobility.

At the other end of the political spectrum, such 'special' measures have been castigated for being too radical, rather than for not being radical enough. The label of 'affirmative action' has been applied pejoratively to a range of measures to widen access for those from minority ethnic groups, which are perceived as a form of 'political correctness' resulting in lower standards in higher education and discriminating against those from the majority culture. The searcher for evidence of a genuine shift towards a more international, multicultural and egalitarian system of higher education in Europe has thus to tread a very careful path through a minefield of marginalization on the one hand and political correctness on the other.

The avoidance of both these perils requires recognition that neither the application of so-called 'equal' rules to those from diverse cultural backgrounds, nor their location in a 'special' category outside the 'normal' rules, constitutes progress towards a multicultural higher education. For this to be achieved, the rules themselves must change. This requires inclusive policies designed to meet the needs of those historically marginalized or excluded, as much as those of dominant ethnic groups. Equality of opportunity thus becomes systemic, integral to a pluralistic higher education culture, where diversity is celebrated and 'special' provision for any group is unnecessary. What is required to achieve such a model and are there signs that European higher education is progressing towards it?

There are examples of current policy and practice designed to implement systemic change, but nowhere in Europe do they represent a comprehensive alternative. These include: race relations legislation; progress towards ethnic monitoring; progress towards a multicultural higher education; resourcing a multicultural higher education.

Race relations legislation

Race relations legislation could provide protection against discrimination in education and employment as in other aspects of society. This may not be essential to the achievement of a multicultural higher education, but it helps. In Europe such legislation is in a continuum including the few countries with comprehensive and effective legislation; a larger number where it is limited or ineffective; many with no legislation at all, which thereby legitimizes discrimination; and those with legislation which actively discriminates against particular groups, for example, through regulations denying eligibility for national status to minority ethnic groups in the country of their birth.

In much legislation, as in the UK, the onus is on individuals to demonstrate discrimination in the courts. The Commission for Racial Equality (CRE) has won cases proving discrimination against staff and students in higher education, although their limited funding enables them to pursue only a few. Moreover, the commitment of the police force and the judiciary, both overwhelmingly white and male, to enforcement of the legislation is often regarded as lukewarm at best. Nevertheless, the impact of successful cases and the publicity that they receive operate to discourage discrimination and provide a reference point for non-discriminatory policies in higher education.

A few countries are moving towards race relations legislation where the onus is not on the individual to prove discrimination, but on organizations, including employers, to demonstrate that there is none. Far from leading the field as a graduate employer of minority ethnic staff, the record of higher education is poor. Even in countries and universities with a sizeable proportion of minority ethnic students, there is no comparable diversity among academic staff, while minority ethnic staff at senior management levels are so rare as to have curiosity value. Until a breakthrough can be achieved here, the higher education curriculum will remain monocultural. In the Netherlands, where 'racial-ethnic minorities are virtually absent among faculty and staff members', the Act on Equal Treatment 1994, which provides 'a clearly codified norm of equal treatment', seeks to promote change at all levels of employment, although it is considered to be too soon to evaluate its effectiveness (Essed, 1997). There are also other encouraging signs, including the recent introduction of race relations laws in Switzerland, a country formerly conspicuous for their absence, but here again their impact remains to be seen.

Progress towards ethnic monitoring

As noted above, this practice is a rarity in European higher education. Its absence enables prejudice to thrive on ignorance and is inconsistent with higher education's claim to academic objectivity and detachment, which cannot be associated with a preference for not finding out the facts. One encouraging sign here is the Monitoring Pilot Project set up by the Council of Europe as an outcome of its Access to Higher Education in Europe Project. This project, undertaken at institutional level, involves universities in western and eastern Europe and seeks to identify and compare problems in the monitoring process of under-represented groups, including those from ethnic minorities, with a view to offering transferable solutions and identifying a compatible system. The project recognizes that monitoring systems are not easy to introduce and can be difficult to implement. It emphasizes therefore the importance of: proceeding with the involvement of those with a legitimate interest, including representatives of the different groups to be monitored; having regard to legitimate concerns over data protection and privacy; and avoiding the 'creation of cumbersome and complex systems which staff will be reluctant to implement and which will arouse proper concerns about cost and feasibility'. The pilot project plans to report in the year 2000 and in the meantime to involve and gain support for this work from the EU, UNESCO, the German Studentenwerk, the European Access Network and other international organizations (Woodrow, 1996).

Monitoring provides the hard evidence needed to demonstrate under-representation, plan strategies to address it, set targets and calculate progress towards them. It is clear that 'arguments based on sentiment, on perceived need, on pleas for mercy or similar do not get a hearing against sound documentation' (Barlow, 1995). The achievement of effective and comparable monitoring systems will demonstrate visibly what kind of values are paramount in higher education.

Progress towards a multicultural higher education

A few examples here demonstrate how varied progress in changing values has been. In Spain, where until the end of Franco's era higher education conformed to 'a concept of centralist and unitarist Spain, with uniform structures of the State, and with aspirations to cultural homogeneity', considerable progress is recorded. At the University of Barcelona, for example, where Catalan is now the official language but with both Catalan and Spanish as the working languages, there is close co-operation with other universities in the region to preserve the Catalan language and culture. The University of Barcelona is seen as representing a very different model, indicative of 'a plurilinguistic, pluricultural, plurinational Spain' (Pons, 1995). Yet this new model of higher education remains singularly unresponsive, not only to the largest minority group in Spain, the gypsies, but also to more recent minority groups of North African origin, many of whom have settled in Catalonia. It would be encouraging to think that the inclusion of one formerly rejected culture would be the breakthrough point for the inclusion of others, but unfortunately this is not so. It is clear that even a 'multicultural'

higher education discriminates between one culture and another. In this case, what the Catalans have, despite their different language and traditions, that the gypsies and the North Africans do not, is a closer socio-economic, physical and cultural affinity with the dominant group, which gives them greater acceptability among conventional norms.

In Finland, where there is a strong drive towards equality of opportunity, the strategy for achieving a multicultural higher education has been by use of quotas. At the University of Helsinki, for example, where teaching is bilingual, there are staff and student quotas for those of Swedish origin, now 5.8 per cent of the total population in the country and the largest minority group. In 1995, twenty-eight chairs were reserved for Swedish-speaking professors, a practice which, if implemented for minorities in other countries, would transform the power structure and culture of European higher education. In addition, there are sizeable quotas for Swedish-speaking students in six out of the eight faculties and a Swedish-speaking institute of social studies in the faculty of political science. Overall, the proportion of Swedish-speaking people studying in the universities is slightly greater than their incidence in the country as a whole. There are similar student quotas for the Sami people, who comprise 0.03 per cent of the population, at the Universities of Lapland and the University of Oulu, which are located closest to their communities (Valimaa, 1996). However, two policies restrict the drive towards a multicultural higher education in Finland. The first is that take-up of the quotas is not always realized, because of the requirement of all students to pass the university entrance examination, which can be taken in Swedish or Finnish. There is an additional weighting for Sami students, but entry requirements otherwise make no response to their different background, culture or earlier educational experience. The second limitation again concerns the gypsies who comprise an estimated 0.2 per cent of the population, but for whom there are no quotas for higher education places, which are allocated only on the basis of language, Swedish legislation, as noted earlier, disallowing the use of race or ethnic origin as criteria.

Several countries in central and eastern Europe have begun to make some higher education accessible to the gypsies. In Hungary, where the Romany community constitutes an estimated 5 per cent of the population, government resources have been targeted to mother-tongue teacher training programmes for Romany students, in recognition of their very low participation rates in the education system as a whole. In Romania, the Social Work Faculty of the University of Bucharest runs a scheme under which Romany students are accepted onto courses irrespective of entry qualifications. Monitoring student performance on these courses has shown that after two years of study the achievement of the Romany students does not differ from those with the formal qualifications for entry (Woodrow and Crosier, 1996). Although these are only isolated examples, they demonstrate what can be achieved by the provision of resources and the importance of recognizing student potential on entry, as distinct from past educational achievement. Values in higher education will have significantly changed when, instead of being isolated examples, such initiatives are incorporated within flexible entry systems, which recognize the different starting points and backgrounds of applicants.

Resourcing a multicultural higher education

The change to a multicultural higher education is sometimes portrayed as a resource intensive process which, however desirable, is not practical in the present financial climate. Such a change can be achieved not so much by an increase in the overall investment in higher education, as by a redistribution of the resources currently available. Moreover, financial incentives to institutions are perhaps a more palatable method of 'making the talk walk' in terms of equal opportunities. There are signs of increasing awareness in Europe of the Australian 'Fair Chance For All' system, by which the government funding per student is additionally weighted for those from under-represented groups, including minority ethnic groups. The location of home minority ethnic students, in a similar category to that of black students in the lucrative and competitive overseas market, would rapidly change their value and do much to transform the student profile in European higher education. In this respect, recent proposals by the Higher Education Funding Council for England (HEFCE) for funding for under-represented groups are encouraging. Circular 21/96 'Funding Teaching' proposes to allocate additional weightings, not directly to students from minority ethnic groups, who overall

are not under-represented according to HESA statistics, but to mature students, those with non-traditional entry qualifications and, if an appropriate methodology can be found, to those from low socio-economic backgrounds (HEFCE, 1996). If similar policies were adopted on a Europe-wide scale, they could do much to change attitudes in higher education towards minority ethnic groups.

The other aspect of resourcing which presents a barrier for many minority ethnic students is, of course student funding. Here again the solution is redistribution, so that the present system of access by ability to pay is replaced by a system of payment by ability to pay. The Recommendations of the Council of Europe Access Project propose: 'Student funding, whether through grants or loans would be in inverse proportion to student/parental ability to pay, taking into account any additional financial requirements, for example those with disabilities, or those with dependents'. Any fees charged would be for those from higher income backgrounds only (Woodrow, 1996).

Such processes of redistribution would do much for those minority groups where class differentiation goes hand in hand with racial discrimination to exclude them from participation in higher education and hence from graduate career opportunities.

Conclusion

To return to the two questions posed at the start, the evidence overwhelmingly points to higher education as a force making for the social exclusion rather than the social inclusion of minority ethnic groups. Examples of the promotion of cultural diversity in higher education are scattered and isolated. But however depressing this conclusion, nevertheless it achieves something of significance and that is the recognition of the realities of the situation. These are seldom acknowledged and often categorically rejected. Yet 'the first step towards rectifying the situation of the under-representation of certain groups such as ethnic minorities and lower socio-economic status groups is for governments and educational institutions to recognise that the problems exist' (Harkin, 1994). Resistance to this recognition is considerable. As the indignant reaction of some rectors and ministers to our survey indicates, there is a tendency to perceive investigation into questions of ethnicity and higher education as being a potential cause of increased friction between different ethnic groups and to discourage it accordingly. The reaction to proposals for ethnic monitoring or quotas is to ask whether we can really 'expect the introduction of racial distinctions to advance the goal of the elimination of racial distinctions?' (Singer, 1993). The answer of course is that the distinctions are already there and to pretend that they are not is a means of perpetuating them. It is already clear that European higher education serves to maintain the position of elites in society and all the equal opportunities statements in existence cannot conceal that its admissions policies, employment practices, curricula and resource distribution contribute to severe inequality between ethnic groups, to divided communities and hence to increased racial tension. Once this inequality is acknowledged, we can get on with the process of addressing it, of creating a higher education that will be of benefit to all and to which no ethnic group has a greater claim than any other.

References

Aarna, O. (1995) Tallinn Technical University for Tolerance in Europe. In *Proceedings of the CCHER Forum Role Conference. Ljubljana.* Strasbourg: Council of Europe.

Barlow, A. (1995) Initiatives in addressing more equitable participation in higher education: the Australian experience, in *Proceedings of the EAN Cambridge Convention and Council of Europe Workshop: Addressing Under-Representation in European Higher Education.* Strasbourg: Council of Europe.

Bimrose, J. (1995) *Guidance and Counselling for Higher Education.* Strasbourg: Council of Europe.

Commission for Racial Equality (CRE) (1994) *Further Education and Equality.* CRE: London.

Essed, P. (1997) Widening access in Europe: racial-ethnic minority access to Dutch higher education. In R. Taylor, (ed.) *Opportunities for Black People in Higher Education.* Leeds: University of Leeds, Department of Continuing Education.

Harkin, S. (1995) *Proceedings of the Parma Conference. Access to Higher Education in Europe.* Parma: University of Parma.

Higher Education Funding Council for England (HEFCE) (1996) *Funding Method for Teaching from 1998–99.* Circular 21/96. Bristol: HEFCE.

Higher Education Statistics Agency (1995) *HESA Data Report. Students in Higher Education Institutions.* Cheltenham: HESA.

Martiniello, M. (1996) Ethnicité, *Agenda Interculturel* 143 Brussels: Action Interculturelle.

Mora, J. G. (1995) Access to higher education for under-represented groups in Spain. *Proceedings of the EAN Cambridge Convention and Council of Europe Workshop: Addressing Under-Representation in European Higher Education.* Strasbourg: Council of Europe.

Policy Studies Institute (PSI) Survey (1994) *Ethnic Minorities and Higher Education: Why Are There Different Rates of Entry?* London: PSI.

Pons, J. M. (1995) Linguistic policy at the University of Barcelona. In *Proceedings of the CCHER Forum Role Conference, Ljubljana.* Strasbourg: Council of Europe.

Singer, P. (1993) *Practical Ethics.* 2nd ed. Cambridge: Cambridge University Press.

Smilgevicius, A. (1994) Minorities in Lithuania – Lithuanian minorities in other countries. Paper given at *Educational Workshop on Cultural Minorities. Bautzen.* Strasbourg: Council of Europe.

Valimaa, J. (1996) *Indigenous Minorities in Higher Education.* Jyvaskyla: University of Jyvaskyla, Institute for Educational Research.

Wimberley, J. (1995) Introduction to the themes. *Proceedings of the EAN Cambridge Conference, Addressing Under-representation in European Higher Education.* Strasbourg: Council of Europe.

Woodrow, M. (1996) *Quality and Equality: Values and Policy in European Higher Education. Report of the Project on Access to Higher Education in Europe. Part 1.* Strasbourg: Council of Europe.

Woodrow, M. and Crosier, D. (1996) *Access to Higher Education for Under-represented Groups.* Strasbourg: Council of Europe.

10 Values Education and Cultural Diversity

PAULO RENATO SOUZA

> The education we speak of is training from childhood in goodness, which makes a man eagerly desirous of becoming a perfect citizen, understanding how both to rule and be ruled righteously.
>
> Plato, *Laws*, I, 643E

Introduction

It is surely a truism to say that the second half of the twentieth century has been marked by swift and deep transformations in the economic, political and cultural fields which have brought about new requirements to be fulfilled by those who wish to participate in society as full citizens and to share the socially generated wealth and knowledge, finding a place in the professional world.

The complexity of modern life, the great amount of information made available through the media, the weakening of family ties and of life in community, along with a marked flattening out of traditional values around a common market value denominator, have created for the educational system new responsibilities which are well beyond its traditional role. This consisted in guaranteeing the acquisition of basic skills such as reading and writing and of a well-defined body of contents in well-delimited fields of knowledge.

In the new context, the school has now the responsibility of developing sociability, of promoting a democratic and highly critical participation in political life, of creating the capacity to link and organize information, of preparing to compete in an ever more exacting labour market, of facilitating access to ever more abundant cultural goods and of inducing the capacity to engage in continuous learning and reformulation of what has been learned already.

In what concerns the developing countries of Latin America, such as Brazil, the situation is really challenging. Here it is not only a question of changing the traditional school so as to offer a wider and more thorough education to children who come from families with a long tradition of school attendance; it is a question of setting up institutions which will prove able to incorporate in the educational process those children whose families have no tradition of schooling. This has to be carried out with paucity of means and lack of a sufficiently qualified body of teachers. At the same time, the high rates of population growth and the increase in the number of mandatory schooling years make it necessary to promote a rapid widening of the educational system's coverage.

Brazilian society carries an authoritarian mark. During a long period as a colony of Portugal and after independence as an empire, the economy was based on slavery. Brazil has a long tradition of paternalistic political relations and has undergone long periods of non-democratic government. It is thus a society marked by strongly hierarchic social relations and by privileges that reproduce a very high level of social exclusion. The high rate of population growth during the last thirty years has, among other factors related to the process of economic development undergone by the country, made it impossible to provide the needed education that would enable the ever-growing population to participate in the life of society.

Furthermore, the challenge has to be faced of recuperating young people and adults who were left at the margins of the educational process, enabling them to recuperate some of the lost time in acquiring the skills and knowledge needed to enter and to face a highly competitive labour market.

The great territorial dimensions of the country

and the specific character of the different regions, determined by historical evolution, have led to a many hued cultural diversity which it is also imperative to take into consideration. To the native Indian population, Portuguese and African stock were added, from the beginning of the century onwards, large contingents of immigrants from Europe and Asia. These immigrants settled in different regions, bringing with them their language, culture, and ways of life. Thus, the country harbours several cultural subgroups that require special attention from education planners to adjust curricula, calendars and timetables to the differences of each region and even of population subgroups.

The federal government has recently started a wide and deep process of educational reform, which includes amendments to the constitution and the approval of new legislation by Congress. Nevertheless, any such process of reform depends, as we know, primarily and fundamentally on reforms that must occur in the classroom; thence the importance of curricular design as a tool to change.

Responsibility for public primary education, including administration of schools and academic organization, falls to the states, the federal district and the municipalities. Primary education is mandatory for all children between the ages of 7 and 14 and is provided free of charge in public establishments, including primary studies for those individuals who did not have access to education at the appropriate age. The curriculum at this level of education is structured around a common core defining nationwide subjects, with a changeable part, established by the normative bodies of the schools, according to their needs and possibilities, in order to take into account local peculiarities.

The full curriculum is set up on the basis of subjects determined at the national and regional levels. Each school is responsible for adopting the method for teaching, as well as for the arrangements required for the ordering and sequence of their respective curricular contents.

In these circumstances, the union's role in primary education is mainly concentrated on providing stimulus for the improvement of quality of education in its various aspects, including general provisions regarding financing and school management, evaluation, distribution of textbooks and school meals and distance education, as well as in offering the guidelines for a national curriculum. National Curricular Standards have been drawn up

that include cross-curricular subjects such as Social Life and Ethics through which issues such as ethics, sex education, the environment, health, economic studies and ethnic plurality can be systematically addressed in the classroom. These themes are included in the curriculum not as independent subjects, but as a part of the conventional areas of study, so as to be present in all of them, relating their contents to issues of actuality. For instance, in the area of the sciences, bodily differences between the sexes may be taught, conveying at the same time respect for individual characteristics.

Education, as a social praxis, is the responsibility not only of the school but of society as a whole through its numerous institutions such as the family, the churches, the media and the workplace.

Social reality, being made up of different social classes and groups, implies the existence of different political allegiances, different values and points of view. It is thus contradictory, plural and has many possible layers of meaning. Its positive values and negative attitudes are therefore also contradictory. However, bearing in mind the fact that society is a historical process permanently on the move, it is possible to understand that these negative attitudes are potentially transformable by social action. It is here that we meet again the role of the school. The school cannot change society by itself, but it can become not only a place of reproduction of social relations but also of resistance to or transformation of these same relations. It can do this by collaborating with other social institutions and groups.

Taking the school as a social institution, we note that it is affected by the same contradictions that run through society. Thus it carries the marks of its time and of its historical and political situation. In these circumstances, we cannot expect the school to transform society without a political-pedagogical plan of action, which will take into account the need to evaluate its performance and deliberately and systematically to move in the direction of change.

The successful accomplishment of this plan depends on understanding that the teacher–pupil relation is a political one and raises the same questions of democracy that are raised in society at large. In the daily relations at school, there is a constant affirmation of opinions, values and positions; some acts are sanctioned, others are not. The teacher's personal demeanour in the classroom, for example, denotes certain modes of behaviour and very often the taking of a stand over what concerns questions of ethical importance. The norms that guide school life are also indicative of behaviour and an ethical stand in that they may admit relations of co-operation and solidarity (among adults, among children, between adults and children), or impose hierarchical rigidity between instances, stimulating individualism, competition and success to be obtained at any cost.

Textbooks, for example, transmit messages, explicitly or implicitly, about values and social roles. It has been noticed that very often women are presented as mother and housewife, whereas men move about in the world of work, outside the home. Men are almost never depicted having affectionate relations with their children or doing housework. Thus conceptions of the social roles of each sex are transmitted to the children.

In the same way, the choice of curricular content can include or exclude specific questions that will enable students to acquire a critical understanding of reality and to use it as a tool to think, to ponder and to decide for themselves about the pressing problems of social life. Alternatively, the choice of contents can give prominence to the transmission of abstract concepts as data to be learned by rote, aiming only at promotion. Thus, evaluation has to be directed to ascertaining the students' capacity for thinking and not their capacity for storing information.

During this process particular attention needs to be given to the ways in which teaching and learning come about, that is, to the methods, the didactic options, the organization and scope of activities that make up the educational experience. This is a key question in favouring the development of autonomy, of good interrelations between groups and of fostering social participation inside and outside the school.

It has to be noted, nevertheless, that contradiction is intrinsic to any social institution and that it is not desirable to pretend to eliminate contradictory values and behaviour in school and teacher practice. This is not a simple process and there are no ready formulae for success. It is rather a question of constantly working together, of establishing an adequate linkage between teaching and learning sustained by a wish to go forward and to transform reality. The results are not controllable either by the school or by any other institution. They will be fused in the crucible of history.

The school's contribution should be to develop a plan of action for education which will foster the development of skills and capacities leading to a critical understanding of reality and to the possibility of creatively transforming the adverse conditions of society. Such a plan should be guided by the following lines:

1   A clear stand should be taken in relation to social questions and the educational task should be interpreted as an intervention in the social and physical environment:
2   Values should not be treated as ideal concepts:
3   This perspective should be held in mind while teaching the curricular contents.

The inclusion of social themes in the school curriculum is not a new question. Given their great importance in the overall education of students, these themes have often been discussed and sometimes included in the areas linked to Social Sciences and to Natural Sciences. Some of them, for example, Environment and Health, have even come to constitute new areas of study. The National Curricular Standards adopt such a view and include these themes in the curriculum in such a way as to form an adequately articulated whole that is open to new themes. Their didactic treatment tries to do justice to their complexity and dynamism and to give them as a place in the curriculum that is as important as the conventional areas. In this way the curriculum will gain in flexibility and openness: such themes may receive priority or significance according to regional or local peculiarities and new themes may be included in the future. The group of themes by the Standards proposed, includes Ethics, Environment, Cultural Diversity, Health and Sexual Education. Ethics constitutes the backbone around which the other themes cluster.

These themes were chosen from many other important issues according to the following criteria:

- *social urgency*: those questions that, by their gravity, prove to be an obstacle to the practice of citizenship and to be an insult to human dignity;
- *national scope*: those questions that prove relevant for the country as a whole;
- *adequacy* for being taught during basic schooling.

The study of Ethics implies the taking of a stand in relation to values. The central question of Ethics concerns justice, understood as inspired by values of equality and equity. Within schools we find Ethics in the relationship between teachers, pupils, staff and parents. It is also found in the other curricular subjects since the acquisition of knowledge is not a pure activity, detached from all other values. It can be found in the area of the other cross-curricular themes which, as is obvious, are involved with values and norms.

In short, the school must be engaged in reflection on the multiple sides of human conduct and one of its major aims must be the stimulus for the development of moral autonomy, as a condition for ethical reflection. Under these circumstances, four content blocs were chosen for special attention: mutual respect, justice, dialogue and solidarity.

Cultural diversity

> Nature and education resemble each other. For education transforms man and thus creates for him a second nature.
>
> Democritus

Cultural diversity is also a major concern. Brazilian society is made up of different ethnic groups and of immigrants from various countries. The country's regions have their own characteristics and harbour some deep cultural differences. This great diversity makes it inevitable that prejudice and discrimination should be found in social and cultural relations. In these circumstances, the school should stress the great wealth contained in ethnic and cultural diversity, making known the specific cultural trends that constitute this precious heritage of Brazilian society. In this sense the school should be a place of dialogue, where the students learn about community life and respect for different forms of cultural expression.

Brazil harbours within its territory approximately 206 Indian groups, a very large population of descendants of African slaves and as large a population of descendants of immigrants of various origins, including large contingents of Japanese, Italians, Germans, Spaniards, French, Jews, Chinese, English, Hungarians, Syrians, Lebanese and Armenians. These groups have brought with them many different languages and are the sources of contact with different cultural traditions, social organization, and ways of relating to nature. The city and the country are also a source of diversified world views, of life rhythms, of modes of transmission of values and of forms of solidarity. This complex and highly fertile process is often ignored or deformed,

particularly when confronted with the larger and more powerful trends of what is called the industry of cultural goods.

Where this diversity is present in the schools, it has been ignored or minimized. There are many reasons for this phenomenon. The high-pitched nationalism that was characteristic of authoritarian political government in Brazilian history favoured the creation of a homogeneous society, in which process the schools played a relevant role. During the 1930s when official policies aimed to assimilate the immigrant population, official documents registered a great concern with what was called the nationalization of their descendants, as well as a subtle but clear-cut racism. These official attitudes were accompanied by mythical views of Brazilian reality, which interpreted the country as blessed with both cultural homogeneity and by a racial democracy. The concept became widely disseminated that Brazil was a country without differences, originally formed by three races – the Indians, the Whites and the Negroes – which had virtually disappeared in their individuality by virtue of strong mixing. This social myth was transmitted by the schools and through textbooks. There also arose the myth that Brazil was open to other inflows of population, in what was deemed a racial democracy. This veiling of reality and of discriminatory practices in Brazilian society pushed into a shadowy zone all the suffering and exclusion which was endemic in society in general.

These trends made a deep mark on the history of schooling in Brazil and have helped to consolidate attitudes and mentalities of which people are generally unaware. This has led to distorted expectations in relation to student performance. Children and adolescents were expected to conform to the pattern of the 'average student'. All dissonant behaviour was regarded as outside the norm and undesirable. Various researches undertaken in this field have demonstrated that there is a high degree of correlation between this expectation on the part of teachers and student performance. The 'average student' proved to be a self-fulfilling prophecy. There was no incentive to do better than the average. However, those children and adolescents from the poor strata of society are expected to perform as well as the average. This puts an enormous strain on their schooling. They find themselves unable to cope and end up dropping out of school. Children are also expected to display an urban behaviour, seen as the only form required and accepted by the school. Thus educational policies have been unfortunately inattentive to regional differences, to social classes and to the specific traits of traditional social groups.

It is important to note that some pedagogical theories have contributed to deepening mistaken attitudes on the part of teachers. These theories have tended to perceive school failure as exclusively due to 'lack of appropriate conditions' for learning, which is a subtle way of undervaluing students and their groups of origin. These educational practices and theories have shifted the responsibility for failure from the school to the student. Together with inadequate curricula and poorly trained teachers, they have left a scar on schooling in Brazil. Among other necessary structural changes, it is imperative that traits peculiar to regions, ethnic groups, schools, teachers and students should be taken into consideration.

The gap between what has been historically preached as the aims and values of democracy on the one hand, and social practices marked by domination, exploration and exclusion on the other, requires an ethical stand on the part of both the school and of the teacher. The suppression of these distortions in the educational field is one of the greatest challenges to educational practice.

In a world which is rapidly moving towards a global society in the economic field, with the attendant still wholly unknown social consequences, it is of the utmost importance to take into consideration and to value the various groups that make up national society. It is important for each student to be assured of being accepted, of having a space to make himself known through his own characteristics and those of his cultural group, and of being able to share with the other students the experiences lived through outside the school, but which nevertheless can be a relevant contribution to the learning process. This means offering children an environment marked by respect, by interest in their modes of expression, by the absorption of the contributions that they bring to school. This philosophy should apply not only to the children, but also in relation to the staff and teachers. This demands sensibility with regard to others and perspicacity in addressing various situations in practice and involves making teachers aware of their fundamental role in this process.

Conclusion

The Ethiopians say that their gods are snub-nosed and black, the Thracians that theirs have light blue eyes and red hair.
                                    Xenophanes, frag. 171

The inclusion of Cultural Diversity in the National Curricular Standards thus proposes to review and to transform unacceptable, unconstitutional and deep-rooted practices. At the same time, it is intended to stimulate the widening and deepening of knowledge of the different groups of population in Brazil, their histories, their values and the lives of their members. Work done with students is directed towards the elimination of causes of suffering, constraint and eventually of social exclusion of the child due to cultural differences. Pedagogically, the theme provides very interesting opportunities to link school, local community and society at large, thus transporting daily and local issues to the wider field of national concerns and vice versa. It is both an aim to be achieved and a means in the educational process.

The teaching of history and geography is especially apt to be carried out from a point of view of diversity. Territorial occupation and population trends can be studied through the history of ethnic groups in Brazil. A complex and fruitful task, this method of teaching can give the students a notion of Brazilian economic development, its sources of wealth, the resulting progress as well as the effects of poverty and injustice on many layers of the population. Basic issues to be addressed include: occupation and conquest, slavery, immigration and internal migration. It will also be important to study the continents that gave origin to the various groups which make up the Brazilian population. Knowledge of the lives of Indian groups, present in the country since time immemorial, is a way of valuing their existence and of ascertaining their rights. The students should be made aware that these groups are not homogeneous and have their own distinctive traits, being the sources of rich cultural diversity. This can be achieved through the inclusion of aspects of their cultures in the school curricula, as well as through a strengthening of Indian schools and their methods of teaching.

Understanding the processes that led to the formation of the European nations and the relations between their history and the age of the great sea voyages of the sixteenth century which gave rise to the close-knit interrelations between their political history and that of the Americas, will give teachers and students the necessary references in terms not only of specific contents but also of the structure and dynamism of mutual influence. This is particularly important at present, when international issues interfere in the daily lives of our citizens in many and variegated manners. Similarly, knowledge of the millenary complexity of the history of the African and Asian continents is of great relevance as a factor of information and education.

The fact that the question of cultural differences has been largely overlooked by the educational system has proved a means of strengthening and maintaining social inequality. Social and economic injustice is supported by ethnic prejudice and discrimination in such a way that it becomes difficult to know if discrimination is due to the ethnic or social factor or to both. It is thus imperative that the question be approached theoretically and in concrete situations from multiple angles.

Culture is a set of symbolic codes through which specific values and a whole world view are transmitted from generation to generation and accepted by a group. The members of a group are reared within this set of symbolic codes from early infancy. Every culture is in a constant process of regeneration, by which new symbols are introduced, others left behind or transformed and new values set up. The social group incessantly transforms and reformulates its cultural codes, adapting the traditional heritage to new circumstances historically given and created by the life of society. Culture is not something fixed and crystallized to be carried by the individual as a burden which may, in certain cases, be a source of stigmatization. In this connection, we should remember that the process of change, intrinsic to any culture, has sometimes inaccurately been seen as a denigration of traditional culture, as a deviation and loss. It must be clearly understood that this process is very different from the forced imposition of foreign elements on a culture from outside.

The theme of cultural diversity can also be worked through by means of the different types of languages that in society take communication well beyond its verbal form. Linked to anthropological elements, this type of work can lead to the correct understanding of the importance of the existence of different linguistic codes and of their interrelation, as a means of integration and expression available to the student. It can be easily taken up during the

study of the Portuguese language, in Arts and in Physical Education, giving place to an enriching appraisal of regional linguistic and artistic manifestations, as well as games and plays. The practice of music, dance and arts in general, linked to the various regional groups, seen as relevant means of expression, help children and young people to grasp the extension and wealth of the country's cultural heritage. At the same time, it fosters the development of their own individual capacity for expression.

When we talk about discrimination, we know that one of its many and complex psychological causes is fear. It is of extreme importance that this fear should be addressed and thought about in order to recognize it for what it really is: the expression of insecurity, often springing from archaic motives. From the side of the discriminator, fear emerges as a reaction to the unknown, seen as menacing. Those who have a different skin colour or speak an unfamiliar language confront other members of society with an unknown reality. These people are seen as 'strange', as 'strangers' and, escaping any attempt at classification, are thought of as 'weird'. Fear feeds on itself: the more one fears the more one shuns the feared object. The way to fight this vicious circle is by means of information, which can be disseminated through texts, videos, newspapers, newsletters. From the side of those discriminated against, fear emerges as a feeling of being constantly menaced. Its extreme manifestation is the fear of being physically eliminated. Discrimination always carries contents of violence, even if only in a symbolic form. These contents give rise to exclusion and fear of elimination. Thus it is of the utmost importance to provide students with elements that help them to shun social exclusion in daily practice and to adopt attitudes in accordance with equity.

It is possible to fight discrimination and its attendant sequels through adequate school programmes. Nevertheless, it should be remembered that these problems are not essentially questions of individual behaviour, but of social relations historically brought about and enjoying a measure of stability and permanence. In these circumstances, the school must become a space of resistance to these undesired historical practices, helping to create other forms of social relationship, by means of interaction between educational work in the classroom and relations among students, teachers and staff. Social questions should be viewed critically and in a responsible manner whenever they come up. The school should thus foster confidence, permitting teachers and children to understand that the cultural characteristics they share with their group can be accepted as part of their life circumstances and not prove an obstacle to the development of their personal potentiality.

Respectful mutual knowledge must include many modes of communication, as well as the opportunity for the student to take on the role of the teacher in matters that concern his cultural background. Teachers should co-operate with them, learning at the same time as the other members of the class.

This is a relevant activity in creating awareness that society, in all its complexity, is an object of constant study, providing the occasion for everyone to learn.

All these reforms – of which curricular formulation is only a small albeit important part – represent the formidable task that the federal government has set itself. In a country the size of Brazil, with a total of around 1,000,700 teachers in primary and secondary education who are frequently inadequately trained, there are understandably enormous difficulties to overcome. This should not deter us from beginning to carry out the many reforms that are so urgently and sorely needed.

11 Values: The Western Australian Experience
An Overview of a Three-year Project

KAREN CAPLE

Introduction

The National Professional Development Programme (NPDP) Values Review Project in Western Australia has been proactively investigating the extent to which values can be explicitly integrated into a school curriculum, in particular one framed within an outcomes based context.

The NPDP Values Review Project was one of eighteen projects undertaken in Western Australia over a three-year period through Commonwealth government funding, all under the co-ordination of the WA Cross-sectoral Consortium (1994–6). This consortium comprised representatives from each of the WA government, independent, Anglican and Catholic school authorities, the government and non-government teachers' unions, representatives from professional and subject associations and the WA Council of Deans of Education.

The National Professional Development Programme (NPDP) was a Commonwealth initiative where funds were made available to the states and territories, over a three-year period, for teacher Professional Development (PD) activities. These funds supported national initiatives in education, by recognizing the importance of ongoing teacher renewal to improve educational outcomes for students. The activities undertaken were to address the following goals:

- facilitate the use of curriculum statements and profiles for Australian schools, key competencies and the teaching of accredited vocational education courses in schools:
- assist the renewal of teacher discipline knowledge and teaching skills and help teachers to improve work organization practices and teaching competencies within schools;

- enhance the professional culture of teachers and encourage teacher organizations to take a higher profile in promoting professional development;
- promote partnerships between educational authorities, teacher organizations, principals' associations and universities in the provision of professional development opportunities for teachers.

Foundations in 1993

A perceived lack of an explicit values dimension in the National Statements and Profiles being developed for National Curriculum Framework in 1993 motivated a group of individuals from the non-government schooling sector in Western Australia, to initiate the Values Project. Prior to this, the Education Department of WA had commenced working on Student Outcome Statements (SOS), a set of desired outcomes in eight learning areas for monitoring student achievement. Both of these initiatives signalled a concern as to the lack of an explicit values dimension.

At this time, Rev. Dr Tom Wallace, Chaplain and Education Consultant for the Anglican Schools Commission in WA, convened a meeting to discuss this apparent lack of values within the proposed outcomes being developed at both national and state levels. A number of questions were raised and discussed at this meeting:

- Could SOS be modified to include a more specific reference to values?
- Which values should be identified in each of the Learning Areas?
- Could values be integrated into a student

outcomes framework that was sequentially developed into eight levels?

- How could both teachers and schools integrate values more effectively and explicitly into classroom practice and school life?

Thus the NPDP Values Review Project was born with the general aim of determining the extent to which values could be explicitly integrated into a curriculum that may be framed by Student Outcome Statements and current curriculum practices.

After funding was granted by the Commonwealth and directed to the WA Cross-sectoral Consortium for distribution, the Project was initiated and managed by a group, reflecting the partners represented in the Consortium. This Management Group[1] was initially termed a Reference Committee and has helped guide and advise on the work and direction of the Project since 1994.

Values – What are they?

The first major step for the Project was to explore the possibility of obtaining some central starting point and consensus position in relation to those values that should be integrated into a curriculum. The notion of what is a value revolved around two key definitions:

1 Values are determined by beliefs we hold. They are the ideas about what someone or a group thinks is important in life and they play a very important part in our decision making. We express our values in the way we think and act (Lemin *et al.*, 1994, p. 1).
2 Values are the priorities individuals and society attach to certain beliefs, experiences and objects in deciding how they will live and what they will treasure (Hill, 1994).

A values framework

Early in 1995 the Project was successful in publishing the *Agreed Minimum Values Framework* document that took into account both the multicultural and pluralistic natures of our society. The work on this document commenced late in 1994 with a group of consultants[2] given the task of developing some form of framework to represent a baseline agreement in values that could assist individual groups to identify the values which are specific to their needs and be able to integrate them into a curriculum. This document represented a consensus position on values within the non-government schooling sector.

The framework is presented in three levels: Ultimate, Democratic and Educational values. The theistic or religious position was expressed within the *Ultimate Level*, concerning those values with a view of God and the place of humanity in the world. While each faith group has its own respective beliefs, a large amount of consensus or agreement on values was attained within this Ultimate level.

The values listed under the *Democratic Level* were seen as a procedural notion, that of negotiating a values agreement at a practical level within society. As a minimum, democracy consists of a society in which all groups have equal rights to participate in the political process, as long as they do not infringe upon the rights of others. For this reason, it was suggested that people holding different Ultimate values may be prepared to accept a number of different values whose practical justification is the maintenance of a viable democratic state and sustainable environment.

The *Educational Level* represented even more consensus agreement on values in relation to knowledge. This level draws upon the values intrinsic to the knowledge it seeks to impart, and also the ethics of providing instruction to human beings within the constraints of a compulsory classroom. The *Agreed Minimum Values Framework* states:

> The educational value that rescues all values education from the tendency to relapse into indoctrination is the commitment to build students up in their capacity to reflect critically on the value traditions to which they are heir, and to make informed personal choices about them.

Within these three levels, four themes are generated:

- life perspectives;
- individual;
- society;
- natural world.

Under these themes are listed the sixty values contained within the framework, with all values being defined to give a context for their existence. For example, equality, is defined as: 'We affirm the equal worth and basic rights of all persons, regardless of differences in race, gender, ability, and religious belief.' These value words have been used collectively by the Project, as listed below, to generate debate and consensus on an agreed values dimension within educational initiatives, planning and curriculum development. The value words listed within the *Agreed Minimum Values Framework* are as listed in their four themes: in Table 11.1.

This NPDP Values Review Project *Agreed Minimum Values Framework* document is now currently being used as a tool for individual schools, systems or sectors, communities or religious groups to create or refine their own values framework to suit their own needs and purposes. The framework has provided the foundation to all work undertaken within the Project in relation to curriculum development and trialling, in both areas of Classroom Practice and School Planning.

An audit of values

The next step of the Project was to conduct an audit of the educational outcomes for students developed in Western Australia, entitled Student Outcome Statements (SOS), to determine first whether there was some explicit reference to values, and second, whether or not these SOS contained any obvious value conflict for non-government schools and teachers within each Learning Area.

The study by thirty-seven teachers from the non-government schooling sector clearly indicated that values, using the *Agreed Minimum Values Frame-*

work document as a guide, were not explicitly accommodated within the SOS. It was concluded that the SOS seemed to provide a fairly neutral framework into which teachers could integrate particular key values if they wished. Teachers noted that a surprising number of values integrated into their classroom practice were indeed implicit in many of the SOS. However, very few were explicit. The explicit reference to three clusters of values in the Learning Area[3] of Studies of Society and Environment seemed to fit within the Project's framework (AMVF). The work of this audit is contained within the document *Values Audit Trials on Student Outcome Statements* (NPDP, 1995).

1995 School trials

This small, initial study involved teachers from nine non-government schools exploring the possibility of integrating values derived from the AMVF, explicitly into their classroom practice. These case studies involved six key Learning Areas, one whole school case study on Language and Communication and one case study by a principal on a whole school approach to values integration. These case studies included samples of lessons, programmes and worksheets from the trial teachers and are contained in the NPDP Values Review Project document *Values in the School Community: School Trials*

Table 11.1 Value words

Life perspectives	Individual	Society	Natural world
After-life	Access	Authority	Conservation of the environment
Family	Caring	Benefits of research	Development
Freedom of worship	Citizenship	Community	Diversity of species
God as Creator	Compassion	Conflict resolution	Domains of knowledge
God as Self-revealer	Empowerment	Contribution	Environmental responsibility
Knowledge	Equality	Critical reflection	Exploitation
Personal meaning	Imperfection	Diversity	Nature is good
Religion	Individual differences	Family	Quest for truth
Religious freedom	Individual uniqueness	Morality	Rehabilitation
Religious quest	Learning climate	Multiculturalism	Science and values
Search for knowledge	Open to learn	Participation	Stewardship
Spirituality	Opportunity	Reconciliation	Sustainable development
Study of world views	Responsibility	School as community	
Value systems	Responsibility and freedom	Social justice	
	Social nature	The Common good	
	Tolerance	Value dimension	
		Welfare	

Source: *Agreed Minimum Values Framework*, NPDP Values Review Project, 1995

(1995), completed by Dr Norrine Anderson on contract to the Project.

The case studies from this trialling demonstrated clearly that values are inherent within education and can be integrated more explicitly when they are clearly articulated in programmes and classroom practice. The following reflections from three of the trial teachers, highlight that values are an integral part of schooling:

> Peter took into his class a newspaper article describing an error in an IVF case where twins, one white and one black, had been born to a Dutch mother. Peter invited discussion, and it was clear students were seeing a need to be responsible. Said one: 'It's really sad that people do not realize that they are playing God and it is people who have to live with it.' (Report of a Science lesson, p. 27).

> I do believe that when teaching values, you have to be honest but you have to be careful in terms of giving your views and careful not to indoctrinate kids and make them feel your view is the only view. If they ask you what you think you have to be honest enough to say 'Well, this is what I feel, and this is why I feel that and this is how I've come to that conclusion. However the discussions that come from your parents may be different and you need to look at why Mum and Dad say and where they are coming from.' (A teacher of Social Studies, p. 82).

> I try to create an environment where kids will value commitment, endeavour and a striving for excellence, valuing each other and themselves. All our music rehearsals are at 7.30am in the morning. So there's a pretty big value statement they're making just being there. Then you watch them under pressure. I think that's a very important way of learning to value themselves. (A music teacher, p. 78)

This document reflects the importance of this initial trialling completed by the Project during 1995. Anderson points out, for example, 'the possibilities for the integration of subjects through values education' and the significant impact of the trial and the application of the values framework in helping to direct the professional development of staff and providing a coherence to planning at the school level.

The final two paragraphs from the document are particularly important to reflect upon:

> Those of us who are both teachers and parents will readily acknowledge the frustrations of young ado-

lescents for whom the school offering is 'boring' and for whom the constraints of conforming behaviour above all else denies any possibility of engagement with education. The *Agreed Minimum Values Framework* affirms the need to equip students with the tools to examine world-views, both religious and non-religious, especially those dominant in their background and school community. It acknowledges the need of all persons for a sense of personal meaning, and encourages critical reflection on questions constituting the self in relation to the natural and social worlds. It affirms the tentative and limited nature of socially constructed knowledge, and the need to make students aware of this.

A focus on critical thinking, creative imagination, and interpersonal and vocational skills would indeed enhance those 'basic skills' which comprise the current curriculum. Potential for critical reflection on both the cultural heritage and the attitudes and values underlying current social trends and institutions would go a long way to equip young people to respond to their society. In other words, it is time to bring into our schools a postmodern view of the knowledge and learning that might more appropriately prepare them for the 21st Century. The *Agreed Minimum Values Framework* provides a starting point for this much needed reform of schooling.

The development of value outcome statements

To address the issue of values being omitted from the Student Outcome Statements (WA version), a writing trial of creating new outcome statements or rewriting existing outcome statements was conducted in late 1995. A small team of experienced teachers was brought together for each of the eight Learning Areas to explore the ways in which the current SOS could be amended to include a more specific reference to values. The work of this trial was contained in the NPDP Values Review Project *Report to the State Reference Committee on SOS: Integrating Values into Student Outcome Statements* (Confidential Report).

In summary the report's findings were:

- Some existing SOS could be rewritten to include a more explicit values dimension.
- In some Learning Areas it was possible to develop new strands or substrands to carry values development through the eight levels.

In the light of the case sometimes put forward that to assess values outcomes is to endorse indoctrination, this trial signalled that this need not be so, especially if the emphasis is on measuring capacity rather than commitment. This trial also highlighted that the availability of the *Agreed Minimum Values Framework* has made the task of integrating values into curriculum writing much easier.

This was a valuable exercise by the Project in relation to highlighting the need for a values perspective to be integrated into outcome-based education. It is noteworthy that since this report was presented in December 1995, values have become a part of the agenda in relation to current developments within the Interim Curriculum Council (frameworks) and the Education Department of WA (refinement of SOS).

School trialling 1996

In 1996 the work of the Project continued and consolidated its trialling by undertaking two main focus areas:

- Teachers and Classroom Practice;
- School Planning.

Teachers and Classroom practice trial

The Teachers and Classroom action research trial involved 44 teachers from both primary (31) and secondary (13) backgrounds in government (24) and non-government (20) schools. It assisted teachers to integrate their chosen, self-determined set of values into their classroom practice. This chosen set of values, using the *Agreed Minimum Values Framework* as a tool in conjunction with their own School Vision Statement, was integrated explicitly into the teachers' programmes. The aim of this action research trial was to investigate and document how these values were integrated into their teaching and classroom practice.

A curriculum package written by a contract writer[4] in consultation with the Projects Management Committee, was developed and trialled by the teachers. This package was a process for teachers to follow and contained strategies and resources for teachers to use. Schools involved in the trial were:

All Saints College	Mirrabooka Primary School
Australian Islamic College	Neerigen Brook Primary School
Beldon Primary School	Palmyra Primary School
Belmont Senior High School	Parkerville Primary School
Caversham Primary School	Perth College
Chrysalis Montessori School	Port Community High School
East Maddington Primary School	St Brigid's College
John Septimus Roe Anglican Community School	St Mary's Anglican Girls School
Kingsway Christian College	St Matthew's Narrogin
Lance Holt School	St Patrick's Primary School
Maddington Senior High School	Swanbourne Primary School
	Wembley Primary school

The curriculum package that was developed and is now available for purchase contains both the trialled process and individual case studies. The process developed proved to be an excellent pathway for classroom teachers to follow for explicitly identifying and integrating values into their classroom practice.

Table 11.2 outlines the process section of the NPDP Values Review Project *Values in Education: Classroom Curriculum Package*:

Table 11.2 Classroom practice trial planning process

1 *Introduction*	• Rationale for teaching values
	• Definition of terms
2 *Getting started*	• Integrating values into teaching
	• Articulating values
	• Creating your own School Values Statement
3 *The classroom environment*	• The worlds of a teacher
	• What is your own values stance as a teacher?
	• How can you establish an appropriate classroom environment to promote values development?
	• How do children learn best?
	• What kind of language do you use as a teacher?
4 *Programming*	• Ten steps to creating your own programme unit of work
	• Action Research model
5 *Assessment and reporting*	
6 *Strategies and resources*	

Source: *Values in Education: Classroom Curriculum Package*, Grellier, 1997

Results from the trial[6]

Each teacher involved in the trial derived a set of core shared values from documents that existed in the school at the time, from publications from their schooling sectors and from the *Agreed Minimum Values Framework* to create their own School Values Statement[5]:

> I presented a suggested list of values from the *Agreed Minimum Values Framework*, together with a copy of the Framework to my colleagues at a staff meeting. The selection of values was a challenging task but I was guided by the School Aims and Objectives booklet, our Pastoral care Policy and the curriculum initiatives we had put into practice in the Junior School.   (Year 5 teacher)

> I worked alone and began by going to our School Code of Ethics and highlighting all of the words that I felt held a value. I then circled the values from the *Agreed Minimum Values Framework* that interested me. From these I created a priority of values that I felt were the most fundamental.   (Year 7 teacher)

> The statement was created through a consultative process involving the values trial teachers, who presented a draft statement to the school staff for endorsement. Parents were also consulted through a Parents and Citizens Association meeting and endorsed the statement. The values incorporated within the statement were selected from the school performance indicators, school behaviour management policy and the *Agreed Minimum Values Framework*.   (Years 1–7 teachers)

> Selection of 'Trial Values' was quite a difficult task so I can see that a School Values Statement really must be in place first before teachers can be expected to introduce values as a matter of course . . . Creating a School Values Statement is a big task and needs the full commitment of a coordinated and supportive committee.   (Year 6 teacher)

Most teachers were surprised at how easy it was for them to integrate values. Rather than making vast changes to their programmes and teaching styles, they added the extra dimension of values through carefully chosen questions or activities:

> I had already planned my program in Society and Environment for the Term, so I had to decide which values I wanted to cover 'post programming'. I broke down each lesson to find out where values would fit best, and then altered the focus of the lesson.   (Year 3 Teacher).

> Integrating values into my teaching was not

difficult. It involved some thought at the planning stage of programming merely because it was different. It involved teaching in a different way – therefore different activities needed to be arranged. This was refreshing for both my class and me. Many useful classroom activities would not have been undertaken if values teaching had not occurred.   (Year 3 teacher)

Others stressed that they had always programmed with values in mind but that this trial allowed them to make these values explicit:

> I appreciated the opportunity to make more explicit something I had been doing anyway. I think it is really important that we'd make our own values overt and that we give the students opportunities to explore and formulate theirs.   (Year 9 teacher)

> I have no difficulty in programming values into my lessons. It is something I have always done in the past. It is inherent in the very 'social' nature of the subject, but in the present context I find the highlighting of 'values in education' certainly makes more conscious of the need for closer correlation with student outcomes.   (Year 2 teacher)

The classroom atmosphere was considered vital by many, particularly as fostered by the teacher's own attitudes, value stance and relationship with the students:

> The development of a positive classroom climate does not happen immediately but over a period of time and as a result of the consistent promotion and demonstration of positive values and behaviours. Its development is fundamental to the success of any values based programme and the most powerful determinant is the teacher – being genuine and sincere will not solve all the problems but will help you to develop the trust which will allow a student to at least explore different values and the notion of choice.   (Year 4 teacher)

> I consciously avoided standing in front of the children and informing them of the values that we were 'going to learn'. The aim was for the children to experience the activity first and then draw their own conclusions from the following discussions. I tried to alter my normal lesson as little as possible and not make the value teaching too obvious. It was hoped that the message would be better absorbed with a subtle approach.   (Year 6–7 teacher)

Several teachers commented that they were still in the process of developing a new approach to class activities, which they found exciting but challenging:

> It is taking me some time to become used to my new role in discussions. I even have to watch my body language. I'm so pleased I decided to incorporate the values into my philosophy programme because philosophy lessons see me as the facilitator, modelling procedures of inquiry but also taking a stance of committed impartiality – this has been emphasized during the trial. (Year 5 teacher)

> I avoided directly teaching a particular value. Instead, I used activities which helped students to consider and reflect on a variety of points of view which enabled them to develop an opinion and belief. Sometimes I found this difficult because I held a particular belief very strongly. (Year 6 teacher)

A large number of teachers reported that students were strongly involved and interested in the trialling, even groups of students who tended to be negative towards school:

> There was more involvement by all students in the lessons. It was noticeable that there was a keener response from those students who are normally reluctant to participate in discussions. Although there was an improvement in the oral discussion level, this improvement did not flow through to the students' written work. (Year 6 teacher)

> I believe that more students were on task and producing worthwhile work while working on these projects than one might usually expect. (Year 9 teacher)

> The language that they used when discussing interpersonal issues changed noticeably. Their reflective writing also demonstrated their increased understanding. (Year 9 teacher)

The complete account of the process trialled and the practical outworkings of the theory are contained in the NPDP Values Review Curriculum Package (1997), available from the Project Office.[7]

School Planning trial

The School Planning trial involved the Principal and the School Planning Team from 20 schools, again cross-sectoral representation from government (10) and non-government (10) schools. The trial assisted individual schools clearly to identify the key values of their school and then facilitated the integration of these values into the school community through the process of school planning, policy development and curriculum design. The process of selecting the appropriate key values to form a School Values Statement for each individual school was an important feature of the trial, using existing school documents and the NPDP Values Review Project Agreed Minimum Values Framework. This trial process was facilitated into schools by four key facilitators, trained by the Project, through individual meetings and workshops with the Principal and members of the School Planning team. The Schools involved in this area of the trialling were:

All Saints College	Mirrabooka Primary
Australian Islamic College	School
Beldon Primary School	Neerigen Brook Primary
Belmont Senior High	School
School	Palmyra Primary School
Chrysalis Montessori	Parkerville Primary School
School	Port Community High
East Maddington Primary	School
School	St Brigid's College
John Septimus Roe	St Matthew's Narrogin
Anglican Community	St Mary's AGS Junior
School	School
Kingsway Christian	Swanbourne Primary
College	School
Lance Holt School	Wembley Primary School
Maddington Senior High	
School	

This component of the trialling has complemented the action research completed within the Classroom Practice trial detailed in the above section. Individual schools that undertook both components of the trialling experienced a level of commitment far greater than those schools involved in only one facet of the trial.

The NPDP Values Review Project *Values In Education: School Planning Package* (1997) developed from the trialling contains a process component, in addition to individual case studies containing examples of good practice in terms of School Values Statements, strategies for integrating values explicitly into the areas of Policy, Pastoral Care and Priority, and also informed comments on consulting the school community at large.

Table 11.3 outlines the process section of the NPDP Values Review Project *Values in Education: School Planning Package.*

Results from the trial[8]

Participant schools had various reasons and interests for undertaking the trial in this area of school planning:

Table 11.3   School values planning process

1 *Introduction*	• Rationale for teaching values
2 *Why values integration is important*	• Values are fundamental in schools
	• Reaching agreement of a set of shared values
	• The case for Spiritual Values in education
	• Benefits for members of the school community
	• A whole school approach
3 *The pathway*	• How to initiate values integration in your school
	• Creating your School Values Statement
	• Communication and consultation strategies
	• Implementing your School Values Statement
4 *Ongoing strategies*	
5 *Resources*	

It was apparent that our school policy document did not clearly state the values that we as a staff were wishing to focus on in the school. We saw that value words and phrases were buried in the official Mission Statement and Performance Indicators. (Parkerville Primary School)

As part of a system-wide, cyclical process of school review and renewal over a period of 5 years, our school was about to review its Vision Statement and related Aims and Goals. This Values Review Trial matched closely the process of review needing to be carried out, and also supported the classroom trial being conducted within the school. (St Matthew's Catholic School)

We have long sought to overtly articulate the 'hidden curriculum' of our school and this Values trial seemed to be an ideal vehicle to pursue this goal. (Chrysalis Montessori School)

A major step within the process developed was the recognition that each school should examine its current position on values and build upon this foundation:

Although we had never before had a written Values Charter or Statement, we knew that there were certain beliefs, attitudes and actions that were held and practised within the school ... this lack of a written statement however, made it difficult to impart specifically the values and beliefs that underlie the school's operations. (Lance Halt School)

The educational priorities in our school included an ongoing focus for managing student behaviour and implementation of a whole school approach for catering for children with learning difficulties. Both of these priorities affirm important values for an individual child, which if highlighted by a separate values statement would gain focus in their own right. (Parkerville Primary School)

We reviewed our Schools Vision Statement to assess the inherent and explicitly expressed values it contained. (St Matthew's Catholic School)

In the establishment of a School Values Statement during the trial process, the emphasis was placed upon extensive consultation to gain a shared or 'owned' School Values Statement within each school:

Initial meetings, including our first staff meeting were held with our key facilitator. We identified the values stated within existing documents in a whole staff workshop, e.g. performance indicators. We then brainstormed other values and the list was displayed in the staffroom for a week. During this time the staff, including support staff (e.g. library, canteen, teacher aides) and members of the P and C, were able to add any values they felt were important to the school community. At the end of the week all staff and P and C were given the opportunity to vote on the six values they felt were most important for our school. The School Values Planning Team then developed six statements which would make up our School Statement. (Mirrabooka Primary School)

One to initiate the project and a second to work on the formulation of a possible implementation plan (... a facilitated workshop with the key facilitator ...). The basis, process and purpose of the review were expressed to the *parish*, through the Parish Priest; the *parents*, through the P and F association and School Board meetings; the *staff*, at staff meetings; the *upper students*, through class discussion related to the questionnaire and other related issues; and *past students*, through a willing ex student at the local high school. (St Matthew's Catholic School)

The second phase of the trial was to 'action' the School Values Statement into school planning, by exploring strategies of explicitly integrating the core values selected by the school:

This fits with our current School Philosophy. As a Priority School a large part of our emphasis in the last three years has been on Self Esteem – children getting to know themselves and respect others. These programmes will continue with perhaps more reflection on the values as stated. (Mirrabooka Primary School)

For us, this Project was not to be a list of unattainable values that set about to change the children's behaviour form current practice. Rather we would identify those values seen in our everyday actions, reflected by the way we as a community interact and by the best practice of our classroom teachers. We believe we develop those values listed in our SVS by the following practice: whole school meeting, rules, cross age programmes, social skill sessions, education of the whole child, staff, community and relationships. (Lance Holt School)

We have decided to increase the teaching of philosophy and develop the concept of Classroom, Community of Inquiry. We will also continue with our positive affirmation and plan accordingly – award structure affirmation days, opportunities for students to mix effectively across age groups and to work collaboratively. Values will be also public via the newsletter, assemblies, Chapel services, our school publications. Values will continue to be on every agenda for staff planning. (St Mary's AGS)

Throughout the trialling period a number of highlights were apparent, both intended and unintended:

Staff receptiveness to the idea of values in education as well as the input by parents of the P and C. (Mirrabooka Primary School)

The opportunity to work very closely with parents on a project in which we all had a keen interest and from which occasions arose in which parents rather than teachers facilitated meetings for other parents. (St Matthew's Catholic School)

The most significant highlight was the chance to discuss the 'deeper' issues at length. The chance to explore this was richly rewarding and very interesting. (St Brigid's College)

The rapport and creativity that was developed and encouraged amongst group members made the process enjoyable for all those concerned. The final draft is a useable and valuable document which appears to have been well received and supported by all staff. This will have a very positive impact on the school planning process and on the perception of the school in the community. (East Maddington Primary School)

The initial concern about the process of priority selection being turned into a positive commitment for Values as a school priority. (Palmyra Primary School)

The main highlight was the opportunity to review our existing structures and processes and evaluate the extent to which the values were finding their way into every day practice in the organisation. (Kingsway Christian College)

The development of a School Values Statement gave us the opportunity to openly discuss values education in a government school. Many teachers believed this was outside their job description. (Parkerville Primary School)

The trial's highlight was the staff reflection, commitment to action and especially the staff team unification that was brought about by the trials implementation. (Australian Islamic College)

Despite the highlights of the trial, some schools experienced difficulties:

Our only difficulty was in keeping the focus strictly on values as distinct from attitudes and beliefs. (St Matthew's Catholic School)

Not a serious or obviously apparent difficulty, but there are a few staff members not so convinced or supportive. (Swanbourne Primary School)

Yes, some staff have philosophical issues with 'values in education': these have yet to be resolved: concern expressed with accountability in this area. (Beldon Primary School)

Initially we had to overcome the concept that 'values education' meant 'religious education'. Once this idea was expanded to include democratic and educational values, most people were happy to explore further. (Parkerville Primary School)

We had no difficulties in recognizing the importance of values in education. The only difficult area for our community is the concept of GOD, particularly as expressed in the Ultimate section of the *Agreed Minimum Values Framework*. Whilst we did not wish to ignore this section, we did seek to separate spirituality from any set religion. To us, the values we uphold in daily action are indeed an expression of any meaningful definition of God. (Chrysalis Montessori School)

In addition to the highlights of the trial, a number of schools commented on the effect that the trial had on the wider school community:

There appears to be a greater consciousness about the importance of bringing values more into the fore. (Mirrabooka Primary School)

Renewed and increased awareness of, and interest in, the values promoted by our school. (St Matthew's Catholic School)

The group are very enthusiastic and are considering values much more explicitly and implicitly in all their professional duties. Parents appear to be pleased that the school has a statement of values which they appear to endorse. (East Maddington Primary School)

It has brought parents and staff into a closer working relationship and a relationship that has shared values. The school is a happier environment. There have been fewer disciplinary problems. (St Mary's AGS)

It has already broadened the perspective of teachers on the curriculum. 'Extra' activities have been viewed as integral and fundamental curriculum initiatives. (Chrysalis Montessroi School)

The values effort has provided a unified staff focus on the one Project as well as providing an opportunity for staff to review and renew their commitment to these values ideals. (Australian Islamic College)

Created an excitement among students in terms of gaining fair treatment by teachers in the classroom. They saw this as a means by which relationships between students and teachers would be improved. (Kingsway Christian College)

NPDP Values Review Conference[9]

Students, schools and values: exploring values outcomes for schools in the twenty-first century

On 1 June 1996, the Project held a one-day conference for principals, school administrators and educators engaging local, interstate and overseas speakers on the issue of values and their importance in education. Professor David Aspin (Monash University, Melbourne) spoke on the nature of values and their place and promotion in schools. He emphasized that values are already there within schools, in all the activities that make up the life of a school.

Professor Brian Hill (Murdoch University, Perth) addressed the issue of designing a values curriculum for schools. He regarded values education as unavoidable and that the use of a democratic charter (i.e. NPDP Values Review Project Agreed

Minimum Values Framework) of values was a must in the selection of key values for content areas within the curriculum. Dr Mal Leicester, a guest of the Project from Warwick University (UK), presented the UK perspective on values education. She detailed the work, both past and present, being undertaken in the UK and some European countries on this issue of values within education, in addition to providing valuable insight and feedback on the NPDP Values Project. It is important to note here that the level of work being undertaken here in WA by the NPDP Values Project has not been carried out anywhere in the world to date, according to Dr Leicester.

The conference was both affirming for the work being undertaken by the Project and also provided an avenue for showcasing to all present the need for a values dimension in all current educational initiatives.

Other associated initiatives in Western Australia

The NPDP Values Review Project has achieved additional unintended outcomes in curriculum developments in Western Australia (WA). A cross-sectoral independent body, the Curriculum Council of Western Australia, has been formed by the government to review and formulate curriculum frameworks for all schools in WA. This council has adopted the position of having an explicit values dimension in its framework, and has created a Values Position Paper (or Charter) based on the Project's Agreed Minimum Values Framework. Throughout 1997 the framework writers and consultation groups will address this explicit values dimension in each of eight curriculum frameworks, in addition to the overarching framework.

The Education Department of WA (government school system), creators of the Student Outcome Statements (WA version) mentioned earlier, are undertaking a curriculum review of these outcomes and are now ensuring that values are appropriately represented in each of the eight Learning Areas of Student Outcome Statements.

Conclusion

The National Professional Development Programme in Australia has provided a valuable pathway for the Values Review Project to undertake major developments in the field of values in education. The establishment of the Agreed Minimum Values Framework has been recognized as a first and its usage in two aspects of trialling has been unmatched.

The Packages available from the Project, *School Trialling* and *Classroom Practice* (incorporating the *Agreed Minimum Values Framework*) are assets to any educational or community group throughout the world, recognizing multicultural diversity in all facets.

Notes

1 The Management Group of the NPDP Values Project:
  Rev. Dr Tom Wallace (Chair), Anglican Schools Commission
  Mr Glenn Bennett, Education Department of WA
  Ms Karen Caple, Project Co-ordinator
  Assoc. Professor Cynthia Dixon, Edith Cowan University
  Dr Ian Fraser, Association of Independent Schools (WA)
  Mr Tony Giglia, Catholic Education Office of WA
  Mr Peter Havel (Inaugural Project Co-ordinator), Kingsway Christian College
  Mr Tim McDonald, Australian Association of Religious Education
  Mr Chris Reimers, Catholic Education Office of WA
  Mrs Frances van Riessen, Secondary Education Authority

2 The consultants involved in the establishment of the Agreed Minimum Values Framework were:
  Dr Mark Debowski, Australian Islamic College
  Assoc. Professor Cynthia Dixon, Edith Cowan University
  Professor Jack Dwyer, Notre Dame University
  Mr Peter Havel, Project Co-ordinator
  Professor Brian Hill, Murdoch University
  Father Gerry Holohan, Catholic Education Office of WA
  Mr Yaakov Levi, Carmel Jewish School
  Rev. Dr Tom Wallace, Anglican Schools Commission

3 Key Learning Areas: in Western Australia the curriculum has been categorized into eight Key Learning Areas, derived in part from investigations into a national curriculum. These are: the Arts, English, Health and Physical Education, Languages other than English (LOTE), Mathematics, Science, Studies of Society and Environment, and Technology and Enterprise.

4 The curriculum writer contracted to undertake the formation of the process package was Ms Jane Grellier from Jane Munroe and Associates.

5 A School Values Statement as defined by the NPDP Values Review Project is a simple collection of values to affirm a set of shared values for the school community and exists as a subset of a school's development plan or vision/mission statement.

6 The curriculum package *Classroom Practice* (1997) developed by the NPDP Values Review Project, is available from the Project Office. This package contains the trialled process and full annotations of the 44 case studies from the trialling. An expanded account of this trial can be found in *Explicit Values in the Classroom. Is it Possible?* (London: Cassell).

7 The NPDP Values Review Project Office is located at:
  Association of Independent Schools of WA
  3/41 Walters Drive
  Herdsman Business Park
  Osborne Park WA 6017
  Western Australia
  Telephone: 08 9244 2788
  Fax: 08 9244 2786
  E-mail:aiswa@ais.wa.edu.au

8 The NPDP Curriculum Package *School Planning* (1997) is available for purchase from the Project Office. An expanded account of this trial can be located in *Values in School Planning. Can they be Explicit?* (London: Cassell).

9 The Conference held in Perth Western Australia has been reproduced onto four videos which can be purchased from the Project Office.

References

Anderson, N. (1995) *Values in the School Community: School Trials*. Osborne Park: NPDP.

Hill, B. (1994) *Teaching Secondary Social Studies in a Multi-cultural Society*. Longman Chesire: Melbourne

Lemin, M., Potts, H. and Welsford, P. (eds) (1994) *Values Strategies for Classroom Teachers*. Hawthorn Victoria: ACER.

NPDP Values Review Project (1995) *Agreed Minimum Values Framework*. Osborne Park: NPDP.

NPDP Values Review Project (1997) *Values in Education: Classroom Curriculum Package*. Osborne Park: NPDP.

NPDP Values Review Project (1997) *Values In Education: School Planning Package*. Osborne Park: NPDP.

NPDP Values Review Project (1995) *Values Audit Trials on Student Outcome Statements*. Osborne Park: NPDP.

Set of 4 videos: *Values in Education*, featuring four keynote conference speakers. (*Western Australia*) *1995*. Osborne Park: NPDP.

12 Biculturalisms (and Antiracisms) in Education in New Zealand
An Overview

JENNIE HARRÉ HINDMARSH

Increasingly, Pakeha-dominated educational organizations in New Zealand have been faced with challenges, from within and from outside, to change their structures, processes and outcomes to become more 'bicultural'. These challenges have not been confined to education – organizations in all spheres of New Zealand society have been engaged in a similar journey. The term 'biculturalism' has been constructed with particular localized meanings. In New Zealand 'biculturalism' generally refers to Pakeha (non-indigenous) attempts to address the racisms and inequities which have been colonizing and oppressing Maori, the tangata whenua (indigenous peoples). In addressing such racisms and inequities, biculturalisms are conceptualized as ways to develop structures and processes which 'honour Te Tiriti o Waitangi' (the Treaty of Waitangi), the founding document of the country signed between many rangatira (chiefs) and the British Crown in 1840 (see Glossary in Table 12.1).

While acknowledging the way in which our pursuit of policies and practices based on some contemporary ideas of 'biculturalism' and 'antiracism' have challenged and loosened the strangle hold of Pakeha-dominated structures in education – opening up new organizational, political and cultural spaces – it can also be observed that the more things appear to have changed, at a more fundamental level the more they have been staying the same. Predominantly, attempts to develop more bicultural institutions most often have not led to the hoped for radically different relationships of power and control. However, in some traditionally Pakeha-controlled community, continuing and professional education organizations, more radical shifts in relationships of power and control have occurred and there is much to learn from reflecting

Table 12.1 Glossary of Maori terms used

Term	Meaning
Aotearoa	New Zealand
Hapu	Sub-tribe
Iwi	Tribe
Kawanatanga	Governorship
Maori	Indigenous peoples of Aotearoa
Mana Motuhake	Autonomy, independence
Mana whenua	Respect the authority of the tangata whenua
Pakeha	Descendants of European (mainly British) colonizers
Rangatiratanga	Chieftainship, sovereignty
Tangata whenua	Local or indigenous people
Te reo	Maori language
Te Tiriti o Waitangi	Treaty of Waitangi
Tipuna	Ancestors
Whanau	Extended family
Whenua	Indigenous rights

with those involved in these situations (Harré Hindmarsh and Irwin, in press).

At the same time Maori developments based in their constructs of rangatiratanga, mana whenua and mana motuhake (sovereignty, self-determination and autonomy as tangata whenua) have developed a momentum and an energy of their own. These processes increasingly have challenged Pakeha to re-examine our concepts and strategies of 'biculturalisms' and 'antiracisms' and our place in relation to Iwi (tribal) and Maori development. No longer can Iwi or Maori development constructs and actions be lumped together with bicultural development as if the two are the same process. Critical revisionist analyses have led to a careful distinction between contemporary constructs and actions of biculturalisms, of Iwi/Maori development and of the relationship between them (Harré Hindmarsh and Irwin, in press).

The focus of this chapter is to reflect critically on the range of assumptions and meanings embodied in the constructs of biculturalisms (and associated concepts of antiracisms) as developed and acted upon by Pakeha in the contemporary education world of Aotearoa New Zealand. In the process it will be argued that, rather ironically, some of the most common assumptions and meanings of biculturalism and antiracism have reified Pakeha interpretations of the world and ways of addressing injustices – a neocolonialist form of racism.

The inadequacies of contemporary biculturalisms and associated concepts of antiracisms in New Zealand are not a new or original 'insight'. For example, Jane Kelsey, a lecturer in law at the University of Auckland, has been developing this argument since at least 1987. In 1991 she observed that despite years of anti-institutional racism activities, the actual effect of 'biculturalism' has been to maintain Pakeha control and to stifle Maori self-determination.

> Biculturalism is a policy (although often not a prac-tice) whereby Maori staff and cultural behaviours are accommodated within the broader framework of neo-colonial institutions, while Maori com-munity agencies are given superficial administrative responsibility but remain dependent and subservi-ent to Pakeha power brokers. It is a soft option which avoids addressing Maori self-determination and provides a modern day, more culturally sensi-tive and saleable form of discrimination. Many who consider themselves progressive stress the need for Pakeha to understand and embrace this bicultural-ism – and assume the extent of any further conces-sions to Maori will depend on how far and fast Pakeha are prepared to move along this path. (Kelsey, 1991, pp. 43–4)

This observation pricks the euphoric bubble of liberal Pakeha action which has been a central fea-ture of much of what we have done in the name of biculturalism and antiracism – especially in the 1980s and early 1990s. Even if we have redefined the problem as ourselves and our institutions, many of us have not changed the assumption that we con-tinue to be the saviours of Maori, and Maori con-tinue to be conceptualized as the object, the victim, incapable of independent thought and considered agency, forever dependent on Pakeha action, grace and favour – powerless. The racist arrogance of these outcomes and the assumptions upon which they are based is sobering for those of us who

thought we were 'doing good' with the very best of intentions.

In a final irony of Eurocentrism it has been believed that all the effort which could create a true bicultural symbiosis (to say nothing of a multi-cultural society) can only come from European ini-tiatives (Ballara, 1986, p. 169). This is insulting to Maori owned and driven self-determination and development, to the abilities of Maori people, to Maori concepts and to Maori interpretations of our histories and strategies. The patterns of our history are repeating themselves as we have continued to ignore and silence Maori.

We in New Zealand are not alone in facing the limitations of our forms of antiracisms in the name of biculturalisms. Others along with us are facing the potential of our contemporary constructs to 'strategically silence' (Gilroy, 1987, p. 12) those who have been colonized and oppressed and the urgent need critically to re-evaluate and revise white/western concepts and strategies to address racisms and colonialism.

For example, at the same time as Kelsey began publishing her radical doubts in New Zealand, in England Gilroy (1987, p. 12) cast doubts on anti-racisms there. He commented on the masking, silencing and absence of black histories, writings and involvement in the development of sociological studies of racisms and the strategies of antiracisms in Britain. Furthermore, he argued that the new concepts of 'race' and 'ethnicity' as 'cultural abso-lutes' as promoted by some blacks and antiracists risked endorsing the essentially racist theories and politics of the New Right (Gilroy, 1987, pp. 13, 17). Similarly Rattansi has suggested:

> Now is a time to take stock and reflect on the the-oretical, pedagogic and political foundations of multiculturalism and antiracism ... We need to understand the extent to which oppositional practices have, wittingly and unwittingly, shared the assumptions of the dominant state-led strat-egies. (Rattansi, 1992, p. 11)

With others, Rattansi also argues that we need to revisit critically the conflation of concepts of 'cul-ture' and 'ethnicity', the relationship between these and 'race' and politics and the limitations of ration-alism and essentialism. They take critical revisionist thinking further, to propose that we develop more localized constructs and initiatives to replace pre-scriptive (to date, western) universalisms (Donald and Rattansi, 1992; Rattansi, 1992; Cohen, 1992;

Rizvi, 1993). It is argued that it is an erroneous remnant of pre-modern and modern colonialist and imperialist assumptions to assume there are objective, universal, international meanings and experiences of 'racism', of 'antiracism', 'biculturalism' and 'multiculturalism'. These cannot be understood as disembodied abstract phenomena. Rather, it is suggested that we must grasp the historical and cultural specificities of racisms and responses to these, grounded in our particular histories and social, political, economic and meaning systems (Donald and Rattansi, 1992, p. 5).

In this chapter I focus on the particulars of racisms, antiracisms, multiculturalisms and biculturalisms peculiar to our specific, local New Zealand histories of colonialism, neo-colonialism and the related developments of our socio-political and economic structures and meaning systems. The chapter is in two main parts. The first part provides an historical overview against which the specificities of our bicultural meaning systems, the focus of the second part, must be understood. The first part ends with a summary of the phases through which Maori–Pakeha relationships have passed since 1840, using education as a specific example. In the second part I provide an overview of the range of local constructs of 'biculturalisms' (and 'antiracisms') – the range of meanings they have acquired and associated action strategies in the contemporary New Zealand post compulsory education organizations. The relationship between biculturalisms and rangatiratanga-based Iwi/Maori development; Maori and Pakeha places, spaces and relationships in these; and limitations to strategies for action within education are sub-themes in this discussion. In developing this overview, it is acknowledged that there is no universal truth to be discovered here. This chapter is directly and authentically grounded in the historical and cultural specificities of my position – as a Pakeha woman involved in a range of post compulsory education contexts in contemporary New Zealand.

Maori–Pakeha relationships: a brief historical overview

Mohi Tawhai spoke prophetically to a gathering of Maori and Europeans/Pakeha at the Hokianga discussions of the Treaty of Waitangi on 12 February 1840.

Let the tongue of everyone be free to speak: but what of it. What will be the end? Our sayings will sink to the bottom like a stone, but your sayings will float light, like the wood of the whau tree, and always remain to be seen. Am I telling lies? (Mohi Tawhai, 1840, quoted in Orange, 1991, p. 11)

European, white western concepts, meanings and ways of being and acting have come to dominate the most overt aspects of the country, floating most prominently on the surface of Aotearoa New Zealand. Initially this process was fuelled by our Eurocentric racist constructions of 'Maori', consistent with nineteenth-century theories of 'savagery and civilization', 'evolution' and a hierarchy of 'biological races' – where the Maori were constructed as the 'noblest savages' of those inferior to Aryan Europeans (Salmond, 1991; Ballara, 1986).

Now Pakeha dominance is fuelled from the new forms of racism – hidden in liberal, humanistic and some bicultural and antiracist constructions of Maori and Pakeha 'culture'. Throughout this history Iwi/Maori constructions of their and our world have continued to be present but, until at least recently, largely out of the consciousness of most Pakeha and some Maori who have been 'successfully assimilated', transformed into 'brown-skinned Pakeha'.

Commonly, in our new forms of racism, Maori worlds have been constructed, given meaning, either as a static 'cultural heritage' to be preserved in an unchanging state by 'proper' Maori and in museums and by 'cultural groups and entertainers', or as 'therapy', a means to give identity to 'problem' 'identity-less' Maori (in a caring humanistic way) – thus to 'help' Maori feel good about themselves in the current social structures (Wetherell and Potter, 1992, pp. 128–34).

In the process we Pakeha have assumed a range of oppressive positions in relation to 'Maori culture'. We treat Maori culture as an arena for skill acquisition by 'magnanimous' and 'sensitive' Pakehas – 'culture buffs'; as a challenge for us to identify a 'Pakeha' 'culture'; and/or as an extension of the 'white man's burden' in which it is a Pakeha duty to give Maori opportunities to use and express (selections of) their 'culture'. We surround Maori to provide them with paternal leadership and guidance, encouraging the 'passive' Maori to revive their culture and thus themselves – so long as they do not demand any substantial change to our relationships of power, control and sovereignty. In these contemporary liberal constructions of 'the race relations problems' in our country and how best to respond, Pakeha maintain control of Maori culture in the guise of well-meaning liberalism or radicalism. At the same time some are constructing a more liberatory discourse of 'Maori', 'Pakeha' and 'culture'. These alternative discourses are an important source of resistance, expression of difference and reclaiming sovereignty (Wetherell and Potter, 1992, pp. 134–9).

The meeting of the two worlds which have now become known as those of the 'Maori' and of the 'Pakeha' is understood to have begun in 1642 with the brief visit of the Dutch exploration led by Abel Tasman, who named as 'New Zealand' the islands which Nga Iwi Maori referred to as Aotearoa and Te Waipounamu. This was followed in 1769 with the first of three visits from England led by James Cook and the visits by French, the first two led by Surville in 1769 and Marion du Fresne in 1772.

This is not the place to develop a detailed account or analysis of the history of events from there on. (See Orange, 1987, pp. 6–31 for a brief summary of the period up to 1840 and the remainder of her book for detail thereafter, as centred on the Treaty of Waitangi; and Ballara, 1986 for a study of Pakeha Eurocentrist racisms 1814 to 1980s.)

'Maori' and 'Pakeha': some notes on definitions

When the Europeans arrived on their shores the tangata whenua thought of themselves as members of their hapu or iwi. 'Maori' then meant 'normal, ordinary, of the usual kind', which Pakeha were not. The terms Maori and Pakeha were thus drawn on by Maori to distinguish the tangata whenua from the newcomers (Sharp, 1990, p. 50).

Today the terms Maori and Pakeha are highly contested – in response to and as a product of disputes regarding relative identities, belongingness and political commitments, partly in relation to debates about Maori sovereignty and biculturalisms – often sourced to Te Tiriti o Waitangi/Treaty of Waitangi. They are also contested internally as each 'group' is not homogenous. There are complexities of differences and similarities between and within

groups of 'Maori' and 'Pakeha'. Differences and similarities located on the dimensions of, for instance, class, gender, sexuality and political ideologies are often silenced or subjugated as we focus on themes such as biculturalisms and racisms.

The idea of being Maori has been constructed by the indigenous peoples out of many tribal identities, in response to the Pakeha presence (Sharp, 1990, pp. 50–1; Greenland, 1991; Ritchie, 1992), and since then has been constructed by Pakeha as an enclave of 'cultural' 'difference' in a sea of Pakeha pervasiveness, 'normality' and 'society' (Wetherell and Potter, 1992, p. 136). Contemporary expressions of being Maori are both a response to and product of the current political and economic circumstances of the tangata whenua; constructed in either an oppressive or liberatory mode, the latter finding expression in the ideas of nationhood/sovereignty (Spoonley, 1991, p. 157). Through identifying as Maori a cultural distinctiveness and tangata whenua status is asserted as a basis for sovereignty claims and resistance and opposition to Pakeha. Identification as iwi/hapu expresses whakapapa and turangawaewae within the tangata whenua world and the success of the tangata whenua to resist and survive Pakeha constructions of their culture/s – the ultimate expression of rangatiratanga.

The idea of being 'Pakeha' has become a way of grouping, distinguishing and referring to white New Zealanders of European, usually British, descent (Wetherell and Potter, 1992, p. 3). However, many to whom it applies shun the label while some welcome it. Associated with the biculturalism and antiracism activities of the 1980s and 1990s there has been an emphasis on using 'Pakeha', an interest in what it means and who claims or rejects it as an identity (Spoonley, 1991, p. 157). A survey in 1986 by Project Waitangi, a Pakeha movement combining church and political antiracist groups, found that the idea of being Pakeha did not greatly appeal to the majority of non-Maori. Those who did positively identify as Pakeha were commonly members of some church, feminist and/or antiracist groups, and some liberals. For those not so positive, being grouped by others was not welcomed and the grouping did not express their commitments – rather their commitments were to being 'Kiwi' or 'New Zealanders' (Sharp, 1990, pp. 64–5; Wetherell and Potter, 1992). Some therefore suggest that the contemporary self-identifying construction of being Pakeha is primarily a political and ideological commitment, either liberal or radical, which has evolved through the biculturalism and antiracism debates. It is centred on antiracist analyses of Maori–Pakeha history and the construction of a contemporary identity located here, rooted in a liberal or radical ideological commitment to redress the injustices (Spoonley, 1991, p. 160).

In this environment of contested identities, nationhoods, sovereignty, injustices and relationships, the term tauiwi has also emerged to refer to 'all foreign' not just 'white foreign', that is all non-Maori or non-indigenous peoples (Henare and Douglas, 1988; Sharp, 1990, p. 65). This was a notion introduced around Treaty of Waitangi politics to distinguish between those who descend from the indigenous signatories and those who have settled here since, either as descendants of British settlers or those who immigrated through the policies of the British Crown/NZ government – the other side of the 'Treaty partnership'. This term has also been contested by those objecting to being grouped by others in relation to Treaty and biculturalism debates – an objection often expressed as 'after all we're all New Zealanders aren't we?'.

It has also been contested on the grounds that it can lump together Pacific Islands peoples with settlers from beyond the Pacific rather than with their Maori 'cousins', and by some as it fails to distinguish between those who descend from the Crown partner in Te Tiriti/Treaty and settlers from other lands ('ethnic minorities') who also experience racisms, but which differ in their historical and cultural specifities from those experienced by Maori and may be silenced by being categorized with the majority group.

Thus Maori, Pakeha and Tauiwi are politically contested labels in the contemporary context – the points of debate being integrally linked to the themes of sovereignty, biculturalism and multiculturalism. These constructs give prominence to our national preoccupation with the failure to find a way of 'settling' these themes, and at the same time have come to symbolize political positions in relation to how the 'problem' is defined and the 'solutions' posed. While fully recognizing this, in line with common usage and for pragmatic reasons the term Maori is used broadly in this chapter to refer to the tangata whenua and the term Pakeha to descendants of the Crown partner in Te Tiriti o Waitangi/Treaty of Waitangi and the Declaration of Independence document.

1770 to 1835

In the seventy years prior to Te Tiriti o Waitangi/Treaty of Waitangi of 1840 the 'British and Maori were no strangers to each other . . . British frontiers of trade and Christianity advanced to New Zealand' (Orange, 1987, p. 6). By the 1830s there were thousands of transient British people coming and going and by 1839 2,000 people had settled, mainly in coastal areas of the north (Orange, 1987, p. 6). During this period, the Iwi who had had most contact with the British selectively adapted their ways of life to accommodate the new trade opportunities and needs that presented themselves with the meeting of the two worlds. In 1834 most northern chiefs met to choose a national flag and to declare and create an independent Maori state. In 1835, encouraged and advised by the representative of British Crown in the face of a perceived threat from French interests, they declared themselves an independent state. These were the first steps taken to develop a concept of a united Maori nationhood and sovereignty (compared with Iwi bases for sovereign power), based on European ideas of sovereignty and governance (Orange 1987, pp. 19–31).

Te Whakaputanga o Te Rangatira o Nu Tirene/Declaration of Independence

The 1835 Declaration of Independence was made up of four clauses. The first clause states that the United Tribes declared the country an independent state (whenua rangatira); the second that all sovereign power and authority was to reside totally in the hereditary chiefs and heads of tribes in their collective capacity, that they would not allow any legislative authority or function of government to be exercised unless appointed by them and acting under the authority of laws made by the United Tribes; the third that chiefs agreed to meet in Congress annually to form laws, to preserve peace and order, and to regulate trade, and invited the Southern Tribes to join them; and the fourth sent a copy to the King of England thanking him for acknowledging their flag (1834) and asking him to continue to protect them from all attempts on its independence in return for their friendship to and protection of British settlers and traders. The Crown Office acknowledged the document but soon after the tide began to turn.

The turning point: 1837 to 1839

Between 1837 and 1839 the balance between competing British interests – humanitarian, missionary, commercial and colonialist, all overlaid with Eurocentricism which considered Maori inferior and uncivilized (Ballara, 1986) – shifted to favour the commercial and colonialist. These interests demanded intervention and, preferably peaceful acquisition of land, power and control. This was justified in relation to what was considered as a deteriorating situation of lawlessness, Eurocentric racist views of Maori inferiority and French threats. During 1838 British attitudes changed to seek more jurisdiction or even total sovereignty over all or part of a country whose indigenous peoples were perceived as enfeebled, incapable of agreeing and governing themselves. In 1839 Hobson was sent from the Colonial Office to intervene, preferably through a treaty, to give effect to this shift in British attitudes – somewhat apologetically given previous indications from the Crown that they recognized the independence of a Maori New Zealand in which a place for British settlers needed to be negotiated (Orange, 1987, pp. 23–31). 'No longer were they, Hobson and the rest, considering a Maori New Zealand in which a place had to be found for the British intruders, but a settler New Zealand in which a place had to be found for the Maori' (Orange, 1987, p. 31).

This was the first significant turning point in our shared history, to which we must return in the search for a U-turn, if we are fully to address the issues we attempt to address through 'biculturalism' and 'antiracism'.

Te Tiriti o Waitangi/Treaty of Waitangi: 1840

It was in this context that the Treaty of Waitangi was drawn up and signed in 1840. Such 'treaties with indigenous peoples were not unusual in the history of British imperial expansion' (Orange, 1987, p. 1; Ritchie, 1992, p. 136). However, unlike many others the Treaty of Waitangi lives on (Henare and Douglas, 1988; Renwick, 1993, p. 24). It has been the focus of Maori protest and resistance against cultural invasion and assimilation and, together with an increased awareness of the Declaration of Independence and other symbols of 'nationhood' in the early 1840s, a focus for Maori

claims to rangatiratanga/sovereignty and nationhood in the contemporary context (Walker, 1989). It has also become the basis upon which Pakeha antiracists work towards biculturalism and decolonization (Kelsey, 1987; Yensen et al., 1989; Ritchie 1992).

However, the meaning of the document has always been highly contested as there are two texts to the Treaty which do not say the same thing – one in Te Reo Maori and one in English. It was the Maori version that most Maori signed. In international law, under the *contra preferentum* principle, it is ruled that in the event of any ambiguity of meaning a provision should be interpreted against the party that drafts it and that the indigenous language texts take precedence.

Each version has three articles, with a fourth statement added to Te Tiriti (i.e. the te reo Maori version). The preamble to Te Tiriti states that the Queen of England was to protect the chiefs and subtribes, preserve their chieftainship and their land to them, and to maintain peace and good order. Essentially, Te Tiriti guaranteed Maori rangatiratanga or kingdomship/sovereignty in return for granting to the Crown the limited right of governorship (kawanatanga). The added fourth statement read to the Chiefs guaranteed protection of the several European faiths and Maori customs. Many Maori thus understood 'that the shadow of the land goes to the Queen, but the substance remains with us' (Nopera Panakareao, 1840).

In contrast the Treaty states that Maori ceded sovereignty to the Crown (article one) and retain rangatiratanga/possession of their lands and estates, forests, fisheries and all other properties they collectively possess (article two). In both versions Maori agreed to sell land only to the Crown (article two) and were also granted the rights of British subjects (article three). Given the events that quickly followed the signing of Te Tiriti o Waitangi/Treaty of Waitangi, eighteen months later, Nopera Panakareao confided that he feared 'the substance of the land would pass to the European and only the shadow would remain with the Maori people' (Nopera Panakareao, 1841).

1840 to the 1990s

'Let's work together,' said the shark to the kahawai. 'Great,' said the kahawai with a trusting smile. 'Fool,' thought the shark as it opened its mouth and swallowed the kahawai . . . 'That's partnership,' said the politician. 'That's integration,' said the bureaucrat. 'That's assimilation,' said the Maori. (Reedy, 1993, p. 273)

Since 1840 and the rapid increase in British settlers Maori–Pakeha relationships have been predominantly characterized by the denial of autonomy, sovereignty and an economic base for Maori. Until recently the Te Tiriti/Treaty has been absent from most people's consciousness, as though destroyed or at least in a deep sleep (Ritchie, 1992, pp. 134–5), and even more so the Declaration of Independence (Maori Congress, 1993).

Assimilation has been attempted, in various guises: in policies to 'save' and 'civilize' Maori; integration policies; policies of multiculturalism; and more recently, those of forms of 'bicultural partnerships' – the latter particularly expressed in terms of honouring one or other interpretation of one or other version of Te Tiriti o Waitangi/Treaty of Waitangi. Almost all these policies have been based on the assumption that the goal is to find a more just place for Maori in a Pakeha New Zealand. Few have genuinely entertained the flip side of this: that the goal is to find a more just basis and place for Pakeha in a Maori Aotearoa New Zealand, a possibility entertained from Maori perspectives in 1835 and expressed by those labelled as 'extreme Maori radicals' in the 1980s (e.g. Awatere, 1985).

The example of education

Assimilation in many guises can be demonstrated by providing a brief sketch of the development of formal education between 1840 and the 1990s, a process repeated in many arenas of social policy. Formal state education policies in Aotearoa New Zealand began 'with racism at its core, and that . . . is still alive and well today' (Alton-Lee *et al.*, 1987). Analyses of the racism evident in the development of education policies are available in works such as Barrington (1988), Davies and Nicholls (1993), Irwin (1989, 1992), Penetito (1988), Simon (1990, 1992), and Smith (1992). Here, a brief summary is provided, from which key themes and issues for a critical revision of our concepts and strategies for pursuing change are extracted as a starting point for the second part of this chapter.

From rangatiratanga to assimilation
Prior to the 1840s missionaries and Maori established village schools to develop literacy in te reo

Maori and to learn and teach Christianity. Maori also continued their traditional formal and non-formal education systems to maintain and develop their culture, skills and knowledges, and drew on the mission schools to develop skills to trade and to negotiate with the British.

However, from 1847 to 1960 assimilationist policies for Maori education, as defined by the Pakeha state, quickly gained dominance. For example, the agenda of the cultural assimilation of Maori was first overtly evident in the 1847 subsidies for Maori Mission Boarding Schools. To gain state funding these schools were to provide religious (European) and industrial training and instruction, in English, away from Maori 'village' – whanau and hapu – influences (Simon, 1992). This emphasis on using formal schooling to 'civilize', that is assimilate, Maori to English ways, language and knowledge was continued through the Native Schools Act (1867) and amendments.

During this and the pre-1847 period many Maori were keen to learn Pakeha knowledge and language – not to be assimilated but to deal with threats to their sovereignty and resources arising from an increasing Pakeha presence (Simon, 1992, pp. 2–6). In all events Maori epistemologies, language and processes were 'structurally excluded' (Banks, 1994, pp. 49–50). Those who did comply with the agenda of assimilation found that they still remained structurally excluded, because of the Eurocentric racisms integral to the society. Two conflicting agendas for the development of education policies had emerged. The Crown's agenda, which rapidly assumed dominance, was colonization, control and assimilation; the agenda of Maori was rangatiratanga, development, empowerment and resistance. These two agenda remain with us today.

To integration
From the 1930s, government education policy was moving from an assimilation to an integration focus, a shift formally recommended by the Hunn Report in 1960. In that report, integration was to 'combine (not fuse) the Maori and Pakeha elements to form one nation wherein Maori culture remains distinct' (Hunn, 1960, p. 15).

Integration was understood to imply some continuation of Maori culture, that is those 'fittest elements (worthiest of preservation)' (Hunn, 1960, p. 15), and even those elements were expected gradually to disappear as the goal of assimilation to the civilized Pakeha ways was achieved (Ballara, 1986, p. 134).

During this period Pakeha and many Maori were still, and increasingly, preoccupied with how to improve the position of Maori within a Pakeha-dominated society (largely through education), rather than with how to resist and challenge the encroachment of that society on Maori (Simon, 1992, p. 21). Basically, this was akin to 'multi-culturalism' and 'biculturalism' policies evident in Britain and the USA. In Britain, it is referred to as the 'three Ss' policy – of more saris, samosas and steel bands in schools (Troyna, 1993). In our land we select/ed aspects of the 'three Ts' – taha, tikanga and te reo Maori – to be introduced to the curricular to increase the 'pride' of Maori. It was considered that their 'despondency' was blocking Maori from the taken for granted goal of achieving in the dominant Pakeha world, on its terms (Simon, 1992, pp. 14–15) – 'culture as therapy'.

To resistance and rangatiratanga: biculturalism and treaty principles

However, in more recent times, especially since the 1980s, there has been a reassertion of disillusion-ment with Pakeha-dominated education policy development processes, content and outcomes for Maori. Many Maori had been seeking to develop and expand their own education, on their own terms and based on Maori strengths. Maori had been seeking Maori-controlled education – Maori education in, by and for Maori (Penetito, 1988) – embedded in Maori bodies of knowledges, mean-ing systems and processes, and drawing upon 'Pakeha wisdom' where appropriate to the promo-tion of rangatiratanga. The state had been seeking to replace Maori culture and knowledge with that of the Pakeha and to have Maori succeed on Pakeha terms. Neither had been successful. The policies of assimilation and integration had failed both their own agenda and the oppositional agenda of resistance and rangatiratanga.

This realization represents a crisis in education, and in our society in general. Competing def-initions of this crisis, and thus of the solutions required in education policies are evident, yet again reflecting the two agendas of 1840. On the one hand, we have cleverly repackaged assimilationist and integrationist 'policies for Maori education' (Penetito, 1988) in the rhetoric of 'equal education opportunities' (Sharp, 1990, p. 187), some con-structs of 'biculturalism', 'towards multicultural-

ism', 'honouring the principles of the Treaty' and more 'taha Maori' (Durie, 1989, p. 283). Under such policies Maori staff and cultural behaviours are accommodated, but still within the broader frame-work of neo-colonial institutions (Kelsey, 1991, p. 44). More resources are made available, for example, for bilingual units in schools and for Maori defined as illiterate but not enough and still at the ultimate will of Pakeha decision makers, with the ultimate goal of Maori doing better in a Pakeha rather than a Maori world. The integrationist edict of 'unity within [Pakeha-dominated] diversity' is still fundamental. Unity within a Maori-dominated diversity is never entertained as even a remote possibility, let alone as an equally valid option.

On the other hand, at the same time, revitalized 'Maori education policies' (Penetito, 1988) based on rangatiratanga, resistance and Maori or Iwi development have emerged from Iwi and multi-tribal bases (Irwin, 1992; Smith, 1992; McCarthy, 1995; Harré Hindmarsh and Irwin, in press). These policies and programmes continue to be based on Te Tiriti o Waitangi guarantees of protection of unqualified chieftainship, Maori interests, land as an economic base, citizenship rights and customs: Maori nationhood or tino rangatiratanga.

The same conflicts of interest evident around 1840 remain over the goals and meanings of 'edu-cation': whose takes precedence; whose means and strategies take priority; and whose knowledge and values are to be legitimated (Penetito, 1988, p. 100); and what is the place of each to the other, where and when. Pakeha policies continue to control Maori but Maori interests and resources are gathering to resist more strongly and to create powerful alternatives in Maori, for Maori – spiritually and practically inspired by the 1835 Declaration of Independence, Te Tiriti o Waitangi of 1840 and the analyses and visions of the tipuna (ancestors) who initially maintained their culture while educating themselves to succeed in parts of the Pakeha world they chose to succeed in, on Iwi terms.

In the process Pakeha are having to confront some key questions – about our place, the assump-tions in our meaning systems and thus our bodies of knowledge, concepts, processes and strategies, and about our own development. Typically, our responses have been threefold: to try to do more of the same, yet better – to continue in the 'do-gooder Pakeha' mode of the missionary and humanitarian and displaying 'patronising ethnic welfarism'

(Harré Hindmarsh 1992, 1993, p. 62) based in Eurocentric racism (Ballara, 1986); to become impotent, guilt-ridden wimps (Harré Hindmarsh, 1992, 1993, p. 62); or to find an appropriate space and place from which to work for tino rangatiratanga through genuine Maori political and economic self-determination (Kelsey 1987, 1991; Jones, 1992; Conference of Churches, 1993; Harré Hindmarsh, 1992, 1993) and thus for a more positive and just Pakeha place in Aotearoa New Zealand.

Biculturalisms (and antiracisms) in education organizations

The variety of Pakeha responses in education organizations to the historical issues outlined above is a reflection of and are reflected in the range of ways in which we explain 'the problem' and thus 'solutions' and which are subsumed in our contemporary constructs of 'biculturalisms' (and 'antiracisms'). In recent decades, biculturalism has been made to mean many different things (Harré Hindmarsh, 1993; Durie 1994; Harré Hindmarsh and Irwin, in press), with different antiracism strategies associated with these different meanings. It has been argued in the local context that biculturalism must be construed as superior to multiculturalism – an imported abstract notion not grounded in the local historical and social specificities of New Zealand.

The term biculturalism was first imported to New Zealand in the 1960s from French Canada as part of a critique of integrationist policies (Schwimmer, 1968). However, it was not until the 1980s that it was used widely in Pakeha circles in association with liberal and radical antiracism activities initially imported from Britain and the USA (Spoonley, 1988; Wetherell and Potter, 1992, pp. 215–22). In contrast to the use of the term in the 1960s, biculturalism has now assumed unique local meaning. Honouring the Treaty of Waitangi, historically part of Maori constructs of the problem and solutions, has now assumed centre stage in constructs of 'biculturalism'. There is also a focus on Pakeha and their organizations becoming bicultural rather than on Maori, who are often said to be bicultural already and to be seeking rangatiratanga or more autonomy.

Three predominant constructs of biculturalisms are identified here: two forms of liberal biculturalisms (increased Maori participation and unequal partnerships) and the more radical approach of more equal partnerships, referred to in some quarters as 'parallel development'. The liberal meanings of biculturalism do not promote fundamental changes to relationships of power and control. They have dominated our education organizations' structures and processes, if not in rhetoric – especially in state institutions. Some traditionally Pakeha non-government organizations, having tried to achieve change in the early 1980s through increasing Maori participation in their structures and processes – a liberal model – are leading the way in constructing and implementing more radical meanings of biculturalism in their philosophy, structure and processes. To achieve this, these groups are drawing on concepts based in rangatiratanga and subsuming particular meanings of biculturalism (and antiracism) within that frame. Iwi and Maori organizations are basing their development in rangatiratanga (Melbourne, 1995; Archie, 1995) – for case study examples see Harré Hindmarsh and Irwin (in press) – an approach which Durie (1994) suggests we conceptualize as post-biculturalism.

Multiculturalism and biculturalisms

Today, biculturalism rather than multiculturalism is considered to be the primary and initial goal of the antiracism movement in Aotearoa New Zealand. While there was a tussle between multiculturalism and biculturalism up to the early 1980s (Spoonley, 1988, pp. 103–4), since then it has been widely promoted that biculturalism is the key issue, and if addressed adequately multiculturalism will follow as a matter of course. The argument in this approach is that the 'relationship between the dominant Pakeha group and the Maori as tangata whenua needs to be renegotiated, especially in the light of the Treaty of Waitangi. It precedes and dominates all other political issues in this area and ought to be addressed as a necessary first step' (Spoonley, 1988, p. 104).

'Multiculturalism' is also a concern to proponents of biculturalisms in that it is considered a soft option politically. As do some overseas writers (e.g. Sivanandan, 1985; Troyna, 1993), proponents of biculturalisms criticize multiculturalism for constructing the issues liberally, as those of addressing prejudice and developing 'tolerance of difference' and 'diversity' – rather than radically, as issues of 'oppression'. Locally it is argued that multiculturalism maintains Pakeha dominance and minority interests of others who then are constructed to compete for a share of resources with each other (Spoonley, 1988, p. 105). Furthermore and importantly, in the Aotearoa New Zealand context, multiculturalism is further criticized as offering Pakeha an avenue to avoid the 'historical and social imperatives of the Maori situation' (Ministerial Advisory Committee, 1986, p. 19) and the Treaty of Waitangi – the 'moral, political and social obligations' which require Maori and Pakeha to negotiate (Spoonley, 1988, p. 105). Multiculturalism subsumes the issues of colonization, of indigenous and non-indigenous relationships within that of cultural pluralism.

'We're all New Zealanders' and 'One Law, One Education System for All' are the slogans of those Pakeha supporting the position of groups such as the One New Zealand Foundation. They interpret issues between Te Tiriti partners as principally issues of law and order. Another cornerstone of this position is that all peoples are to be treated equally and to deny any special status to the tangata whenua. Any attempts to redress Maori grievances under Te Tiriti are defined as privileging Maori unfairly. This position promotes multiculturalism rather than biculturalism.

Liberal biculturalisms

The goals of liberal biculturalisms in education organizations range from integration to a type of unequal partnership. Integrationist biculturalism – 'window-dressing' (Ministerial Advisory Committee, 1986, p. 22) or the 'shop front' approach (Dialogue, 1991, p. 16) – occurs at a personal, organizational and national level. Initially we Pakeha appropriate the visible trappings of Maori culture in our personal and organizational processes in the name of the Treaty and bicultural sensitivity (Jones, 1992, p. 296), and as visible symbols of our emerging Pacific/bicultural discourse-identity and our move away from our British/European roots. To put it cynically: personally, we are into 'kia ora', wearing bone pendants and using kete (kit bags); organizationally, our institutions are displaying more Maori art work, signs in te reo Maori and employ a Maori staff member; nationally, we display an image of a bicultural Maori–Pakeha identity through events such as the opening of the Commonwealth Games in Auckland and in

the national exhibitions at the last two EXPOs. But if little else changes in structural power relationships and in political, epistemological and legal sovereignty this remains a form of liberal *bi*cultural diversity, expressing a modern form of cultural racism.

The main goal of this approach is 'the introduction of a Maori perspective into the culture of the institution but as an addition to the overall culture of the organization rather than as an integral part of its core business' (Durie, 1994, p. 7). This approach often develops from the first step taken – that of Pakeha developing more awareness of Maori culture and history and incorporating these cultural trappings to 'add local colour and flavour' to education. It is akin to a multicultural, cultural diversity approach.

Most Pakeha-dominated education organizations were demonstrating such an integrationist form of biculturalism by the late 1980s (Harré Hindmarsh and Irwin, in press). Some continue to do so and others are beginning their journey to biculturalism with this as an initial phase in the 1990s. Some other education organizations have become frustrated by the severe limitations of this approach to the achievement of their vision for a bicultural system in which Maori are initially a subcomponent then a more independent and autonomous parallel body in the organization. These processes of moving through the other two constructs of biculturalisms have culminated to date in Maori and Pakeha striving for a more equal and interpendent form of partnership within the organization (e.g. see case studies of National Women's Refuges, Anglican Social Services Family Centre and the Adult Reading and Learning Assistance Federation in Harré Hindmarsh and Irwin, in press).

Liberal biculturalism with the goal of (unequal) partnership takes the form of 'bicultural symbiosis' (Ballara, 1986, p. 169). Here, the main objective is a workforce that is more representative of Maori and an organization which provides a structural opportunity for a Maori component, unit or caucus to develop as part of its central mission and structure (Durie, 1994, p. 7; Harré Hindmarsh and Irwin, in press). The partnership is unequal in that the dominant Pakeha partner holds the balance of power. Decisions, processes and goals of the Maori department, unit or caucus must be fit into an over-capping Pakeha system and be approved by the Pakeha in dominant organizational positions.

At the most such 'bicultural reformism' (Sharp,

1990) goes some way to Maori feeling more culturally safe and represented in at least some part of the organization. However, Maori in organizational settings which are implementing either of these forms of liberal biculturalisms soon feel overstretched, abused and dumped on (Ministerial Advisory Committee, 1986, p. 22; Dialogue, 1991, p. 17; Harré Hindmarsh and Irwin, in press). The way in which 'culture' is conceptualized (e.g. as heritage, therapy or ideology as discussed earlier in part one of this chapter) in these constructs of biculturalism is crucial to the extent to which the 'partnership' empowers or oppresses Maori. Either way, such liberal constructs depoliticize the issues to those of organizational tolerance, understanding and sharing between Maori and Pakeha. The construct remains centred on assumptions that more cultural respect, understanding, mutual sharing, communication and tolerance – at an administrative and management level – will shift the power relationships and structures.

Liberal and radical antiracism activities, initially imported from the USA and Britain (Spoonley, 1988; Wetherell and Potter, 1992, pp. 215–22), have been used to move towards the goal of developing biculturalism and honouring the Treaty, through strategies which focus on changing Pakeha 'racism' at personal and organizational levels. Initially in the 1970s and early 1980s a liberal form of 'antiracism' was used (often that of Racism Awareness Training promoted by Katz in the USA and many early antiracist programmes in Britain) and provided an analytical flame for the liberal biculturalisms noted above. Liberal humanist antiracisms reconstructed 'the problem', not as the 'Maori problem' but as 'Pakeha prejudice' and the 'solution' as: 'a good dose of painful self-probing and hard work on oneself, systematically identifying and eradicating stereotypes, guilt and delusions of white superiority' (Wetherell and Potter, 1992, p. 215). Pakeha were reconstructed as agents/ subjects and objects of both the problem and solution, who must act to change their attitudes in the interests of biculturalism.

However, the limitations of this liberal antiracism were quickly revealed in practice. These limitations have been referred to in various ways – in terms of its reductionist assumptions that: racism is a combination of original sin, mental illness and culturally and/or biologically determined; power is a personal matter and individuals can solve social problems (Sivanandan, 1985, p. 29; Spoonley, 1988,

pp. 110–25); and that the individual can separate from the social and the political (Rizvi, 1993, p. 12). Liberal antiracism is also limited by its tendency to leave Pakeha paralysed with guilt and institutions unchanged (Kelsey, 1987); to take cultural relativism to a dangerous extreme (Spoonley, 1988, p. 113); to leave Pakeha in a wimpish and exploitative dependency on oppressed people to think for them and to tell them what to do (Rankine, 1983, p. 37; Spoonley, 1988, p. 114).

Essentially these liberal biculturalisms (and antiracisms) result in a more humanistic and 'culturally sensitive' and 'tolerant' form of individual, cultural and institutional racism: more of the same – and can be portrayed as in Figure 12.1:

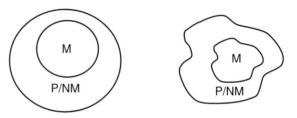

Figure 12.1   Liberal biculturalism (M = Maori; P/NM = Pakeha/Non-Maori)

While this position often represents important first steps for Pakeha organizations, and thus in this sense is not to be scoffed at, the danger is that we Pakeha remain stuck here. This may be an important first step in the recognition of the value of a culture other than our own and of the injustices which riddle the history of our country. However, it does little to alter radically the structures and relationships of power and control.

Radical biculturalisms: parallel development

Through critical reflection and revised action in some organizations a range of more radical constructs of biculturalism are being developed and implemented (e.g. see case studies of the Adult and Community Education Association, National Women's Refuges, Family Centre, Adult Reading and Learning Assistance Federation and Project Waitangi in Harré Hindmarsh and Irwin, in press). The focus of more radical constructs is to reframe the solution in terms of 'honouring Te Tiriti as read through the Declaration of Independence' and the problem as issues of epistemological, constitutional/legal and political 'sovereignty', 'self-determination' and 'autonomy'. In acting on this focus, it then develops into how Maori and Pakeha can develop working relationships which are more just and interdependent, while respecting autonomy.

In more radical constructs of biculturalisms the focus is on developing parallel sub-organizations/organizations which use different approaches and vehicles to achieve the same overcapping and agreed aims (Durie, 1994, p. 8). Case studies in Harré Hindmarsh and Irwin (in press) illustrate that the first structural steps in more radical biculturalisms are commonly the development of twinned Maori–Pakeha positions (e.g. co-training managers, co-chairpersons), equal numbers of Maori and Pakeha on decision-making bodies, separate caucuses with equal voting rights and fifty–fifty resource allocation within the organization – 'bicultural distributivism' in Sharp's (1990) terms. In some fields of education Pakeha have agreed to support the development of parallel, separate sub-organizations or caucuses, each operating under its own approach and mechanisms, to achieve common goals under a national umbrella. For example, kohanga reo at the preschool level, kura kaupapa Maori (primary schools) and whare wananga (tertiary institutions) have been supported and funded through the Ministry of Education's education system (Irwin, 1992). Here, pan-Maori or Iwi institutions deliver a service to their own people – but still under the auspices of a Pakeha-dominated Ministry and government which has a large say in the parameters for operation, whether funding will be allocated and for how long.

These biculturalisms, rooted in more radical ideas of limiting the spheres of Pakeha power and control (kawanatanga) and of supporting greater Maori self-determination (towards rangatiratanga), have loosened Pakeha power structures and opened up the way for new forms of dialogue and relationships. They have enabled Maori to develop organizations or sections of organizations which operate under tikanga Maori, some in te reo Maori. However, these forms of biculturalism stop short of honouring Maori sovereignty in the fullest sense of the word. They have not been successful at 'addressing the constitutional relationship between the iwi and hapu and the Crown – between the relative authority of tino rangatiratanga and kawanatanga' (Kelsey, 1991, p. 44).

In essence, Pakeha constructs are still reified and have 'the last word'. This is so because we are all operating in a constitutional context which gives ultimate authority to a Pakeha-dominated and form of government, upholding as supreme Pakeha or western ways of interpreting the world, of acting and western values. Thus while on an institutional or personal level some may have developed relationships of dual determination, this is within the constraints of the Crown assuming sovereignty, not kawanatanga.

This range of Pakeha positions and perspectives has developed in a context where, internationally as well as nationally, governments, organizations and individuals who are descendants of colonizing powers living in the colonized lands are finding it harder and harder to avoid the daily implications of issues of relationships of power and control. It is also harder to avoid knowing about and facing the need to redress injustices to indigenous peoples and to find a more just place for ourselves in these countries.

Radical bicultural activists have been influenced by notions of institutional and cultural racisms, as well as personal racism (Ministerial Advisory Committee 1986, p. 19). Reflecting its location in the discourse of critical theories, antiracisms focusing on institutions have construed 'racism' more in 'structural and politicized terms', and 'race' as a 'false representation of reality'. This form of antiracism suggests solutions lie in developing a more accurate analysis of, and programme to change, structures of power. As elsewhere (e.g. see Troyna, 1993 in relation to Britain), however, in practice the 1980s' use of the construct focused on the structures in single institutions, oversimplifying institutional racism and abstracting it from its historical and wider political meanings (Rizvi, 1993, p. 11).

While radical biculturalisms informed by anti-institutional racism have had the effect of loosening the Pakeha power structures in some state and more non-government organizations, very rarely have they (to date) shifted fundamental epistemologies, decision-making power and resource distribution – the 'ideological culture' and 'legal sovereignty'. Commonly, the outcome of programmes of anti-institutional racism forms of biculturalism has been marginalized and disillusioned Pakeha and Maori activists, with organizational power intact (Kelsey, 1987, p. 7; Spoonley, 1988, pp. 117–18).

As with liberal modes, there is often an inflated and naive expectation of the power of a group or individual to change institutions because of the shared individual–social dualism (Rizvi, 1993, p. 12; Troyna, 1993) inherent in both liberal and critical discourses. There is a lack of distinction between beliefs and actions and a lack of recognition of the complexity of the relationship between the two (Rizvi, 1993, p. 12). We can hold 'politically correct' antiracist bicultural beliefs, liberal or radical, and still act in racist monocultural ways (for Pakeha examples see Wetherell and Potter, 1992). We can act in ways which appear to symbolize 'politically correct' antiracist biculturalism without the commitment and beliefs – as isolated or momentary strategies to defuse and divert immediate tensions.

Racism (as sexism in critical feminist theories) is often inflated or 'stretched to impose a brittle coherence on multi-faceted phenomena, thus avoiding the need for more diverse and discriminating forms of analysis' (Donald and Rattansi, 1992, p. 3). It can also impose a reductionist, limiting and homogenizing construction on Maori and Pakeha 'cultures' and politics, and a reductionist explanation that the issues of all their members are reducible to issues of racism and culture, in the same way (but with more 'politically correct' content) as do assimilationist and multiculturalist or integrationist constructions (Donald and Rattansi, 1992, pp. 3–4). Gender, class, sexuality and age divisions are ignored in the institutional racism slogan of 'prejudice plus power' and in the liberalist construct, as is the differential access to power within both the dominant and oppressed group (Rizvi, 1993, p. 11).

To summarize to this point: the radical constructs of biculturalism are sourced in critical theories and analyses of institutional racism. They are manifested in actions which range from the creation of twinned Maori and Pakeha partnership positions – for example co-chairs, equal numbers of Maori and Pakeha on decision-making bodies, separate caucuses with equal voting rights within the originally Pakeha organization; to the separation of organizations into 'parallel', equally resourced Maori and Pakeha sub-organizations/organizations under the umbrella of a jointly negotiated mission.

The operative idea within these constructs is 'distributive biculturalism'. Some conceptualize this as involving equal or unequal distribution of decisions and resources, others extending it to equal distribution of political, but not legal/constitutional sovereignty:

The doctrine of distributive biculturalism [argues that] distributions of things in Aotearoa/New Zealand should be made primarily between the two main cultures, Maori and Pakeha, and that since Maori and Pakeha were *ethnie* worthy of equal respect, the distributions should be equal between them. It was not numbers of persons within each *ethnie* that weighted the balance; it was the equal value of each culture . . . In regard to the distribution of political authority, it was (so to say) representative ethnocracy rather than representative democracy that was sought for. (Sharp, 1991, p. 227)

We define biculturalism as the coexistence of two distinct cultures, Maori and Pakeha, within New Zealand society with the values and traditions of both cultures reflected in society's customs, laws, practices, and institutional arrangements, and with both cultures sharing control over resources and decision making. While this definition is deliberately silent about where the balance of power should lie, we reject the simplistic and inflexible maxim that a partnership demands a fifty–fifty sharing of resources. (O'Reilly and Wood, 1991, p. 321).

A successfully functioning bicultural nation is one in which at least two separate peoples, defined by cultural boundaries, can maintain their different ideologies and cultural heritages, supported by an equitable share of the resources of the state, while still regarding themselves as part of a national community. In practice, in New Zealand, this would mean that Pakeha of European origin regarding themselves as one cultural entity and Maori regarding themselves as another cultural entity, shared the resources of the state in mutually supportive roles by agreed equitable division, with the aim of maintaining their separate cultural heritages through education and other institutional means, while still regarding themselves as partners in one national community (Ballara, 1987, p. 106).

In all these constructs the concept of 'culture' is pivotal – but which concept? The assigning of separate but equal (in terms of power and value) Maori and Pakeha spaces is required and it is assumed that both 'cultures' combine in one nation. This meaning of biculturalism can be represented diagrammatically as shown in Figure 12.2.

Moving to post-biculturalism

In whatever form, the liberal and radical biculturalisms of the 1980s and 1990s have not satisfied

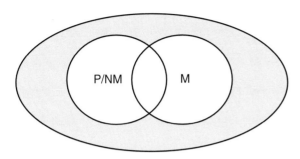

Figure 12.2 Radical biculturalism (M = Maori; P/NM = Pakeha/Non-Maori)

Maori demands and also have antagonized many Pakeha. These biculturalisms are not tino rangatiratanga (Kelsey, 1991, pp. 44–6) – the primary concern of Maori since the meeting of our worlds. By placing as central the international constructs of personal prejudice or institutional racism, such biculturalism 'avoids addressing the constitutional relationship between iwi and hapu and the Crown – between the relative authority of tino rangatiratanga and kawanatanga. It therefore has nothing to do with the Treaty' (Kelsey, 1991, p. 44). It yet again reifies western constructs drawn from outside our historical specificities; rather than drawing on the indigenous constructs based firmly in those historical specificities.

For this reason, Durie (1994, p. 8) suggests that we refocus our energies in New Zealand to develop what he terms post-biculturalism. Here, the prime operative concept becomes rangatiratanga (sovereignty) rather than 'culture'. It is argued that biculturalisms inevitably undermine Maori aspirations for greater self-sufficiency and determination and reduce Iwi competiveness with Pakeha state and non-government agencies to provide service to their own peoples. In effect Maori and their resources become appropriated in the interests of Pakeha, even if the goal of biculturalisms had been to promote Maori interests. At the most, biculturalisms have made Pakeha organizations more 'Maori friendly' and 'culturally sensitive and responsive', but have diminished Maori self-determination (Durie, 1994, p. 9).

The bicultural model that has come closest to this approach has involved the establishment of an organizational constitution which sets up two (Maori and non-Maori, as in the case of Women's Refuge Constitution 1988) or three (Maori, Pakeha and Pacific, as in the cases of the Anglican Church Synod 1990 and the Lower Hutt Family

Centre) distinct cultural structures which operate under their own tikanga, come to their own decisions, own an equal share of the assets and have an equal voice as an 'ethnie' in joint organizational decision making and resource distribution. Some such organizations have set up clear accountability systems in terms of both 'ethnie' and 'gender'. For example, the other two groups are accountable to Maori if the issue is principally one in their sphere; all men to women if it is a women's issue (e.g. Lower Hutt Family Centre, Waldegrave and Tamasese, 1993). To operate effectively a high level of commitment, trust and respect is required and constant dialogue and negotiation – and tolerance of pain and confusion at times – in the spaces between and surrounding all the spheres, and in maintaining the boundaries and sovereignty of each sphere, yet some interdependence.

For some years the Maori Council, and now the Maori Congress, have been calling for similar constitutional changes in state government – thus honouring Te Tiriti as read through the Declaration of Rangatiratanga. For example, in 1993 the Maori Congress announced in a press release that it was mounting a two-year public education campaign to 'encourage the acceptance of a separate Maori parliament' based on the Declaration of Independence and the Treaty of Waitangi as 'a positive part of our history and future development' (Maori Congress, 1993).

Whether expressed in a state or an organizational constitution, the place and role of the 'other/s' in relation to one's own sphere and in any intersovereign spheres must also be addressed. In some current expressions of this construct, Maori spheres sometimes include Pakeha on Maori/Iwi terms, who are accountable to Iwi/Maori controlled kaupapa while retaining a Pakeha identity (Smith, 1992; Salmond, 1991; Ritchie 1992). Some of the alternative models for such relationships have been constructed as 'tiaki (mentor model)', 'whangai (adoption model)', 'power sharing and empowering outcomes models' (Smith, 1992). This works best when the relationship is based on conceptualizations like those found in the second clause of the Declaration of Independence – where rangatira/Maori retain sovereign power and authority and require accountability of those appointed by Iwi/Maori and acting under the authority of laws (and lores) made by them to this sovereignty. Likewise, in Pakeha spheres located within such an arrangement Maori are to be included on 'Pakeha' 'non-racist' 'terms' – which begs us to define 'Pakeha', 'non-racist' and what terms or concepts we use. Can we create such a sphere?

Fears and ambivalence are often expressed by both Maori and Pakeha about instances where Pakeha have worked and do work in Maori-controlled contexts – that Pakeha will repeat history, colonize from within, use the process for their own interests and not those of Iwi/Maori and/or deny or lose their identity and history as Pakeha (King, 1985, p. 179). Examples are often given from people's own networks of this occurring. Even when counter-examples are given of trustworthy and non-exploitative 'bicultural Pakeha' and successful collaboration within the interests of Iwi/Maori world/s, shades of doubt and suspicion linger – a deeply felt legacy of the past 159 or so years. We need to be well tested over time. Both interactive options, when located in each other's sphere, require each to be genuinely respectful and knowledgeable of the ways of the other and of their respective rights to exercise legal and political sovereignty in that territory. Perhaps this intercultural sub-sphere is where a sub-construct of antiracist biculturalism is necessary?

With this construct of post-biculturalism there is a concomitant shift to Maori focusing on rangatiratanga-based Iwi/Maori development, within separate enlarging Maori/Iwi organizational, social, economic and political 'spaces' while retaining the need also to be more justly included in Pakeha contexts. This begs the question of 'the relationship between rangatiratanga and kawanatanga in local and national expressions' (Nairn, 1993). The 1835 Declaration (clause 2) constructed kawanatanga as being exercised within the domains of Rangatira and under their collective authority/legal sovereignty. This provides a model for the relationship between Maori and Pakeha within those spheres defined as Maori/rangatiratanga and as Pakeha/kawanatanga (and ultimately the state). If we return to the historical constructs of rangatiratanga and kawanatanga, it follows that Iwi/Maori define what is tika, that Pakeha must trust and respect them to do so in a just way for all (Nairn, 1993) – a full turn of the tide.

This construct of sovereignty in a post-biculturalism era, if it is called that at all, can be represented as in Figure 12.3.

This sovereignty construction differs significantly from all biculturalisms. It is based in constitutional

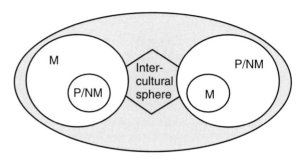

Figure 12.3 Post-biculturalism sovereignties (M = Maori; P/NM = Pakeha/Non-Maori)

sovereignty, two (or more) groups alongside each other claiming separate 'nationhood', equal spheres and mutually negotiating both where and how they may overlap, by what they may be overlapped and surrounded, and the place, if any, of the 'other/s' in each sphere. All are thus engaged in redefining alternatives to live by which seek a more just place for both Pakeha and Maori in Aotearoa New Zealand, and in each other's realms rooted in Te Tiriti/Treaty. In contrast, in the former constructs the focus is solely on more just inclusion of Maori (as a 'culture' rather than a 'nation') in Pakeha spheres, with unchallenged constitutions. In the latter construct Maori and Pakeha are conceptualized as two sovereign groups/nations with their own forms of government, united under the umbrella of a mutually negotiated kaupapa – the issue is constructed as one of political and legal 'sovereignty' and 'nationhood'. In the former Maori are constructed as a 'culture' seeking fairer personal and structural inclusion and spheres of autonomy within the Pakeha organization-nation-state – in the form of a cultural rather than nationhood partnership, with or without reference to the Treaty. In terms of English constitutional discourse, the former constructs seek to expand Maori 'political sovereignty', to impose limits on the sphere of control exercised by Pakeha 'legal sovereignty' (McHugh, 1989, pp. 42–9); the latter to accord both Maori and Pakeha their own spheres of legal sovereignty, each also engaged in negotiating their political sovereignty – the limits they can impose to check the legal sovereignty they and the other exercises.

Concluding reflection

In this chapter, from the position of being Pakeha in Aotearoa New Zealand, I have reflected on the assumptions and range of meanings in which the concepts of biculturalism and antiracism are embedded. This has brought me face to face with the limitations of these constructs and with yet another layer of oppressiveness and colonization, new forms of racism implicit in our attempts to promote change. I have felt uncomfortable with the ramifications of some of what we have been doing in the name of biculturalism and antiracism for some time now and hope that through a process of critical reflection we can face the limitations and issues to conceptualize fresh directions more clearly.

As the net of our memories, our histories, is hauled in for checking by the 'Maori renaissance' and the questioning of 'bicultural' and 'antiracist' activities, we are rediscovering and revising our understandings of the floats and the stones, and the relationships between them: the way they have been and are woven together by the threads of our co-existence; the respective places, value and functions of the stones and the floats; the purpose/s for which the net may be recast, and by whom; the holes that need mending – or are there so many that the whole net must be rewoven?

This process is intimately linked to the Maori pursuit of 'Maori/Iwi development' and 'nationhood/sovereignty' based in their concepts of rangatiratanga, mana motuhake and mana whenua (Awatere, 1985; Ritchie, 1992; Te Whaiti, 1993). The way forward for Maori is solidly embedded in these Maori concepts. This raises questions for us to ponder in the light of the limitations of biculturalisms and antiracisms which some Maori and Pakeha have experienced and faced. Do these Maori concepts and strategies for regaining and asserting whenua rangatiratanga and mana rangatiratanga (chieftainship, independence, sovereignty) and mana motuhake (autonomy) – more firmly grounded in our local socio-historical context, particularly in the Declaration of Independence and Te Tiriti o Waitangi and the patterns which followed – offer a more sound alternative to those of biculturalisms and antiracisms which have their sources in more abstract western international concepts, strategies and interests? Is there any local meaning of biculturalism which has a place alongside rangatiratanga and Iwi/Maori development, in pursuit of complementary goals? What is the place, if any, of Pakeha in relation to and in these processes, and in relation to each other?

References

Alton-Lee, A. *et al.* (1987) Take your brown hand off my book: racism in the classroom. *Set* 8. Wellington: NZCER.

Archie, C. (1993) Have the Anglicans found the answer? *Mana* Jan.-Feb., 36–9.

Archie, C. (1995) *Maori Sovereignty: The Pakeha Perspective.* Auckland: Hodder Moa Beckett.

Awatere, D. (1985) Maori Sovereignty. *Broadsheet,* Auckland.

Ballara, A. (1986) *Proud to be White?* Auckland: Heinemann.

Ballara, A. (1987) Biculturalism and multiculturalism. In R. Smithies (ed.), *Ten Steps Towards Bicultural Action: A Handbook on Partnership in Aotearoa-New Zealand.* Wellington: Catholic Commission for Justice, Peace and Development.

Banks, J. A. (1994) *Multiethnic Education: Theory and Practice.* Boston: Allyn and Bacon.

Barrington, J. (1988) Learning the dignity of labour: secondary education policy for Maori. *New Zealand Journal of Education Studies* 23 (1), 45–58.

Binney, J. (1989) The Maori and the signing of the treaty. *Towards 1990.*

Cohen, P. (1992) 'It's racism what dunnit': hidden narratives in theories of racism. In J. Donald and A. Rattansi (eds), *'Race', Culture and Difference.* London: Sage in association with Open University.

Conference of Churches in Aotearoa New Zealand (1993) Tino Rangatiratanga: a public questions occasional paper, revised July 1993. In *ACCANZ Kitset: Constitutional Reform.* Auckland: National Office.

Davies, L. and Nicholls, K. (1993) *Maori and Education.* Wellington: Ministry of Education.

Dialogue (1991) 'Biculturalism'.

Donald, J. and Rattansi, A. (1992) Introduction. In J. Donald and A. Rattansi (eds), *'Race', Culture and Difference.* London: Sage in association with Open University.

Durie, M. H. (1989) The Treaty of Waitangi perspectives for social policy. In I. H. Kawharu (ed.), *Maori and Pakeha Perspectives of the Treaty of Waitangi.* Auckland: Oxford University Press.

Durie, M. (1994) Understanding biculturalism. Paper given at Kokiri Nga Tahi Hui – Side by Side Seminar: Maori and Pakeha Working Together, Sponsored by the Race Relations Office, Gisborne.

Fay, B. (1987) *Critical Social Science: Liberation and its Limits.* Oxford: Polity Press and Blackwell.

Gilroy, P. (1987) *There Ain't No Black in the Union Jack.* London: Hutchinson Education.

Greenland, H. (1991) Maori ethnicity as ideology. In P. Spoonley, D. Pearson and C. Macpherson, (eds), *Nga Take: Ethnic Relations and Racism in Aotearo/New Zealand.* Palmerston North: Dunmore Press.

Harré Hindmarsh, J. (1992) The Treaty of Waitangi in lifelong learning? *Lifelong Learning in Aotearoa,* 3, 4–7.

Harré Hindmarsh, J. (1993) Jennie Harré Hindmarsh. In J. Manchester and A. O'Rourke (eds), *Liberating Learning: Women as Facilitators of Learning.* Wellington: Women's Suffrage Centenary Project.

Harré Hindmarsh, J. and Irwin, K. (in press) *Partnerships in Practice: Case Studies of Maori and Bicultural Development.* Palmerston North: Dunmore Press.

Henare, M. and Douglas, T. (1988) Te Reo me Te Tiriti Mai Ra Ano: the treaty always speaks. In *The April Report: Future Directions, Vol III, Part One. Te Kohana a Te Karauna mo Nga Ahuatanga-a-Iwi, Report of the Royal Commission on Social Policy.* Wellington: Government Printer.

Hunn, J. (1960) *Report on the Department of Maori Affairs.* Wellington: Government Printer.

Irwin, K. (1989) Multicultural education: the New Zealand response. *NZ Journal of Education Studies* **24** (1), 3–17.

Irwin, K. (1992) Maori education in 1991: a review and discussion. *NZ Annual Review of Education.* Wellington: Victoria University of Wellington.

Jones, D. (1992) Looking in my own backyard: the search for white feminist theories of racism for Aotearoa. In R. Du Plessis *et al.* (eds), *Feminist Voices: Women's Studies Texts for Aotearoa/New Zealand.* Auckland: Oxford.

Kelsey, J. (1987) The Treaty of Waitangi and Pakeha responsibility – directions for the future. *Race Gender Class* **5**, 42–50.

Kelsey, J. (1991) Tino Rangatiratanga in the 1990s. *Race Gender Class* **11–12**, 42–7.

King, M. (1985) *Being Pakeha.* Auckland: Hodder and Stoughton.

Lambourn, B. (1990) Parallel development in women's refuge: the non-Maori perspective. Paper given at the Women's Studies Conference, Rotorua.

Leicester, M. (1993) *Race for a Change in Continuing and Higher Education.* Buckingham: Open University Press.

McCarthy, M. (1995) He Hinaki Tukutuku: Whare Wananga and the State. MEd thesis, Victoria University of Wellington, Wellington.

McHugh, P. (1989) Constitutional theory and Maori claims. In I. Kawharu (ed.), *Waitangi: Maori and Pakeha Perspectives of the Treaty of Waitangi.* Auckland: Oxford.

Maori Congress (1993) Maori parliament campaign starts. *Evening Post* 28 October.

Melbourne, H. (1995) *Maori Sovereignty: The Maori Perspective.* Auckland: Hodder Mao Beckett.

Ministerial Advisory Committee on a Maori Perspective for the Department of Social Welfare (1986) *Puao-Te-Ata-Tu (Day break).* Wellington: Government Printer.

Nairn, M. (1993) Transition and Tikanga. *Programme on Racism Newsletter* **33**, 1.

Orange, C. (1987) *The Treaty of Waitangi.* Wellington: Allen and Unwin.

O'Reilly, J. and Wood, D. (1991) Biculturalism and the public sector. In J. Boston *et al.* (eds), *Reshaping the State: New Zealand's Bureaucratic Revolution.* Auckland: OVP.

Penetito, W. (1988) Maori education for a just society. In *The April Report: Social Perspectives, Vol IV. Te Komihana mo Nga Ahuatanga-a-Iwi, Report of the Royal Commission on Social Policy.* Wellington: Government Printer.

Rankine, J. (1983) Not just them out there. *Broadsheet* October, 37–40.

Rattansi, A. (1992) Changing the subject? Racism, culture and education. In J. Donald and A. Rattansi, (eds), *'Race' Culture and Difference.* London: Sage in association with Open University.

Reedy, T. (1993) The shark and the kahawai. In W. Ihimaera (ed.), *Te Ao Marama 2: Regaining Aotearoa.* Auckland: Reed.

Renwick, W. (1993) Decolonising ourselves. *British Review of New Zealand Studies*

Ritchie, J. (1992) *Becoming Bicultural.* Wellington: Huia Publishers, Daphne Brassell Associates Press.

Rizvi, F. (1993) Critical introduction: researching racism and education. In B. Troyna *Racism and Education.* Birmingham: Open University Press.

Salmond, A. (1991) *Two Worlds: First Meetings between Maori and Europeans 1642–1772.* Auckland: Viking Penguin.

Schwimmer, E. (1968) The aspirations of the contemporary Maori. In E. Schwimmer (ed.), *The Maori People of the Nineteen-Sixties: A Symposium.* Auckland: Longman Paul.

Sharp, A. (1991) *Justice and the Maori: Maori Claims in New Zealand Political Argument in the 1980s.* Auckland: Oxford University Press.

Simon, J. (1990) The place of schooling in Maori-Pakeha relations. PhD thesis, University of Auckland.

Simon, J. (1992) State schooling for Maori: the control of access to knowledge. *ARRE/NZARE Conference Proceedings,* Australia: Deakin University.

Sivanandan, A. (1985) RAT and the degradation of the black struggle. *Race and Class* **26**, (4), 1–33.

Smith, G. (1992) Tane-Nui-a-Rangi's legacy . . . propping up the sky . . . Kaupapa Maori as resistance and intervention. In *AARE/NZARE Conference Proceedings,* Australia: Deakin University.

Spoonley, P. (1988) *Racism and Ethnicity.* Auckland: Oxford University Press.

Spoonley, P. (1991) Pakeha ethnicity: a response to Mäori sovereignty. In P. Spoonley, D. Pearson and C. Macpherson *Ngä Take: Ethnic Relations and Racism in Aotearoa-New Zealand.* Dunmore Press, Palmerston North: Dunmore Press, pp. 154–70.

Te Whaiti, P. (1993) Rangatiratanga. MEd Thesis, Victoria University of Wellington, Wellington.

Troyna, B. (1993) *Racism and Education.* Birmingham: Open University Press.

Waldegrave, C. and Tamasese, K. (1993) Culture and gender accountability in 'just therapy' approach. *Journal of Feminist Family Therapy: International Perspectives,* Spring.

Walker, R. (1989) The Treaty of Waitangi as the focus of Mäori protest. In H. Kawharu (ed.) 1989, pp. 263–79,

Wetherell, M. and Potter, J. (1992) *Mapping the Language of Racism: Discourse and the Legitimation of Exploitation.* London: Harvester Wheatsheaf.

Yensen, H. *et al.* (eds) (1989) *Honouring the Treaty: An Introduction for Pakeha to the Treaty of Waitangi.* Auckland: Penguin.

13 Two Tracks to Citizenship in the USA[1]

DONALD A. BIGGS, ROBERT COLESANTE and JOSHUA SMITH

At the turn of the twentieth century the USA was inundated with voluntary and involuntary immigrants. An avalanche of 27 million voluntary immigrants from southern and eastern Europe arrived between the end of the Civil War and US entry into World War I. These new citizens settled in the cities and learned how to construct their lives as Americans. However, they often confronted people who had real misgivings about their "foreign ways" and insisted that they immediately adopt "American Ways." These immigrants were expected to learn how to live their lives as ordinary American citizens. How did they do this? We suggest that they used narrative thought to construct their life stories as Americans, and figure out the meaning of "being American" (Bruner, 1986, 1990).

Narrative thought was used to describe their day-to-day realities and to get a sense of what it means to be an American in particular situations that arose in their lives. This kind of thought is interpretive and deals with "meaning making" rather than computational or algorithmic thought (Feldman *et al.*, 1993). Narrative construction depends on both intrinsic cognitive operations and canonical forms that exist in a culture. Our construction of meanings is done within a culture that shares a literature, visual arts, music, oratory, myths, and religious practices. These provide a shared framework and canonical forms for interpreting our daily experiences. We will argue that the voluntary and involuntary immigrants utilized very different narrative frames to interpret the meaning of American citizenship in their daily lives. These interpretive frames are evident in the folk psychology of "white citizenship" and "black citizenship" in our culture. The culture provided voluntary immigrants a narrative model of citizenship that encouraged them to work hard and adopt "American ways" in order to reap the benefits of citizenship. The culture provided involuntary immigrants with a narrative model of citizenship which told them that no matter how hard they worked, they should not expect to get the same benefits of citizenship as white American citizens.

The goals of this "folk psychology" approach to citizenship education were primarily:

- to create a "common American" out of the polyglot of immigrants in the country;
- to assure that citizens of color did not become part of the national molding process.

As is true of most folk psychology beliefs, the contradictions inherent in this "common-sense approach" to citizenship education were not recognized by most citizens. Instead, it was only common sense to impose Anglo-centered views on hapless immigrants and to maintain separate black and white worlds in the USA.

The culture, through its folk psychology, provided narratives about American citizens, how and why they acted as they did and how they dealt with troubles. These cultural canons depicted the ordinary way to live one's life as an American citizen and the new immigrants used them to construct their daily lives as Americans. These cultural conventions were a part of their children's stories, popular music of the day, and an emerging literature about Americans. Together these new immigrants also constructed a collective concept of "we Americans" that has played a major role in determining the nature of American citizenship for the last 100 years. They often told each other stories about how "Americans" who work hard, get a good education, and save for rainy days can achieve the American dream. They read "rags to riches" stories in school texts like the McGuffy readers to provide reasons for living their lives as good citizens.

From the end of the Civil War to the beginning of the twentieth century, the country was also inundated with an avalanche of involuntary immigrants or former slaves who were "freemen" and new citizens of the USA. They wanted to be Americans, but their skin color and the racism in the dominant culture made it difficult for them to become fully accepted as "real Americans." The black churches played a significant role in educating these new American citizens. Their idea of citizenship for black Americans did not emphasize complete assimilation because they recognized that the white culture in the USA would not accept blacks as full citizens of the country. Instead the white folk culture offered a number of racist caricatures for black Americans to emulate. Many of these involuntary immigrants wanted to be Americans but did not want to be "colored folks." The black churches spearheaded a social movement for public education in the South between the end of the Civil War and the late 1870s that reflected their shared beliefs:

1 Education should help blacks avoid exploitation and oppose racism.
2 Education should develop ethnic pride by teaching African and African-American history.
3 Education should lead to greater and more varied ways of participating in American society (Cross, 1995).

At the end of the reconstruction period, whites had regained complete control of the educational system in the South. They set up separate schools to ensure that blacks knew their place and learned a cultural etiquette that was calculated to maintain separate black and white ways in society. In 1896, Homer Plessey brought his case to the Supreme Court. He told about how he had to sit in segregated cars on trains passing through Louisiana and that this kind of segregation violated his constitutional rights under the Fourteenth Amendment. The response from the Supreme Court, labeled "The Separate but Equal Doctrine," legalized Jim Crow laws in the USA and defined the meaning of American citizenship for black Americans until 1954 when *Brown vs. Board of Education of Topeka* declared school segregation to be unconstitutional.

In spite of Jim Crow laws in the South and de facto segregation in the rest of the country, involuntary immigrants tried to figure out how they could become Americans and enjoy the rights afforded to citizens in this country. They found the white American cultural canons were based on negative ethnic stereotypes. So, if they used these cultural conventions to shape their lives as Americans, they should expect to play demeaning roles in society because they were inherently different from the voluntary immigrants who could all expect to achieve the American dream. After a period of assimilation, voluntary immigrants learned that their cultural and ethnic differences were not obstacles to achieving the American dream. By contrast, the white cultural message to involuntary immigrants was that their so-called racial differences would always limit their opportunities as American citizens. If these involuntary immigrants wanted to succeed in the American society, they could live their lives as typical negroes or second-class citizens. But if they found these "racist role expectations" unacceptable, they had to resist or oppose becoming Americans. As a result, many developed mixed feelings about whether they wanted to be Americans. Instead some turned to their own black culture for guidance about becoming proud black Americans. Gospel music, rural blues and sophisticated jazz validated their experiences. Slave narratives proclaimed the victory of the black spirit over oppression and persecution. These powerful black cultural narratives provided protection from a white culture that told them that they would always be "second-class" citizens, no matter what they accomplished.

At the turn of the twentieth century the country developed a folk psychological narrative about citizenship education using the metaphor of a "melting pot." During the last 100 years, the schools have promoted a variety of academic models of citizenship education. Yet many ordinary citizens still use the melting pot metaphor to explain why they consider the presence of diversity a threat to the "peace and quiet" of their lives and why they think the schools should mold youth into "like-minded" citizens who get along with each other.

In 1908, a play *The Melting Pot* by Israel Zangwill, an English writer of Russian Jewish origin, opened in Washington DC. The title of the play became an American icon that gained a great deal of popularity with the press, politicians and ordinary American citizens. The idea of taking immigrants and somehow melting them down and molding them into Americans made sense to Americans in their new steel mills, so why should the same idea not work in their daily lives. The assumption was that immigrants would get along better if they were forced to drop all their foreign pretenses and act like "Americans."

Zangwill had a vision of a melting pot:

> America is God's crucible, the great Melting Pot, where all of the races are melting and reforming! – Here you stand in your fifty groups with your fifty languages – and your fifty blood hatreds – A fig for your feuds and vendettas! Germans and Frenchmen, Irishmen and Englishmen, Jews and Russians – into the crucible with you all! God is making the American.   (In Schlesinger, 1992, p. 11)

In the final scene of this play, the Jewish hero David and his Christian love are on the roof garden of a lower Manhattan settlement house when he gestures toward the city: "There she lies the Great Melting Pot – Listen can't you hear the roaring and the bubbling? Ah, what seering and seething: Celts and Latins, Slavs and Teutons, Greeks and Syrians – Blacks and Yellows."

Zangwill's metaphor of an American melting pot became the symbol for the Americanization movement in the early 1900s. Presidents such as Theodore Roosevelt and Woodrow Wilson played on the chauvinistic sentiments that were inherent in the melting pot metaphor. Wilson proclaimed that Americans who thought of themselves as belonging to particular national groups were not "thorough" Americans (in Schlesinger, 1992). Roosevelt, who was given to hyperbole, outdid himself when he said that "Americans were children of a crucible that does not do its work unless it turns out those cast into it in one national mold" (in Schlesinger, 1992).

This concept of one national mold never has included all citizens all the time. Our African American citizens were trying very hard to be molded into American citizens. But they were not allowed to be part of the mix. For most of the twentieth century in the USA, African-American citizens were excluded from the national mold. They were not viewed by the white American culture as "people like us." So they were segregated from other citizens to make sure that their black ways did not mix with the white ways. The German Americans and Japanese Americans also found themselves not included in the American melting pot when the political situation boiled over with chauvinistic fervor during World War I and World War II.

The "melting pot" represents a cultural canon or

a narrative model that American citizens have used since the 1900s to think about citizenship and diversity. It became part of the ordinary and "common-sensical" knowledge of the culture that was translated as "fitting in." This kind of knowledge, in contrast to propositional or school knowledge, is assumed to be true. It is just the way things "should be." Everyone just knew that ethnic diversity was a threat to political stability and was un-American. The idea was that citizens could "get along better" if they adopted common American values, customs and beliefs and repressed any of their foreign characteristics.

During the twentieth century citizenship education in the USA has involved two instruments of American culture. The first is folk psychological narratives about how Americans live their lives. The second is the public schools and their roles in political socialization and instruction of future citizens. Voluntary and involuntary immigrants learned how to be Americans by utilizing folk psychological narrative canons from their culture to shape their daily lives as citizens. They also learned to be American citizens through civic instruction programs and activities in the schools. These instructional programs primarily relied on propositional thought or logical argumentation to convince students of abstract principles or truths about civics (Bruner, 1986). Since its inception, education for citizenship has been a major objective of the public schools in the USA (Adler, 1983; Bellah *et al.*, 1991).

The American "common-sense" approach to citizenship

The folk approach to citizenship education in the USA has provided a track for black citizens that assigned them to membership in a negative social group. As a result, Dubois (1969) argues that the personalities of black Americans could not develop without creating a deep internal division. He describes the process of becoming an African-American as becoming both an American and not an American. To identify with "Americans" as a reference group is possible for all citizens, but such identification carries with it a powerful form of self-rejection for African Americans (Gaines and Reed, 1995). No black person in the USA can expect to be an American citizen in the same sense as white Americans.

Dubois pointed out that using the concept of

race to classify and evaluate human beings gained prominence only after the institution of New World slavery. Those differences that could be used to distinguish persons of European and African origin (e.g. skin color) were invested with social and psychological meaning that greatly exceeded their actual bearing upon individuals' social and psychological makeup. Racial categorization can be viewed as a cultural tool that persons in power use to identify others as inferior and to justify treating them as "inferior" (see Gaines and Reed, 1995).

In *The Souls of Black Folk* Du Bois (1969) suggested that his existence in the USA as a black citizen was defined as "a problem" every day in his life:

> Between me and the other world there is ever an unasked question: unasked by some through feelings of delicacy; by others through the difficulty of rightly framing it. All, nevertheless, flutter round it . . . Instead of saying directly, How does it feel to be a problem? They say, I know an excellent colored man in my town . . . or, Do not these Southern outrages make your blood boil? At these I smile or am interested. . . . To the real question, How does it feel to be a problem? I answer seldom a word. And yet, being a problem is a strange experience.   (Du Bois, 1969, p. 44)

The involuntary immigrants or former slaves were not to expect to become the same kind of Americans as the voluntary immigrants. Indeed, the culture painted a very dismal picture of what these new citizens could expect to achieve as Americans. They were not to act like white Americans or they would be ridiculed as "coons" and if they acted like black Americans, they would be ridiculed as "sambos", "mammys" or "colored folks."

Negative stereotypes of black Americans caused individuals to become anxious about inadvertently confirming them in their own eyes or in the eyes of others (Steele and Aronson, 1995). These negative stereotypes present a source of potential threat to one's self-esteem and feelings of competency. Consequently, black Americans might be expected to avoid situations in which they know others harbor negative stereotypes about them. As a result "stereotype threat" has contributed to de facto segregation in the USA. In the past, black Americans were most concerned about stereotype threat. However, white Americans are now increasingly aware of the negative stereotypes that black Americans hold about them. As a result some of them are becoming anxious that they will inadvertently confirm white "racist" stereotypes in their own eyes or the eyes of others.

The schools and citizenship education

Before 1890, one could argue that early Americans learned to be citizens by participating in public life rather than by taking classes in school. The educational institutions reflected differences of ethnicity, religion and social class and there was strong public opposition to "state power" in education. At the turn of the twentieth century, advocates for compulsory education used the German empire as a model for how education could be used to mold citizens and preserve the authority of the state. However, this German ideal of duty to the state was often in conflict with long-held American ideals about "individual rights." During the nineteenth century compulsory education was endorsed in principle but not widely enforced (Tyack, 1988).

At the close of the nineteenth century, the typical child in the USA could expect to attend school for five years. The US Commissioner of Education, William T. Harris, trumpeted this accomplishment and indeed he had a right to be proud. At that time, the USA led the world in its provision for mass education. After 1890, public attitudes toward compulsory schooling became more positive and by the mid-1930s, young people were typically required to attend school until the age of 16 (Tyack, 1988).

Compulsory schooling in the early years of the twentieth century was advocated as a means of educating immigrant children in crowded cities. It was viewed as a mechanism for creating and legitimating citizens. The schools were to transform all kinds of people into citizens by teaching common history and a common ideology in a common language. Tyack (1988) made the following observation about the role of schools in citizenship education:

> Characteristically, Americans intensified their attempts at political socialization in schools whenever they perceived a weakening of loyalties (as in World War I), or an infusion of strangers (as in peak times of immigration), or a spreading of subversive ideas (whether by Jesuits or Wobblies or Communists). Interest in compulsory attendance seems to correlate well with such periods of concerns. (Tyack, 1988, p. 335)

Schooling in the USA has always included a civic agenda. Thomas Jefferson wanted to create state primary schools to make loyal citizens of the young. Noah Webster wrote a federal catechism to teach republican principles to children. Horace Mann contended that the common schools would provide youth with traits of character and loyalties required for self-government.

Citizenship education

For the most part, US citizenship education during the twentieth century has been viewed by ordinary citizens as molding diverse peoples into one common American type. However, educators developed three intellectual perspectives on citizenship education in schools (Giroux, 1983). Two models in citizenship education based on a technical/instrumental view of knowledge are the "cultural transmission" model and the "social science" model. The former represents the oldest tradition in citizenship education. The idea is to transmit the "best of the culture" from one generation to the next. These cultural "canons" of knowledge are held to be sacrosanct and not open to question. Students are presented with a view of past, present, and future that is in some ways idealistic, and may not necessarily be historically accurate. This model closes its eyes to the faults of a society and uses modified forms of indoctrination to reify the "glorious collective past." The idea is to promote a sense of national pride. Cultural knowledge is imparted to students as cultural "truths" that are to be learned and not to be questioned. No student is to ask whether George Washington really did cut down the cherry tree. The social science model of citizenship education is more rigorous in its approach to defining the content of citizenship education. What counts in this approach is so-called objective facts about society. However, the social science perspective does not question the conditions under which they were constructed and does not examine the connections between these facts and social control. Both the "cultural transmission" model and the "social science" model of citizenship education fail to raise questions about how knowledge citizenship is constructed and by whom.

The hermeneutic approach to knowledge emphasizes how the texture of everyday life in a society contributes to our understanding of each other and the world around us. The tradition in citizenship education that has been most influenced by the hermeneutic perspective has been described as the "reflective inquiry approach." It teaches that citizens cannot escape the burden of making decisions in a democratic society. Students are encouraged to explore their own values and define problems within the context of their experiences, or to relate social problems to their day-to-day lives. The problem-solving process is the principle tool used in teaching citizenship education. This approach may question, but only in relatively narrow terms, the nature of existing social arrangements in society.

The emancipatory approach to knowledge teaches students to criticize what is restrictive and oppressive in society, while at the same time encouraging them to support actions in the service of individual freedom and well-being. If citizenship education is to be emancipatory, it begins with the assumption that its goal is not to fit students into the existing society. Citizenship education needs to stimulate the passions, imaginations, and intellects of students so that they will be moved to challenge social, political, and economic forces – to display "civic courage." Agnes Heller (1967) argues that citizens should think and act as if they live in a real democracy. The fundamental bravery of this way of life is not military heroism but civic courage. A citizen who is capable of saying no to the dominant prejudices and if necessary to public opinion has the virtue of civic courage. In this approach to citizenship education, students learn not only how to weigh the existing society against its own claims, but they are taught to think and act in ways that speak to different social possibilities and ways of living. The development of civic courage is by far the bedrock of any emancipatory approach to citizenship education.

In one contemporary view of civic education, which is similar to the "melting pot" model, truth and critical inquiry are subordinated to the aim of forming individuals who can effectively conduct their lives within the society and also support their political communities. The notion of support for political communities is a major criterion for judging the adequacy of civic education. Galston (1989) argues that civic education should not include an open critical study of history. Instead, the study of history should be more enabling and moralizing, describing heroes who confer legitimacy on social institutions and provide models for emulation. In this model, civic education is not to be justified as a means of fostering critical reflection on beliefs, values, and ways of life inherited from parents or cultural communities. McLaughlin (1992) uses Galston's model of civic education as an example of a minimal interpretation of "education for citizenship" that provides social-political information and attempts to develop very specific virtues (such as voluntarism). There is nothing in this view of education for citizenship that calls for critical reflection or moral reasoning about conditions in society that inhibit persons from being full members of a community. Obviously, this kind of minimalist interpretation for citizenship education can be open to criticism as being no more than "pure" indoctrination.

A strikingly different contemporary view of civic education is that students should learn how to participate in and influence those public affairs which define the common good (Newmann, 1979). Without the competence to influence the state, their inalienable right to do so cannot be exercised. Civic competence is this ability to exert influence in public affairs. Citizens have to be able to identify common issues of concern to citizens and become advocates to institutions of government. A citizen's attempt to exert influence can be viewed as a process in which the individual identifies goals or desired outcomes, such as electing a candidate for a school board. The person then takes the next step and works for support of these goals through organizing, bargaining, and various methods of persuasion. In building support, it may be necessary to revise goals so as to produce outcomes consistent with them. All attempts to exert influence in a democratic society should be ethically justified. The goal of civic education is to assist citizens in having some impact on public affairs consistent with intentions which they develop through a process of rational, moral deliberation.

Although schools in the USA have historically considered citizenship education to be an important part of their mission, far too often in the history of the country the model behind civic education has been the patriotic metaphor of a "melting pot." As a consequence, civic education has often sounded more like an exercise in "indoctrination" than in critical thinking (Andrain, 1985). In a review of the relevant research on civic education courses, the effects on tolerance and understanding of democratic living have been nil (Langton and Jennings, 1968; Ehman, 1980) or slight (Remmers, 1963). The reason for this may be inherent in the undemocratic structure of the school and its teaching of citizenship. In some cases, civic education has been a hodge podge of political slogans about loyalty to our country under all conditions of "rightness" or "wrongness." In other cases, civic education has presented our democratic traditions as a rationale for unfettered individualism. Issues of the common good have been represented as simply questions of loyalty to your country. The "common good" is defined as those rules, norms and values determined by "them" rather than "us." Students learn about their "individual goods" as if they existed in isolation from the rights of their neighbors.

Conclusion

Citizenship education in the USA has involved both the folk psychology of the culture and the schools in the country. The American folk psychological approach had two tracks, one for "white citizens" and one for "black citizens." Those who did not understand this "common-sense" distinction between citizens ran the risk of being ostracized or even violently attacked. Present conditions in the USA still reflect these folk divisions in daily life. White and black Americans at the turn of the twenty-first century may work together or even go to school together, but for the most part they do not live together, go to church together or play together. When this is questioned, both black and white citizens will often reply, "We are more comfortable with our own kind."

In order for white and black students to become citizens of a pluralistic society, they need to identify with the common good of their community. They must be able to communicate across their "backyard fences" with a wide variety of other citizens. Unfamiliarity and lack of communication among citizens breeds a lack of concern for others and poor citizenship. We are less apt to show "good will" or "fairness" to other citizens who are "strangers" to us. Thus citizenship education must ultimately include communication about life in the community and interactions with others who have different perspectives. Through such positive interactions, students can learn about the importance of tolerance in a democratic society. Democratic education is at the heart of citizenship education in a pluralistic society because it is a mechanism that brings all citizens together to discover their common humanity through solving the problems of common concern (see Mosher *et al.*, 1994).

What are the consequences of the two-track approach to citizenship in the USA? In light of history, it is not at all surprising that black youth still find it difficult to accept the idea that vocational and academic success will yield the same benefits for them as for white youth. As a result of their cultural experiences, many black students resist those who call upon them to "work hard" in school so that they too can achieve the "American dream." They also resist those who call upon them to be hard working, responsible citizens of a country that continues to provide lower expectations for them. Indeed, it is also not surprising that many black youth believe that schooling in the USA has always been for the benefit of white youth and not for them.

One of the main reasons that contemporary black youth may believe that working hard in schools and at their jobs will not yield benefits for them is that they are members of caste-like minorities that have been socialized under a dualistic model of citizenship (Ogbu, 1986; Fordam and Ogbu, 1986). Their historical and contemporary experiences have taught them that black citizens should not expect the same benefits from work and education as white citizens. Whites have been socialized to be "optimistic" about the possibilities of improving their lives if they work hard in school and at their jobs. Blacks have been socialized to be "realistic" about what they can expect from working hard. This dualistic approach to citizenship continues to foster the development of two segregated communities in the USA who view themselves not only as different but unequal partners in the American democracy.

Note

1 This chapter was originally presented at the Association for Moral Education Conference, University of Ottawa, Ontario, Canada, 13–16 November 1996.

References

Adler, M. (ed.) (1983) *Paidia: Problems and Possibilities*. New York: Macmillan.

Andrain, C. F. (1985) *Social Policies in Western Industrialized Societies*. Berkeley, CA: Institute of International Studies.

Bellah, *et al.* (1991) *The Good Society*. New York: Knopf.

Bruner, J. (1986) *Actual Minds, Possible Worlds*. Cambridge, MA: Harvard University Press.

Bruner, J. (1990) Culture and human development: a new look. *Human Development* **33**, 344–55.

Cross, W. E. Jr. (1995) Oppositional identity and African American youth: issues and prospects. In W. D. Hawley and A. Jackson (eds) *Toward a Common Destiny: Improving Race and Ethnic Relations in America*. San Francisco: Jossey-Bass.

Du Bois, W. E. B. (1969) *The Souls of Black Folks*. New York: Signet. (Original work published 1903.)

Ehman, F. A. (1980) The American school in the political socialization process. *Review of Educational Research* **50**, 99–119.

Feldman, C., Bruner, J., Kalmar O. and Renderer B. (1993) Plot, plight and dramatism: interpretation at three ages. *Human Development* **36**, 327–42.

Fiske, S. T. (1993) Controlling other people: the impact of power on stereotyping. *American Psychologist* **48** (6), 621–8.

Fordham, S. and Ogbu, J.U. (1986) Black student's school success: coping with the "burden of acting white". *Urban Review* **18** (3), 176–206.

Gaines, S. O. Jr. and Reed, E.S. (1995) Prejudice from Allport to Du Bois. *American Psychologist* **50** (2), 96–103.

Galston, W. (1989) Civic education in the liberal state. In Nancy L. Rosenblum (ed.), *Liberalism and the Moral Life*. Cambridge, MA: Harvard University Press.

Giroux, H. (1983) Critical theory and rationality in citizenship education. In H. Giroux and D. Purpel (eds), *The Hidden Curriculum and Moral Education*. Berkeley CA: McCutcheon, pp. 321–60.

Heller, A. (1967) Marx's theory of revolution and the revolution in everyday life. In *The Humanization of Socialism: Writings of the Budapest School*. London: Ellison and Busby.

Heller, A. (1974) *Theory of Need of Marx*. London: Ellison and Busby.

Langton, K. P. and Jennings, M. K. (1968) Political socialization in the high school civics curriculum in the United States. *American Political Science Review* **62**, 852–67.

McLaughlin, T. H. (1992) Citizenship, diversity, and education: a philosophical perspective. *Journal of Moral Education* **21** (3), 235–50.

Mosher, R. *et al.* (1994) *Preparing for Citizenship: Teaching Youth to Live Democratically*. Westport CT: Praeger.

Newmann, F. M. (1979) Skills in citizen action: an English-social studies program for secondary schools. In R. L. Mosher (ed.), *Adolescents' Development and Education*. Berkeley CA: McCutchan, pp. 418–33.

Ogbu, J. U. (1986) The consequences of the American caste system. In U. Neisser (ed.), *The School Achievement of Minority Children: New Perspectives*. Hillsdale NJ: Erlbaum.

Raywid, M. A. (1983) Family choice arrangements in public schools: a review of literature. *Review of Educational Research* **55**, 435–67.

Remmers, H. H. (ed.) (1963) *Anti-democratic Attitudes in the American Schools.* Evanston IL: Northwestern University Press.

Schlesinger, A. M. Jr. (1992) *The Disuniting of America: Reflections on a Multicultural Society.* New York: W. W. Norton.

Steele, C. M. and Aronson, J. (1995) Stereotype threat and the intellectual test performance of African Americans. *Journal of Personality and Social Psychology* **69** (5), 797–811.

Tyack, D. B. (1988) Ways of seeing: an essay on the history of compulsory schooling. In R. M. Jaeger (ed.), *Complementary Methods for Research in Education.* Washington DC: American Educational Research Association.

Vogt, W. P. (1997) *Tolerance and Education: How Education Influences Attitudes and Beliefs.* Thousand Oaks CA: Sage.

14 Changing Values and National Identities in the Caribbean and their Effect on Language Education Policy

PETER A. ROBERTS

For the child, from the outset, the process of acquiring literacy in the formal educational context is simultaneously a process of acquiring discipline and learning to conform. Learning the alphabet, for example, means acquiring a set of symbols and a relationship between sounds and those symbols which is accepted as natural. Learning to spell means learning to write words in the same way that everybody else writes them. Learning to construct a proper sentence, paragraph and essay means learning rules and learning to follow rules which everybody else follows. Moreover, this process takes place in a formal context, the classroom, which requires a high degree of conformity from all who are in it. There is a high degree of conformity in the Caribbean classroom in the grouping and appearance of the children as a result of age grading and the wearing of school uniforms, among other things. Conformity in the Caribbean classroom is therefore both apparent and taught. This conformity is pursued in the Anglophone Caribbean, a region where each country has a different and in most cases complex language history.

The language of instruction in all Anglophone Caribbean schools is English and English is also studied by all children as an academic subject. The pass rate, on average, in the Caribbean Examinations Council English 'A' examination, which is taken by children around the age of sixteen and generally used in the world of work as a kind of passport, is about two-thirds of those who sit the exam. Weaker students who would have been deemed to have no chance of passing the exam as well as drop-outs are not included in this average. In general, therefore, there is a high failure rate which is usually associated in the minds of the population at large with the degree of distance between the school language and the language of the home

– a degree of distance which varies from very great to marginal depending on the class and upbringing of children in these countries with their different language histories.

Conformity in official language is seen as facilitating national cohesion in the USA and in the case of Canada lack of cohesion (i.e. bilingualism) is seen as doing the opposite. In the case of Britain, monolingualism evolved as a fact of life and was implemented in the colonies in the Caribbean, not only in the same spirit, but also as a way of consolidating colonial gains. In other words, territories gained by the English from the French in treaties had to be made English. This was achieved by making English the sole official language in business and facilitated by using English as the language of instruction in schools to ensure that the young, in contrast to their parents, became English. It was intended that the general population should change to suit the official language and not the reverse. This policy was not altered after the different countries gained their independence from Britain, even if different arguments have been put forward today to justify the policy that English be retained as the official language of instruction in school.

In addition to the fact that English was instituted as language of instruction in Caribbean schools for hegemonic reasons for the mass of the population, the process of schooling and the teaching of literacy were introduced in the nineteenth century partially as a method of control to replace slavery. Roberts (1997) presents evidence of the close relationship in the Anglophone Caribbean between literacy and control as well as the way in which education for slaves (and then ex-slaves) was perceived and used as a conduit for the inculcation of religious and social values to maintain the power relationships in the status quo. One of the clearest demonstrations of this intent is seen in the publications of the Ladies' Negro Education society immediately after emancipation, which contained the following as reading material for the young children of the liberated slaves:

> These people were once slaves, but now they are apprenticed to their master for six years, after which they will be free. All their little children who are not yet six years old, are free already. Then, too, they have an hour and a half more every day to work for themselves. So they feel very grateful to God, their King, and their country, and wish to show their love and thankfulness, by being better servants to God and their kind **Massa** than they were before. Besides they remember that God has said in his Holy Word, 'If any will not work, neither let him eat.' They each want to do sixty holes before sunset, and they gladden their labour by repeating the texts which they have learnt at church, or at the Sunday and Night Schools.
>
> I hope you are very grateful to God, who has put it into the heart of the King and the good people of England to think about the salvation of the Negroes, and that you try to show your gratitude by being industrious and obedient, and strive to serve and please God in all things.

This close relationship between literacy (i.e. early reading material), submission, 'good' behaviour and success which formed a part of the primary school and Sunday school curricula from that time on contributed to a value system in the Caribbean which underscored conformity as the foundation of success in modern society. In addition, the institution of English as the language of instruction in schools and, as a consequence, the use of literature imported directly from England created in the Caribbean among the general population an admiration for English values.

Everyday experience within the acculturative process in the Caribbean taught slaves and their descendants to adopt certain strategies if they wanted to survive and prosper in the societies in which they found themselves. One of these strategies which complemented the process of conformity towards a foreign model is captured in the Haitian Creole proverb *Couleuvre qui caché, vini gros*. Literally it means 'the snake which is hidden becomes big/fat'. Ardouin, in whose 1853 history of Haiti it appears, gives it a French translation (*pour éviter un danger, il ne faut pas se laisser voir*) which translates into English as 'to avoid a danger, you must not let yourself be seen'.

For many Caribbean people at home and abroad, especially in the face of the monolithic presence of the English language and English derived culture, this proverb translates into a strategy of invisibility where the Caribbean person is in the role of the *couleuvre*. Caribbean proverbs consistently use animal imagery for effect. Although it seems peculiar for people to cast themselves in the image of a snake, the proverb captures a certain reality which Caribbean people live out daily in the public and formal domains of society and have lived out for centuries. It is a certain reality which has a poignant immediacy when a person is downtrodden, seen as a danger and always under attack.

The proverb represents a general strategy of invisibility or conformity for survival and progress which is mirrored in various ways, primarily in the behaviour of the lower working classes. However, what can betray individuals who adopt this strategy is their speech. The most immediate 'revealer' (and therefore constant threat to invisibility and conformity) in social interaction is one's speech. Immediately upon speaking one's national and regional identity and social class are labelled according to one's accent, and often one's level of education and intelligence according to the choice of words. The Creole speaker in the Anglophone Caribbean is acutely aware that language is a recognized badge of identity which will determine reactions, privileges accorded or denied, jobs, placement, preference, acceptance and rejection. This awareness is based on knowledge and everyday experience not only within the Caribbean but also outside the region. It also has a long history: for example, by Samuel Mathews (1793, pp. 132–3), in telling jokes about Creoles in London, begins:

> Three West Indians, young gentlemen of fortune, went to a public house, in London, to dine, they resolved to keep their being Creoles a secret.   (Mathews, 1793, pp. 132–3).

Mathews then related how the lack of knowledge in their choice of words revealed their identity and effectively reduced their social status. In fact, Creole speakers then and now know that many English people actually associate Creole speech characteristics with deficiency, and some actually find such speech annoying. Today such attitudes are not restricted to the English. American television, for example, often uses subtitles to 'translate' the speech of West Indians living in the USA into 'normal' language, even though West Indians interact with and are understood by Americans in their everyday lives and even though they are more intelligible to the television public than many non-English speaking white Europeans attempting to speak English.

There is a very long history of humiliation as a result of linguistic identity in various societies in the New World and it is on this experience that the strategy of avoidance has been based. Attempts to avoid public humiliation as a result of language problems and the sad consequences of these attempts have been highlighted on the island of St Lucia by Alleyne (1961). He presented the case of people being brought before the court to answer charges even of a very serious nature and preferring to conceal monolingual French Creole competence, that is, their inability to understand English, the language of the court, rather than to acknowledge publicly that they did not understand English. (Note that the court would have provided them with interpreters if they had indicated that they could not understand English.) They were in a sense saying 'gaol rather than linguistic humiliation'. This illustrates the depth of feeling attached to language choice and performance in the public domain and the need to conceal a perceived 'deficient' linguistic identity which makes one stand out negatively.

As other examples from within the Caribbean one can take typical cases from Trinidad or Barbados. In Barbados, for example, some working-class St Lucians, Vincentians and Dominicans choose to speak like Barbadians (which for them must be doubly bitter) in order to avoid the typical Barbadian stereotyping of them as 'low islanders'. Migrants from all the islands living in one metropolis or another (i.e. London, New York, Miami) and having to compete for jobs and privileges with other immigrants as well as citizens quickly come to the conclusion that, in order to avoid constant humiliation by being asked to repeat what they said, to be understood more easily and to have a better chance of earning a daily living, they must 'do as the Romans do, when in Rome' and mask their native linguistic identity in public.

While lower working-class adults have to make choices, particularly when they are in the unskilled category, their children are confronted by problems which are equally if not more difficult because of tenderness of age, over-sensitivity and lack of experience. When children have not yet fully acquired the duplicity of adults, they can be cruel in their social dealings with others whom they do not like or understand. Those on the receiving end know this. In the Caribbean itself when a lower working-class or rural child moves into an urban secondary school the experience may initially be traumatic because the child's normal speech is somewhat removed from the language required in the classroom. If the child begins by adopting evasive tactics in the classroom, this continues for the length of secondary school experience.

In the case of immigrant children in big city schools, they quickly find that as soon as they open their mouths in the classroom, they are no longer considered if their accent is different. So, in order to avoid public humiliation, rejection or open confrontation, some of them opt to conceal their linguistic identity (meaning their inability to produce mainstream or appropriate social class speech) at all costs and suffer the educational consequences, rather than to be identified as 'nerd', 'jerk', or whatever the current teenage word of disapproval may be. Others seek safety in the solidarity of a strong group, which consequently may lead to undesirable behaviour. In other words, since language is one of the most prominent features of identity, Creole-speaking children may either try to conceal their normal speech by adopting that of the dominant culture or may seek to stand out by emphasizing their own or by adopting an alternative, clearly different one.

In the classroom the danger (i.e. humiliation) may come not only from peers but also from the source of authority – the teacher. Again, there is a long history which can be attached to this. In 1774 Long described the strategies of punishment which should be used by masters to slaves:

> The force of ridicule, on the contrary, brings upon them the cutting sneers of the other Negroes, and always turns the edge of their contempt and rage from their master, to themselves; and hence they may smart more severely under such reprehension, than they would under the scourge. (Long, 1970/1774, pp. 411–12)

If instead of 'master' you read 'teacher', then it is obvious what effect such a tactic will have on a lower working-class or immigrant child, who by speech, behaviour or dress falls outside the pale of conformity. In order to avoid such 'dangers', the lower working-class or immigrant child may choose not to be seen, as the proverb suggests. The child will avoid the eyes of the teacher and when directly asked a question will use body language. The teacher will immediately reprimand the child, will insist on words, and the child will keep words to a minimum. Even up to university level it is difficult to get the majority of students to talk freely in the classroom. In Britain, Canada and the USA many Caribbean children have been identified as timid and even unintelligent because of their lack of (linguistic) assertiveness.

The long recognized practice by West Indians of trying to conceal national identity is not totally unrelated to the fact that they are often not officially counted among the speakers of English. In other words, by being linked formally in their national identity to a colonial language (English), by being perceived to be 'bad' speakers of this language, and by being observed to imitate other people's speech in public and formal contexts, West Indians are not usually regarded as native speakers of English and included (in international presentations and statistics) as such. Thus, a major characteristic of their national identity is left unstated and the status immediately accorded to an English-speaker is withheld in the case of West Indians. In public formal domains therefore it seems as if they spend most of their lives conscious of this initial languagelessness which is thrust upon them. It is a perceived 'deficiency' that some continue to try to overcome whenever they journey abroad or interact with foreigners by imitating their interlocutors. In sophisticated contexts among themselves, many Creole speakers, aided by values and practice in the educational system, have traditionally essayed different ways to circumvent the undeclared status to their 'best' native speech by adopting other ways of speaking. The practice may have declined over the last thirty years but it is still a significant factor.

Complementing the strategy of avoidance, therefore, has always been the practice of imitation, a practice which is imbued with very positive values. This is seen, for example, in the history of speech-making in the Anglophone Caribbean. In the first half of the nineteenth century, Bayley (1833, p. 585) remarked: 'In the West Indies there is a sort of rage for this table elocution, and there are some gentlemen who really speak well, but who, unfortunately, have also a propensity for speaking **long** (half an hour for instance).'

Caldecott, at the end of the same century, noted:

But life in the West Indies had, of course, its aesthetic side in some form. The chief amusements were Conversation and Dancing. The conversation which chiefly filled the hours of social intercourse of the men was, after its kind, more artistic than the conversation of a community which is largely absorbed in reading. In furtherance of it great dinners were in vogue, and every opportunity was seized for holding them. . . Seated round a table loaded with the varied products of these fertile regions, with the chief native liquor, rum, supplemented by imported wines and spirits of Europe, the hearts of West Indian Planters expanded with the chief enjoyment they knew, and tale and song and practical joke, too, filled up the long evening hours.   (1970/1898, pp. 39–40)

The models for speech-making in the West Indies in the 1780s were decidedly British and male. This is clear from the way in which the evidence of notable speech-making in the law courts in the West Indies is presented. Luffman (1789, pp. 148–9), in his treatment of Antigua, says: 'The solicitors are advocates also. A Mr. Burke . . . stands foremost for energetic declamation; Mr. Hicks and Mr. Wise, for ingenuous argument; the language of the latter is elegant possessing, at the same time, the luxurious flowers of rhetoric and fine oratory.'

So impressed was Luffman with the language skills of these gentlemen that he continues:

It is to be deplored that such abilities should be confined to so small a circle as this island, abilities, which would possibly enable the possessor (if at the bar of the Westminster courts) to raise himself to the first eminence in his profession. (Luffman, 1789, p. 149)

References to 'energetic declamation' relate back to the oratory of people like Edmund Burke, Charles James Fox, William Pitt and to the case of Warren Hastings and the celebrated speeches of Richard Sheridan.

What is interesting about the development of facility in speech-making among the white population is its relationship to a similar facility among the black population. The late nineteenth- and twentieth-century phenomenon of performance English, which is documented throughout the Anglophone Caribbean as part of the culture of the black population, is linked by Abrahams and Szwed (1983, p. 79) to British traditions: 'This kind of speech is regarded as a borrowing from British sources rather than as an adaptation of African style to New World language, setting, and occasion.'

It seems clear that the early references in the literature by Long (1970/1774, pp. 426–7) and Edwards (1794, p.83) to oratory or speeches among the slaves, even though they were not instances or the kind of performance English that became a cultural characteristic of the black population in the latter part of the nineteenth century, were a developmental phase. More generally, during their 'entertainments', balls and parades at Christmas time, in their imitation of whites, the slaves proposed inappropriate toasts, exhibited 'genteeler behaviour' and acted like their masters. In addition, the slaves watched and participated in English farces put on by the local whites and became familiar with their 'theatricals', their costumes, their toasts, their speech and their high society behaviour.

However, their behaviour was seen as ludicrous and their attempts at artistry were ridiculed:

> The better sort are very fond of improving their language, by catching at any hard word that the Whites happen to let fall in their hearing; and they alter and misapply in a strange manner; but a tolerable collection of them gives an air of knowledge and importance in the eyes of their brethren, which tickles their vanity, and makes them more assiduous in stocking themselves with this unintelligible jargon.   (Long, 1970/1774, pp. 426–7)

Yet, what emerges as significant in this speech-making and in the creolization process is the role of imitation. Local whites were seen to be imitating the English and blacks were seen to be imitating local whites. On the other hand, local white women, remarkably enough, were said to be imitating their slaves: 'You are accused of several great foibles, such as valuing yourself too much on your Negroes, lisping their language' (Barbados Gazette, 1732).

Poole (1753, p. 280) also noted that white women's speech was like that of the slaves. He believed that this reflected 'want of proper care in their education', a view echoed two decades later by Edward Long in Jamaica. His proposed solution for the problem of white Creole women who did not go to England was 'a boarding school for these girls . . . where they might be weaned from the Negroe dialect' (Long 1970/1774, p. 250). This was a time when overseas education for the children of the white planters was the norm, but principally the males were sent to be educated. So, for women, imitation of 'bad' models was to be replaced by imitation of 'good' models. Imitation, therefore, seemed to be a fact of life and a general practice from the early years in English Caribbean colonies.

In the construction of English colonial society, women and slaves, because of their perceived language and other deficiencies, were relegated to lower roles, which did not involve decision-making and ruling; that level of society was for white men only. Moreover, the education system introduced by the English into their Caribbean colonies in the nineteenth century was specifically geared to produce workers for the medium and lower levels of society. Within the ruling class itself, the social divisions that were characteristic of social gatherings in England were preserved and strengthened. Note what Pinckard (1806) said about the seating at dinner parties in the very English island of Barbados:

> Instead of the different persons being, pleasantly, intermixed, it is too common to see the ladies grouped together in a crowd at the upper end of the table – the officers and strangers, just arrived from Europe, placed at one side, – and the gentlemen of the island, who are mutual and familiar acquaintances, at the other side.   (Pinckard, 1806, p. 103)

The separation of the sexes was so clear that, according to Pinckard, even before dinner the women did not join the men and after dinner they had to retire so that the men could 'enjoy their bottle'. This was a policy of exclusion by the dominant, not one of avoidance by the dominated. By the beginning of the nineteenth century the Barbadian social scene was male dominated with women relegated to the background. Interestingly enough, the social separation of the sexes said to be characteristic of Barbados contrasted with practice in Trinidad, if Carmichael (1969/1833, p. 322) is to be believed: 'Drinking to excess is unknown in good society in Trinidad; the gentlemen join the ladies in the drawing-room, in a quarter of an hour after they have retired.' Trinidad society, unlike Barbadian society, had not been overwhelmingly influenced by the British and their ways.

Differences in language competence served to maintain social distinctions in British colonial society; the differences in education perpetuated this. The monitor or pupil–teacher system used in local education ensured the propagation of a creolized language among women and the coloured population while foreign education for white males pre-served the primacy of British English (in theory more than practice) among the ruling clique of males. Imitation of foreign English by West Indians up to today can therefore be interpreted not only as an attempt to avoid the detection of Creole identity but also as a continuity from the early days of education, as imitation of the ultimate model.

The opposite direction can be identified as an alternative form of avoidance behaviour, manifested not in the kind of evasive tactics mentioned, but in those which seem quite the opposite. Reisman explains this apparent contradiction in his presentation of ambiguity and ambivalence on the island of Antigua:

> Yet lower class status, for rural villagers, is not just a position which one happens to occupy. It is also an **assertion.** There are both positive and negative aspects to low status membership. So there are a number of contexts in which, rather than simply conforming to the deference patterns accompanying such status, one asserts the status – and its lowness – by unruly, disorderly and non-English behaviors associated with it. (Reisman, 1970, pp. 135–6)

This manifestation of the strategy is therefore what is regarded as 'ignorant' behaviour and presented as the other face of avoidance. It is not surprising therefore that strong assertiveness is not encapsulated in any popular adage in the Caribbean – it is not seen as wise in historical folk experience. Even if it is perceived on the international scene as characteristic of Americans, it is still often regarded by older people in a negative light. It is associated with 'the ugly American' at the level of the individual and with the 'big stick' American at the national political level. In addition, even if assertiveness attracts some admiration, it is seen as one of the acquired benefits of those who are powerful and have succeeded, but not necessarily encouraged as a method for success. In other words, it has never been presented as a model of positive behaviour for the masses of Caribbean students and it is not a preferred feature of the Caribbean classroom. However, avoidance behaviour, in both its evasive and assertive forms, is now increasing in Caribbean classrooms and among Caribbean students overseas.

Today, the most troubling manifestation of avoidance behaviour differs from the familiar class-based one: it is gender specific. Gender-specific analyses of the values of Jamaican schoolgirls by Miller (1967, 1969) and of Jamaican schoolboys by Figueroa (1976) were not explicitly comparative, but they reflected a growing perception of differences between boys and girls in their values and scholastic achievement. By the late 1980s and early 1990s Miller had shifted his attention to the plight of males (Miller, 1991, 1994). Today the differences in performance between boys and girls are seen as constituting a problem across the Caribbean region. This problem is not only directly addressed as Caribbean-wide in academic papers (e.g. Parry, 1996) but is also discussed in the media and as a popular topic (e.g. Layne, 1997).

The consequences of what is here called 'avoidance behaviour' are seen in the marked decline in academic performance of males in the formal educational system. This decline is noted at the secondary level in the results of public examinations and also at tertiary level in the graduation statistics of the University of the West Indies where female graduates have come to outnumber male graduates in every faculty except one (Engineering). In Barbados specifically, this decline is popularly attributed to the almost universal implementation of co-education (in the early 1980s) in the secondary school system, but since there was no such parallel measure in other islands where the same phenomenon is observed, co-education cannot be used as a general explanation. Social progress for women surfaces in arguments as the main causative factor: the perceived decline is negatively correlated with the rise of feminism over the last thirty years and more specifically with the increasing numerical dominance of female teachers in primary and secondary school classrooms, teachers whose notions of conformity and discipline in the classroom are believed to conflict with traditional male student behaviour. While there may be substance to these arguments about the reaction of males to recent gains by females, the most critical factor in the decline has to be the change of attitude in boys towards English. Speaking standard English is regarded by many of them as a kind of denial of self whereas the use of non-standard dialect, or some deliberate modification of it, is adopted as more desirable and appropriate. This disregard for the language of instruction has negative consequences across all subjects in the secondary school programme.

In the case of Caribbean children in metropolitan

schools avoidance behaviour is manifest in the following:

- denial of native identity;
- adoption of overt symbols of the perceived superior or host culture, including public language of display (greetings, cursing);
- adoption of negative attitudes towards school and standard English, the language of instruction – some teenagers view standard English and success in school as white behaviour;
- adoption of an alternative culture, e.g. Jamaican culture;
- opting out among boys and lack of motivation for academic work;
- absenteeism and involvement in antisocial behaviour.

In contrast to the more traditional avoidance with imitation, there is today then more avoidance with assertiveness, that is, what would seem to be more 'ignorant' behaviour. In actual fact, this change highlights a difference in choice between imitation and assertiveness.

Reisman's (1970) view of 'assertion' in the West Indies (on the part of the dominated, black population) is presented within a framework of African survivals in which 'unruly' and 'disorderly' are explicitly associated with 'non-English behaviors' and presumably with African behaviours. In fairness to Reisman, although he does not specifically say so, unruly, disorderly, ignorant behaviour was in the popular perception and in the acculturative process associated with Africa. When imitation and assertiveness are used as poles of behaviour, it is not only that they have been traditionally associated with English on the one hand and African on the other, it is also that they bear some relationship to popular perceptions of national identities in the Anglophone Caribbean. In line with this conception, if the Anglophone territories are set out on a continuum based on level of retention of African features, Jamaica can be identified as having the highest level, with Barbados at the opposite pole.

In other words, Jamaicans and Barbadians can be seen to have opposite tendencies as far as life strategies are concerned. For even though Jamaica and Barbados both had a long history of British rule and are fairly similar in their racial composition, Jamaicans and Barbadians are perceived to be diametrically opposed in their national character, that is, in the way they are popularly spoken about. Barbadians are seen as more colonized, non-

confrontational, law abiding, more English in speech, generally literate and generally level headed. Jamaicans are more highly visible and more creative, and are seen as more confrontational and assertive, less law abiding, less generally literate and more Creole speaking. This contrast between Barbados and Jamaica is not only a popular perception but is also highlighted in the literature. Note, for example, that in the argument between Hancock (1980) and Cassidy (1980) about the difference between Jamaican English and Barbadian English, both concede that there is a sharp difference between the two varieties of English. Hancock argues in the case of Barbados: 'I maintain that then, as now, it was a local metropolitan, rather than creolized, variety of English that was spoken by both blacks and whites on the island' (Hancock, 1980, p. 22).

Hancock contrasts this 'metropolitan variety' in Barbados with a creolized variety in Jamaica.

Alleyne (1980) also presents a linguistic contrast between the two islands but for him it is rooted in a broader cultural contrast:

In Barbados, the emancipated slaves remained for the most part on sugar plantations. Whereas the plantation as a social institution afforded little opportunity for primary social contacts between master and slave and between manager and fieldworker, it provided the locus for a relatively high degree of interaction when compared with the small farming communities set up in the remote hills of Jamaica by former slaves who left the plantations in large numbers after emancipation. In Barbados, the relatively high demographic strength of Whites, the topography of the island, and the early development of secular and religious education (Barbados now has one of the highest literacy rates in the world) also contributed to the rapid movement of all Barbadians through the stages of linguistic acculturation . . .

In Jamaica, and to a lesser extent in Antigua and Guyana, the process of acculturation has not advanced as far as it has in Barbados. (Alleyne, 1980, p. 186)

This is essentially a continuation of an earlier analysis which Alleyne (1971) had presented:

We have Barbados, the U.S.A., Antigua, on the one hand, where conditions favoured the greatest departure from African modes of life.

The correlations of this linguistic picture with other aspects of culture are numerous. Take the example of religion. African religion survives in its pure state in cults like **Cumina** in Jamaica . . . This kind of worship is entirely absent from the modern United States of America or Barbados. (Alleyne, 1971, p. 181)

As is evident in Alleyne's argument, there is a basis in the observable daily lives of Barbadians and Jamaicans for popular perceptions of polar differences between the two peoples.

While these types of generalization do not hold for all Jamaicans and Barbadians, they tend to correlate with academic performance (i.e. the results of public examinations) as well as with poverty and crime statistics. They also set up Barbados as a model of orderly behaviour as well as a successful island, which tends in the regional perspective to lend support to and preserve traditional language educational policy.

Such generalizations about national identity usually have a historical basis and in the case of these two islands it can be seen as a difference in the intensity and pervasiveness of English influence in spite of both being under English colonial domination for the same length of time. So, the difference between the two islands has been explained in terms of the fact that Jamaica was bigger and had mountainous terrain which allowed for maroonage, while Barbados was small and flat and did not allow for maroonage. In addition, the primary school system of education effected by the Church of England was more general and widespread in Barbados than it was in Jamaica. Even if the popular idea that the slaves who went to the two islands were different in their ethnic character cannot be shown to be true, it can be demonstrated that during the slave period, for maintenance and increase of population, Barbados relied more on natural increase than Jamaica, which depended more on importation of new African slaves. The cumulative effect of this over the years was that the acculturative process in Jamaica was much slower. Added to these basically socio-cultural factors, it should be borne in mind that Jamaica was nearer to and more affected by revolutionary events in nineteenth-century Haiti and events on the other (Spanish) islands of the Greater Antilles than was Barbados. The acculturative process (i.e. the adoption of English values and behaviour) in Jamaica was therefore not as 'successful' as it was in Barbados.

Barbados was the first English Caribbean colony where the natives were identified by name, 'Barbadians' (Oldmixon, 1708, p. 14). What was really extraordinary about Oldmixon's reference, however, was that it also associated the black, slave population with the term: '40,000 of them [Negroes] are Natives of the Island, as much Barbadians as the Descendants of the first Planters, and do not need such a strict Hand to be held over them as their Ancestors did' (Oldmixon, 1708, p. 14).

At the beginning of the nineteenth century, M'Callum (1805, p. 338) referred to Barbados as 'the oldest and most civilized of our Slave Colonies'.

In the latter half of the century, Underhill (1970/1862, p. 97) said: 'Barbados is often called Little England, and the Barbadians are proud of their highly cultivated and prosperous island.' This description clearly applied not only to the white population but also to the black for, as Pinckard (1806, p. 76) explained earlier, the native-born slaves there voiced the same sentiment: 'Me neder Chrab [Carib], nor Creole, Massa! Me troo Barbadian born.'

So, overall, while Barbadian characteristics are associated with the English, Jamaican assertive behaviour is often interpreted by other West Indians as a manifestation of 'ignorance', which is believed to be a characteristic of Jamaicans. In this distinction between the national identities of Jamaica and Barbados, one can see therefore that the conception of Barbadian is consistent with imitation and can be placed at one extreme and that of Jamaican with assertiveness at the other extreme.

Antigua, the country that Reisman (1970) was dealing with, and the older British Caribbean colonies have small populations without any well-known and immediately identifiable national identities, probably because they fall between the two extremes. The other nations in the Anglophone Caribbean, those which only came definitively under British colonial rule at the end of the eighteenth century or the beginning of the nineteenth, are conceived of differently. What characterizes these later British colonies is a greater degree of and more deep seated ethnic, cultural and religious differences. Trinidad and Guyana have East Indians and their languages as a major component of their identity and Trinidad also has a history of French and French Creole. St Lucia and Dominica have a dominance of French Creole and Grenada residues of the same. Such components do not allow for a unidimensional scale of (English) imitation and (African) assertiveness. For instance, it is interesting to note that in Trinidad in the second half of the twentieth century there has been more military-type violence associated with Africanness than in Jamaica, yet Trinidadians are not conceived of negatively or associated with 'ignorant' behaviour. In fact, they are associated with a Carnival and calypso (i.e. carefree) mentality.

It may seem then that the imitation–assertiveness paradigm is limited in its usefulness because, even though the English/imitation relationship applies to all the colonies, the African/assertiveness relationship applies only to Jamaica. The fact is, however, that Jamaica has been a catalyst for development in the Caribbean. Many Caribbean young people of various cultures today identify with assertiveness because they view the identity of Jamaica in a very positive light. Assertive behaviour is now accepted by the young not as negative but positive. In this reversal, the national identity of Jamaica is identified with Marcus Garvey and Bob Marley, popular, internationally known, revolutionary-type heroes tied to Africanness. In Britain where Jamaican identity, through speech, is adopted by West Indian born youths or those born of West Indian parents, this is the result of the knowledge that there is safety in numbers and that Jamaicans, because of their perceived aggressive behaviour, are more feared than other West Indians or blacks in Britain. Today young West Indians have become aware of the economic value of Jamaican identity because of the dominance of Jamaican music, the Jamaican and specifically Rastafarian speech in it and the associated African imagery. As a result, Jamaican speech is imitated widely outside Jamaica. This not only puts in a different light the consequences of the behaviours that Reisman (1970) refers to as 'non-English', but also identifies non-English with African and gives validity to the imitation–assertiveness paradigm.

The Jamaican–African-assertiveness relationship, symbolized in figures such as Bob Marley and Marcus Garvey, is for the Caribbean young person linked at the international (American) level to a figure such as Malcolm X, who had a strong (black) Muslim and African connection. Malcolm X differs from figures such as Martin Luther King and Mohammed Ali, who were not immediately connected to Africa and were basically non-violent in their behaviour. As such, King and Ali have been heroes for older Caribbean persons while Malcolm X was not. His confrontational, assertive rhetoric is now being re-evaluated by Caribbean youth in a positive light. The Jamaican–African

connection is of course most powerfully symbolized in the person of the Rastafarian and his spiritual head, Haile Selassie of Ethiopia. In addition, the most powerful international figure associated with violent struggle in the last decade is Nelson Mandela of South Africa. The assertiveness of these figures and the confrontational Jamaican have not been the inspiration for most older Caribbean people.

In the adults' negative conception of assertiveness and positive conception of conformity through imitation and avoidance, the person whose experience and behaviour has been the focus of attention is either a lower working-class person in his/her own country, a migrant from a poorer Caribbean territory to one a little better off, or a migrant from the Caribbean to Britain, Canada or the USA. These constitute the vast majority of Anglophone Caribbean people and their experience is the norm. This has varied according to their actual situation, but through the experience of being workers rather than bosses common responses and a common philosophy have evolved. Even those Caribbean people who are not poor and downtrodden are not completely excluded. In this case disadvantage is not determined by class. There is a history of racial exploitation which makes it clear that the reality of being at a higher level of Caribbean society is no more than being a generation or two removed from the plantation and the fields. In addition, the fact that the Caribbean colonies were established to serve and service greater powers has caused Caribbean people to see themselves in the position of the exploited. In other words, national identity in the Caribbean is part of the notion of 'Third World' which is generally regarded as politically and economically subordinate, even powerless. It is this kind of experience and the cautious philosophy for improvement that it has inspired which have determined current language education policy.

The strategy of avoidance coupled with imitation and rejection of assertiveness have for a long time been at the heart of a reality of language education policy in the Caribbean: no local native (variety of) language (in the case of the Anglophone Caribbean) has become the sole official and de facto language of instruction in schools. Even today none seems likely to become so; this role is generally identified with the English language. Although some applied linguists have attributed the persistence of this policy to political inaction, among the acknowledged reasons for its persistence is clearly the fact that the speakers of Creole themselves have been resistant to the idea of an upgrading of the Creole to make it a school language. This negative valuation older Creole speakers have to the use of Creole in public formal domains generally, and in the formal education system specifically, was assumed by applied linguists to be based on ignorance and a long history of colonial indoctrination. This is a misguided assumption, for the Creole speakers' valuation has always been based on everyday experience, pragmatic values and proven strategies.

The implementation or non-implementation of an exclusive Creole language policy lies with the Creole speakers themselves. The fact is that Creole speakers are more sophisticated and rational than they are thought to be. They know that their Creoles are essentially lower working class and that formal education is not. Their attitudes to the past and the future are less romantic, less exotic and more practical in the context of a world which they consider for the most part hostile. Even when told of the advantages of primary school children being educated in their native language, many older Creole speakers remain unconvinced of the overall advantages of Creole education because they see no real advantages. However, the high value attached to standard English by adults is now being challenged by new values. The re-evaluation brought about by Jamaican 'ignorant' behaviour is being applied to each territory in turn by its young people. In popular behaviour (music, radio call-in programmes, literature) assertiveness is increasingly becoming a model to be followed.

This change is based to some extent on imitation of current fashion but more on conscious choices made by young people. The strategies they adopt are a result of actual experience in the formal educational setting and elsewhere. In the internal struggle which each child/student faces in the classroom, though choices made can be set out in a framework of cultural values which highlight continuities or changes, faithfulness to national, regional or social class identity is not a strongly motivating factor. Value in the choice made is related to perceived success and personal survival. It is because of the perceived success of what Reisman referred to as 'non-English behaviors' that attitudes towards standard English have changed.

It is not a foregone conclusion, however, that the move away from standard English as the model for success will become 'consciousness' behaviour, and as such adopted generally by girls through their normal interaction with boys. One indeterminate factor right now is that in the re-evaluation of 'ignorant' African behaviour the major models (e.g. Marley and Malcolm X) are male. This is coupled with the fact that the decline in male academic performance is often interpreted as a negative reaction on the part of males (boys) to the gains of feminism. However, this present interpretation, which links boys' academic performance to assertiveness and re-evaluation, must support the argument that girls will eventually adopt the same attitude and that the differences in performance will become insignificant. If this happens, then further changes will have to be accommodated in the educational system and policy will be driven from the bottom rather than dictated from the top. Policymakers will have to devise ways to incorporate the new values into language education policy.

There are a number of educational problems arising from the contradiction between re-evaluated 'ignorant' behaviour and traditional policy. One significant problem is that Caribbean people of all social levels have always been migratory; they see their world as an extension from the place where they were born to one or more metropolitan centres. For them, education has to facilitate freedom of movement. When Caribbean children move to big cities and confront school in these alien cultures, they suffer some shock of not being 'normal'. However, their (former) colonial and (now) outward-looking education will have partially prepared them and their parents. They have a home and neighbourhood culture which sustains them and provides them with coping strategies. Caribbean governments seem to have always been educating their people to move about freely, to fit in wherever they go. It would not be sensible policy now, in the era of the 'global village', for the language competence of Caribbean people to be restricted to their place of birth.

Another problem is that Creole languages in the Caribbean will not become the languages of the powerful, even if they feature more prominently in the expression of heritage and the preservation of dignity. In fact, historical evidence in the Anglophone Caribbean, that is, observation of the process of decreolization, points to their decline or fusion with the standard language. Re-evaluation may slow this process but tourism and the media will ensure its continuation. However, it is already being seen that assertion of ethnicity, with native language as a major factor, is becoming more necessary in the global village as a method of preserving self and community. In view of these realities, it seems logical that policy should be consistent with both the perceived evolution and assertion of ethnicity.

Another problem brought about by the change is that since the benefits of assertiveness have been accompanied by several ills, educational policy would have to de-link assertiveness (and the kind of creativity which it facilitates) from the negative values which it also inspires in the Caribbean. Re-evaluation has created an illusion of licence in general behaviour. In relation to the classroom specifically, the greater use of native language has fostered the myth that achievement can take place without conformity, discipline and hard work. Such illusions and myths have to be dispelled.

Solutions to the contradictions caused by change – adults' negative views of assertiveness and young people's experience of the benefits, the male decline in academic performance and female success, assertion of ethnicity and decline of language, local Caribbean needs and migrant needs – will not be provided by a language education policy. In fact, these opposing forces and the arguments supporting them will cause a continuation of what may appear to be an ad hoc education policy. Nevertheless, it seems appropriate to suggest that Creole language should be formally represented in the school to the extent that this facilitates learning and makes secure the confidence and cultural heritage of the majority of children. Creole languages and Creole ethnicity must, however, be seen as a stage in the continuous process of evolution of language and ethnic identity. They cannot be promoted as permanent ethnic or linguistic states or as having characteristics which are immutable. Synthesis and syncretism, which in academic literature are constantly associated with the Caribbean and are the historical product of evasion and imitation of the foreign, are now being replaced by assertion of native Caribbeanness. While this Caribbeanness is now seen as a spiritual and emotional constant, it has to be made more rational in the face of inevitable evolution and in consequence of the demands of a technological 'global village' and the information age.

References

Abrahams, R. and Szwed, J. (eds) (1983) *After Africa*. New Haven and London: Yale University Press.

Alleyne, M. C. (1961) Language and society in St Lucia. *Caribbean Studies* **1** (1), 1–11.

Alleyne, M. C. (1971) Acculturation and the cultural matrix of creolization. In D. Hymes (ed.), *Pidginization and Creolization of Languages*. Cambridge: Cambridge University Press, pp. 169–86.

Alleyne, M. C. (1980) *Comparative Afro-American: An Historical-Comparative Study of English based Afro-American Dialects of the New World*. Ann Arbor: Karoma.

Ardouin, A. B. (1958/1853) *Etudes sur l'histoire d'Haïti suivies de la vie du Général J. -M. Borgella*, 2nd edn, F. Dalencour, ed. 5 Rue Saint-Cyr, Port-au-Prince, Haiti.

Bayley, F. W. N. (1833) *Four Years' Residence in the West Indies During the Years 1826, 7, 8 and 9*. 3rd edn. London: William Kidd.

Bennett, L. (1966) *Jamaica Labrish*. Sangster's Book Stores, Jamaica.

Caldecott, A. (1970/1898) *The Church in the West Indies*. London: Frank Cass.

Carmichael, Mrs C. (1969/1833). *Domestic Manners and Social Condition of the White, Coloured, and Negro Population of the West Indies*. 2 vols. New York: Negro Universities Press.

Cassidy, F. (1980) The place of Gullah. *American Speech* **55**, 3–16.

Edwards, B. (1793–4) *The History, Civil and Commercial, of the British Colonies in the West Indies*. London.

Figueroa, P. M. E. (1976) Values and academic achievement among high school boys in Kingston, Jamaica. In P.M.E. Figueroa and G. Persand (eds), *Sociology of Education: A Caribbean Reader*. Oxford: Oxford University Press.

Hancock, I. F. (1980) Gullah and Barbadian: origins and relationships. *American Speech* **55**, 17–35.

Layne, A. (1997) Gender and academic performance in primary and secondary schools in Barbados. Public lecture at the Cave Hill Campus of the University of the West Indies, 29 April.

Long, E. (1970/1774) *The History of Jamaica, or General Survey of the Antient and Modern State of that Island: With Reflections on its Situations, Settlements, Inhabitants, Climate, Products, Commerce, Laws and Government*. London: Frank Cass.

Luffman, J. (1789) *A Brief Account of the Island of Antigua . . . Written in the Years 1786, 7, 8*. London.

Mathews, S. (1793) *The Lying Hero or an Answer to J. B. Moreton's Manners and Customs in the West Indies*. St Eustatius: Edward L. Low.

M'Callum, P. F. (1805) *Travels in Trinidad*. Liverpool.

Miller, E. L. (1967) A study of body image; its relationship to certain physical, social, cognitive and adjustment variables in a selected group of Jamaican schoolgirls. Unpublished PhD thesis. Mona: University of the West Indies.

Miller, E. L. (1969) A study of self concept and its relationship to certain physical, social, cognitive and adjustment variables in a selected group of Jamaican schoolgirls. Unpublished PhD thesis. Mona: University of the West Indies.

Miller, E. L. (1986) *Marginalization of the Black Male: Insights from the Development of the Teaching Profession.* 2nd edn. Mona, Kingston: Canoe Press.

Miller, E. L. (1991) *Men at Risk.* Kingston: Jamaica Publishing House.

Oldmixon, J. (1708) *The British Empire in America.* London.

Parry, O. (1996) Schooling with fooling: different approaches to educational underachievement of Caribbean males. Paper presented at the 21st Annual Conference of the Caribbean Studies Association, San Juan, Puerto Rico, 27–31 May.

Pinckard, G. (1806) *Notes on the West Indies.* 3 vols. London: Strahan and Preston.

Poole, R. (1753) *The Beneficient Bee: or, Traveller's Companion.* London.

Reisman, K. (1970) Cultural and linguistic ambiguity in a West Indian village. In N. E. Whitten, Jr and J. F. Szwed (eds), *Afro-American Anthropology: Contemporary Perspectives.* New York: Free Press, pp. 129–44.

Roberts, P. A. (1997) *From Oral to Literate Culture: Colonial Experience in the English West Indies.* Jamaica: The Press UWI.

Underhill, E. B. (1970/1862) *The West Indies: Their Social and Religious Condition.* Westport CT: Negro Universities Press.

15 Pluralism and Linguistic Diversity
Policy Trends in Africa

CLINTON D.W. ROBINSON

Introduction

The place of cultures and cultural differences in today's world is high on the social agenda. The issues come into clear focus in education where students from differing cultural backgrounds mix together every day, where they join in a common learning exercise and where their attitudes towards each other and their cultural background are being formed. Defining and developing education for a multicultural world are identified as the central challenges for educational planning for the twenty-first century in the conclusion of the Delors Report *Learning: The Treasure Within* (1996). As part of this concern, this chapter will look at the place of linguistic diversity and language policy, with special reference to the African context.

The multilingual complexity of Africa poses special challenges to the design and implementation of education. The large number of distinct ethnic groups, some numbering only a few thousand and each speaking its own language, introduces considerations different from those pertaining to northern contexts. These issues, however, have never been high on the international educational research agenda. Northern research issues have been the dominant focus for which resources have been available (Little, 1996). This has meant the continuation of colonial policies and practices which were derived from European situations, quite different linguistically from Africa. Explanations of language policy inertia have revolved around issues of power and political elitism (Corson, 1993; Ouane, 1995; Tollefson, 1991).

Yet large socio-political questions of cultural mismatch and historical influence beg more basic questions about values. What value is attached to language in situations of diversity? What particular values underlie decisions about language use and promotion? Whose values prevail? One reason why questions like these have not figured more prominently in addressing decisions about language in education in Africa is the lack of detailed attention to the numbers and uses of languages (Adegbija, 1994). This has meant that decisions have been made on other criteria, without close consideration of the structure of language diversity (Cooper, 1989).

This chapter will explore these issues, first by a discussion of pluralism, values and the place of language. A presentation of language diversity in Africa will follow in order to show more clearly the linguistic reality. I will then examine some approaches to language policy and ask how far they may be considered pluralist. Cameroon will provide a detailed example of a country of high linguistic diversity and will be contrasted with Zaïre, Tanzania and South Africa.

Pluralism, languages and values

Pluralism

Every society, indeed every community of whatever size, is plural in nature, in that it is made up of different groupings. Plurality as a fact does not however necessarily lead to pluralism. Pluralism is a question of attitude towards differences, relationships between different groupings and evaluation of differences. It rests on the recognition of differences, rather than denying them or minimizing their importance, seeking to make such recognition a positive feature of social life and behaviour, and looking for a commonality which might underpin the acceptance of diversity. Kekes (1994) argued that this commonality is our common humanness with its universal requirements:

> There *are* human differences, but they are *human* differences . . . the Dinka and we, radical feminists and ayatollahs, Tibetan lamas and stockbrokers are all human beings, and therefore they are – we are – united at a deep level of our being. The minimum requirements of our welfare are the same. These requirements create a case for meeting them, and that case will be found persuasive by all reasonable people who pause to reflect on it.   (Kekes, 1994, p. 59, original emphasis)

Kekes is worth quoting at length, since he introduces, but does not acknowledge, another commonality, that of the 'reasonable person'. It is that common value on which the universal appeal of his argument rests. In other words, the common core of a pluralist approach is that 'reasonable people' can agree on what minimum human welfare requires. Those who cannot agree then presumably become 'unreasonable', therefore different, and the pluralist search for a common vantage point begins again. Nevertheless, the notion of the 'reasonable person', also a concept in English law, may have practical value in the pluralist debate; it would be hard to sustain the debate without it. However, I shall leave further discussion of its basic validity to moral theorists.

Turning now to situations of linguistic diversity, a pluralist approach does not shy away from the intricacies of a linguistic situation and is not threatened by a multiplicity of languages. The detail of such diversity is rather to be explored and appreciated. Evaluation begins as choices have to be made about how far diversity, linguistic in this case, contributes to the quality of life. We should note that this is not yet a question of the priority of resources, but of what this diversity offers in qualitative terms. Edwards (1985, p. 105) answers this by defining a pluralist approach as a 'sensible middle road between segregation and homogenisation' and sees 'group harmony' as a central tenet of pluralism. In practice there must be much sympathy with this position, since the alternatives are ultimately less than human: assimilation or complete ethnic separation. The latter has been the basis for the so-called ethnic cleansing of the 1990s. The theoretical difficulty remains, in the domain of any diversity, linguistic or otherwise. As Larmore (1994, p. 70) puts it, '*how* are the values weighed against one another?' He sees no answer to this question

beyond returning to ideas similar to those of the 'reasonable person', termed a 'moral perception'.

The disagreement over the evaluative function of a pluralist position is manifest in different approaches to linguistic diversity in Africa. Conceptions of how it contributes to a quality of life differ widely. African languages were and remain important to those who speak them; of greater importance to colonial – and some post-colonial – policymakers has been their own maintenance of power or convenience of administration. More recent concerns for social cohesion have brought these two positions closer together, as is clear in attitudes towards pluralism in education.

While pluralism admits and appreciates difference, the question is how to turn this into a tool which builds social cohesion rather than exacerbating it. Education has this responsibility:

> Education serves as a vehicle for cultures and values, creates an environment where socialization can take place and is the melting-pot in which a common purpose takes shape . . . Faced with the breakdown of social ties, education has to take on the difficult task of turning diversity into a constructive contributory factor of mutual understanding between individuals and groups. (Delors, 1996, pp. 53–4)

This report also reflects the pluralist tension between acknowledging difference yet 'upholding the principle of homogeneity implicit in the need to observe common rules' and yet makes 'learning to live together' one of its four pillars of education. It is not my aim here to review the literature or debate the issues raised by multicultural education, a task admirably performed by other contributors to these volumes. Rather, I will examine how far a pluralist stance is reflected in the language policy framework in Africa, with reference to linguistic practice in education.

Before exploring other dimensions of pluralism – culture, globalization and human rights – I offer the following working definition of pluralism on the basis of the foregoing discussion: pluralism is the active recognition and appreciation of cultural differences, based on respect for human dignity, ensuring space for dialogue about conflicting opinions over values.

Cultures

There is a tendency in some popular circles to posit

the possibility of a pristine state of a culture which is sufficient in itself and untouched by contact with other cultures. This has been the basis for a popular perception of Latin American indigenous groups isolated in the tropical rain forest. In such situations those of a culturally pluralistic stance may seek the maintenance of cultural purity, so that each culture can sustain its distinctiveness. Whether such isolation and resulting cultural purity has ever been the case is moot (cf. Edwards, 1985, p. 106), and certainly intercultural contact is the norm with resulting mutual influence and change. As Kukathas puts it:

> Cultures must be seen, then, as distinguishable ways of life which are the product of the interaction of individuals within cultures and among cultures. Because they are the product of interaction, and are subject to numerous influences, cultures are also mutable.   (Kukathas, 1994, p. 6)

Such a definition of cultures will profoundly affect attitudes and policies of cultural pluralism. First, it implies that there is not and can never be a status quo which can be preserved or serve as an authoritative cultural map of a region or state (de Cuéllar, 1995). Second, it accepts the validity of each culture and of their influence on each other. While this may be an organic and steady process under normal circumstances, it becomes traumatic in situations of gross inequality of power – military, economic, cultural, political. The struggle between recognizing the truth of Kukathas' contention and merely acquiescing to any kind of cultural contact and change is a tension at the heart of cultural pluralism and policies based on it. Questions such as the following are the abiding stuff of the pluralist debate in multi-ethnic and multicultural situations:

- How far is one culture beginning to dominate another?
- What measures can be taken to limit cultural invasion?
- How far is cultural domination being pursued as a policy and by whom?
- Why should a 'small', 'minority' culture have any fewer rights, resources, privileges and power than a 'large' and 'mainstream' culture?

These questions can be asked directly, *mutatis mutandis*, of language issues and they underlie the evolution of language policies in a number of African states, as we shall see.

Discussion of pluralism tends to isolate values into systems which may then be compared and

contrasted. The obvious danger of over-categorization is that overlap between systems – shared, common values – is downplayed. A further danger exists in distilling values to such an extent that their actual outworkings are neglected, as Featherstone contends:

> So it is important when we seek to examine the quest for fundamental values not to err too much on the side of abstraction and assume a plurality of different value positions as coexisting in some ideal value sphere which confronts the individual with an agonizing choice between potentially meaningful (or meaningless) alternatives. Values only effectively exist if they are used practically and mobilized by various groups of people.   (Featherstone, 1995, p. 74)

In terms of pluralist policies this represents a call for an integration of rhetoric and reality. In terms of analysis it calls for a recognition of the discrepancy between avowed commitment and actual practice, and thus that reflection about values be measured against their actual manifestation in society. Featherstone is also making the point that people rarely choose values as a complete abstract set, but as a means of living their lives in a meaningful way. He contends that values are manifested particularly through the means of cultural transmission; while he is concerned with cultural intermediaries, such as the media, artists and so on, language is a sine qua non of such transmission. Thus policies about language and languages reveal much about the real value accorded to cultures.

Is cultural pluralism as a basis for policy merely a recognition of the presence and validity of distinct cultures, or does it imply in any way a promotion of cultural diversity? Diverse cultures may be seen as enriching our lives by bringing in new and different values as fresh perspectives on what life is about (Kekes, 1993). A pluralistic stance on the part of governments recognizes that each cultural group's greatest good is pursued by allowing/promoting values specific to them. In the linguistic sphere the difference is between seeing linguistic diversity as a problem to be managed or an asset to be developed (Robinson, 1996a).

Globalization

This must be debated in relation to globalization. How far does globalization rest on a very broad consensus of values? Or does it rest on 'core values that all humanity could uphold: respect for life, liberty, justice and equality, mutual respect, caring, and integrity' (Commission on Global Governance, 1995, p. 336)? In other words, is globalization as such an expression of multicultural stance? Is the fact that we can talk about globalization at all an indication that many across the world accept diversity of values as an overriding value? It is important to specify whose perspective is in focus here. While international academics and civil servants may identify some sort of 'globalized' culture within which diversity finds its place, rural communities in Africa or India may find globalizing tendencies threatening or incomprehensible.

One interpretation of globalization is associated not with diversity but with homogenizing influences, with the assumption that somehow the world is moving towards a global monoculture (UNRISD, 1995). As soon as we ask, like Knutsson (1996, p. 113) 'whose perception of the global – and what ought to be globalized – are we talking about?', then it becomes clear that certain countries, sections of the population and institutions are able, by means of particular media, to promote products, information and messages all over the world, and others are not. From the point of view of the 'recipient', these are not part of some global culture, but 'localized expressions or manifestations or something from another part of the globe that attracts me. . . or is powerful enough to influence [me]' (Knutsson, 1996, p. 114).

Featherstone argues that globalization should not be equated with homogenization, particularly in the cultural sphere. It is rather a force which opens up a 'dialogical space in which we can expect a good deal of disagreement, clashing of perspectives and conflict, not just working together and consensus' (Featherstone, 1995, p. 103). As he goes on to point out, homogenizing influences are a result of unequal power relations, and therefore of dominance and cultural arrogance. Not everyone has equal amounts of 'dialogical space', even though equity may be well accepted in principle. Language is a crucial part of this debate, since the growth of the use of English has been associated with the increasing global reach of powerful and well-resourced media. Thus English has both been a means of such penetration and has led to the desire to learn it on the part of ever greater numbers of people. Discussion of this extension of English reflects the globalization debate – some heralding its importance as a unifying/homo-genizing factor, others seeing it as an instrument of neo-colonialist approaches (Pennycook 1994; Skutnabb-Kangas and Phillipson, 1995). In the language debate the starting point of the local-language speaker is frequently neglected. Just as Knutsson, quoted above, called for a clearer definition of what globalization means for the 'recipient', so the situation of the local-language speakers – with their communication needs and patterns, individual and collective multilingualism, and specific linguistic environment – is neglected. This difference of perspective will be apparent again in discussing the development of language policy.

The value of language

How far does language matter as a value? It is already clear that attitudes and policies about languages reflect attitudes to cultures and to pluralism. What kind of value is attached to language? Is it one of the universal, constant, minimum requirements of human welfare? Clearly the capacity for language is a basic human and social phenomenon, but it is not at this level that language becomes a value. Rather than language being a value in itself, value is attached to language when questions are asked about different languages, about languages in their social context, particularly in situations where a number of languages are present in the same social space. Thus languages are valued for their relative usefulness, beauty, prestige, tradition, literature, or significance to certain people; a language may even have 'utility and exchange value' in economic terms (Coulmas, 1992, p. 53ff). Any value which people attach to a particular language depends therefore on its connection with other aspects of the speaker's life: their relationships, group membership, economic aspirations, religious practices or political circumstances. Owing to these multiple and often overlapping links, the value attached to a language does not depend on the nature or quality of the language itself, nor on the human capacity for language, but on what specific languages do and represent for people – thus on instrumental and symbolic functions. These two functions are observable in every instance of language use and are inseparable. In instrumental terms language is a tool, enabling us, for example, to pass messages, issue orders, transmit information, or express ourselves poetically. The focus is on the content carried by the language and the potential impact on the hearer. In its symbolic role language is a badge, identifying the speaker and signalling to the listener information about solidarity and distance, power and status, culture and background. It is the symbolic function which is heavily value laden. While there is some discussion, based on the Sapir-Whorf hypothesis (Mandelbaum, 1963; Carroll, 1972; Edwards, 1994), about whether any language can perform any instrumental purpose, it is generally agreed that all languages can, in one way or another, express the same information and serve as a channel for any message. Some languages are richer in certain vocabulary areas than others, some are more or less complex grammatically, but ways can be found to express any idea. It is in this sense that linguists maintain that all languages are equal and, in their instrumental role, cannot be assigned an intrinsically different value (Hymes, 1992; Edwards, 1994).

Socially, the situation is quite different. In social space languages, and varieties of a single language,[1] represent identity, power relations and the multiple dimensions of personal and institutional relationships. As symbols of such significance, languages evoke loyalties, excite feelings and conjure up images of self and others. Whatever the content of the message which the language carries, its very use is value laden, and this is particularly true in multilingual environments.

Of particular interest to the linguistic dimension is the pluralist debate over conflicting values. Because languages are value laden there is often an assumption that they may be in conflict. This however is rarely the case since multilingual competence is a basic human capability. Where language competition forms the basis of policy, it is seen as impossible to promote a plurality of languages, since promoting one will lead to the eclipse of the other. While certain languages are felt to compete – for instance, French and English on a worldwide scale (Ager, 1996; Wardhaugh, 1987) – a better basis for policymaking is the recognition of the different uses and contexts (domains) in which each language functions best.

Since this chapter is written by an English speaker for an English-speaking (or English-reading) public, a brief parenthesis is in order here. Debate rages over to whom English belongs (see Phillipson, 1992; Quirk, 1985) or whether it belongs to anyone at all. In other words, for whom does English represent a powerful expression of identity? What does it symbolize for native speakers from the UK,

Canada, Australia, the USA, etc? All speak different varieties of English. Furthermore, while each group may have feelings of loyalty to a local variety of English, they all understand and (may) speak a variety which is shared with the 500–700 million speakers of English as a second or foreign language. This 'international' variety does not belong to anyone, and thus has little or no function of identity. It does, on the other hand, have very high symbolic value in terms of power. It can be difficult for both these reasons for users of (international) English to appreciate the strong feelings of group membership and cultural identity which are evoked by speakers of minority and indigenous languages. In such situations, language is the primary symbol and marker of identity – the badge par excellence that signals membership of a relatively small group and maintains the boundaries. For speakers of English, it is frequently other cultural markers, along with local linguistic features, which make up a composite identity symbol. In terms of values, English-speaking elites may find it harder to understand the strong feelings evoked by local languages, since they have acquired such power and status through their mastery of English. This is well known, but becomes an issue where those same elites are responsible for setting policies for minorities and indigenous groups.

Linguistic rights

This leads to consideration of human rights, not only in an individual sense, but of the 'collective rights of culturally distinct peoples' (Stavenhagen, 1990, p. 73). Even though language is the most salient marker of minority and indigenous groups, it has only recently moved into prominence in the human rights movement. The Declaration of Linguistic Rights, signed by eighty-five institutions and international non-governmental organizations in Barcelona in June 1996 and presented to UNESCO as a potential international convention, sees linguistic rights as 'individual and collective at one and the same time', and takes the language community as its basic unit of analysis:

> It adopts as its referent the case of a historical language community within its own territorial space, this space being understood, not only as the geographical area where the community lives, but also as the social and functional space vital to the full development of the language. (Universal Declaration, 1996, p. 9)

These points of departure echo Khubchandani's (1995, p. 314) contention that 'linguistic rights are essentially *cultural*' (original emphasis), related to social groupings sharing a collective identity of which language is not only an element, but a powerful symbol. A concern for linguistic rights implies a pluralist view of social organization and aims to establish an appropriate framework. The Universal Declaration of Linguistic Rights 'aims to encourage the creation of a political framework for linguistic diversity based upon respect, harmonious coexistence and mutual benefit' (Universal Declaration, 1996, p. 7).

The linguistic human rights movement gives focus to the promotion of cultural pluralism in two particular ways:

1 It recognizes the centrality of language as the carrier/vehicle and symbol of cultures, with the implication that attention must be given to language as a crucial factor in enabling the culture to sustain a public presence alongside others.
2 Attention to language focuses on a prominent boundary marker of cultures, thus making it more difficult for states, elites or majorities to lump together people who perceive themselves to be distinct. While acknowledging how remarkably difficult it is in certain situations to establish the boundaries between different languages, language must be considered as one boundary-marking factor, along with other ethnic distinctives.

This discussion has addressed values, language and pluralism in general and not with specific reference to education. This is because the values on which language policies rest – in education or more generally – reflect societal values and approaches to cultural, ethnic and linguistic diversity. Education is however one of the prime sites in the institutional fabric of society where the effects of language policy are felt. In what follows an analysis of Africa's linguistic diversity will serve as a basis for examining the use of African languages in education. The subsequent section will present a detailed analysis of the language policy of Cameroon, with reference also to other countries of the continent.

Linguistic diversity

Of a total of 6,703 living languages in the world, 2,011 are found in Africa, according to the most

recently published research (Grimes, 1996). The distribution of languages worldwide is as follows:

- The Americas 15 per cent;
- Africa 30 per cent;
- Europe 3 per cent;
- The Pacific 19 per cent;
- Asia 33 per cent.

The much lower linguistic diversity of the north, relative to the south, explains in part the lack of attention which this question has received in research circles. While language issues in education are high on the northern research agenda, with resulting concern for changes in policy (cf. the recent recognition of Ebonics, a black American English variety, as a medium of instruction in some Californian schools), the complex situations of the south and their implications have attracted neither resources nor effort in the same measure. This state of affairs crucially affects the debate, since a lower level of research results in lower awareness of the issue on the part of policymakers. It is not infrequent to hear educational policymakers from the south dismiss the language issue with the contention that 'there are just too many languages' (Tadadjeu, 1989). It is at precisely that point, however, that northern biases are revealed and that the particularities of southern situations require fresh approaches. The northern bias emerges in the assumption that the use of languages in education will necessarily have to fit educational systems inherited from the west. This assumption works against the search for radical ways forward which integrate sound pedagogical principles with high linguistic diversity.

Measuring linguistic diversity is an area of research in itself. Numbers of languages must be correlated with levels of population, but not in a direct way. Following earlier work (Robinson, 1993), linguistic diversity is measured here based on the population size of the largest language group in each country. Thus the most highly diverse country linguistically will be the one where the largest language group represents the smallest proportion of the population. All other language groups therefore represent smaller percentages.

Table 15.1 lists countries of sub-Saharan Africa according to three levels of diversity on the same measure.

Ever since the earliest days of formal education initiated by missionaries in Africa, the question of linguistic diversity has been on the agenda.

Table 15.1 Countries of sub-Saharan Africa grouped according to largest language group as percentage of population

<22%	22–50%	>50%
Cameroon	Angola	Botswana
Central African	Benin	Burundi
Republic	Burkina Faso	Congo
Chad	Ethiopia	Djibouti
Côte d'Ivoire	Gabon	Equatorial Guinea
Kenya	Gambia	Eritrea
Liberia	Ghana	Lesotho
Mozambique	Guinea	Mauritania
Namibia	Guinea Bissau	Rwanda
Nigeria	Malawai	Somalia
Tanzania	Mali	Sudan
Togo	Niger	Swaziland
Uganda	Senegal	Zimbabwe
Zaïre	Sierra Leone	
Zambia	South Africa	

However, until the end of the 1980s the debate was overshadowed by the legacy of colonialism. This legacy meant that the language situation was seen as a problem to be solved, rather than as an educational asset to be explored. It is noteworthy that the educational value of beginning a child's education in the mother tongue is not even a subject of debate in, say, Germany, but continues to be debated in Africa, as an educational issue. While the question of resources is a thorny issue where languages are many, the search for ways forward is not helped by confusing economic and educational/pedagogical arguments.

As we shall see when examining language policy in Cameroon, the continued focus in educational circles in the colonial era was the place of the metropolitan language. The use and non-use of African languages were debated in relation to the promotion of French, English, Portuguese, etc. This left the majority of states at the time of independence with educational systems that gave heavy weight to learning the metropolitan language and which rewarded mastery in it with the most powerful and prestigious social positions. African languages were neglected; an implicit value judgement was made against them, manifested in two ways, using Cameroon as an example:

> Success in education is dependent on success in French, and therefore intellectual training and advancement have nothing to do with the local language and culture; rather, education is a process of distancing oneself increasingly from local culture; education never comes to the child by means of the local language.

The local language and culture are of little or no intellectual interest or value, since they are never the object of systematic enquiry or description in school.   (Robinson, 1996a, p. 106)

Generations of African teachers and students have absorbed implicit messages of this kind, resulting in internalized attitudes of cultural inferiority. This is all the more confusing when calls are made by those outside the educational system for a recognition of cultural diversity, whether for reasons of national politics or cultural development (cf. MINFOC, 1985). Clearly neglect of local languages and cultures and their rejection by implication is an anti-pluralist position and cries out for clarification of the values which should underpin the educational system in situations of high linguistic diversity. Arguments about pedagogical processes and best practice are powerful but will remain at the level of rhetoric unless those within the educational systems of Africa are clear about the values which are driving policymakers, politicians and educational planners. It is true to say that reasons of pedagogical practice will only carry weight when built on the bedrock of conviction about the basic value given to cultural and linguistic diversity. I now turn to this question.

Pluralism and language policy in Africa

Africa provides a particularly rich and interesting context in which to examine how far cultural pluralism is or has become a value which influences national policy. Language policy is an area par excellence in which such values become apparent. In discussing policy the arguments for and against the use of African languages will not be repeated here. They are well summarized and documented by others such as Bokamba (1995), to whom the reader is referred for further literature on the topic (cf. also Robinson, 1996a). I build on the premise that, as Bokamba concludes, 'the best language policies for African states are multilingual ones' (p. 23) where African languages find their place alongside official languages. My concern is to ask how far the development of this kind of policy is based on pluralist approaches.

Further, the colonial history of Africa has meant a confrontation of quite different cultures, and above all with western culture which saw itself as qualitatively different from African cultures. Speaking of the rise of rationalism, Featherstone comments:

It was assumed that Western nations which had first developed and applied this knowledge were well ahead in the process of social development and . . . that the project had an inherent and demonstrable superiority . . . In the last analysis this meant that everyone throughout the world would have to acknowledge the superiority and universality of the project of modernity. Such was the dream of (Western) reason. (Featherstone, 1995, p. 72)

At the time of independence for many African countries (around 1960) the focus was not on the intrinsic value of the languages and cultures within their borders, but on the building of a united, efficient and 'modern' nation-state. The models for such an enterprise were of course the European states who had been their colonial masters. Part of this model was the dominance of a single language in national public life, even to the point of assuming that such nation-states were monolingual. Writers such as Haugen (1972) and Sutherlin (1962) promoted the desirability of a single language as factors of national unity and administrative efficiency. While African states recognized the plurality of ethno-linguistic groups within their borders, there were no precedents or patterns of how to integrate their use into national institutions. Cultural distinctives were celebrated in terms of tradition and folk history, but rarely allowed expression in the political sphere. These approaches are reflected in the evolution of language policies. Cameroon will serve as a detailed example, with briefer reference to Zaïre, Tanzania and South Africa for contrastive purposes.

Cameroon

Cameroon is particularly interesting from the point of view of linguistic and cultural pluralism. Its 13 million people speak a total of 270 languages (each of which has its dialectal variants); both French and English are official languages, reflecting its colonial tutelage under France (Cameroun) and Britain (Southern Cameroon). Geographically and climatically the country has three clear zones: tropical rain forest in the south, grasslands and savanna in the centre and west, and dry sahelian conditions in the north. These differences are reflected in living and farming patterns as well as in distinct cultural practices. The languages fall into three major language families: Bantu/Bantoid (south and west), Adamawa (east and centre), and Chadic (north). Christianity (54 per cent), Islam (28 per cent) and

traditional religion constitute the main religious groupings.

In this context there has been debate since the earliest records about language diversity. With the arrival of missionaries in the eighteenth century and the colonizing powers in the nineteenth century the debate focused on the use of languages in the administrative and educational systems. Bearing in mind the working definition of pluralism suggested earlier, we will assess how far changing language policy in Cameroon reflects a pluralist stance.

The lack of records does not allow us to trace the pre-colonial history of language use in Cameroon. One can only surmise that the daily use of languages was structured by the needs of communication and by political realities. Thus people probably learnt to whatever level necessary those languages which were useful to them – those of neighbouring groups, larger groups, groups into which they married or from which they took spouses. On a political level conquering groups, such as the Fulani of northern Cameroon, brought their language which spread in the area as a lingua franca.

The basis on which Christian missions, Catholic and Protestant, chose and used languages was initially the desire to communicate as clearly as possible with the local population for evangelistic purposes. This meant using local languages, and early written documents in Cameroonian languages date from this time (Stumpf, 1979). This policy was extended to education, but soon encountered the question of how many languages to develop and use for this purpose. Moving away from the principle of using those languages which communicate best, both Catholic and Protestant missions selected certain languages for use both as church languages and as the medium of instruction in education. However, in the latter domain, the metropolitan languages of the colonial powers – first German (1884–1916), then French and English (after 1916) – became important. Although each colonial power gave some attention to teaching in local languages, the metropolitan languages were in fact promoted through incentives to students and by the prestige accorded those who found work with the colonial administration. By the 1950s, just a few years before independence, local languages had disappeared from the formal education system (Robinson, 1996a).

In terms of multicultural approaches, Christian missions recognized the value of local languages, though this was tied up initially with the desire to communicate a message, rather than with an appreciation of diverse local identities. Nevertheless, the missionary movement, in Cameroon as elsewhere, came to take a real interest in local languages and cultures for their own sake, resulting in monographs and descriptions (see Basel Mission, 1988). In a sense this never developed to a multicultural position, since the question of how to recognize each ethnic identity as well as promote co-operation and dialogue between groups was never resolved. The promotion of some languages for broader communication was an attempt to cross ethnic lines, but introduced power differentials which were keenly felt by local people whose languages were not selected. The colonial administrations, in spite of some support for local languages generally and in education (Robinson, 1996a), gradually increased the emphasis on the metropolitan languages in education, as a means of tying both people and social institutions to the colonial power.

Significantly, little changed at independence (1960). Faced with 270 languages and a divided colonial heritage, the new national government downplayed diversity and emphasized unity. Linguistically, this meant continued promotion of French and English, which were the only languages mentioned in the constitution (Republic of Cameroon, 1972) and so the languages of education. Bilingualism in English and French was espoused as a unifying initiative and measures were taken to promote this (Bot Ba Njock, 1981; Chumbow, 1980). The notion of selecting a single Cameroonian language as a national language was not seriously considered, as no one language was an obvious candidate and it would have been invidious, not to say politically explosive, to make an arbitrary choice (Tadadjeu and Sadembouo, 1982; Tadadjeu, 1987).

Beginning in the 1980s the language policy debate, with particular reference to education, started to change shape. An experimental university programme[2] in bilingual (i.e. local language/ official language) was launched and showed, over the next ten years, that such an approach to education in a highly multilingual country was feasible and effective (Cairns, 1987; Gfeller, forthcoming; Tadadjeu, 1990). In addition, political stability enabled the language issue to resurface out of a concern for communication needs, for instance, in rural development, without the overtones of incipient social divisiveness. Thus a number of political

pronouncements were made about the usefulness of Cameroonian languages in various communication sectors: agricultural extension, radio, press, etc. These culminated in an endorsement of linguistic diversity by the president: 'At an ethnic level the development of national (i.e. Cameroonian) languages, special vehicles of ethnic cultures, must be encouraged. It follows that each language expresses the culture which it carries' (Biya, 1986, p. 116).

For the first time the link between cultural and linguistic development was acknowledged at this level, and ethnic identity not only recognized but 'encouraged'. The dual basis of a national multicultural policy – expression of local identity within a common framework – became explicit in what followed:

> Developed in this way, these cultural gems will be transferred on to the national stage to the great benefit of all. It is therefore appropriate to let all our linguistic flowers blossom, as a necessary and indispensable phase in the history of making up our national cultural bouquet. We are therefore opting for the integration of each Cameroonian into his or her community by means of their mother tongue, on the understanding that this is only a strategic step towards better integration into the national community.   (Biya, 1986, p. 116)

The emphasis on nation building is clear, but this paved the way for political implementation of an unequivocal policy for the use of local languages in education almost ten years later. The 1995 National Forum on Education adopted 'the teaching of national languages and cultures at school, this being a factor of national integration' (Republic of Cameroon, 1995, p. 22) and summarized the 'type of person to be trained' as one who is, among other things, 'literate in at least one national language, steeped in his culture yet open to the world' (ibid., p. 21). This was followed later the same year by the promulgation of a new constitution in which linguistic diversity and national languages are explicitly endorsed:

> Preamble: Proud of our cultural and linguistic diversity, an enriching feature of our national identity. . .
> Article 3: The official languages of the Republic of Cameroon shall be English and French, both languages having the same status. The State shall guarantee the promotion of bilingualism throughout the country. It shall endeavour to protect and

promote national languages.   (Cameroon Tribune, 1995, p. 7)

These pronouncements, which are gradually moving towards implementation, provide a basis for a pluralist approach. However, economic considerations and the lack of written development of some Cameroonian languages weigh heavily in the balance and may prevent full realization. These are the issues which must be the subject of research and further experimentation in such a way that local communities are drawn into the debate and the practice of multilingual approaches.

Zaïre

Zaïre stands in contrast to Cameroon both by the relationships between its languages and the outworkings of its policy. It has a total of 221 languages (Grimes, 1996), with French as the official language. During the colonial period French was used alongside local languages, with the administration developing a bilingual approach. This came to an official end at independence with the declaration of French as the single official language of the new republic. In contrast to Cameroon, four local languages came into focus as regional lingua francas: Swahili, Ciluba, Kikongo and Lingala. The policy debate was coloured in the colonial period by Belgium's own language tensions, although familiarity with a degree of bilingualism at home may have made the colonial authorities more open to the African–French bilingualism which did in fact develop. Kazadi (1991) documents the pre-independence debate on language policy within Zaïre, but laments the fact that it was not based on serious consideration of educational, sociolinguistic or functional parameters.

Ager (1996) characterizes Zaïre's policy as a pyramid with French at the top, the four regional languages in the middle and all the other Zaïrean languages at the bottom. In education, the four 'semi-official' languages were used until 1962 when a decree insisted on the use of French alone, purportedly in the interests of national unity and harmonization. This was modified in 1986 with the stipulation that 'national languages [i.e. the four regional languages], or languages of the child's environment, and French are the languages of education' (Kazadi, 1992). With the many economic, political and social problems which confront Zaïre, language policy development is not in focus. The

tense stand-off between president and prime minister has effectively eviscerated policy formulation in any area, not to speak of the virtual withdrawal of government from implementing policies or providing education and other services.

Against this background mention should be made of an educational project which serves as an example of grass-roots multilingual practice in Zaïre (Gfeller, 1997; Robinson and Gfeller, 1997; Robinson, 1996b). In the north-west of the country an adult education and literacy programme is being implemented among the 2 million speakers of Ngbaka who are spread over an area the size of Switzerland. Its design sheds practical light on the place of linguistic diversity in an educational initiative. The programme thus uses three languages:

1 *Ngbaka*: the local language of the area, the language of daily social intercourse in the 1,000 villages of the region.
2 *Lingala*: the national language used in this part of Zaïre, used as a means of inter-ethnic communication, and commonly used in larger towns.
3 *French*: the official language, the language of the education system and of government administration; little used in daily interaction either in towns or villages. High prestige because of its international connections and written, documentary functions.

Literacy instruction and adult education use Ngbaka as the medium of instruction, through all the levels. Lingala and French are introduced in oral and written form, with the emphasis on the functions for which people are called upon to use these languages. The emphasis on the local language goes further than Zaïre's official policy has ever gone, even though such an approach provides a more secure basis for mastery of the regional language and French. In effect, the programme is setting its own policy environment – witness the increasing demands of other linguistic groups who have become aware of the Ngbaka success. Educationally, the programme exemplifies two principles: first, working from the known to the unknown by starting with the local language and maintaining it as the medium of instruction throughout; second, the educational process is embedded in local linguistic and communication patterns, introducing languages in ways and for functions which mirror everyday usage. Thus the multilingual and multicultural behaviour of daily life forms the basis of the educational programme and is reinforced by it. Local practice such as this may well serve as a model for a more pluralist policy, once policymaking is again on the agenda.

Tanzania

The history of language policy in Tanzania is well-documented and only its essential features will be rehearsed here (Polome, 1979; Robinson, 1992; Rubagumya, 1990, 1994). Tanzania is often held up as an example of an African country which has managed to establish one of its own languages as the national language. From pre-independence days Kiswahili was promoted as a lingua franca and then as the national language of the country. English, the colonizer's language, was retained as the language of the upper educational levels and as the official language of diplomacy, the higher courts and international trade. The issues of language policy which Rubagumya and Lwaitama (1990) raise are those relating to the relative status of English and Kiswahili and how far Kiswahili will continue, or should continue, to take over functions which, at independence, were occupied by English. Their proposal for 'alternative policy options' calls on Tanzania, and other African countries, to reinforce efforts to develop the use of indigenous languages in order to 'disseminate both elementary and advanced technical information in languages in which most of their peoples are fluent' (Rubagumya and Lwaitama, 1990, pp. 151–2).

What is fascinating in this debate is the negligible space given to the discussion of the 130 or so other African languages in Tanzania (Grimes, 1996). This is all the more surprising in that the extension of Kiswahili has depended not only on the relationship with English, but also on the displacement from some village functions of the local ethnic languages. Batibo (1995) points out that the kiswahilization of education left some children and adults with just as much of a linguistic barrier as if they had had to begin schooling in English, particularly in non-Bantu speaking areas. More significantly, from the point of view of validating and learning from the diversity of Tanzania's cultural fabric: 'The ethnic languages could be sources of historical and cultural information about Tanzania as well as sources of Kiswahili enrichment. Their marginalization and even elimination may deprive Tanzania of important national heritage' (Batibo, 1995, p. 72).

Referring to a move towards political pluralism, Batibo points to a 'decision by some political parties to revive ethnic sovereignty' (1995, p. 76) as a sign that ethnic languages may to some extent be revitalized. Insofar as language is used as a symbol of aggressive ethnic indentity, such revitalization cannot be said to promote pluralist approaches in education or in society generally. If, however, local languages can find their place alongside Kiswahili as an expression of a dual local–national identity, then the cultural self-confidence and openness to wider dialogue on which pluralist attitudes rest may be reinforced.

South Africa

In the context of this chapter it seems appropriate to add a note about the situation in South Africa. So long excluded from the family of black African nations, change in South Africa has created space for rethinking what it means to be a multicultural and plural society and how truly pluralist policies can be both designed and implemented. During the wilderness years other African countries felt that, once apartheid disappeared, South Africa could become a motor for development in economic and other spheres. Thus its policy development in the area of language is followed with interest and expectation. Alexander (1995) spells out South Africa's basic pluralist position with regard to the ethno-linguistic issue:

> Our future as a nation is indisputably a multi-lingual one. All suggestions of a monolingual future do not simply go against the global trends but contain within themselves the dangerous seeds of future ethnic conflicts. A consistently democratic approach to the language question has to be based on the sound linguistic premise that all languages are equal in their capacity to serve as means of communication, as means of thought and as bearers of culture, as well as on the sound political premise that any attempt to suppress the rights of languages will inevitably give rise to the most bitter resistance.   (Alexander, 1995, p. 40)

This position has led to the formulation of a policy recognizing eleven languages. The constitution makes reference to the state's responsibility to develop all official languages and promote their use; in education it grants the right to 'instruction in the language of his or her choice where this is reasonably practicable' (cited in Ridge, 1996, p. 20). This last phrase is problematic, as Ridge goes on to discuss, but the thrust of policy and the constitution is fundamentally pluralist. South Africa's policy statements in this regard go beyond those of the other African contexts mentioned here and are more thoroughly consistent (Webb, 1996). The efforts to promote awareness of language issues and the state's pluralist stance are laudable; I am aware of no other country where a popularizing magazine is regularly published in the area of language policy. Produced by the National Language Project, *Bua!* debates the South African situation, presents arguments about multilingual approaches (generally supportive of them) and reports on situations in other parts of Africa. Heugh (1996) reports that a Language Plan Task Group has been set up to develop a national language plan. Its deliberations thus far have adopted the following principles: equity, access, language as an economic resource, extension of language services, development of African languages, promotion of minority and heritage languages. The educational implications are for a bilingual or perhaps trilingual ('trifocal', Alexander, 1995, p. 41) language policy. The constitutional statements and the high level of activity in the language policy area do not guarantee full implementation on the ground of a thoroughgoing pluralist policy. There is however a greater prospect of success in an environment where the language issue, within the ethno-political debate, has such prominence. Whether South Africa's language policy in education is transferable to other African countries remains a moot point. However, other countries would benefit from aiming at the same level of debate.

Summary

Examination of Cameroon's language policy showed a gradual move towards a more pluralist position, to the point where implementation must follow if new policy statements are to go beyond rhetoric. Zaïre's policy vacuum has enabled local, pluralist initiatives to develop, with policy implications for the future. Tanzania, heralded as one of the few countries in Africa to break the colonial linguistic yoke, has not at this point developed a pluralist stance which provides space for all the country's ethno-linguistic groups. South Africa has gone the furthest in espousing an explicitly pluralist policy and demonstrates the clearest will

to turn it into action in educational and other spheres.

Valuing diversity?

In conclusion, what direction are language policies in Africa going in terms of pluralism? Recalling the earlier working definition of pluralism as 'the active recognition and appreciation of cultural differences, based on respect for human dignity, ensuring space for dialogue about conflicting opinions over values', how may current trends be evaluated? How far is cultural and linguistic diversity valued and how does this fit with wider trends across the world?

It is clear that policymakers have increasingly adopted a pluralist approach towards diversity. In political terms this means a greater public debate about ethnicity. In some places this is leading to political divisions along ethnic lines, as democratization takes root (Robinson, 1996c). In educational terms the stage is set for new initiatives and bold steps. There is good reason for optimism that African languages may become the medium of instruction and, in consequence, that African cultures may begin to shape the curriculum and bring school and community closer together. In other words, there is an opportunity to join pluralist approaches with sound educational principles so that multicultural and multilingual education gives a chance for the expression of cultural identity as well as for intellectual advancement.

This is taking place in a world context where globalization may overwhelm local initiative or help provide space for it. Delors (1996, p. 46) is of the opinion that 'the requirements of globalization and cultural identity should be seen as complementary rather than contradictory'. Little (1996) sees new space opening up for the local within a global rather than a merely national framework. These trends favour pluralist approaches, but it remains to be seen how far local cultural space can be maintained in the light of global cultural penetration by powerful media and products.

Thus it is urgent to reinforce movement towards multicultural policies and approaches in education to prepare the next generation to affirm its African identity in the face of globalizing forces, and to affirm very local identity in highly diverse societies. This must be an educational process, and not merely a policy orientation. Since African languages are such powerful symbols of the cultures they represent, their use is a key element in this process.

Acknowledgement

I am indebted to Fiona Varley for her invaluable assistance in researching and editing this chapter. Responsibility for content and opinions is entirely my own.

Notes

1 This is not the place to rehearse the debate on what constitutes a 'single language' or on the difference between 'language' and 'dialect'. For more on this see Romaine (1994), Edwards (1994), Trudgill (1983).
2 PROPELCA, Projet de Recherche Opérationnelle pour l'Enseignement des Langues au Cameroun.

References

Adegbija, E. (1994) *Language Attitudes in Sub-Saharan Africa*. Clevedon: Multilingual Matters.

Ager, D. (1996) *'Francophonie' in the 1990s*. Clevedon: Multilingual Matters.

Alexander, N. (1995) Nation building and language in the new South Africa. In M. Pütz (ed.), 29–43.

Basel Mission (1988) *Guide to the Basel Mission's Cameroon Archive*. Basel: Basel Mission.

Batibo, H. M. (1995) The growth of Kiswahili as the language of education and administration in Tanzania. In M. Pütz, (ed.), 57–80.

Biya, P. (1986) *Pour le libéralisme communautaire*. Lausanne/Paris: Pierre-Marcel Favre/Editions ABC.

Bokamba, E. G. (1995) The politics of language planning in Africa: critical choices for the 21st century. In M. Pütz, (ed.), 11–27.

Bot Ba Njock, H. M. (1981) Maîtrise des langues nationales et maîtrise du développement. *Revue Science et Technique* **1** (3), 83–92.

Bua! Periodical of the National Language Project. Salt River, South Africa.

Cairns, J. C. (1987) Experimental Mother Tongue Literacy Program, Cameroon: Report of Pre-Evaluation Mission. Unpublished report.

Cameroon Tribune (1995) The amendement constitution. 6003, 26 December, 7–9.

Carroll, J. (1972) *Language, Thought and Reality: Selected Writings of Benjamin Lee Whorf*. Cambridge MA.: MIT Press.

Chumbow, B. S. (1980) Language and language policy in Cameroon. In N. Kofele-Kale (ed.), *An Experiment in Nation-Building: The Bilingual Cameroon Republic since Reunification*. Boulder: Westview Press, pp. 281–311.

Commission on Global Governance (1995) *Our Global Neighbourhood*. Oxford: Oxford University Press.

Cooper, R. L. (1989) *Language Planning and Social Change*. Cambridge: Cambridge University Press.

Corson, D. (1993) *Language, Minority Education and Gender*. Clevedon: Multilingual Matters.

Coulmas, F. (1992) *Language and Economy*. Oxford: Blackwell.

Cuéllar, J. Perez de (ed.) (1995) *Our Creative Diversity*. Report of the World Commission on Culture and Development. Paris: UNESCO.

Delors, J. (ed.) (1996) *Learning: The Treasure Within*. Report to UNESCO of the International Commission on Education for the 21st Century. Paris: UNESCO.

Edwards, J. (1985) *Language, Society and Identity*. Oxford: Blackwell.

Edwards, J. (1994) *Multilingualism*. London: Routledge.

Featherstone, M. (1995) *Undoing Culture*. London: Sage.

Gfeller, E. (1997) Why should I learn to read? Motivations for literacy acquisition in a rural education programme. *International Journal of Educational Development* **17** (1), 101–12.

Gfeller, E. (forthcoming) *La société et l'école face au multilinguisme. L'intégration du trilinguisme extensif dans les programmes scolaires du Cameroun*. Paris: Khartala.

Grimes, B. (1996) *Ethnologue: Languages of the World*. Dallas: SIL.

Haugen, E. (1972) Dialect, language and nation. In J.B. Pride, and J. Holmes (eds), *Sociolinguistics*. Harmondsworth: Penguin.

Heugh, K. (1996) The impact of two NGOs on language policy and planning in South Africa: a case-study. In *Dunford Seminar Report: Accountability in Governmental and NGO Projects and Programmes*. London: British Council.

Hymes, D. H. (1992) Inequality in language: taking for granted. *Working Papers in Educational Linguistics* **8**, 1–30.

Kazadi, N. (1992) *L'Afrique afro-francophone*. Aix-en-Provence: Institut d'Etudes Créoles et Francophones.

Kekes, J. (1993) *The Morality of Pluralism*. Princeton: Princeton University Press.

Kekes, J. (1994) Pluralism and the value of life. In E.F. Paul, F.D. Miller and J. Paul (eds), *Cultural Pluralism and Moral Knowledge*. Cambridge: Cambridge University Press, 44–60.

Khubchandani, L. M. (1995) 'Minority' cultures and their communication rights. In T. Skutnabb-Kangas and R. Phillipson (eds), *Linguistic Human Rights*. Berlin: Mouton.

Knutsson, K.-E. (1996) Social field and cultural constellations: reflections on some aspects of globalization. In L. Arizpe (ed.), *The Cultural Dimensions of Global Change*. Paris: UNESCO, pp. 109–33.

Kukathas, C. (1994) Explaining moral variety. In E.F. Paul,

F.D. Miller and J. Paul (eds), *Cultural Pluralism and Moral Knowledge.* Cambridge: Cambridge University Press.

Larmore, C. (1994) Pluralism and reasonable disagreement. In E.F. Paul, F.D. Miller and J. Paul (eds), *Cultural Pluralism and Moral Knowledge.* Cambridge: Cambridge University Press.

Little, A. W. (1996) Globalisation and educational research: whose context counts? *International Journal of Educational Development* 16 (4), 427–38.

Mandelbaum, D. (1963) *Selected Writings of Edward Sapir.* Berkeley: University of California Press.

MINFOC (Ministère de l'Information et de la Culture) (1985) *L'identité culturelle camerounaise.* Yaoundé: MINFOC.

Ouane, A. (ed.) (1995) *Vers une culture multilingue de l'éducation.* Hamburg: UNESCO.

Paul, E. F., Miller, F. D. and Paul, J. (eds) (1994) *Cultural Pluralism and Moral Knowledge.* Cambridge: Cambridge University Press.

Pennycook, A. (1994) *The Cultural Politics of English as an International Language.* Harlow: Longman.

Phillipson, R. (1992) *Linguistic Imperialism.* Oxford: Oxford University Press.

Phillipson, R. and Skutnabb-Kangas, T. (1995) Language rights in postcolonial Africa. In T. Skutnabb-Kangas and R. Phillipson (eds), *Linguistic Human Rights.* Berlin: Mouton.

Polome, E. C. (1979) Tanzanian language policy and Swahili. In E. C. Polome, *Language Society and Paleoculture.* Stanford: Stanford University Press, pp. 88–100.

Pütz, M. (ed.) (1995) *Discrimination Through Language in Africa?* Berlin: Mouton.

Quirk, R. (1985) The English language in a global context. In R. Quirk, and H. G. Widdowson (eds), *English in the World.* Cambridge: Cambridge University Press.

Republic of Cameroon (1972) *Constitution of the Republic of Cameroon.* Yaoundé: Secretariat General of the Presidency of the Republic.

Republic of Cameroon (1995) *National Forum on Education: Final Report.* Yaoundé: Secretariat General of the Presidency of the Republic.

Ridge, S. G. M. (1996) Language policy in a Democratic South Africa. In M. Herriman, and B. Burnaby (eds), *Language Policies in English-Dominant Countries.* Clevedon: Multilingual Matters.

Robinson, C. D. W. (1992) *Language Choice in Rural Development.* Dallas: International Museum of Cultures.

Robinson, C. D. W. (1993) Where minorities are in the majority: language dynamics amidst high linguistic diversity. *AILA Review* 10, 52–70.

Robinson, C. D. W. (1996a) *Language Use in Rural Development: An African Perspective.* Berlin: Mouton.

Robinson, C. D. W. (1996b) Language policy from the bottom up: reclaiming language use in Africa. Paper given at 6th International Conference on Minority Languages, Gdansk, Poland, 30 June–5 July.

Robinson, C. D. W. (1996c) Winds of change in Africa: fresh air for African languages? Some preliminary reflections. In H. Coleman and L. Cameron (eds), *Change and Language.* Clevedon: Multilingual Matters.

Robinson, C. D. W. and Gfeller, E. (1997) A basic education programme in Africa: the people's own? *International Journal of Educational Development.*

Romaine, S. (1994) *Language in Society* 17 (3); 295–302 Oxford: Oxford University Press.

Rubagumya, C. M. (ed.) (1990) *Language in Education in Africa.* Clevedon: Multilingual Matters.

Rubagumya, C. M. (ed.) (1994) *Teaching and Researching Language in African Classrooms.* Clevedon: Multilingual Matters.

Rubagumya, C. M. and Lwaitama, A. F. (1990) Political and economic dimensions to language policy options in Tanzania. In C. M. Rubagumya (ed.), *Language in Education in Africa.* Clevedon: Multilingual Matters.

Skutnabb-Kangas, T. and Phillipson, R. (1995) *Linguistic Human Rights.* Berlin: Mouton.

Société Internationale de Linguistique (1987) *Alphabétisation expérimentale en langue maternelle: Rapport final.* Yaoundé: SIL.

Stavenhagen, R. (1990) *The Ethnic Question: Conflicts, Development and Human Rights.* Tokyo: United Nations University Press.

Stumpf, R. (1979) *La politique linguistique au Cameroun de 1884 à 1960: comparaison entre les administrations coloniales allemande, française et britannique et du rôle joué par les sociétés missionnaires.* Bern: Peter Lang.

Sutherlin, R. E. (1962) Language situation in East Africa. In F.A. Rice (ed.), *Study of the Role of Second Languages in Asia, Africa and Latin America.* Washington DC: Centre for Applied Linguistics.

Tadadjeu, M. (1987) Les origines historiques d'un défi. In Société Internationale de Linguistique, *Alphabétisation expérimentale en langue maternelle: Rapport final.* Yaoundé: SIL, pp. 7–14.

Tadadjeu, M. (1989) *Voie Africaine: Esquisse du Communautarisme Africain.* Yaoundé: Club OUA Cameroun.

Tadadjeu, M. (ed.) (1990) *Le Défi de Babel au Cameroun.* Collection PROPELCA 53. Yaoundé: Université de Yaoundé.

Tadadjeu, M. and Sadembouo, E. (eds) (1982) *Recherche en langues et linguistique au Cameroun.* Yaoundé: Centre de Recherches et d'Etudes Anthropologiques.

Tollefson, J. W. (1991) *Planning Language, Planning Inequality: Language Policy in the Community.* London: Longman.

UNRISD (United Nations Research Institute for Social Development) (1995) *States of Disarray: The Social Effects of Globalisation.* Report for World Summit for Social Development. Geneva: UNRISD.

Trudgill, P. (1983) *Sociolinguistics.* Harmondsworth: Penguin.

Universal Declaration of Linguistic Rights (1996) Adopted by the World Conference on Linguistic Rights, Barcelona, June 1996.

Wardhaugh, R. (1987) *Languages in Competition.* Oxford: Blackwell.

Webb, V. (1996) Language planning and politics in South Africa. *International Journal of the Sociology of Language* 118, 139–62.

16

Values, Policy and Practice in the Education of Maori in Aotearoa/New Zealand[1]

KEITH SULLIVAN

Introduction

The school is a microcosm of society at large. At school we teach children how to co-exist within the social world of friendships and relationships, how to prepare for work, how to survive in the economic world and how to be part of society with its boundaries and rules. In weaving these patterns of understanding, we teach children a set of values and a way of interpreting the world. Our far from perfect liberal education system in which the child is nevertheless held paramount has evolved out of a decent, responsible society in which the social good has largely been supported by the public sector. This education system is under attack from New Right philosophies in which education is seen as a commodity, teachers are seen as providers, pupils are regarded as consumers and success is measured by outcomes. This goes against the grain of respected educational and management research which shows that it is through co-operation, mutual support and assistance that people not only survive but also flourish (for example, see Johnson and Johnson, 1987; Michaelson, *et al.*, 1989; Zubhoff, 1988).

Increasingly we are aware that education is neither neutral nor value free, that what is imparted to our children is not merely facts but also points of view which reflect particular ways of seeing and understanding the world. Curriculum is a manifestation of the values that underlie any education system, and grows directly out of policy. What is taught in terms of specific skills is adjusted as appropriate, for instance, children today are taught the skills to keep up with the increased sophistication of computer hardware and software. On the other hand, the core of values and policies which reflect and constantly challenge the health and equity of any society is developed and implemented

by a less clear process. However, in both cases the concrete choice of emphases in syllabus and chosen values, whether directly or by implication, determines the nature of education and in as much influences society in the long term. These choices are therefore ideological and it is consequently important to understand both the content of the value system underlying our current education system and the processes by which they either become or do not become policy statements and are implemented as programmes.

In New Zealand, work on values education has been sporadic. However, Waikato University's 1993 'Values in Social Studies Project' was timely as government was developing a national curriculum and designing subject curricula. These curricula are the culmination of a reform process which started by creating a quasi-market approach to education and where the various curricula have been ranked, classified, standardized and compartmentalized by the New Zealand Qualifications Authority (and measured as unit standards; see Philips, 1993). The project's research monograph 1, *Values Education and Social Studies* (Keown *et al.*, 1993) provides a useful overview of the contemporary issues in values education both in New Zealand and overseas. The document uses Australian (ACER) research to identify important distinctions between values, beliefs and attitudes, and calls on the work of New Zealand academics (Alton-Lee and Nutall, 1991; Codd, 1980a, 1980b; Snook, 1980a, 1980b) to provide a contextual and international overview with reference to the work of educationalists such as Robb (1992a, 1992b). I will not elaborate on the specifics of their arguments here as this will be covered elsewhere in this series. However, what is apparent is that the issues surrounding values education and values in education need to be more extensively considered and debated; and that the cultural pluralist dimension, particularly in relation to issues in Maori education, is all but absent. We are moving towards a very standardized way of looking at knowledge and, by implication, valuing only those aspects of education that lead to achievement. Those who do not succeed are not valued, and as there is a greater percentage of those from ethnic minorities who do not 'succeed', such issues are a key concern of antiracist discourses.

This chapter explores values in education and cultural pluralism in Aotearoa/New Zealand. It provides first a case study of the historical development of education for Maori; second, a comparison with other settings, particularly Britain and the USA; third, a paradigm approach for better understanding the relationship between values in education and their expression in terms of policy and programmes. This analytical tool, derived from the rigour of critical theory,[2] provides the basis for reflection and consideration in order to provide humane solutions to inequalities of access and participation for Maori in education in Aotearoa/New Zealand today. The chapter exemplifies both how to deconstruct from programmes to policies and their underlying values, and conversely how to create policy and programmes based on a given set of values. The use of the paradigms helps to identify disparities between values, intentions and outcomes, to indicate specifically when disparities occur and to suggest possible solutions.

The multicultural–bicultural debate

In 1993, prominent Maori politician (later Deputy Prime Minister) Winston Peters unveiled his plan for a better future for the Maori people of New Zealand. It was entitled *Ka Awatea* (a new dawn) and was strongly supported by the National (Conservative) government as it seemed to echo its intention to 'mainstream' Maori, to bring them more centrally into all aspects of New Zealand life and to provide a new dawn for a better future.

The new dawn was presented as a proactive response to a perception of poor performance by Maori, notably in education. Although on first appearances *Ka Awatea* seemed laudable, a positive suggestion for solving an apparent problem, a closer inspection indicates that from an educational perspective it ignores the history of policy and practice for Maori as well as contemporary Maori

responses to culture loss, inequality and social difficulties. In the midst of statistical indicators of poor Maori performance and a perception of this performance as 'truth', Maori-driven initiatives such as kohanga reo (early childhood language nests), kura kaupapa Maori (Maori immersion) schools and whare wananga (Maori universities) that have sprung up as part of a Maori move to develop separate but parallel education systems within a bicultural setting (see Irwin, 1989, 1990; Smith, 1990) indicate another interpretation of Maori performance and another 'truth'. The biculturalism which has sustained these developments and this 'truth' is part of an approach that is largely Maori driven but is also widely supported by Pakeha (European New Zealander) educators, and is particular to Aotearoa/New Zealand. It is based upon the idea that our nation is founded upon a partnership between Maori and Pakeha that dates back to the signing of the Treaty of Waitangi in 1840, and it is intended to redress past injustices and to honour cultural diversity. Biculturalism, by its intentions and practices, is antiracist, and approaches to Maori education are premised on an understanding that there was a thriving and successful Maori form of education before European contact which needs to be revitalized and revalued on an equal footing with European education. In relation to this response, *Ka Awatea* seems patronizing, culturally insensitive and ill conceived.

Within this democratically and locally driven context, Parata (1993) identifies the mainstreaming behind *Ka Awatea* as the old discredited assimilationist approach dressed up as something new; old wine in new bottles, rather than a new dawn. 'Mainstreaming assumes that Maori are the same as the rest of the population and that if they are treated the same they will behave the same.' What is more, this mainstreaming approach is a multi-ethnic echo of the neo-liberal concept of the level playing field where gender, ethnic and social class issues are all 'equalized' by the provision of a free market.

Further to this, mainstreaming is tied up with a conservative interpretation of the concept of multiculturalism. Whereas biculturalism asserts the value of difference and is philosophically embodied in initiatives like kohanga reo, this version of multiculturalism is reactive and premised on the notion that we are all New Zealanders and that no group including Maori should be treated preferentially, as we all have interesting ethnic roots that need to be nourished and acknowledged. Vasil (1988) suggests that rather than being genuine, such concerns are reactionary and use multiculturalism as a blind, a way of avoiding addressing the difficult challenges that biculturalism brings with it:

> Some Pakeha, who in the past had rarely thought of New Zealand as anything other than a white Western nation, now faced with Maori demands for its recognition as a bi-racial and bicultural nation, insist on arguing with a certain vehemence that New Zealand, in view of the existence of many ethnic minorities, can properly be viewed only as a multicultural and multi-racial society. They insist that in fairness the identity and cultures of the other ethnic components – the Chinese, the Indians, the Greeks, the Dutch, etc. – cannot be ignored. They argue that if the separate culture, language and identity of the Maori were to be given a special recognition, the same privilege could not be denied the others. This new-found concern for the interests of the non-Maori ethnic minorities in New Zealand by the Pakeha must be looked at closely. (Vasil, 1988, p. 1)

In a general sense, what this scenario tells us is that in New Zealand today there are at least two ideologies competing for the dominant position. Each has a different vision for New Zealand and each has an investment in establishing the credibility of its position. The metamorphosis of any such position into policy is likely to be mediated by many forces such as political context, the strength of pressure groups and public feeling, and economics. For instance, although the government may be inclined towards a multicultural perspective, Maori political strength is such that it would probably be seen as politically unwise for the government to push its stance too strongly because of potential repercussions.

Policy development in Maori education

If we examine the historical development of policy attitudes towards the education of Maori, it is apparent that there have been several distinct but overlapping stages since the signing of the Treaty of Waitangi. Peters and Marshall (1989) identify five such stages: assimilation, integration, cultural difference, multiculturalism and biculturalism.

> The history of policy can be seen in a number of clearly discernible successive phases: an 'assimilationist' approach to race relations which predominated up until the late 1950s; a focus on a policy of integration implicitly based on a notion of cultural deprivation during the 1960s and early 1970s. This was followed by a transitional period where emphasis was shifted from 'cultural deprivation' and 'the problem of the Maori child' to a concept of 'cultural difference' which emphasised Pakeha tolerance of non-Pakeha culture; and, finally, an attempt to formulate a multicultural policy with the attendant notion that 'cultural diversity' should be valued. Most recently, there have been some signs that we are moving into a policy era of 'biculturalism', primarily as a result of Maori initiatives. (Peters and Marshall, 1989, p. 142)

Irwin (1989) similarly identifies five stages, although she categorizes them differently. Like Peters and Marshall, she calls the first phase from early settlement until 1960 assimilation. She posits the Hunn Report (1960) as the initiator of the next or integration stage. Her third stage, however, she terms cultural pluralism rather than Peters and Marshall's cultural difference. Irwin then identifies her fourth stage as biculturalism, in which the central concern is the need to sort out the Maori–Pakeha partnership and to continue the surge of Maori educational development through this bilateral partnership so that multiculturalism, the fifth stage, can be reached.

Unlike Peters, Marshall and Irwin, I argue that there have been four successive stages in Maori educational policy and practice: assimilation, integration, multiculturalism and biculturalism. While Peters and Marshall's summation is useful, I would argue that acknowledgement of cultural difference (depending on the degree of tolerance) is a characteristic of multiculturalism rather than a policy stage in its own right. Therefore I would incorporate 'cultural difference' into the multiculturalism phase and recast Irwin's cultural pluralist phase as multiculturalism.[3]

Since these 1989 analyses and as Marshall and Peters suggest, New Zealand has clearly moved into a Maori-initiated and driven bicultural stage which has meant a reframing of thinking about Maori educational policy and practice.[4] While it may be useful to identify biculturalism as a stage on the way to multiculturalism in that it indicates an evolving response to a complex philosophical question (as Irwin does), this approach ignores the predominantly bipolar nature of New Zealand society and the racism which often hides within concerns about multiculturalism.

I would therefore argue that in this particular

context biculturalism is a full stage in its own right rather than a transitional stage on the way to multiculturalism, a biculturalism that upholds the Treaty of Waitangi and permanently acknowledges Maori as tangata whenua (the people of the land) and all that this entails. I also argue that a rethinking of the nature of the bicultural partnership should provide the philosophical and cultural impetus for effective policymaking, redressing the ethnic inequalities of Aotearoa/New Zealand and building a proactive path to the future.[5]

In making comparisons with other countries, it is clear that each setting has its own particular circumstances and values that dictate that country's policies and counter-policies, that one approach is not intrinsically better than another but that values and policies are context driven. For instance, in relation to the development of educational policies that respond to the oppression of blacks in Britain, Brandt (1986) identifies four phases: assimilation, integration, cultural pluralism and antiracism. From a black British perspective, it is clear that the antiracist–multicultural debate has similarities with the bicultural–multicultural debate in Aotearoa/New Zealand, that the multiculturalists could be accused of being essentially tokenistic and appearing to be enlightened but, in fact, being unwilling to address the underlying issues of racism within the British school system. In this case antiracism is the appropriate response. While Brandt is speaking on behalf of the black British immigrant community rather than an indigenous group, it could be argued that what his antiracist phase shares with biculturalism and what distinguishes them both from the other phases is that the impetus and input come from the oppressed group, i.e. from the black and the Maori communities respectively. Similarly, while Banks (1988) argues for the development of multiculturalism as an appropriate response in the USA, the particular context of Aotearoa/New Zealand demands primarily a bicultural framework, which is informed by many of the same issues as multiculturalism elsewhere.[6]

Ideological development of multi-ethnic education in Aotearoa/New Zealand

The four educational stages of assimilation, integration, multiculturalism and biculturalism are prem-

ised on sets of values that logically lead to policies and programmes. Although they each have an implied special character rather than a chartered policy, it is possible to identify the specific policies and programmes that fit within their philosophical frameworks and which have been developed under them. What is more, they are similar to policies and programmes that have been developed elsewhere in the world. Over time, there has been a tendency to move from a reactionary, conservative, even racist, perspective to more liberal and even radical stances. The framework that I have developed (Figure 16.1) incorporates Banks's (1988) ten paradigms as an analytical tool and arranges them along a continuum from reactionary to radical, and also places them within the framework of the four stages that I have identified. These paradigms were developed from Banks's understanding of American and British responses to multi-ethnic demands over time.[7] They also equate with New Zealand policy and practice which has been largely influenced by the American and British developments.

In my analysis, the first three of Banks's paradigms fall under the heading of assimilation and the fourth and fifth under the heading of integration. Of the remaining five, I would argue that the cultural difference paradigm clearly relates only to the multicultural stage, and the antiracist to the bicultural stage (the radical paradigm could be considered an extreme form of biculturalism). I would also argue that the language and cultural pluralism paradigms could fit within either the multiculturalism or biculturalism stages, that is, there is some overlap.

The usefulness of the paradigms

Banks's adaptation of Kuhn's paradigms is useful for understanding the relationship between values in education and policy and programmes. A pictorial way of understanding paradigms is to compare a paradigm with an onion. The programmes are on the surface of the onion. They are visible, we can see them at work. If a couple of layers are peeled away then the policies which support the programmes become visible. While they cannot be seen on the surface they are logically linked to the programmes. Beneath the policies at the core of the onion are the set values out of which both the policy and the programmes grow. Paradigms are also useful because:

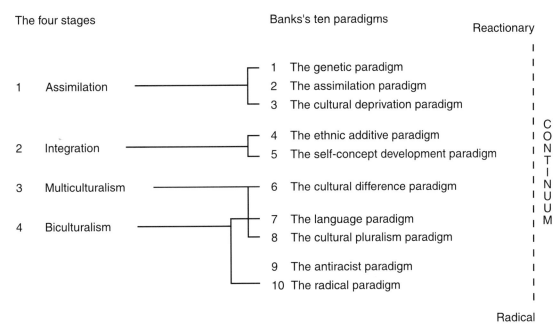

Figure 16.1   Historical and ideological responses to the education of Maori in Aotearoa/New Zealand

1   They are developed as a way of conceptualizing and explaining a particular phenomenon at a particular time. As our understanding develops or circumstances change, these paradigms are superseded by newer and more appropriate models.

2   They are particularly useful because they are logical and easy to understand, that is, if a particular ideological or philosophical perspective is identified, then there is usually a clearly discernible path from this to the development of related educational policies and to their practice in the classroom. An understanding of this process can help to reveal or unmask the intentions of the policies of pressure groups or government (and their underlying value systems).

3   When used with my four-stage theory, Banks's paradigms provide us with insights at the macro and micro levels. In other words, the four-stage theory provides an overview of what has happened or is happening during a particular time period. The paradigms complement this by dealing with a more specific understanding of the ideologies and their consequences, i.e. the former is generalized and impressionistic, the latter is more analytical and particular.

It should be pointed out, however, that single-factor paradigms such as these are over-simplified and there is not a strict one-to-one adherence between the stages and the paradigms. There is often an overlap between policy and practice, but they are presented in this analysis in a single-factor fashion so as to facilitate understanding. In order to develop a complex response to a complex situation, several paradigms can be and have been wholly or partially used to develop a multi-factor paradigm, as suggested by Banks. Further to this, although such models are useful in helping us understand how things work, it should be kept in mind that in the real world things are never as straightforward and simple as they are portrayed in models.

The four stages and their accompanying paradigms

The assimilation stage[8]

In New Zealand the period starting from the signing of the Treaty of Waitangi and ending with the Hunn Report (1840–1960) can be classified as a period of assimilation. During this time Maori systems of knowledge and teaching were ignored, and until the beginning of the twentieth century the

Maori population was rapidly decreasing. Assimilation in the New Zealand state school system was characterized by the attempt to Europeanize Maori through excluding Maori culture from the curriculum and by banning the use of Maori language in state schools. Despite Maori academic successes, most notably at Te Aute College, a private Maori boys' boarding school, a policy of adapted education dominated in which Maori were treated as intellectually inferior to Europeans and prepared for 'an appropriate station in life' (similar to the treatment of Afro-Americans in the American South and by colonizers in Africa; see Barrington, 1976, 1988). In rural Maori schools, basic skills were taught along with certain aspects of Maori culture (although not Maori language) and Maori students were encouraged to stay in their home areas. Barrington states:

> The new policies placed particularly strong emphasis on agricultural and gardening activities. In the view of the Director of Education, T.B. Strong, the best means for the Maoris to realize the full benefits of civilization was for them to cultivate their land. Thus, 'we should provide fully a type of education that would lead the boy to become a good farmer and the girl to become a good farmer's wife'. ... Teachers in Maori schools were enjoined to 'study the social life, music, recreation and arts and craft of the Maori people' and to occupy the greatest amount of time in history lessons with stories of Maori and New Zealand history. (Barrington, 1976, p. 3)

The underlying philosophy of this form of education was that the overwhelming majority of Maori were suited only for a particular type of work, largely physical and unskilled, the implication being that this was appropriate for their limited abilities and lesser intelligence. Further to this, that with their limited abilities it was best for Maori to be assimilated into European society, although it was also understood that they would never rise beyond a basic level.

Although there was an attempt to include Maori material in these schools, the new policies introduced in 1930 remained assimilationist and also illustrate the genetic paradigm which is a facet of assimilationist philosophies. The policies also indicate the attitudes of superiority and patronage exhibited by the Pakeha policymakers. I have placed three of Banks's paradigms under the umbrella of assimilation: the *genetic, assimilation* and *cultural deprivation* paradigms.

The genetic paradigm

This paradigm is an extreme example of the underlying thinking of assimilationism. Supporters of this paradigm attribute educational failure of minority groups to their genetic makeup. In 1969, Arthur Jensen, professor of psychology at the University of California at Berkeley, suggested that the reason compensatory programmes such as Head Start and Follow Through (which had been designed to increase the IQ of Afro-Americans living in the urban ghettoes) had failed was because the people for whom they were designed were genetically inferior.[9]

The genetic paradigm is a racist paradigm. Because supporters of this paradigm believe that the reason some groups do not perform well in school is solely genetic, they have no commitment to educational equality for ethnic minority students and use the argument to avoid implementing educational programmes which aim to address equity issues. They believe that there is no real need for ethnic minority programmes. In contemporary New Zealand, supporters of this paradigm would say that there is no need for kohanga reo and kura kaupapa Maori because if a genetic difference exists between Maori and Pakeha then this cannot be alleviated by such educational programmes.

A logical policy of this paradigm is that within a state school system students are assigned to streamed classes according to their intelligence as demonstrated in IQ and other tests of mastery. As a result of such policies, a highly disproportionate number of ethnic minority children end up in low academic streams. This puts into effect the self-fulfilling prophecy syndrome.[10]

If, in this setting, the self-fulfilling prophecy is accepted as the probable reality, then one can conclude that streaming tends to perpetuate inequality. It supports the dominant hegemonic structure of society, maintains class and ethnic stratification, and teaches low-stream students to accept their low status.

The assimilation paradigm

This model is another conservative stance that predates Jensen's articulation of the genetic argument (although this can be implied in the policies developed). This approach to education dominated government policy in various forms in Aotearoa/New Zealand from the onset of colonization up until the 1960s.[11]

The underlying philosophy of the assimilationist

paradigm is not as blatantly racist as the genetic paradigm. Its basic tenet is that minority group children will benefit most from their education if they are absorbed into the dominant culture. This is, of course, an approach that assumes cultural superiority. In Aotearoa/New Zealand, Maori children were expected to give up their ethnicity, culture and language and to take on the characteristics of the dominant culture. In order to get ahead in the dominant Pakeha world, they would be expected to learn the ways of the white patriarchy in order to succeed.

An underlying theme of the assimilationist policy is that encouraging ethnic identity of minority groups (indigenous or otherwise) undermines national unity and conversely encourages the development of little enclaves or ghettoes of people who could be at odds with the national interest. Cultural and linguistic difference in this setting is not valued but is seen as a threat.

The main goal of assimilationist education is to teach minorities the values and behaviour of the majority culture, and part of the process is the surrender by minority groups of their ethnicity, culture and language in return for access to all the goods of the dominant society. Educationally, assimilation is achieved largely through the specific aims and shape of the curriculum, which is geared to the culture and style of the dominant group. The reality for those coerced into denying their cultural and linguistic heritage is that this sacrifice does not provide access to the promised areas. The result is alienated and unhappy individuals caught between cultures. Bordieu (cited in Harker, 1990) charges that the acculturated individual does not reap the promises of assimilation, i.e. success within the mainstream culture. Instead, although he or she may acquire some dominant group cultural capital, the school system sees that the individual does not generally rise above the second of five levels in which inequalities are perpetuated.[12]

Cultural deprivation paradigm

As we move away from the conservative end of the scale, the next paradigm encountered is the cultural deprivation paradigm (often referred to as the deficiency syndrome). In this paradigm, the family and culture of ethnic minority (and indigenous) children are seen as not providing either adequate stimulation or preparation for education, which the middle-class Pakeha home in Aotearoa/New Zealand is seen as doing. Therefore such children arrive at school ill prepared and disadvantaged and consequently continue to be increasingly disadvantaged as they pass through the various stages of the education system. These children are seen then as starting their education from a position of deficit. Their own culture and language are seen as deficient and inferior and as holding them back.

The aim of education policy for this paradigm is to address these perceived deficits, and so school programmes are developed to provide children with the tools to help them to catch up. Head Start in the USA was such a compensatory programme intended to be behaviouristic and intense. There is an implied assumption in this paradigm that the minority culture is dysfunctional, and that not only does it prevent children from acquiring the correct socialization (cultural capital), but also retards their cognitive development.

The intentions of the cultural deprivation model are arguably not as negative as the genetic paradigm in that they do not dismiss the ethnic minority child as being genetically fixed and therefore unchangeable. This model does, however, dismiss the child's culture and background as inferior. In Aotearoa/New Zealand, then, this would translate that Maori children perform poorly in school because their culture, specifically related to their iwi (tribe), hapu (sub-tribe) and whanau (extended family) are seen as being deficient. The suggested path would be to provide Maori children with various compensatory programmes in order to give them better access to the skills provided in the family setting of middle-class Pakeha society. The intentions of the programme are obviously culturally imperialistic but are cloaked in well-intended equity-based policies aimed at giving the child a fair chance. Policies and practice from this paradigm, in particular, held sway for a very long time and experienced a revival in the 1980s.[13]

The integration stage

The integration stage can be characterized as the start of the acknowledgement of cultural diversity. Educationally there is some appreciation of things different, but only through the eyes of the dominant society. Ethnic minorities are idealized as the 'noble savage', i.e. they are regarded as exhibiting the simple and honest values that have been lost in the dominant society. They represent a simpler lifestyle, the dominant society in its more primitive form. So, in other words, indigenous and other groups are valued for what they appear to represent for the dominant society rather than what they are in their own right. It is a superficial appreciation of cultural diversity. Thus Street-Porter (1978, pp. 50–1) describes integration as 'a modest tokenism, an acceptance of that which is quaint in minority culture but a worried rejection of those cultural aspects that seem not just alien but feel threateningly so'.

As Irwin (1989) suggests, the Hunn Report heralded the introduction of integration into Aotearoa/New Zealand education. She describes integration as follows:

> A less crude, less racist version of assimilation. Whereas the racist, ethnocentric judgements about cultural superiority were an overt part of the ideology of assimilation, they became covert aspects of integration. Contrary to the view that policy-makers would have us believe, such notions are not removed from new policy areas, they are simply disguised. Integration is described as a more liberal and humane version of facilitating the interaction of two cultures. Lack of equal opportunity is recognised and a new promise of equality of opportunity made. (Irwin, 1989, p. 4)

The Hunn Report (1960) acknowledges integration as 'New Zealand's policy for the future' and defines it as 'to combine (not fuse) the Maori and Pakeha elements to form one nation wherein culture remains distinct' (p. 15). The report is a clear example of attitudes that typify the integrationist stage:

> Integration, as stated, implies some continuation of Maori culture. Much of it, though, has already departed and only the fittest elements (worthiest of preservation) have survived the onset of civilisation. Language, arts and crafts, and the institutions of the marae are the chief relics. . . . Every Maori who can no longer speak the language, perform the haka or poi, or take his place on the marae, makes it just so much harder for these remnants of Maori culture to be perpetuated. (Hunn, 1960, p. 15)

Within this integrationist stage, two of Banks's paradigms fit: the ethnic additive and the self-development paradigms.

The ethnic additive paradigm

This model is marginally better than the assimilation paradigm. It attempts to meet the needs of the children rather than leaving them to sink or swim in the curriculum of the dominant group. This may be done by the addition of some cultural facets to the curriculum or by the provision of a programme to meet needs not met by the home culture or family. It involves a small move towards the acceptance of the rights and validity of indigenous and ethnic minority cultures, assuming that ethnic bits can be added to the curriculum without either re-contextualizing them or fitting them into a culturally appropriate philosophical base.

Typically, this attributes values to a culture when it was 'simpler, nobler and more honest'. In other words, the model is romantic, unrealistic and patronizing. 'Interesting' rites and customs are studied and mythological heroes are identified. Ethnic units are provided in social studies, and the cultures of other groups are acknowledged, but only in a marginalizing and superficial way.

Often this sort of acknowledgement adds up to a form of 'cultural commodification' – making commodities of people's cultures be it material, mythic or cognitive. This is seen in Aotearoa when the All Blacks perform the haka or children are taught waiata and poi dances at school as an indication of that school's acknowledgement of Maoritanga.[14] These items are presented out of context and the mana and spirituality are ripped out of them.

The self-concept development paradigm

This paradigm moves beyond tokenism in that it assumes that indigenous ethnic-minority children have low self-esteem because of the inequitable and controlling socio-economic reality that confronts them. The remedy is to increase the child's self-esteem by curriculum developments that emphasize the contributions of ethnic minorities to the national culture and show ethnic heroes as national heroes. So it introduces elements of the culture as the ethnic additive paradigm does, but also attempts to address the psychological needs of the child. While the intentions within this paradigm may be good, it can be argued that such changes need to come from within the culture, rather than from the outside by non-ethnic 'experts'.

The multicultural stage

The multicultural stage is characterized by the beginnings of the acknowledgement of cultural diversity in a more substantial fashion. There is the start of a true recognition of different cultural styles and the language of ethnic minority/indigenous groups is seen as central to cultural survival. Irwin (1989, p. 7) defines multiculturalism in the following way: 'A multicultural society . . . is one in which all cultural groups are able to make sense of the world, communicate with each other and plan and live their lives as they see fit.'

The British Swann Report (Department of Education and Science, 1985) provides the following description of multiculturalism:

> We consider that a multicultural society such as ours would in fact function most effectively and harmoniously on the basis of pluralism which enables, expects and encourages members of all ethnic groups, both minority and majority, to participate fully in shaping the society as a whole within a framework of commonly accepted values, practices and procedures, whilst also allowing and, where necessary, assisting the ethnic minority communities in maintaining their distinct ethnic identities within the common framework. (Department of Education and Science, 1985, p. 15)

Cultural difference is the only paradigm that relates solely to multiculturalism, while the language and cultural pluralism paradigms possess qualities which could fit either within a multicultural or bicultural framework. This is because the relationship between multiculturalism and biculturalism is dependent on context. In the Aotearoa/New Zealand setting, biculturalism is appropriate with all its attendant paradigms because of the tangata whenua/tauiwi[15] relationship, while elsewhere multiculturalism or antiracism may be the crucial and necessary approach.

The cultural difference paradigm

This paradigm acknowledges the importance of a group's unique world view. Here, language, values, mores, patterns of organization and cultural characteristics are acknowledged and seen as 'functional for them and valuable to the nation state' (Banks, 1988, p. 97). Their development in schools is supported in policy and practice, i.e. there is now an acceptance of diversity as an enriching rather than a divisive characteristic. The aim of the paradigm is to change the school through the existing power structures so that it both respects and legitimizes the cultures of students not part of the dominant culture.

The bicultural stage: towards an educational partnership

Biculturalism in Aotearoa/New Zealand is characterized as a partnership between the two main groups, Maori and tauiwi. It is about power sharing and mutual respect. Along with the language and cultural pluralism paradigms, the antiracist paradigm fits within this stage.

The language paradigm

A further step in taking away blame for failure from ethnic minorities can be found in what Banks terms the language paradigm. This goes a step further than the cultural difference paradigm in not only acknowledging the importance of language but also in developing policy and programmes for its teaching and its recognition as a taonga, a treasure. The paradigm stresses the importance of the first language for the educational survival of indigenous ethnic minority children, i.e. children do not succeed in the school system because they are not educated in their first language. The policies encourage the development of bilingual and language immersion programmes.

The cultural pluralism paradigm

Cultural pluralism has a similar theme to the cultural difference paradigm but is more developed. It recognizes education as having an important role not only in acknowledging but also actively promoting ethnic identification – in Banks's words, 'to promote the maintenance of groups; to promote the liberation of ethnic groups; to educate ethnic students in a way that will not alienate them from their home cultures' (1988, p. 97). In concrete terms, this means the creation of ethnic studies courses that are philosophically and ideologically based, and ethnically based schools that focus on 'the maintenance of ethnic cultures and traditions' (p. 97), i.e. cultural pluralism supports bilingual and/or separate development.

Maori departments at universities, kura kaupapa Maori schools, kohanga reo, whare wananga and Pacific Island language nests are examples of this approach. Ethnically based studies are created as means and ends in their own right rather than as meaningful additives to what remains, in essence, a monocultural education system.[16] This paradigm could well work in partnership with the language paradigm to develop an emancipated language/culture programme.

The antiracist paradigm

Banks terms this the racism paradigm. Other than the radical paradigm, the antiracist paradigm provides the most challenging approach to multi-ethnic education. All previous paradigms value the indigenous ethnic minority culture to varying degrees, from not at all, in the assimilationist and genetic paradigms, to very valued in the cultural pluralist paradigm. However, in none of these instances is the dominant culture charged with any responsibility for an inequitable system of education, or in the larger sense, with a social system in which minority individuals cannot really succeed. In the worse case scenario of the assimilationist and genetic paradigms, the minority cultures are held responsible for their own situation, i.e. the victim is blamed. In the more liberal scenarios, those holding power are prepared to take steps in varying degrees to 'give a helping hand' (in the case of the cultural difference paradigm) or fully to support the ethnic minority (in the cultural pluralism paradigm). But in none of these does the dominant group accept responsibility for the creation of the inequality.

The antiracist paradigm shifts the blame for school failure onto the dominant society. It suggests that the reason there is educational inequality is because of racism, and that the school should play a major role in eliminating personal and institutional racism both in schools and in the wider society. This should be done through antiracist workshops and courses for teachers, and antiracist lessons for students, with an examination of curriculum materials, personnel, teaching attitudes and school norms.

The radical paradigm

This is, as the name suggests, the most challenging of all the paradigms. I would argue that its aims could coincide with an extreme form of biculturalism that wishes to overturn contemporary society as it stands to create a better and more equitable world, and to establish a true and equal partnership, not one where despite an appropriate philosophy and good intentions one party still has most of the power. From a radical perspective, schools, as well as society's other central institutions, are seen as purporting to be neutral but in fact represent the status quo and the interests of the dominant group. When addressing educational issues, supporters of this paradigm state that there should be no policy to institute change in education without

addressing the larger issues within the whole of society.

In this scenario, the school is central to the problem and plays a key role in keeping minority groups oppressed. Thus, it is not possible for the school to help liberate oppressed groups because one of its central purposes is to educate students so that they willingly accept their assigned status in society. A primary role of the school is seen as reproducing the social class structure and the values and mores of the dominant group. Exponents of the radical paradigm argue against programmes of multi-ethnic education because they are seen as palliative. They are designed to keep oppressed groups from rebelling against a system that creates structural barriers through institutionalized racism and does not deal with the real issues of ethnic oppression and victimization.

A radical programme for the classroom, the school and the community would be aimed both at raising the consciousness of students, teachers and parents about the nature of capitalist society, its social and economic unfairness and its hegemonic assumptions, and at developing critical and practical oppositional skills and a commitment to overcoming social, economic and educational oppression. In the context of Maori education in Aotearoa, this could be explored through an analysis of the differences between stated education policy for Maori and the actual examination results; and a comparison of these results with other groups, particularly Pakeha. Relative levels of unemployment and a comparison between the types of jobs each group generally occupies, as well as relative rates of imprisonment, would also be revealing. In such an analysis the massive difference between the rhetoric and the actual outcomes in terms of education and social and economic well-being would be made evident. Issues such as institutionalized racism, social class inequality and uneven distribution of power in Aotearoa could also be examined and challenged.[17]

Discussion and conclusion

Education is clearly a site of struggle and the changing policies and reforms in education are an indication of the dominant ideologies and values that emerge at any one time. While in Aotearoa/New Zealand there is clearly a struggle between the notions of biculturalism and multiculturalism, there are also more general ideological positions that compete for the high ground in education: welfare state liberalism, radical educationalism and neo-liberalism (usually referred to as the New Right).[18] In education, the proponents of the New Right have held the high ground for the past fifteen years (in the public sector through government, as well as Treasury and the State Services Commission, and in the private sector through the Business Roundtable and the New Zealand Employers' Federation) and it is their agenda which dominates.

Whereas the New Right has established an economic rationalist and free market structure throughout society, radical educationalists promote the improvement of education and the revision of social structures. Prior to the rise of the New Right, the New Zealand education debate centred on the failure of the welfare state to deliver its promises of equal educational opportunity and social justice through the vehicle of education. Specifically, there was a concern for the three major dimensions of class, gender and ethnicity. The New Right used these radical arguments which were largely accepted by the populace – the arguments of middle-class capture and the failure of the welfare state to deliver the goods (see Treasury, 1987) – but the New Right agenda was very different from that of the radical educationalists who were, in effect, hoisted on their own petard. Through this clever use of political skill, the New Right made sure that the New Zealand education system has been subjected to years of incessant reforms, bringing it in line with New Right ideology. In this process, the welfare state has been largely demolished. Specifically, the process attacked first of all the administration of education in order to dismantle the structures supporting the old system and then the curriculum in order to change the value system inherent in education and, by extension, in society at large. Thus, arguments which in one context may be revisionary and reforming for the good of children, teachers and, in the long term, society, may in another context be used to undermine policies that uphold the social good and eventually to erode the humanistic beliefs and values that underlie those policies.

In the free market of the New Right, individual well-being and success are all important, and there is no social contract or social responsibility. The market and not society decides which is the best 'product'.[19] Michael Jackson and Michael Jordan receive millions of dollars to appear in advertising campaigns. The products they advertise have no great merit and the cost of advertising bears no relationship to the value of the product. As an analogy, in an educational free market, the product most likely to succeed will be that marketed best, but probably not that which is actually the most beneficial to society. If society's job is to envision and implement its values, and its values are held in thrall by an ideology that is essentially anti-humanist, then there seems little chance that it will have the resources to fulfil its tasks and not to be captured by a powerful circumambulatory monetarist machine.

Contemporary scholars such as Giddens (1994) tell us of the collapse of traditional oppositional ideologies and argue that the conservatives are embracing radical market theory approaches and the left is defending the tatters of a welfare state which it was recently attacking. In the global village, social scientists are becoming increasingly interested in postmodern and poststructuralist arguments. Webster (1996) warns that postmodernism is essentially anarchic and in its refusal to support any particular body of knowledge it lays us open to the specific and focused intentions of groups such as the New Right. He observes that postmodernism dissociates itself from unitary bodies of theory (such as critical theory) because of their 'implicit omnipresent hegemony' (p. 234). He then argues that 'After Lyotard, "the post-modern condition" expresses the compromise or collapse of Enlightenment and modern ideals and the fragmentation of social life into pure simulacra, a universe of signs or images which have no referents except other signs' (p. 230). Websters warns that 'the confluence of the postmodern condition across social science disciplines and social theory is persistent and ominous' (p. 231).

An underlying theme of this chapter in examining values in education and cultural pluralism is, as Webster does, to restate the importance of critical theory in our apparently postmodern era. It is crucial to continue to critique thoroughly, to be precise in an era when postmodernism focuses on the imprecise. In such a focus the idea of education as a site of struggle is abandoned to the New Right with its vision of a global free market driven by product and customer demand and its lack of humanism. A critical theory approach provides a useful tool for developing alternatives and solutions in response to the New Right.

Critical theory is radical, humanistic and emancipatory and based on reason. It uses critical analysis, reflection and praxis to find solutions based upon the notions of equality and social justice (what Habermas, 1981, terms the project of modernity). Although both Lyotard's (1984) conclusion that reason and the Enlightenment are just one of many grand narratives, and Giddens's (1994) description of former oppositional ideologies exchanging roles in an emerging global village may contain elements of truth and are interesting in their own right, neo-liberal reforms that simplify to the point of banality our complex world are inexorably marching forward with their inequitable free market scenario. Critical theory has a major role to play not only in countering the changes that are being conceived and implemented, but also in bringing back a discourse which goes beyond the often intricate banalities of the postmodern and poststructuralist debates to provide useful alternatives to the global dominance of economic rationalism.

Although this chapter is a study of the historical development of Maori education, it is also offered as an example of how a critical theory approach can provide a clear picture of underlying values from a 'close reading' of particular policies and programmes and enable understanding of the processes for developing policies and practice from a particular ideological perspective.

Notes

1 This chapter is a much reshaped and updated version of an earlier article entitled 'Bicultural education in Aotearoa: establishing a tauiwi side to the partnership', which appeared in the *New Zealand Annual Review of Education*, 3, 1993.

2 Critical theory is the name given to the theoretical position of the Frankfurt School. The term was first used by Horkheimer in 1937 and the theory was developed in opposition to the then dominant scientific paradigm of logical positivism and is based upon the processes of reflection and practice. During the 1930s its proponents were Adorno, Marcuse, Fromm, Lowenthal, Neumann, Kirchheimer and Reich. The Frankfurt School became influential in the 1950s and reached a peak in the radical student movement of the late 1960s. A second generation of influential critical theorists included Habermas, Wellmer, Schmidt and Offe. Peters *et al.* (1996b) argues that a third concurrent generation was established around the American journal *Telos* and in Australia around *Thesis Eleven*. Critical theory has its roots in the philosophy of Hegel and later in Marx and Engels. See Peters *et al.* (1996a) for an interesting

overview of the debate between critical theory and poststructuralism/postmodernism.

3 Irwin states in her 1989 paper that they are used interchangeably.

4 Having said this, however, it is also true that we have not moved cleanly from one phase to another, either overnight or completely. For example, although I would argue that we are now in a bicultural stage, this does not mean that we all share ideologies or support policies that are bicultural. Rather, there is a mixture of people who support ideologies from the assimilationist, integrationist and multicultural stages, and these ideologies and their policies and practices are in competition with one another even though the present policy emphasis and implementation is bicultural.

5 A useful discussion of the Treaty of Waitangi and contemporary Maori perspectives can be found in Walker (1996) and Kawharu (1989).

6 Sarup (1991) argues in relation to the UK that the debate between multicultural and antiracist supporters is likely to be submerged under the free market policy which seems blind to issues of social class, gender and ethnicity. In New Zealand, although there is a predominance of the free market philosophy, the Maori Renaissance has generated a powerful political base and is able to keep Maori issues high on the political agenda. This is particularly true with the presence of Maori MPs in powerful cabinet positions in both the coalition and subsequent minority national governments.

7 Banks acknowledges Kuhn (1970) and Barnes (1982) for the development and explanation of the paradigm.

8 Although a little awkward, the term 'assimilation' has been used to identify both a stage and a specific paradigm within that stage, and has been adopted instead of Banks's descriptor, assimilationism.

9 See Jensen, 1969; Schockley, 1972; Herrenstein, 1971; Herrenstein and Murray, 1994. This conflict led to a larger debate where those opposing the genetic argument countered that IQ tests were in fact biased towards the knowledge base of the white middle classes. In New Zealand, a similar storm blew up over the use of TOSCA, the test of scholastic ability that was designed by NZCER as a tool to determine which stream students would go into when they entered secondary school. It was claimed that TOSCA was in fact an intelligence test and was culturally biased against Maori students. For more information on the TOSCA debate, see the series of articles and letters (particularly the ongoing jousting between Nash and Reid) in *NZJES* (see TOSCA References). (Timoti Karetu, formerly professor of Maori at Waikato University and later the Maori Language Commissioner, designed the MOTIS test, a Maori-context IQ test parodying the American OTIS test.)

10 The self-fulfilling prophecy works in the following way: those who are placed in higher streams are expected to learn more and do better, they are given more support,

have good self-esteem and do well, as expected. Those assigned to lower streams, however, are given the message that it is expected that they will learn less and perform poorly, and consequently they receive less support, have lower self-esteem and as predicted they do poorly. See Rosenthal and Jacobson (1968) and Rist (1970).

11 It was also predominant in Canada, Australia, the United States and Britain.

12 See Harker (1990, pp. 34–37) for a useful explanation of this process.

13 This illustrates the difficulty in being precise with this model. Peters and Marshall (1989) place this paradigm within their integration stage, even though it is philosophically assimilationist and was adopted chronologically during the integration stage. It also shows the disparity between a government policy of integration and a government policy of assimilation. It may also mean that things were not carefully thought through.

14 It is not the teaching of these items per se, as much as the fact that when taught by Pakeha they are often taken out of context, trivialized and made tokenistic.

15 Maori refer to themselves as tangata whenua, the people of the land, and to those from other places as tauiwi. Pakeha is the term used to refer to Europeans and is more widely used than tauiwi.

16 Although Banks does not identify the indigenous or first language paradigms as central to or even as part of the cultural pluralism paradigm, it is hard to envisage this or the less radical cultural difference paradigm without a strong linguistic component.

17 In the international context, the seminal work of Bowles and Gintis (1967) describes how schools reinforce social class stratification as well as student passivity and an acceptance of their position. This and other more recent examples could serve as tools for analysis and reflection.

18 See Lauder (1990) for a useful overview of competing ideologies and the New Right in New Zealand. See also Sullivan (1994, 1997).

19 See Grace (1990) for a useful discussion of the commodification of education in New Zealand.

References

Alton-Lee, A. and Nutall G. (1991) *Understanding Learning and Teaching Project: Phase Two*. Final Report to the Ministry of Education, Education Department, University of Canterbury.

Banks, J. A. (1988) *Multiethnic Education: Theory and Practice*, 2nd edn. Boston: Allyn and Bacon.

Barnes, B. (1982) *T. S. Khun and Social Science*. New York: Columbia University Press.

Barrington, J. M. (1976) Cultural adaptation and Maori educational policy: the African connection. *Comparative Education Review* 19 (2), 1–10.

Barrington, J. M. (1988) Learning the 'Dignity of Labour': secondary education policy for Maoris. *New Zealand Journal of Educational Studies* 23 (1), 45–58.

Bates, R. J. and Codd, J. A. (eds) (1980) *Theory and Practice in New Zealand Education*. Palmerston North: Dunmore Press.

Bowles, S. and Gintis, H. (1967) *Schooling in Capitalist America*. New York: Basic Books.

Brandt, G. L. (1986) *The Realization of Anti-Racist Teaching*. Lewes: Falmer.

Codd, J. A. (1980a) Moral development and moral education. In R. J. Bates and J. A. Codd (eds), *Theory and Practice in New Zealand Education*. Palmerston North: Dunmore Press, pp. 346–59.

Codd, J. A. (1980b) Values education and the neutrality of the teacher. In R. J. Bates and J. A. Codd (eds), *Theory and Practice in New Zealand Education*. Palmerston North: Dunmore Press, pp. 371–80.

Codd, J., Harker, B. and Nash, R. (eds) (1990) *Political Issues in New Zealand Education*, 2nd edn. Palmerston North: Dunmore Press.

Department of Education and Science (1985) *Education for All*. The Swann Report. Cmnd 9453. London: HMSO.

Giddens, A. (1994) *Beyond Left and Right*. Palo Alto: Stanford University Press.

Grace, G. (1990) The New Zealand Treasury and the commodification of education. In S. Middleton, J. Codd and A. Jones (eds.) *New Zealand Education Policy Today*. Wellington: Allen and Unwin.

Habermas, J. (1981) Modernity versus postmodernity. *New German Critique* 22, 3–22.

Harker, R. (1990) Schooling and cultural reproduction. In J. Codd, B. Harker and R. Nash (eds), *Political Issues in New Zealand Education*. Palmerston North: Dunmore Press.

Herrenstein, R. J. (1971) I.Q., *Atlantic Monthly* 43, 64.

Herrenstein, R. and Murray, C. (1994) *The Bell Curve*. New York: Free Press.

Hunn, J. K. (1960) *Report on the Department of Maori Affairs*. Wellington: Government Printer.

Irwin, K. (1989) Multicultural education: the New Zealand response. *New Zealand Journal of Educational Studies* 24 (1), 3–18.

Irwin, K. (1990) The politics of kohanga reo. In S. Middleton, J. Codd and A. Jones (eds), *New Zealand Education Policy Today*. Wellington: Allen and Unwin.

Jensen, A. (1969) How much can we boost IQ and scholastic achievement? *Harvard Educational Review* 39 (1), 1–123.

Johnson, D. and Johnson R., (1987) *Learning Together and Alone: Co-operative, Competitive and Individualistic Learning* 2nd edn. Englewood Cliffs NJ: Prentice-Hall.

Kawharu, I. A. (ed.) (1989) *Maori and Pakeha Perspectives in the Treaty of Waitangi*. Oxford: Oxford University Press.

Keown, P., McGee, C. and Sands, F. (1993) *Values Education and Social Studies: Research and Development*.

Research Monograph 1. Values in Social Studies Project. Hamilton: University of Waikato.

Kuhn, T. S. (1970) *The Structure of Scientific Revolution*, 2nd edn. Chicago: University of Chicago Press.

Lauder, H. (1990) The New Right revolution and education in New Zealand. In S. Middleton, J. Codd and A. Jones (eds), *New Zealand Educational Policy Today*. Wellington: Allen and Unwin.

Lyotard, J-F. (1984) *The Postmodern Condition: A Report on Knowledge*. Trans. G. Bennington and B. Massumi. Minneapolis: University of Minnesota Press.

Michaelson, L. K., Watson, W. E. and Black, R. H. (1989) A realistic test of individual versus group consensus decision making. *Journal of Applied Psychology* **74**, 834–9.

Middleton, S., Codd, J. and Jones, A. (eds) (1990) *New Zealand Education Policy Today*. Wellington: Allen and Unwin.

Parata, H. (1993) Mainstreaming – a Maori affairs policy? *Institute of Policy Studies Newsletter* **36**, 19–20.

Peters, M. (1996a) Habermas, poststructuralism and the question of postmodernity. In M. Peters, W. Hope, W. Marshall and S. Webster, *Critical Theory, Poststructuralism and Social Context*. Palmerston North: Dunmore Press.

Peters, M., Hope, W., Marshall, W. and Webster, S. (1996b) *Critical Theory, Poststructuralism and the Social Context*. Palmerston North: Dunmore Press.

Peters, M., Hope, W., Marshall, W. and Webster, S. (1996) Introduction: contextualising social theory. In M. Peters, W. Hope, W. Marshall and S. Webster, *Critical Theory, Poststructuralism and the Social Context*. Palmerston North: Dunmore Press.

Peters, M. and Marshall, J. (1989) Te Reo O Te Tai Tokerau: language evaluation and empowerment. *New Zealand Journal of Educational Studies* **24** (2), 141–57.

Philips, D. (1993) Curriculum development in New Zealand. *Educational Review* **45** (2), 155–64.

Rist, R. (1970) Students' social class and teachers' expectations: the self-fulfilling prophecy in ghetto education. *Harvard Educational Review* **40**, 411–51.

Robb, W. M. (1992a) Values education: prevention and cure for some social problems? Unpublished paper given at the 36th Biennial International Conference of the World Education Fellowship, University of Hartford, Connecticut.

Robb, W. M. (1992b) What are values education and citizenship education? Unpublished paper given at the British Comparative and International Society, Annual Conference, York.

Rosenthal, R. and Jacobson, L. F. (1968) *Pygmalion in the Classroom*. London: Holt Rinehart and Wilson.

Sarup, M. (1991) *Education and the Ideologies of Racism*. Stoke-on-Trent: Trentham Books.

Schockley, W. (1972) Dysgenics, genetics and raceology: challenges to the intellectual responsibility of educators. *Phi Delta Kappa* January, 297–307.

Smith, G. H. (1990) Taha Maori: Pakeha capture. In J. Codd, B. Harker and R. Nash (eds), *Political Issues in New Zealand Education*. Palmerston North: Dunmore Press.

Snook, I. (1980a) Moral education: past, present and future. In P. D. K. Ramsay (ed.), *Curriculum Issues in New Zealand*. Wellington: New Zealand Education Institute.

Snook, I. (1980b) Whose Christian values? *New Zealand Journal of Educational Studies* **15** (1), 15–23.

Street-Porter, R. (1978) *Race, Children and Cities*. Milton Keynes: Open University Press.

Sullivan, K. (1993) Bicultural education in Aotearoa/New Zealand: establishing a Tauiwi side to the partnership. *New Zealand Annual Review of Education: Te Arotake a te Ao o te Matauranga i Aotearoa* **3**, 191–222.

Sullivan, K. (1994) The impact of educational reform on teachers' professional ideologies. *New Zealand Journal for Educational Studies* **29** (1), 1–16.

Sullivan, K. (1997) They've opened Pandora's box: educational reform, the New Right and teachers' ideologies. In M. Olssen and K. Morris-Matthews, *New Zealand Educational Policy in the 1990s*. Palmerston North: Dunmore Press.

Treasury (1987) *Government Management, Volume 2, Education Issues*. Wellington: Government Printer.

Vasil, R. (1988) *Biculturalism: Reconciling Aotearoa with New Zealand*. Wellington: Institute of Policy Studies.

Walker. R. (1996) Maori resistance to state domination. In M. Peters, W. Hope, W. Marshall and S. Webster, *Critical Theory, Poststructuralism and the Social Context*. Palmerston North: Dunmore Press.

Webster, S. (1996) Escaping postcultural tribes. In M. Peters W. Marshall and S. Webster, *Critical Theory, Poststructuralism and the Social Context*. Palmerston North: Dunmore Press.

Zubhoff, S. (1988) *In the Age of the Smart Machine: The Future of Work and Power*. New York: Basic Books.

TOSCA References

Ballard, K. D. (1984) The need to focus on the individual child: a comment on TOSCA. *New Zealand Journal of Educational Studies* **19** (2), 157–9.

Ballard, K. D. (1985) Psychometrics versus the individual child: a response to Reid and Croft. *New Zealand Journal of Educational Studies* **20** (1), 93–4.

Beck, L. R. and St. George, R. (1983) The alleged cultural bias of PAT: reading comprehension and reading vocabulary tests. *New Zealand Journal of Educational Studies* **18** (1), 32–47.

Matthews, D. A. (1983) The use of standardised tests: a practitioner's point of view. *New Zealand Journal of Educational Studies* **18** (2), 171–8.

Nash, R. (1983) Four charges against TOSCA. *New Zealand Journal of Educational Studies* **18** (2), 154–65.

Nash, R. (1984) Ability, attainment, prediction and bias. *New Zealand Journal of Educational Studies* **19** (2), 152–6.

Reid, N. and Gilmore, A. (1983) Pupil performance on TOSCA: some additional information. *New Zealand Journal of Educational Studies* **18** (1), 13–31.

Reid, N. and Croft, C. (1984) Replies to Nash and Ballard. *New Zealand Journal of Educational Studies* **19** (2), 162–9.

Reid, N. and Croft, C. (1985) Response to Ballard: final comment. *New Zealand Journal of Educational Studies* **20** (2), 192–3.

Reid, N., Gilmore, A. and Croft, C. (1984) In defence of TOSCA: reply to Nash's 'Four charges . . .'. *New Zealand Journal of Educational Studies* **19** (1), 15–23.

St. George, R. and Chapman, J. W. (1983) TOSCA results from a New Zealand Form 1 sample. *New Zealand Journal of Educational Studies* **18** (2), 178–83.

St. George, R. and Chapman, J. W. (1984) Maori and European ability group placements: TOSCA versus PATs. *New Zealand Journal of Educational Studies* **19** (2), 160–1.

Tuck, B. F. (1983) Education and test of scholastic ability: is there a baby in the bathwater? *New Zealand Journal of Educational Studies* **18** (2), 165–71.

17 An Analysis of the Effect of Recent National Policy Changes on Values and Education in South Africa

ELZA VENTER, KARIN FRANZSEN and ELNA VAN HEERDEN

Introduction

Education is one of the major and much debated concerns in the establishment of 'the new South Africa'. Black education has been one of the main arenas where the struggle for liberation was contested. The concept of people's education was regarded as a symbol of democracy and human rights. It represents a reaction against the effort at social control represented by apartheid education and its infringement on human dignity and freedom. People's values and their perceptions of themselves and others are closely related to their views of knowledge and what the nature of formal education should be. This could be seen in a pre-democratic South African society in which mainly white voices were heard in the education discourse. Other voices which could have contributed to a broader understanding and improvement of critical issues in education have for long not been heard.

With the long-awaited political and constitutional changes taking place in South Africa a different societal structure has been established and a new democratic value system formally and officially embraced. A clear distinction between the pre-democratic and the new democratic South Africa is constantly drawn. Not only does this distinction refer to a shift in political and constitutional conditions, but in more general terms it refers to a major shift in value frameworks and systems which underpin the basis of South African society. The recent changes in national policy can be seen to impact on values and attitudes in all the different areas of education and educational structures. Alternatively, shifts in values have resulted in new policies which closely affect education.

Education in a pre-democratic South Africa

The history of education in South Africa is a history of the conjunction of European and African ways of life (De Villiers, 1994). Education existed in South Africa long before the arrival of the Dutch colonists in 1652. Traditional African education was led by community elders through an oral tradition based on cultural transmission and was closely linked with life experience (Jansen, 1990). As a result of the oral tradition of education elders got involved with the subject they taught and interpreted that subject through narrative.

Ball (1984) identifies two common assertions in accounts of schooling in Africa: first, that western academic schooling was imposed by the colonial powers; second, that their present day education systems are still trapped and inhibited by legacies of the colonial past. However, Ball (1984) points out that 'the indigenous people in Africa were not simply passive recipients but played an active role in attempting to shape the education being offered to them'. Africans regarded education 'to be one source of material superiority of the white colonists, and a route for individual and social mobility' (Ball, 1984).

The following extract from a 1930 essay of Ndabaninga Sithole (cited in Ball, 1984) captures the perceptions of an African pupil of a colonial academic curriculum:

> To us education meant books, writing and talking English, and doing arithmetic . . . At our homes we have done a lot of ploughing, planting, weeding and harvesting . . . We know how to do these things. What we knew was not education: education was what we did not know. We wanted as we said to Ndebele, 'to learn the book until it

remained in our heads, to speak English until we could speak it through our noses'.   (p. 138)

The effect of colonization on perceptions of education is evident in this citation. Knowledge and education, in other words, no longer only took place in the community and through the narratives of elders. Knowledge no longer formed part of a shared discourse, but resided outside the self (and outside the particular community and context). It now became possible for a 'superior other' to transmit objective knowledge to an unknowing subject. It furthermore became possible for students (probably uncritically) to 'learn the book until it remained' in their heads. The student was no longer part of the creation of knowledge as in the case of a contemplative, and communal construction of knowledge, because there was an objective body of knowledge outside which needed to be mastered. The possibility that knowledge resided outside the context of the individual could also affect the way in which the individual saw himself, others around him and the values he and others in his community shared.

According to De Villiers (1994) this encroachment of the European way of life as well as the trauma of the side effects of conflict between Dutch/Afrikaner inhabitants and British imperial strategies were the two threats with which the originally indigenous people in South Africa had to contend. The latter has been a dominant motif in South African political history. It is necessary briefly to discuss the nature and process of this conflict in order also to understand the background against which education in South Africa developed.

After British occupation in 1806, the Dutch-speaking settlers who became known as 'Afrikaners' were faced with enforced English in schools and government, in order to ensure conquest and assimilation. The Afrikaners opted for political and cultural independence by moving into the hinterland of Africa in the latter part of the 1830s (De Villiers, 1994). After the discovery of diamonds in 1867 and gold in 1886, the friction between the newly formed Boer republics and British imperial interests heightened. A form of Calvinistic Christian religion from the Netherlands was entrenched by the Afrikaners to contribute to the beginning of Christian National Education (Taylor, 1987). The Anglo–Boer war of 1899–1902 played a significant role in defining English/Afrikaans rivalry among political, cultural and economic lines.

With regard to black education in the same period, the following developments took place in South Africa (Jansen, 1990). After a period of slave education and simple Christian religious instruction (introduced by European settlers), mission education was introduced in the early 1800s. The era of so-called Native Education stemmed from the 1920s. Native Education was 'characterised by the rapid structural deterioration of black schools and first state-mandated segregated curricula' (De Villiers, 1994). Bantu Education, which it was also called, was introduced in 1953 and consequently derived from the policy of apartheid.

In terms of the Bantu Education Act of 1953, control of black education was removed from the provincial authorities in Natal, Orange Free State, Transvaal and Cape Province and from the mission churches. Full control was placed with the central government's newly created Department of Bantu Education. Bantu education was to take place within the framework of what was called the 'Bantu areas', later to be the designated 'homelands' (Mncwabe, 1993).

Structural pluralism or separatism has always been a significant feature of South African education, but it was vigorously implemented after the National Party's accession to power in 1948 and the passing of the Bantu Education Act of 1953. The school has been used as an instrument to support and legitimize the position of the dominant group and its political interests. The culturally divided population was kept apart to ensure the dominant group's position in all spheres of society. Conformity to and continuity of the ideologies and culture of the dominant group were more important than social change. Christian National Education was the ideology responsible for the transmission of Eurocentric values and culture to everyone in the school system and assimilation became very important (Squelch, 1993).

Hartshorne (1992) sees the years from 1975 onwards as a period of disintegration of black secondary schooling. This disintegration eventually resulted in student-centred unrest of June 1976 in Soweto. Mncwabe (1993) believes that students in Soweto were saying, among other things, that 'they had been let down by their education system and that they wanted education as good as anyone else's'.

Since 1976 various attempts have been made to stand up against apartheid education to create a system for the benefit of all races and cultures in the country, such as people's education, the Open Schools Movement and the opening of previously white-only schools to all race groups (Squelch, 1993). All of these attempts, though praiseworthy, could not do South Africans any good if the intention really to understand and accommodate one another did not exist. If assimilation was the intention, with minimal adjustment on the part of the school, transformation could not take place.

Since June 1976 there has scarcely been peace in black schools. 'School boycotts are more the norm than the exception. There are estimates that on any one school day, approximately 200,000 children scattered throughout the country are boycotting classes' (Mncwabe, 1993).

In 1979 the Education and Training Act was enacted which replaced the Bantu Education Act of 1953. According to Mncwabe (1993), the Act facilitated many practical and material improvements but still 'did not come to grips at all with the isolation of black education, and merely perpetuate[d] the "tradition" of whites taking decisions for the black man'.

In June 1980 the South African government commissioned the independent but state-funded Human Sciences Research Council (HSRC), to investigate the state of South African education. Mncwabe (1993) asserts that the government treated this report 'as a smorgasbord rather than a fixed menu – picking out certain suggestions that it found feasible to implement, leaving out vital recommendations that were supposed to have formed the bedrock of a new education system'.

In 1983 a White Paper was drafted by a government working party, which can be captured, according to Hartshorne (1992), in a slogan 'separate but not equal'. Although the organization of the South African school system has changed a number of times in the past century, in general terms, it can be said that it has always been characterized by ethnically segregated education on all levels and centrally controlled policy and funding (Steyn, 1996). Since 1983 education was organized through three separate 'own affairs' services of the tricameral parliament catering for whites, coloureds and Indians. Education for whites was organized in four semi-autonomous provincial departments. In this era, South Africa had no less than fifteen different ministries of education: four in the so-called 'independent' homelands, six in the self-governing territories, one for the Department of Education

and Training (catering for black South Africans outside the traditional homelands), one in each of the tricameral houses of parliament and one for the Department of National Education (DNE). The DNE was in control of policy as well as budgetary allocations on behalf of the central government and took responsibility for establishing countrywide norms and standards and co-ordinating the functions of the different ministries of education (Department of Education, 1995). Furthermore, each of the education ministries had its own configuration of models of school ownership, governance and funding. Until recent changes, the different ministries and departments have functioned in relative isolation from each other except at top management level (Department of Education, 1995).

The historic pattern of governance in South Africa has been top-down, authoritarian or bureaucratic. Until fairly recently, for instance, representative student organizations were actively discouraged or suppressed in many parts of the system and even teachers' organizations representing predominantly black teachers have operated under severe constraints. Parents and community representatives have at best participated in official advisory and executive structures under paternalistic control. By contrast, in recent years the trend of policy in the self-contained white system has favoured administrative decentralization, professional autonomy for educators and parental ownership and control of schools through governing bodies.

Access to education was rationed on an ethnic and racial basis. Compulsory education for white children had been enforced for decades with the consequence that the adult white population has been literate for generations whereas, by contrast, the black adult population and out-of-school youths had little access to education resulting in a low literacy rate. State provision for early childhood education and for children and adults with special needs has been generally inadequate and racially determined. In most instances, the curriculum, textbooks and teacher education were manipulated for ideological purposes. State-determined history, religion, value systems, culture and gender roles have been imposed. Official policies on teaching methods and examinations have encouraged memorization of information and discouraged both teachers and students from developing initiative and critical thinking skills.

The management and control of education and training systems have always been kept in male hands, across all racial, as well as ethnic subsystems. Discrimination against women in employment practices and of employment conditions prevailed. De Villiers describes the changing situation after 1987 as follows:

> A number of concerned individuals not connected to government met to form forums for action to solve the crisis in education. From these discussions the National Education Co-ordinating Committee (NECC) was formed as an extremely powerful non-governmental agency for investigating the improvement of education. (De Villiers, 1994, p. 231)

One of the projects of the NECC was the National Education Policy Investigation (NEPI) project. This project released a summary and twelve reports with reform proposals. These proposals (NEPI, 1993) centred around decision-making structures and processes, core curriculum and commonality and diversity as burning issues in education.

South Africa's first democratic election followed in April 1994 and since then education has been a major priority of the ANC-dominated Government of National Unity.

The appalling quality in so many of the South African schools, the inequalities of the education system, the under-provision of resources and not least the turmoil and disruption in black schools in the last two decades are among the many factors that have called for the restructuring of the South African education system (Lemon, 1995).

The former ethnically based education departments have been rationalized into nine non-racial provincial departments of education. Each provincial department is a completely new structure and each provincial government entitled to make laws governing education at all levels (excluding universities and technicons which fall within the ambit of national government).

At national level, the DNE has been redesigned into the Department of Education. The new Department of Education is organized in three branches: Education and Training Systems and Resources, Education and Training Programmes and Education and Training Support (Department of Education, 1995), providing for the variety in needs across the spectrum of cultures.

Cultural diversity and diversity in value systems in South Africa

South Africa is a country of many nations, cultures and value systems. South Africans differ in race, religion, heritage and ideology. The ethnic composition of the population of South Africa is extremely complex. In general it constitutes of 73 per cent blacks, 3 per cent Indians, 8 per cent coloureds and 16 per cent whites. The black people can be divided in several ethnic groups such as the Xhosas, Sothos, Zulus, etc., each with their own culture.

There are eleven official languages and fifteen other languages which are recognized in terms of the constitution and need to be 'promoted'. Mncwabe (1990) indicates the diversity of language groups: the black people belonging to the Nguni and Sotho speaking tribes can be divided in five major groups with different dialects. The coloureds and whites speak Afrikaans and/or English and one or more European language(s), while some of the Asians speak Tamil or Hindi.

The religious groupings are equally varied. The main Christian religions are Roman Catholicism, Protestant denominations, some charismatic movements and Pentecostal churches. A number of the African religions encompass ancestor worship, while the most common religions among Indians and some of the coloureds are Hinduism and Islam (see Mncwabe, 1990).

Coombs (1985) defines culture as that which encompasses all aspects of the community's life and gives it its distinctive identity, cohesiveness and continuity, for example, the value system, ideology, social codes of behaviour, technology, political and economic systems, religion, myths and social structures. These are expressed in language, education, literature, art, architecture, food and dress. Very few cultures, however, exist in isolation or remain static over a long period of time. A certain degree of assimilation does occur when cultures meet, although it cannot be enforced by law.

Banks (1989) distinguishes macro and micro cultures in multicultural societies, where the larger, shared core culture is the macro culture and the smaller groups have their micro cultures. He believes that many misunderstandings and conflicts occur because the micro cultures have values somewhat alien to the national core culture and people do not learn to appreciate and respect different cultures and their contribution to the macro culture. Banks (1986) declares that, to a certain extent, both acculturation and accommodation are necessary for diverse groups to maintain their own identities and simultaneously to interact and understand other cultures. People need to develop the skills, knowledge and attitudes to become citizens of their cultural communities, their nation-states and the global community.

The main culture in society often dominates the subordinate cultural groupings through a process known as 'hegemony' which refers to the maintenance of domination not necessarily through force, but more often through social practices, forms and structures such as the church, state, school, mass media, political system and the family (McLaren, 1994).

For decades the white Afrikaans-speaking South Africans through the social structures and mass media dictated which values and cultural norms dominated in the country. The values in the school system, enforced through state policy, were Christian National in nature. Although the white Afrikaners were not the dominant group in numbers, they dominated politics, the church and the school system for years. According to Schoeman (1995) general social stratification and human alienation were reinforced in this way.

The micro cultures in South Africa have become isolated from one another because of the hegemony of the so-called macro culture. Western culture and values dominated for decades, without acknowledging and considering the African origin of the vast majority of people. The western, capitalistic, individualistic view of life is often in direct opposition to the more group-oriented outlook of the African cultures. The task of getting balance in the core culture of such a disparate society is a difficult assignment for its people.

To function in a democratic system, cultural differences and value plurality need to be acknowledged, but somehow, South Africans now also need to recognize similarities. Because of its variety of cultural groups, adequate cultural interaction becomes very important. Young (1990) affirms the necessity to assert the positivity of group difference by inter alia claiming that formerly oppressed groups have distinct cultures, experiences and perspectives on social life with humanly positive meaning (cited in McLaren, 1994). Trinh T. Minh-ha (see McLaren, 1994) states that:

Multiculturalism is not the juxtaposition of several

cultures whose frontiers remain intact, nor is it to subscribe to a bland 'melting pot' type of attitude that would level all differences. It lies, instead, in the intercultural acceptance of risks, unexpected detours, and complexities of relation between break and closure.   (p. 291)

This attitude of unity in diversity is also echoed by Bhiku Parekh (see Aronowitz and Giroux, 1993) who gives the following description of multiculturalism:

Multiculturalism doesn't simply mean numerical plurality of different cultures, but rather a community which is creating, guaranteeing, encouraging spaces within which different communities are able to grow at their own pace. At the same time it meant creating a public space in which these communities are able to interact, enrich the existing culture and create a consensual culture in which they recognize reflections of their own identity.   (p. 207)

With reference to the emphasis on social diversity, Shapiro (1995) asks the following question: 'If we all speak only from within our specific situations and identities (the sexually oppressed, native peoples, the old, the mentally disabled, women) who speaks for humanity?' Perhaps humaneness might be a point to advance towards, instead of only concentrating on differences. A public discourse which includes the experience, needs and hopes of a broad spectrum of people without privileging any one group might be the answer. This discourse should have the healing of society as its concern.

Democracy in South Africa – national policy changes

The years since 1992 have been characterized by dramatic and far-reaching political and constitutional change in South Africa. The Interim Constitution introduced in 1993 laid the foundation of a new democratic constitutional system. The democratic principles introduced by this Interim Constitution have been entrenched in the 1996 Constitution enacted in February 1997.

In a formal sense the Constitution obliges education authorities to ensure that democratic structures, education models and curricula are put in place. In a more informal sense it has to be ensured that democratic values and tolerance are cultivated in schools and that a change in attitudes is brought about.

The impact of the Constitution and Bill of Rights on education is vast and will determine the functioning of the new democratic education system including its particular obligations and limitations (Bray, 1996). The Constitution as supreme law of South Africa defines the state and determines its different structures and powers. Furthermore the Constitution contains a Bill of Rights which guarantees as well as protects the basic or fundamental rights of every individual. As the supreme law, all the other laws are subordinate to it and in all instances must reflect its spirit and intentions. The Constitution in fact represents the balance between the power of the state and the freedom of the individual. The courts of law are the final arbiters between state and individual and as such are empowered to uphold and enforce the Constitution.

Basic education is recognized in the Constitution as a fundamental right, although education is not a 'first generation' right like civil and political rights (Bray, 1996). In South Africa, as in many developing countries, education is regarded as an essential public service rendered by the state, although this fundamental right does not imply that basic education is necessarily free. In terms of the National Qualifications Framework, 'basic education' would involve the first seven years of formal education that in general terms would aim at functional literacy which encompasses the ability to read, write and count as well as elementary economic, cultural and political knowledge (Bray, 1996).

An overview of the prominent policy documents released since the establishment of the new political dispensation in South Africa displays a marked change in attitude and spirit in favour of democratic principles and human rights at all levels and areas of governmental concern.

Section 29 of the Final Constitution of South Africa (1996) determines that:

- every person has the right to basic education;
- equal access to education institutions;
- instruction in a language of choice where it is reasonably possible;
- the right to establish educational institutions of common culture and religion provided that there is no discrimination on the grounds of race.

The White Paper on Education and Training (Department of Education, 1995) identifies the following values and principles for the new schooling system:

- Education and training should be regarded as a human right and the state has the obligation to advance and protect this right.
- Parents and guardians have the primary responsibility for the education of their children and they have the right to be consulted by the state with regards to the form of education. They also have a crucial role to play in the governance of schools.
- The state is responsible to provide advice and counselling on education services and render appropriate care and educational services to parents and young children in the community.
- The goal of educational policy should be to enable individuals to value, have access to and succeed in good quality lifelong education and training.
- Open access to education and training opportunities of good quality to all children, youth and adults must be promoted. Learners should be able to move easily from one learning context to another.
- Owing to inequalities in the past, there should be an emphasis on redress among those people who are disadvantaged or who are vulnerable.
- The principle of equity should be adhered to ensure that all citizens receive the same quality of learning opportunities.
- Quality of education and training must be addressed and is required for all institutions or organizations involved in education and training.
- The rehabilitation of educational institutions is linked to the restoration of ownership of these institutions to their communities by establishing and empowering governing bodies.
- Democratic governance should be reflected in every level of the system and should take place by means of consultation and appropriate forms of decision making.
- To establish a culture of teaching, learning and management, a culture of accountability should be created.
- Independent and critical thought should be encouraged through the curriculum, teaching methods and textbooks at all levels and all programmes of education and training.
- To equip the increasingly large numbers of

youths and adults with education and skills required by the economy, curriculum choice must be diversified, especially in the post-compulsory phase.

- In order to justify the cost of the education system it is necessary to improve efficiency and productivity.

These touch but a few of the specific examples of change in policy which deal directly with education.

The effect of policy changes on values and education

Value plurality and a multicultural education system in South Africa

Multicultural education has been given scant attention in South Africa, mainly because of adherence to the ideology of Christian National Education and a lack of knowledge regarding the theory and practice of multicultural education (Squelch, 1993). Gibson (1976) (see Grant and Sachs, 1995) identifies four types of multicultural education:

> (1) education of the culturally different, or benevolent multiculturalism, which seeks to incorporate culturally different students more effectively into mainstream culture and society; (2) education about cultural difference, which teaches all students about cultural difference in an effort to promote better cross-cultural understanding; (3) education for cultural pluralism, which seeks to preserve ethnic cultures and increase the power of ethnic minority groups; and (4) bicultural education, which seeks to prepare students to operate successfully in two different cultures.   (p. 93)

In South Africa multicultural education should strive to recognize the enrichment of society through cultural diversity. Students need to learn to listen to each other and try to understand the different cultures in order to work together towards a democratic society.

In a formerly divided nation such as South Africa that is now bound together in a newfound, yet fragile unity, schools could play an important role in bringing people together and establishing a semblance of national cohesion. In a post-apartheid South Africa, students need to be educated to live a meaningful life in a society of diversity and change. Through policy changes, public schools have become multiracial and because schools are

transmitters of culture, education should promote and recognize all cultures presented in classrooms and in the wider society. All learners will have to develop the skills, knowledge, competence and attitude to function effectively in a culturally diverse society. It will require a major paradigm shift from most educators and teacher trainers, as well as parents. This kind of transformation is not an easy task – it requires an open mind and a willingness to understand others and to change one's own presuppositions.

The idea of 'empowerment' is often quoted as one of the primary goals of the new education system in South Africa. Squelch (1993) cites Giroux and McLaren to stress the importance of multicultural education for empowerment, referring to a process through which students become able to critically evaluate and select appropriate aspects of the dominant culture as a means to participate in social action and change in the wider society. Students broaden their understanding of themselves, the world and possibilities outside their immediate experience.

Another benefit of multicultural education in South Africa according to Squelch (1993) is that of equity and equality in the provision of education. All students should have an equal chance to maximize their potential, without any institutional discrimination. Equality also implies providing students with an equal chance to succeed in the classroom. Banks (1989) says that the major goal of multicultural education should be to transform the school in such a way that 'male and female students, exceptional students, as well as students from diverse cultural, social-class, racial, and ethnic groups will experience an equal opportunity to learn in school'. Students should be helped to develop positive attitudes toward different cultural, racial, ethnic and religious groups.

The goals of multicultural education in general, but especially in South Africa, should be to develop positive attitudes towards other cultural groups; to understand the contribution each culture could make to society and to reduce cultural prejudice and stereotyping. Individuals should think critically about and appreciate their own culture and value system. The development of cross-cultural communication skills is important. Intercultural competence, including empathy, acceptance and trust, is important to participate meaningfully in a diverse society. Students in a multicultural setting could become change agents (see Lemmer and

Squelch, 1993). Teachers and students should become critical to educational policy and practice. They should be sensitive to a greater understanding of themselves, to the understanding of others and develop a better understanding of how institutions work including their histories of exploitation and repression (Grant and Sachs, 1995).

Sleeter and Grant (1988) (see Grant and Sachs, 1995) argue that education which is multicultural and social reconstructionist should deal with inequalities based on race, social class, gender and disability. Students should be prepared to reconstruct society so that it better serves people of colour, the poor, women and the disabled. McLaren (1994) maintains that teachers need to develop a multiculturalism that is 'attentive to specificity (historical, cultural) of difference (in terms of race, class, gender, sexual orientation, etc.) yet addresses the commonality of diverse others under the law, with respect to global principles of equality and justice'. Aronowitz and Giroux (1993), contend that it is 'crucial for educators to develop a unity-in-difference position in which new forms of democratic representation, participation, and citizenship provide a forum for creating unity without denying the particular, the multiple, and the specific'. Educators need:

> [a] definition of multiculturalism that offers schools the possibility to become places where students and teachers can become border crossers engaged in critical and ethical reflection about what it means to bring a wider variety of cultures into dialogue with each other . . . we need a language of politics and pedagogy that is able to speak to cultural differences not as something to be tolerated but as essential to expanding the discourse and practice of democratic life. (Aronowitz and Giroux, 1993, pp. 207–8)

According to Banks (1989) the implementation of multicultural education acquires certain transformations in schools, which include power relations; interaction between teachers and students; the ethos of the school; the curriculum, including the hidden curriculum; attitudes towards minority groups; grouping practices and testing procedures. Curricula in South African schools were never ethnically pluralistic or culturally relevant, especially for students of colour. Multicultural curricula should enable students to view concepts and issues from different perspectives. Learners should be assisted in listening to and understanding people from diverse backgrounds; they should learn to

think critically and constructively about their society. Multicultural education would indicate the inclusion of multicultural viewpoints in all subjects and the accommodation of all races and value systems in the school in the composition of the students and staff.

Shapiro (1995) affirms that the young should be educated for a socially just, socially responsible, democratic and compassionate community, but at the same time education should not turn into a monolithic, moral straitjacket where educational concerns are narrowly defined. The struggle for a more humane society may mean different objectives in different contexts. In one place it may be literacy, elsewhere it may mean the possibility of jobs and in some other place political participation and empowerment.

People should be enabled to accommodate the cultural diversity of their own society, before being exposed to cultures in the global community. In a world where borders are becoming more and more diffuse, South Africans will have to work hard at accepting each other in order to enter into the global world.

Shifts in values and epistemological emphasis

The human–world–knowledge relationship in early African education could perhaps best be summarized by what Van Manen (1990) describes as 'maintaining a thoughtful and conversational relation to the world'. In this traditional dimension of understanding the world, the student's interpretation and understanding of a narrative later became the source of knowledge of the next generation. What Walsh (1993) refers to as the 'contemplative nature of understanding' rather than the 'concern for generalisation' probably contrasts early African education best with the views of education and nature of knowledge in the colonial period.

It seems as if personal identity, perceptions of knowledge and views of the nature of education are closely interwoven. The thread that combines these different concepts is values: values which the individual attributes both to himself and the community in which he lives and to others and their interpretations of the world (others' knowledge); and the value which an individual can ascribe to an education system.

The status or value (identity) which persons have

in a society could determine whether their views of knowledge and education are acknowledged or not. This could be seen in the way in which knowledge and the nature of education was regarded in pre-democratic South Africa and how it related to the status (or perceived value) of the persons who held that knowledge. The assumption that underlay knowledge production and the transmission of knowledge in a pre-democratic dispensation was that reality can be known objectively and that there could be a best or true interpretation of reality. This led to forms of absolutism and moral smugness in the 'sense that one has an unquestionable hold on what is really essentially true and right' (Higgs, 1995). Also, because the possibility of one true interpretation existed, it led to a cultural imperialism in education that embraces the view that the dominant culture is so superior to alternatives as to make them educationally suspect. What Weinstein (1995) refers to in another context also happened in South African society, namely that obvious, available points of view were marginalized and disenfranchised, which resulted in blatant injustice. An increased awareness of the moral implications of a particular epistemological view led to a current sensitivity for what one regards as knowledge and how that knowledge is produced, used and transmitted in the South African society.

Traces of a so-called mental–manual attitude which became part of the South African education system can also be found in the Sithole extract quoted earlier, 'what we knew was not education'. Knowledge was often removed from the everyday practical context in which students found themselves. Academic learning was valued and given higher status than vocational learning. In education and training systems, the two have been rigidly separated with different curriculum structures, teacher training and qualification structures with little cross-articulation (Department of Education, 1994).

The perception that objective knowledge and education could be found in Eurocentric content, outside the immediate context of the learner, led to the distancing of the black student from his indigenous culture. De Villiers (1994) notes 'the commitment of African aspirations to "progress" through Western education, which is also a commitment to the values, attitudes and orientations of Western culture and a rejection of the traditional forms of African culture'.

The increased awareness of human dignity and

diverse perceptions in a multicultural South African society form part of the change in the moral perceptions of many South Africans. There is an awareness that individuals and their personal contexts and values play a role in the constitution of what is regarded as knowledge or facts. What was previously regarded as the truth or facts (for example, the content of History syllabuses) are now only regarded as interpretations of individuals within a particular context of a broader narrative.

Against this background of an 'Apartheid-colonial epistemology' (Seepe and Lebakeng, 1996), Vilakazi (1995) recommends that African intellectuals in a post-apartheid era should filter international knowledge in order to make it applicable to the South African cultural context. This possibility exists because a paradigm shift has been made and knowledge again (as in the case of pre-colonial education) becomes part of a narrative of a community within a particular socio-political context. In order to accommodate the demand for cultural and contextual relevance, a hermeneutic approach to curriculum development should be preferred to other approaches (Meyer, 1996). A hermeneutic approach entails 'an interpretative and a dialectical mode of engagement, whereby knowledge is at all times subject to scrutiny by means of reason and in each case the proposition which is most plausible and/or intellectually defensible must be accepted' (Meyer, 1996).

Ideology

The dominant ideology in society often tolerates other ideologies to defuse tension, because it can afford to do so. The hegemonic hold of the social system is so strong that it can generally withstand dissension and actually neutralizes it by permitting token opposition (McLaren, 1994).

In South African public schools Christian Nationalism was dogma for decades. The mainly white representatives of the dominant ideology did tolerate the value systems of others represented in society, but never tried to understand them or give them a rightful place in state affairs, schools or the media. With the policy changes came multicultural school systems. The teacher is confronted with diverse cultures and value systems in one classroom.

In a multicultural society teachers need to become critical towards their own values and those of others and assist students in their classrooms to do the same. It does not imply the rejection of particular cultural values, but it does demand the ability to distance oneself from one's own cultural boundaries. 'It is imperative to reflect critically on stereotypes, dogmatic and conclusive answers to certain types of questions, orthodox proposals for the solution of prevailing social and other problems, simplistic interpretations of complicated states of affairs [and] rationalising of social injustice' (Schoeman, 1995).

The ideal pedagogy would be represented by what Giroux describes as a pedagogy where racism, sexism, class exploitation and other dehumanizing social practices are unacceptable:

> This is a pedagogy that rejects detachment, though it does not silence in the name of its own ideological fervour or correctness, acknowledges social injustices, and examines with care and in dialogue with itself and others how injustice works through the discourses, experiences, and desires that constitute daily life and the subjectivities of the students who invest in them.   (Giroux, 1992, p. 101)

Boyd (in Clark Power and Lapsley, 1992) concludes that education itself is a moral claim extended through the activities and role of the teacher. Education is one way for humans to define their humanity, to practise humanity, to maintain humanity and to change humanity. Education is a way to connect oneself to the past and to project into the future.

Effect of policy changes on values and education

The interim South African Constitution (1993) echoes the spirit of democracy and recognition of basic human rights when its states in section 35(1) that it 'guarantees that the court of law will promote the values which underlie an open and democratic society based on freedom and equality'. As can be seen in the exposition above, this intention has been formalized in relevant educational policy documents.

In a new and changed political dispensation, changes in governmental as well as societal structures and instruments are to be expected. It appears that dramatic changes in education policy and practices reflect a particular concern with education and its value as an instrument of change and a vehicle for perpetuating a democratic dispensation. As Bray (1996) puts it: 'Democracy is about people –

empowering people – which in essence means education.'

Conclusion

It would be naive to imagine that policy changes would alter deep-rooted attitudes, practices and existing structures overnight. Negotiating budget allocations, getting the necessary infrastructures in place and deploying the necessary know-how where it is direly needed obviously require extended time and effort.

The change into a democratic society unfortunately does not mean that a political and educational utopia has been created instantaneously. All the problems and concerns cannot be addressed and solved at once. 'Relinquishing such an apocalyptic tale of revolutionary change may be disappointing to those who hunger for the simple, the universal, and the either/or explanation of events. Yet, nor does it diminish our sense of radical possibility and the hope of human transformation and social change' (Shapiro, 1995).

New policies have not been accepted with acclamation from all quarters. Criticism from a practical and economic point of view against many aspects of the educational reform initiatives has been voiced. One could argue that some of the policy changes are over-reactive and counter-productive. The marked emphasis on equality in all respects, for example, could detrimentally affect individual interests, make no provision for learner diversity or even encourage mediocrity, maintaining standards that are equally poor instead of equally superior. Furthermore many of the measures taken seem to be determined by the present moment, without particular concern for long-term effects and needs. However, it is also important to recognize that terms like 'quality' and 'standards' are heavily value laden and may be used as a smokescreen for forms of ideological or cultural exclusion.

References

Aronowitz, S. and Giroux, H. A. (1993) Education still under siege. In H. A. Giroux and P. Freire (eds), *Critical Studies in Education and Culture Series*. Westport CT: Bergin and Garvey, pp. 196–8, 207–8.

Ball, S. J. (1984) Imperialism, social control and the colonial curriculum in Africa. In I. F. Goodson and S. J. Ball (eds), *Defining the Curriculum*. Lewes: Falmer, pp. 117, 138.

Banks, J. A. (1986) Multicultural education: development, paradigms and goals. In J. A. Banks and J. Lynch (eds), *Multicultural Education in Western Societies*. London: Holt, Rinehart and Winston, pp. 19–20, 24.

Banks, J. A. (1989) Multicultural education: characteristics and goals. In J. A. Banks and C. A. McGee Banks (eds), *Multicultural Education – Issues and Perspectives*. Massachusetts: Allyn and Bacon, pp. 6–7, 10, 21.

Boyd, D. (1992) The moral part of pluralism as the plural part of moral education. In F. Clark Power and D. K. Lapsley (eds), *The Challenges of Pluralism Education, Politics and Values*. London: University of Notre Dame Press, pp. 160–1.

Bray, E. (1996) The South African Bill of Rights and its impact on education. *South African Journal of Education* **16** (3), 150–7.

Clark Power, F. (1992) Introduction – moral education and pluralism. In F. Clark Power and D. K. Lapsley (eds), *The Challenges of Pluralism Education, Politics and Values*. London: University of Notre Dame Press, pp. 2–4.

Clark Power, F. and Lapsley, D. K. (eds) (1992) *The Challenges of Pluralism Education, Politics and Values*. London: University of Notre Dame Press.

Coombs, P. H. (1985) *The World Crisis in Education*. Oxford: Oxford University Press, p. 224.

Department of Education (1994) *Draft White Paper on Education and Training*. Pretoria: Government Printer.

Department of Education (1995) *White Paper on Education and Training*. Pretoria: Government Printer.

Department of Education (1996) *White Paper 2 on the Organization, Funding and Governance of Schools*. Pretoria: Government Printer.

De Villiers, S. L. (1994) Guidelines for the development of a curriculum for a multicultural society in South Africa. Unpublished MEd thesis. University of South Africa.

Giroux, H. A. (1992) *Border Crossings – Cultural Workers and the Politics of Education*. New York and London: Routledge, pp. 101, 109, 121.

Grant, C. A. and Sachs, J. M. (1995) Multicultural education and postmodernism: movement toward a dialogue. In B. Kanpol and P. McLaren (eds), *Critical Multiculturalism – Uncommon Voices in a Common Struggle*. Westport CT: Bergin and Garvey, p. 95.

Hartshorne, K. (1992) *Crises and Challenge: Black Education 1910–1990*. Cape Town: Oxford University Press, pp. 73ff., 181–2.

Higgs, P. (1995) Towards a qualitative discourse in education. Paper given at Philosophy of Education Society of Great Britain Conference, New College, Oxford, 31 March–2 April.

Jansen, J. D. (1990) Curriculum as a political phenomenon: historical reflections on black South African education. *Journal of Negro Education* **59** (2), 195–206.

Klapwijk, J. (1994) Pluralism of norms and values: on the claim and perception of the universal. *Philosophia Reformata* **59**, 158–92.

Lemmer, E. and Squelch, J. (1993) *Multicultural Education – A Teacher's Manual*. Halfway House: Southern Book Publishers, pp. 2, 3, 5.

Lemon, A. (1995) Education in post-apartheid South Africa. Some lessons from Zimbabwe. *Comparative Education* **31** (1), 101–14.

McKinney, R. H. (1992) Towards a postmodern ethics: Sir Isaiah Berlin and John Caputo. *Journal of Value Inquiry* **26**, 395–407.

McLaren, P. (1994) *Life in Schools – An Introduction to Critical Pedagogy in the Foundations of Education*. London: Longman, pp. 182, 186, 286, 290, 291.

Meyer, S. (1996) Negotiating legacies and destiny: a reflection on proposals for the Africanisation of university curricula. Paper given at the Kenton Conference, 26 October.

Mncwabe, M. P. (1990) *Separate and Equal Education – South Africa's Education at the Crossroads*. Durban: Butterworths, pp. 7–8, 15.

Mncwabe, M. P. (1993) *Post-apartheid Education: Towards Non-racial, Unitary and Democratic Socialization in the New South Africa*. New York: University Press of America, pp. 4–5, 24, 27, 73ff., 181–2.

National Education Policy Investigation Report (NEPI) (1993) *Education Planning, Systems, and Structure*. Cape Town: Oxford University Press, pp. 102–15.

Schoeman, P. G. (1995) The 'open society' and educational policy for post-apartheid South Africa. In P. Higgs (ed.), *Metatheories in Philosophy of Education*. Johannesburg: Heinemann, pp. 100–101.

Seepe, S. and Lebakeng, T. (1996) Taking front-line responsibility: the role of black intellectuals in tertiary institutional transformation. Paper given at the Conference on Black Perspective(s) on Tertiary Institutional Transformation, University of Venda, April.

Shapiro, S. (1995) Educational change and the crisis of the left: towards a postmodern educational discourse. In B. Kanpol and P. McLaren (eds), *Critical Multiculturalism – Uncommon Voices in a Common Struggle*. Westport CT: Bergin and Garvey, pp. 21, 26, 29, 32–3.

Squelch, J. (1993) Towards a multicultural approach to education in South Africa. In J. le Roux (ed.), *The Black Child in Crisis – A Socio-educational Perspective*. Pretoria: JL van Schaik, pp. 175–8, 187–90.

Steyn, G. M. (1996) Transformation in education and training: a move towards equality and quality. In E. M. Lemmer and D. C. Badenhorst, *Introduction to Education for South African Teachers: An Orientation to Teaching Practice*. Cape Town: Juta.

Taylor, D. J. L. (1987) A critical assessment of the De Lange Report with particular reference to teachers and other groups. Unpublished DPhil thesis, University of Oxford.

Van Manen, M. (1990) *Researching Lived Experience:*

Human Science for an Action Sensitive Pedagogy. New York: State University of New York Press, p.16.

Vilakazi, H. M. (1995) Education policy for democratic society. Paper given at the Conference on Black Perspective(s) on Tertiary Institutional Transformation, University of Venda, April.

Walsh, P. (1993) *Education and Meaning: Philosophy in Practice*. London: Cassell, p. 59.

Weinstein, M. (1995) Social justice, epistemology and educational reform. *Journal of Philosophy of Education* **29** (3), 369–86.

18 Diversity, Values and National Policy in Australia

LORRAINE M. LING

Australian context of diversity

In 1991 the census records showed that there were 3,755,554 overseas-born people in Australia and this represented 22 per cent of the population at that time. There are four major categories under which immigration to Australia may occur:

- family migration;
- skill migration;
- humanitarian entry;
- special eligibility (this category has two subdivisions of immigrants, visaed and non-visaed).

Since World War II (between 1947 and 1991) 40 per cent of the population growth in Australia was due to migration. Between 1987 and 1990 net migration exceeded natural increase in the Australian population. Australia's overseas-born population is generally better qualified than the Australian-born population and school participation rates were generally higher among teenagers born in non-English speaking countries than among either the Australian-born population or the people born in English-speaking countries. This information is cited in a report by the Bureau of Immigration and Population Research (1994) *The Social Characteristics of Immigrants in Australia*:

> People born in non-English speaking countries in general display social characteristics different from those of people born in either English speaking countries or Australia. In general these characteristics indicate that people born in non-English speaking countries are at a social disadvantage when compared with people born in either English speaking countries or Australia. The relative disadvantage experienced by people born in non-English speaking countries is most acute when they have only been resident in Australia for a short time and is most likely associated with the degree to which they have a command of English and the degree to which (and the speed at which) they are able to establish themselves within the work force and the broader community. (Bureau of Immigration, 1994, p. xx)

The report also states that 'in addition to social disadvantage . . . people born in non-English speaking countries have a lower economic status' (p. 159). The report provides a brief overview of the history of immigration in Australia, noting that immigration is a recent phenomenon dating back to the gold rush period in the 1850s and 1860s. Prior to that time the Australian population was only 400,000. By 1900, however, the population had grown to 3.8 million. In 1991 Australia's population was 16,850,540. With 22.3 per cent of that population being born overseas, Australia has one of the largest foreign-born populations.

Australian national policy

The national policy as it pertains to the concept of diversity in Australia will form the focus of this chapter. This issue will be discussed from the perspective of the various groups and individuals who influence the policy construction process and the values which are portrayed by these players will be examined. Currently in Australia there is an overt movement towards privatization and dominance of the market as a driving force for the values which are reflected in policy documents. In the schools, corporate sponsorship is sought to provide sufficient funding for them to compete in the educational marketplace. In tertiary education there is a constant effort to restructure and rationalize departments and faculties so that there is a leaner and more efficient system. In health, governments have increased the user pays component of health funding and have encouraged subscription to private health insurance which provides support for treatment in private hospitals. In industry the same kinds of rationalization, where there is a demand for downsizing which is simultaneous with the demand to produce more with less, are evident. With regard to diversity, there also appears to be a trend towards valuing diversity if it results in increased productivity or some instrumental gain for the nation state. Rizvi (1993), in discussing the Labor government's view of social justice, states that it was cast in terms of the market and the economic good:

> The federal Labor government's social justice policy . . . suggests that freedom, prosperity and equity can only be delivered by the market. With such reliance on the market, the Government's major responsibility becomes that of good management of the social and cultural conditions necessary for capital accumulation. (Rizvi, 1993, p. 132)

Another commentator in the Australian context, Yeatman (1990) also reflects upon the link between economic rationalism and immigration policy in the current Australian context:

> The Labor Government has commissioned substantial reports on immigration . . . these reports accord the agenda of economic restructuring a central place in their recommendations, so that both a specific immigration policy and multiculturalism are strategically aligned with an effective national economic response to the challenges of restructuring. The mixing of the discourses of restructuring and immigration policy on the one hand and of multiculturalism on the other is especially interesting for its introduction of a cultural dimension into the business of restructuring. (Yeatman, 1990, p. 103)

Following the defeat of the Labor government, a Liberal (conservative) government came to power in Australia in 1996. It had been made known in the popular press that the Liberal government favours a reduction of immigration. One of its first steps after coming to power was to close the offices of the Bureau of Immigration and Population Research in some of the capital cities as a step in the process of reducing the extent and impact of immigration in the Australian context. Since the advent of the Liberal government there have been ongoing debates about racist attitudes and remarks by politi-

cians, the general public and the media which gave the event a high profile. The standard for the debate was set by the Racial Discrimination Act which outlawed racial vilification in Australia and thus laid down the code of cultural practice which was seen as acceptable with regard to racial matters. In Australia, racist attitudes may be discerned towards Aboriginals, Asians and other migrant groups. The government attitudes and policies which flow from this, are evident in community attitudes and values. In a 'Newspoll' reported in the national newspaper, *The Australian*, the top concerns of Australian voters were recorded. This revealed that immigration was not the top issue in determining the choice of political parties for the Australian voters surveyed:

> Immigration is not among the top 10 issues that will influence how people vote at the next federal election, despite the race debate of the past five months. A newspoll survey has found that immigration ranked eleventh on the list of vote-influencing issues, with health and Medicare and unemployment regarded as clearly the most important. (*The Australian*, 24 January 1997, p. 4)

The race debate which is referred to in this newspaper report was sparked by the remarks of an independent member of parliament who claimed that the level of Asian immigration to Australia posed a threat to Australian society. This comment was much publicized at the national level as well as at an international level and tended to polarize the population of Australia and to disturb the country's Asian neighbours. This situation was exacerbated by the fact that the Australian prime minister did not disassociate himself from the views of the independent member of parliament, despite demands from many groups for him to do so. His failure to censure the member and, in fact, to defend her right to express her views was taken by many Australians and Asians to be a form of support for the comments which were labelled as racist and anti-Asian. This kind of debate demonstrates that there is still a variety of values operating in Australia with regard to diversity and multiculturalism in particular, and that there is still not a general acceptance of Australia's place in the Asia-Pacific Basin.

There is also an ongoing tension with regard to the rights of Aboriginal people especially with regard to the rights to land title. In a decision which has become known as the 'Mabo decision' (1994),

Aboriginal people were granted rights to the title of land which was traditionally sacred to them and owned by them. Subsequent rights of ownership were classed as co-existing with rather than extinguishing Native Title. The court decision was codified under the Native Title Act (1994). In 1997, however, the prime minister flagged the possibility of changes to The Racial Discrimination Act and to the Native Title Act. This change would involve transferring the responsibility for native title issues from the commonwealth to the state governments. In a rare joint protest the Aboriginal groups and some other ethnic groups combined to oppose the government's possible changes to the Racial Discrimination Act. The chairwoman of the Ethnic Communities Council of NSW said:

> It was the first time ethnic and Aboriginal leaders had combined in an official campaign against the government. 'The Racial Discrimination Act protects all Australians and for the Government to even consider meddling with it would be in virtual contempt of the international obligations.' [The chairwoman said that] they were also hoping the churches would support their campaign . . . 'We have to get the community involved. You have to move the community with you if you're going to make any change.' (*The Australian*, 24 January 1997, p. 2)

However, it was reported, in an Australia Day speech (January 1997) by a prominent Australian writer, Thomas Keneally, that 'Ethnic stereo-typing was a habit Australians had inherited from the "Old World" and one we should be too proud to indulge in with any seriousness' (*The Australian*, 24 January 1997, p. 2).

These selected news items which were published two days before Australia Day 1997, highlight some of the existing debates and tensions which surround the values of Australians as we move into the twenty-first century. While Australia Day has traditionally been celebrated as a national public holiday, in 1997 the premier of the state of Victoria decreed that for his state it would not be a public holiday. This resulted in a situation where all the other states celebrated a public holiday, as did all the employees in Victoria who were covered by a Commonwealth award. The attitude of the Victorian premier exemplifies the obsession with productivity which is currently paramount in the era of economic rationalism and micro-economic reform in Australia. The value then, which is implicit in the Victorian premier's decree, is that the productivity

of Australia is more to be considered than a celebration of the heritage of the nation. This instrumentalist value is present in much of the recent policy which both the national and state governments are constructing and implementing.

It is a salutary thought that in the last decade of the twentieth century the values that are espoused by governments and thus reflected in policy and legislation are based on economic rationalist ideology which sees the market as the driving force for society and that those who are able to produce the required outcomes for the creation of a 'clever country' will be advantaged. Diversity within this climate is valued predominantly as it is able to contribute to the productivity of the nation state rather than as a resource in it own right.

Assimilationist policy

During the 1950s and 1960s in Australia there was an assimilationist policy in place:

> The policy of assimilation was deceptively simple and was couched in liberal democratic terms. It had stipulated that all Australians, regardless of their origin, were gradually to attain the same manner of living, come to share a common culture, live as members of a single Australian community enjoying the same rights and privileges, accepting the same responsibilities and observing the same customs. (Rizvi, 1991, p. 164)

By the end of the 1960s it became clear that the assimilationist policy could not produce the results which it sought. This policy has been criticized as providing a means to further entrench existing disadvantage as migrants invariably occupy the lowest paid jobs in the workforce and are also expected to undertake jobs which Australian-born citizens would not. There was obvious racial prejudice towards migrants and in the school system, learners from non-English speaking backgrounds (NESB) were clearly at a disadvantage.

In the late 1960s the influence of the integrationist 'melting pot' approach, which was favoured by the Johnson administration in the USA began to be exerted in Australia:

> The rhetoric of integration suggested a view of intercultural relations in which all groups lived with each other in a climate of mutual accommodation. The most fundamental problem with this position was, however, that equal participation in which

political structures and institutions were essentially derived from Anglo-Saxon traditions could hardly have been possible. It was recognised that the dice, so to speak, with which the 'melting pot' game was played was already loaded in favour of the existing power structures.   (Rizvi, 1991, p. 165)

The assimilationist and integrationist approaches in Australia were followed by policies of multi-culturalism. This policy rejects the possibility of a common culture and equal participation, as it is recognized that diversity and ethnicity are desirable elements of society. The diverse nature of the population should be regarded as a positive resource to be tapped rather than as a problem which has to be solved by making everybody the same. People are to be valued for their difference, not for their same-ness according to this approach. A report entitled *Multiculturalism for all Australians* (the Zubrzycki Report), issued by the Australian Council on Population and Ethnic Affairs (1982), stated: 'The means to achieve multiculturalism are to be found in two areas: public policy and community attitude . . . multiculturalism must be based on support from the common core of institutions, rights and obliga-tions' (Australian Council on Population, 1982, p. 13).

The Zubrzycki Report (1982) provided the basis for policies in the area of multicultural education. With regard to the attitudes which are necessary for multiculturalism in general the report stated: 'Multiculturalism is a way of looking at Australian society, and involves living together with an aware-ness of cultural diversity. We accept our differences and appreciate a variety of lifestyles rather than expect everyone to fit into a standardised pattern' (Australian Council on Population, 1982, p. 17).

The Zubrzycki Report (1982) claimed that the schooling system is the basis for developing in Australian young people a multicultural attitude. As a result of the report and others which followed, it is now required of each school in the Australian government system to put into place a multicultural education policy and to teach a language other than English (LOTE). Financial support has been pro-vided at both state and federal levels for the provi-sion of LOTE programmes in schools. Despite these programmes and policies some commentators (Foster, 1983) claim that much effort to implement multicultural programmes is tokenism and remains at the level of rhetoric. There has also been little attempt to alter the community structures which might allow for multiculturalism to be more fully

realized. Some of these structures which exist in institutions are still heavily influenced by the Anglo-Saxon tradition and form of organization and so mitigate against the active involvement of some ethnic groups. In schools, for example, the history which has traditionally been studied has been predominantly related to white Anglo-Saxon culture and has paid only token regard for other histories and other cultures. It is also noticeable that within the curriculum of Australian schools there has been scant regard for the Aboriginal heri-tage of the country. Aboriginals remain a disadvan-taged and under-represented group in Australian society and its institutions. In summarizing the effects of multicultural policy on Australian society, Rizvi (1991) claims:

> As a form of ideology [multiculturalism] represents an attempt to celebrate ethnic differences and prac-tices in order to institutionalise those differences, and thus reproduce current patterns of social inequalities. In doing this, multiculturalism tends to obfuscate the common experiences, histories and social and political conditions of migrant groups and hence obscure the degree of common-ality of experience which exists between migrant and Anglo-Australian working class in Australia. (Rizvi, 1991, p. 192)

National policy, then, in moving from an assimi-lationist to an integrationist and then to a multi-cultural stance has not overcome the obvious inequalities and intolerance which are present with-in Australian society. As has been observed earlier in this chapter, in the reports of current racial debates and tensions Australians are divided in their view about diversity and it appears that national policy has not succeeded in reducing that division.

A broader view of diversity

Diversity refers not only to ethnicity, but also to differences in gender, intelligence, physical ability, religion, age and socio-economic background. Australia has put into place various policies which are an attempt to deal with some of these issues of social diversity. For example: The Department of Employment Education and Training (1988) pub-lished a report entitled *Girls in Schools – A Report on the National Policy for the Education of Girls in Australian Schools*; the Department of Finance and the Department of the Prime Minister and Cabinet in 1989, issued a statement entitled *Towards a*

Fairer Australia: Social Justice and Program Management: A Guide; the Department of the Prime Minister and Cabinet and the Office of the Status of Women (1988) produced a document *A Say, A Choice, A Fair Go, The Governments' National Agenda for Women*; the Department of Employment Education and Training (DEET) (1989) issued a *National Aboriginal and Torres Strait Islander Education Policy: Joint Policy Statement*; the Advisory Council on Multicultural Affairs in 1983 produced *Towards a National Agenda for Multicultural Australia*. These policy statements and reports are but a few of the plethora of policies which exist regarding social justice, equal opportunity, equity and access, multiculturalism and the Aboriginal and Torres Strait Islanders. There are also policies pertaining to disability in Australia.

Disability

In the area of disability, the trend is towards 'normalization' and 'de-institutionalization' which has led to the closure of many institutions and special settings in which disabled people have traditionally been placed. There is a marked division with regard to disability in terms of the attitudes and values of the Australian population. There has also been a lack of the necessary support for the de-institutionalization programme by the state and commonwealth governments which, while promoting and advocating this policy, have not provided the level of funding needed adequately to implement it. In fact, it has in some instances been seen by some critical observers as a cynical move on the part of governments around election time, to close institutions and thus claim to espouse and recognize the rights to a 'normal life' for disabled people. This is reported in the media as a social justice initiative on the part of the government, but has been regarded by many who work in the disability field as a political ploy to gain votes and a means of cutting the costs of institutional care. Clients are not correctly or adequately prepared for the transition into the community. Thus many are distressed and disoriented and some suffer severe illness or death due to the sudden change in their life style. It is necessary, therefore, for the government to put into place programmes and policies which allow for the gradual and systematic transition of disabled people from institutions where many have lived all of their

lives into the community. Community attitudes are likely to be more positive if the disabled people who move to their neighbourhood were obviously better prepared and equipped for the change. This is an example of government policy which is not supported with adequate funds and other resources to implement it effectively. The values which this portrays on the part of governments, while on the surface appearing to be about social justice, may be disingenuous.

Integration or mainstreaming

A similar problem to that which exists in the area of de-institutionalization of people with disabilities exists in the area of integration or mainstreaming of students with disabilities into the education system. All schools are required to have an integration policy and may not deny entry to students with disabilities who seek to attend the mainstream school. This has resulted in some debates as to whether the needs of the disabled students are best served in the so-called 'normal school' or whether a special segregated school setting is more effective for their learning. Teachers in the mainstream system are divided in their attitudes towards integration. While in principle most would support it, there is again a severe lack of resources and funding from the government. This results in teachers, parents and learners frequently becoming frustrated and stressed due to insufficient support. Criticism is currently levelled at the corporate restructuring of the area of disability. The influence of the policy of economic rationalism and the strategies of micro-economic reform on the disability field are becoming obvious in Australia. Carpenter (1993) states:

> An economic discourse is now directing the field. *The Handicapped Programs Review* (1985) frequently raised the issues of efficiency, effectiveness and accountability. Services are no longer regarded as a civic or human right but as a commodity for consumers . . . The rationale for service provision has changed from human rights to economic grounds.   (Carpenter, 1993, p. 185)

Carpenter (1993) observes that the various Acts passed by the Australian government – which include the Disability Services Act 1986, Handicapped Persons' Act 1987, Handicapped Programs Review 1985 – have all implied the move to privatize disability services and thus absolve the government from the responsibility for these services. This has the result of placing these services outside the means of many people in the community. Carpenter (1993) claims:

> Privatization has meant that families, especially the caregiver, now bear the costs being offset by the government. They [the caregivers] provide otherwise expensive care without payment and also pay for the care through loss of employment. It is a government cost reduction being paid for mostly by women . . . It is also a cost reduction being paid for by people with disabilities who have extra costs associated with disabilities and needs for specialised technologies.   (Carpenter, 1993, p. 186)

There is then a direct link between the government policy and the level of disadvantage which is experienced by both the disabled and their caregivers. Under the guise of de-institutionalization, the government at the commonwealth and state levels may be perceived to be offloading its responsibilities and obligations for the care of disabled people and placing them on those people and sectors which are already socially and economically disadvantaged. In the name of economic rationalism, the disabled members of the community are being further marginalized rather than being integrated in a genuine sense into the community.

Policy construction

In the previous section a discussion has focused upon the effect of policy on diversity and upon the values which are held for diversity of various kinds. These values are largely formed through the discourse of policy which becomes so entrenched and 'lived' in the social context that it becomes a cultural logic such that it appears to be unproblematic. The process of policy construction involves the influence of a number of interested parties and thus is an arena for the playing out of contests and tensions. When considering the construction of policy, an examination is required of the various domains in which the process occurs.

Policy construction is viewed here as a social process which occurs within and across four discernible domains. These are defined here as the global domain, the macro domain, the meso domain and the micro domain. The global domain may be seen as the international context of policymaking where universal principles and values form the basis for the policies which are developed. This domain is perceived as interacting with the other domains and thus is both constructing and being reconstructed continuously in that interaction. The macro domain is seen as the national context of policy construction while the meso domain refers to the state, provincial or systems level of policymaking. The micro domain is taken here to refer to the specific institution or context in which the policy is particularized and implemented.

The domains approach

There is a dialectical relationship between these four domains so that each is transformed by the others at the same time as each acts upon the others. This constant dialectical relationship between the domains renders the process of policy construction dynamic and complex. Within each of the domains there are specific interest groups between which there are inherent tensions and conflicts. These are referred to here as intra-domain tensions or intra-domain vectors of interest. In addition to these intra-domain tensions, there are at the same time tensions and contests between the domains. These are referred to as inter-domain tensions or inter-domain vectors of interest. A vector has the effect of pulling the action off in another direction and thus these tensions alter the course of the policymaking process. In the kind of context where there are these tensions and contests, policy construction may be seen to be a continuously transformative activity.

Within the four domains in which social processes occur, there are patterns of interaction and episodes which, rather than being linear in nature, are best described as recursive. That is, rather than approaching the context and process of policy construction from a linear, evolutionist perspective, it is asserted here that it is best viewed as a process which may be likened to an open spiral of events that weave in and through each other to produce recurring patterns across time and space. If we are able to recognize these recursive patterns, through a process of critical reflection, we can then monitor our actions so that they are empowered and transformative. When this is applied to the activity of policy construction, reflexivity that stems from a critical reflection upon events and contexts of policy construction potentially enables policy to be created which is transformative and does not reproduce and entrench disadvantage which may exist as a result of previous policies and practices in a specific area.

In addressing cultural diversity adopting the domains approach, it is apparent that there is both an inter-cultural and an intra-cultural dimension to be considered. The concepts which are related to multiculturalism from the perspective of ethnic diversity may be placed in the category of inter-cultural vectors of interest. Policies that address this aspect will focus upon the way a social setting accounts for the diverse nature of the population and the values which are represented in terms of the multicultural composition of that population. This involves not only a view of ethnicity from its own perspective, but a view of diversity in terms of other differences by which individuals and groups are distinguished in society. These include diversity in terms of religion, age gender, socio-economic status, professional status, intellectual capacity, physical capabilities and geographic location. When we speak of cultural diversity it is too simplistic to link this term only with ethnic and racial diversity. In this chapter, cultural diversity is taken to encompass the breadth of social diversity which is present in the Australian social context and in the domains within which policy construction occurs. While the national and state levels of policy construction are the predominant focus of this chapter, the global and micro domains are seen as inseparable from the other two domains and the interests and tensions which occur within and across them. Thus account is taken in this discussion of both the inter-cultural and intra-cultural diversity with particular emphasis upon public policy which attempts overtly to address the differences in values that are reflected in and reified through policy discourse which is developed.

Discourse of policy

Before examining policy discourse as it pertains to the issue of diversity, a brief reflection upon the concept of discourse on which to ground this discussion, will be undertaken. Saussure (1974) advanced the linguistic theory of signs which he termed 'semiology':

> Language is a system of signs that express ideas, and is therefore comparable to a system of writing,

the alphabet of deaf mutes, symbolic rites, polite formulas, military signals etc . . . A science that studies the life of signs within society is conceivable . . . I shall call it semiology.   (Saussure, 1974, p. 16)

This complex study of signs, which is now more commonly referred to as semiotics, focuses upon the premise that an object, thought or concept is as much defined and identified by what it is not as by what it is. For example, we cannot fully conceive of the meaning of dark without reference to light, or comprehend the concept of hot without reference to cold. Thus, instead of perceiving concepts in a linear and polarized manner, they are more logically interpreted in an interactive and recursive manner through their relationships with other concepts which help to give them an identity. Semiotics allows us to deconstruct discourses and to look behind the language at the inherent and perhaps covert meanings which are bound up in the way the symbols of language are constricted. The social and political power of discourse and the way meanings are made and interpreted thus becomes a central and critical element in examining policy:

> A discourse is not just about words or some format arrangement of them. It bears on and informs behaviour, social action and conduct of social relations and provides descriptions, rules, permission and prohibitions of social and individual action. A discourse selectively and to that extent politically asserts that a certain state of affairs is 'this' way and not 'that' way.   (Kress, 1986, p. 39)

When these insights about discourse and the meanings which certain arrangements of signs can portray are applied to public policy interpretation, the activity of policy analysis becomes more deeply critical in its quest to uncover covert agendas, disjunctions and inconsistencies. In the arena of policy construction certain individuals and groups will be advantaged in the sense that their discourse is privileged while other individuals and groups are not heard. The privileging of certain discourses in public policy leads to a situation where already powerful social groups and individuals are able, through the discourse of policy, to ensure that the status quo is not upset and that the existing power structures are preserved. These power structures will be of a social, political and economic nature. In the course of the dialectical relationship between the four domains of policymaking, a discourse is created which predominantly serves the interests of power groups in society. Power groups will also co-opt those who may oppose them and thus ensure that opposition is thwarted. This situation is referred to as hegemony and involves the 'successful efforts of the dominant classes to unify potentially different interests within their own ranks, thereby creating powerful allies who are able to establish their view of the world as universal, thus imposing their own conception of reality on all subordinate classes' (Porter, 1991, p. 15).

Public policy then is a powerful tool for governments and lobby groups to exert effective social control and thus to entrench the existing social stratification. Just as a sign is as much defined by what it is not as by what it is, so it is necessary when interpreting public policy to explore what is not contained in it as well as what is. When looking at the composition of policymaking teams, it is crucial to examine the groups which are not represented as well as to note those which are. In putting a discourse of public policy together, the policymakers are able to juxtapose in a single statement concepts which are inherently contradictory and create a belief in the readers and implementers that there is a logic which does not need to be questioned. Thus policymakers are able to create what may be referred to as a 'cultural logic' which renders the content of policy unproblematic to a point where the public accepts and employs the same policy discourse in everyday discussion. An example of this was seen when the first stage of the major restructure of the education system in Victoria, Australia, occurred in 1979. This was still in a period which may be seen to favour values of social justice, participation and equity as issues to be addressed through social processes such as education. A policy was constructed which set out the directions for the restructure and was built around two concepts: devolution and decentralization. These two notions were juxtaposed in policy as though they fitted in a complementary manner. However, in reflection on these two terms it becomes clear that they do not fit together unproblematically and, rather than being synonymous and interchangeable as the policy was attempting to show, they were contradictory. In espousing both devolution and decentralization, the policymakers established a dynamic tension which helped to prolong the change episode. Decentralization is an administrative concept, advanced in the interests of an efficient means of reaching established goals without implication of

change in the political power. Decentralization may therefore be seen as a means of serving political ends. Devolution, on the other hand, is a political concept propounded with a view to altering the balances in decision making in a manner which alters the bases of political power. This example is provided here as a means to illustrate the way governments can create a discourse which, although conceptually contradictory, is entrenched in the everyday language of the public through its continued and repeated use and iteration. Thus despite a rhetoric of handing over power and access to local sites, there was not a genuine devolution but rather a maintenance of centralized power.

Attention will now focus upon the policy discourse of diversity in the Australian context and an examination of the effect of policy discourse upon the interested parties will be undertaken. The 1980s in Australia saw the beginning of a major educational reform period which was directed through a variety of policies and programmes such as the Transition from School to Work Programme (1980–3) and the Participation and Equity Program (PEP) which replaced it. The Transition programme originated at a time of severe economic crisis and the government was desperate to prove its ability to manage an economy in crisis. In attempting to prove its ability there was a period where the government redirected the blame for the economy and problems such as unemployment so that it fell on the schools rather than upon their own policies and strategies for economic reform. Thus in the discourse of policy and politicians the schools were seen as the main focus for reform and restructure if the ills of society were to be addressed positively. This, however, ultimately created a problem for the government in that there was a movement of students to non-government schools and away from the government school system. The PEP Programme which espoused the rhetoric of social justice and equality was severely slashed nine mouths after it began, through major funding and resource cuts as the economic agenda dominated the policymaking arena, submerging any social justice agendas which may have been overtly or covertly present. In discussing this period and these programmes where governments claimed to be addressing social diversity and disadvantage and were overtly espousing these values, Deaconess (1991) claims:

The rhetoric surrounding both of these programs

was replete with unimpeachable statements about improving the quality (however defined) of education and the life chances of individual students. Yet despite the declamatory language, it is clear that the Transition Education Program was born of crisis, and it displayed every sign that it was a hastily conceived, *ad hoc* program. (Deaconess, 1991, p. 95)

In efforts to bring about micro-economic reform the governments of the time have restructured human service systems such as education along corporate managerialist lines that are reminiscent of the principles of scientific management and structural functionalism which see a strictly hierarchical system of organization, clear and top-down lines of power and control in existence. Within the education system such corporate managerialist reform has occurred so that the public policy objectives are expressed in terms of economic goods rather than in terms of social goods. This has served to re-entrench existing disadvantage and to ensure that the power structures of society are maintained. Angus (1991) claims:

> Educators and community can too easily fall back upon a general faith in managerialism that has been socially constructed in industrial societies through the institutionalization of practices of scientific management in workplaces. These practices, now represented in the discourse of public educational administration in terms of corporate management, need to be recognised as more than neutral managerial devices but as significant contributors to patterns of social relationships in which efficiency and stability are associated with hierarchical authority. (Angus, 1991, p. 248)

In an era and climate of acceptance of corporate managerialism as a way to increase efficiency and effectiveness, policies which promise to rectify economic and social ills are too readily accepted in an unproblematic and unquestioned manner. The drive for efficiency, excellence, quality and competence has largely been born of and fuelled by public policy which has ensured that these concepts are accepted and 'lived' in the community. This leads to a situation where already disadvantaged groups tend to become further disadvantaged as standardized testing programmes, quality assurance reviews, increased accountability, elite forms of education and an instrumentalist approach to schooling exist. The values which are espoused in the rhetoric of policy are those of a 'clever country' where those who are able to contribute to productivity as an efficient economic unit are advantaged. Strike (1985) claims that in the current climate in Australia 'perhaps the real equity issue is the extent to which all children will be expected to play the game of life on middle-class turf' (Strike, 1985, p. 412).

The discourse of policy, then, despite a rhetoric which supposedly addresses diversity and disadvantage, has served, in the Australian context, to ensure that those with access to power retain and reinforce such access and those who have little access to power, continue to be denied it.

Public policy and values

Within any social group the dominant values and beliefs of that group will determine the socialization of learners who are to become active members of a society. Here the issue of identity is central. This involves a sense of belonging to a group and also a sense of place within a given social world. In a multicultural context there are possible conflicts and tensions to be faced when individuals attempt to form an identity for themselves:

> In societies where different ethnic groups have come together, an individual may be subjected to conflicting perceptions of his or her self image. For members of the mainstream, ethnic identity is stable, but for members of minority ethnic groups, because alternative identities are possible, identity conflict may occur. (Partington and McCudden, 1992, p. 44)

In Australian educational policy then there is a tension. This tension is between the concerns which have been outlined here with regard to the policy of multiculturalism and the 'fine-tuning' of that policy. On the other side of the coin, it is necessary to acknowledge that there have been significant steps made in the Australian policy context to address the issue of cultural diversity. The fact that it is an issue to be considered seriously is in itself a recognition of the element of multiculturalism and diversity in the social context of Australia. By comparison with some other social contexts, Australia is well advanced in terms of multicultural policy and strategies. In this regard Australia may thus be viewed as being in a phase of fine-tuning and refinement of multicultural policy rather than being at the basic level of trying to come to terms with the actual concept.

As social values change, so public policy changes

and thus the policies which are articulated will reflect the social, economic and political contexts of that time. In 1989 *An Agenda for a Multicultural Australia* was issued by the Department of the Prime Minister and Cabinet. The goals of that agenda have formed the basis for multicultural policy in schools and other sectors of society since then. There are eight goals articulated in the national agenda:

1 All Australians should have a commitment to Australia and share responsibility for furthering our national interests.
2 All Australians should be able to enjoy the basic right of freedom from discrimination on the basis of race, ethnicity, religion or culture.
3 All Australians should enjoy equal life chances and have equitable access to and an equitable share of the resources which governments manage on behalf of the community.
4 All Australians should have the opportunity fully to participate in society and in the decisions which directly affect them.
5 All Australians should be able to develop and make use of their potential for Australia's economic and social development.
6 All Australians should have the opportunity to acquire and develop proficiency in English and languages other than English, and to develop cross-cultural understanding.
7 All Australians should be able to develop and share their cultural heritage.
8 Australian institutions should acknowledge, reflect and respond to the cultural diversity of the Australian community. (Department of the Prime Minister and Cabinet, 1989, p. 1)

This policy agenda acts as a benchmark against which the government initiatives and policy and practices of institutions in the Australian context may be evaluated. In conjunction with *An Agenda for a Multicultural Australia*, in 1989 the government also issued a *National Education Policy for Aboriginals and Torres Strait Islanders*. The four goals of this policy are:

1 To ensure Aboriginal involvement in educational decision making.
2 To provide equality of access for Aboriginal people to educational services.
3 To raise the rates of Aboriginal participation in education to those for all Australians.
4 To achieve equitable and appropriate edu-

cational outcomes for Aboriginal people. (National Aboriginal and Torres Strait Islander Education Policy, 1989)

These goals of public policy, then, reflect what the government articulates as the values of Australian society with regard to diversity. Given that there is a continuous dialectical relationship between policy rhetoric and lived practices, there will be a constant making and remaking of the values and the practices with regard to diversity in the Australian context. Values are never static in any social order and national values are now more closely than at any time previously influenced by global values. In an era when multinational corporations set the agenda for the global context, the values of economic rationalism will prevail and will affect all levels of public policy:

> Post-colonial theory is not only the product of multiculturalism and decolonization. It also reflects an historic shift from revolutionary nationalism in the Third World, which faltered in the 1970s, to a 'post-revolutionary' condition in which the power of transnational corporations seems unbreakable. (Eagleton, 1996, p. 205)

Diversity, like other social concepts and social processes will largely be viewed as it relates to productivity and competition on the world market. This presents challenges for those who implement public policy. In an effort to value difference and redress disadvantage through human service systems, the outcomes and quality of the system will be judged against an economic and political benchmark rather than a social justice one. This can result in there being two contesting agendas of public policy operating simultaneously. One agenda is that of the policymakers and the other is that of the policy implementers: such is the arena of public policy and social processes which reflects contesting values and conflicting motivations, interests and discourses.

References

Angus, L. (1991) Equality, democracy and educational reform. In D. Deaconess (ed.), *Power and Politics in Education*. London: Falmer.

Australian Council on Population and Ethnic Affairs (1982) *Multiculturalism for All Australians: Our Developing Nationhood*. The Zubrzycki Report. Canberra: AGPS.

Bureau of Immigration and Population Research (1994) *The Social Characteristics of Immigrants in Australia*. Canberra: AGPS.

Carpenter, C. (1993) Corporate restructuring of the Australian disability field. In B. Lingard, J. Knight and P. Porter, *Schooling Reform in Hard Times*. London: Falmer.

Cohen, L. and Cohen, A. (eds) (1986) *Multicultural Education – A Sourcebook for Teachers*. London: Harper and Rowe.

Deaconess, D. (1991) Reform programs and the culture of schools. In D. Deaconess (ed.), *Power and Politics in Education*. London: Falmer.

Department of the Prime Minister and Cabinet (1989) *An Agenda for a Multicultural Australia: Sharing Our Future*. Canberra: AGPS.

Eagleton, T. (1996) *Literary Theory – An Introduction*, 2nd edn. Oxford: Blackwell.

Foster, L. E. (1983) The politics of educational knowledge. In R. K. Browne and L. E. Foster (eds), *Sociology of Education*, 3rd edn. Melbourne: Macmillian.

Kress, G. (1986) Interrelations of reading and writing. In A. M. Wilson (ed.), *The Writing of Writing*. Milton Keynes: Open University Press.

Partington, G. and McCudden V. (1992) *Ethnicity and Education*. New South Wales: Social Science Press.

Porter, P. (1991) The State-family-workplace intersection: hegemony, contradictions and counter-hegemony in education. In D. Hawkins, *Power and Politics in Education*. London: Falmer Press.

Rizvi, F. (1985) *Multiculturalism as an Education Policy*. Geelong: Deakin University Press.

Rizvi, F. (1991) The idea of ethnicity and the policy of multicultural education. In D. Deaconess (ed.), *Power and Politics in Education*. London: Falmer.

Rizvi, F. (1993) Multiculturalism, social justice and the restructuring of the Australian state. In B. Lingard, J. Knight and P. Porter (eds), *Schooling Reform in Hard Times*. London: Falmer.

Saussure, F. de (1974) *Course in General Linguistics*. London: Fontana.

Strike, K. (1985) Is there a conflict between equity and excellence? *Educational Evaluation and Policy Analysis* 7 (4), 406–16.

Yeatman, A. (1990) *Bureaucrats, Technocrats and Femocrats. Essays on the Contemporary Australian State*. Sydney: Allen and Unwin.

19 Ethics, National Education Policy and the Teaching Profession

TERRY HYLAND

Introduction

There are many ways of describing, classifying and characterizing national systems of education. Green (1990), for instance, in examining the rise and development of state educational systems in England, France, Prussia and the USA in the nineteenth century, takes account of political, economic and socio-cultural factors in seeking to determine the 'beginning of modern schooling in western capitalist societies' (p. 4). At the end of a long and painstaking analysis of all the relevant factors, Green concludes:

> major impetus for the creation of national education systems lay in the need to provide the state with trained administrators, engineers and military personnel; to spread dominant national cultures and inculcate popular ideologies of nationhood; and so to forge the political and cultural unity of burgeoning nation states and cement the ideological hegemony of their dominant classes. (Green, 1990, p. 309)

Thus, although educational developments of the nineteenth century are bound to be linked with factors such as the industrialization, urbanization and emergent political democracy of the period, Green maintains that considerations of 'statism' – the desire to consolidate the nation state per se – deserve pride of place among the origins and foundations of contemporary education systems.

Ideas of 'nationhood' (Avis *et al.*, 1996) still figure prominently in the aims of national education systems – overtly so when linked with 'reconstructionist' philosophies (Skilbeck, 1982) such as those in Tanzania and China (Meisner, 1986) in recent times – though educational legislation in Britain over the last twenty years has been informed by a

distinctively 'individualistic' thrust defined by the authoritarian and utilitarian doctrines of the political New Right (Lawton, 1994). The history of education in Britain from the 1970s on might also be interpreted in 'reconstructionist' terms in that it has been characterized by a determined effort to change the culture, language and values of educational debate in line with economistic, instrumentalist and marketized conceptions of the educational task (Chitty and Simon, 1993; Esland, 1996a).

I intend to examine the chief features of this new reconstructionist approach to national education policy in an attempt to identify the key values that inform the theory, philosophy and ideology which underpins it. Following a critical analysis of current strategies and an examination of alternative perspectives, the implications of recent developments for professional values and the work of teachers will be considered. The New Right marketized approach to education and training which emphasizes individualism and monocultural notions of nationhood (Avis *et al.*, 1996) presents a particularly powerful challenge to multicultural strategies in the post-school sector. The ethical aspects of professionalism require that teachers meet this challenge for, as Pring (1992) has pointed out, a pluralist and multicultural society needs educational institutions which both strengthen a commonly agreed framework of values and support different cultural identities.

National policy developments

With the growth of the multi-disciplinary 'policy studies' (Halpin and Troyna, 1994) approach, the sphere of state policy development and legislation in Britain has received more critical attention over the last twenty years than perhaps any other area of educational studies (Ball, 1990; Chitty and Simon, 1993; Lawton, 1994). Commentators have identified a number of key themes and factors in the evolution of policy in British state education over the last two decades, though there are different perspectives and interpretive frameworks utilized to explain and analyse the chief developments.

Halliday (1990) characterizes recent change in terms of three main themes:

- vocationalism (education is centrally concerned with preparation for work);
- managerialism (technical experts are needed to direct the work of teachers, schools and colleges);
- consumerism (education should be guided by the demands of the market).

Cutting across and indeed facilitating all such developments has been the increasingly centralized state control, described as a new nationalization of British institutions by Jenkins (1995), over all aspects of educational policy (Hyland, 1991; Maclure, 1990; Lawton, 1994; Avis *et al.*, 1996). Through the mechanisms of the 1988 Education Reform Act and the 1992 Further and Higher Education Act, government control over all aspects of the education system has been consolidated (Chitty and Simon, 1993). Current policymaking in education has been described by critical commentators such as Gipps (1993) as an 'impoverished' process representing a movement away from 'discussion and evidence'. A standard policymaking process is now one in which 'think tanks promote policy through strong value assertions, and then proceed directly to detailed prescriptions. Argumentation is intuitive; there is an appeal at most to anecdotal evidence but not to research' (Gipps, 1993, p. 36).

In terms of educational ideology, the typologies originally identified by Williams (1961) have proved useful in characterizing recent trends. Three dominant groups were identified originally:

1 *Old humanists*: committed to the ideals of the 'educated man' (see Peters, 1966) and the non-instrumental, intrinsic value of educational activities.
2 *Public educators*: motivated by a social-democratic expansion of educational opportunities for all.

3 *Industrial trainers*: concerned with the primacy of technical vocational studies and the role of training in boosting economic productivity.

In a recent reworking of these basic typologies, Ball (1990, p. 5) has argued that in recent times the 'public educators are in disarray' and that the 'field of education policy-making is overshadowed by the influence of the old humanists and the industrial trainers'. Both these groups are represented on the dominant New Right (Whitty, 1990) of British politics in the form of the 'neo-conservatives' (favouring a traditional curriculum and the preservation of standards) and the 'neo-liberals' (opposed to state interference in education and endorsing the concept of an educational market) though, arguably, it is the consumerist 'market forces' approach which now has centre stage in policy and legislation (Chitty and Simon, 1993).

The increasingly authoritarian nature of New Right policymaking has been reflected in recent years in reforms designed to 'ensure that educational culture should itself be imbued with the values of free-market capitalism, in which commodification, marketization and competitive individualism reign supreme' (Esland, 1996a, p. 39). Although there are strains and tensions within New Right ideology, the notion that educational provision ought to be thought of in the same way as a commercial business subject to market demands and forces has gradually come to influence just about every sphere of educational planning and reform.

The strong version of the thesis asserts that education is a business like any other and that 'markets and private sector management techniques can help provide answers to the perceived problems and deficiencies of the public sector, and that their imposition on schools will result in improvements in standards of provision' (Keep, 1992, p. 102). In order to achieve this, schools and colleges must be 'privatized' (though 'nationalization' seems a more appropriate term in the light of increasingly centralized funding controls) and must 'compete' for business by providing quality 'goods' to be purchased by 'customers'. The mechanisms for marketizing education along these lines have been developing apace with recent state legislation. First of all, schools and colleges are 'freed' from local authority control (the former through the 1988 Education Reform Act and the latter through the 1992 Further and Higher Education Act). Their funding is controlled by central government through quangos (the Funding Agency for Schools and the Further Education Funding Council). Through 'efficiency' measures and the promotion of 'quality' products, regulated by league tables for schools and colleges, it is alleged that the performance of educational institutions will be improved and consumer choice enhanced.

A weaker version of this thesis may be detected in attempts to introduce an 'enterprise culture' (Hyland, 1991; Heelas and Morris, 1992) into the control and management of education. Recognizing that as a public service funded by taxpayers' money education is not quite the same as private sector industry, there is the implication that schools and colleges may operate like businesses by learning from their efficiency procedures and management systems (Keep, 1992). Income generation is a key aspect of this tendency and many institutions, for instance, have developed partnerships with local firms and established projects to boost their funds in the drive to 'achieve the public sector equivalent of profit' (Rustin, 1994, p. 76). In post-school education, the obsession with measures of 'quality' based on industrial standards such as BS5750 (Tysome, 1992) developed as a prominent feature of the new culture.

Specific critiques – both moral and pragmatic – of this marketized approach to education and training will be offered below. For now it is worth noting that a large part of the reason for the recent movement away from market strategies is that – whether we are talking about school (Ranson, 1994) or post-school (Evans, 1992; Hodkinson and Sparkes, 1995) developments – markets have quite simply failed to produce the goods. Thus, we have Barber (1996, p. 19) recommending policies for schools which can create 'a new culture based on trust' and further education colleges being urged to 'replace cut-throat competition with collaboration' (Ward, 1996, p. 29). As Coffield (1997) suggested in a recent analysis of the current 'learning society' project, there now seems to be a 'need to reformulate the social and moral purposes of education' (p. 20).

Ethical basis of national policy

Although, as philosophers of education have demonstrated (Dewey, 1966; Peters; 1966; Brown, 1985), there is a sense in which questions of justice and morality are inseparable from educational

issues, it has been many years since educational policy was based on ethical visions as clearly defined and coherent as the reconstructionist and nationalist policies referred to earlier. Thus, although philosophical idealism could be said to have provided a coherent foundation for educational reforms in the late nineteenth and early twentieth centuries (Gordon and White, 1979), the ethical and theoretical underpinnings of recent educational policymaking are more eclectic and nebulous (Ball, 1990; Lawton, 1994).

The libertarian basis of the New Right's endorsement of a market forces approach to all aspects of public social policy can be identified in the influence of economists such as Hayek and Friedman whose ideas can be traced back to the writings (often narrowly selected) of Adam Smith (Kingdom, 1992; Perryman, 1994). Such theories represent a celebration and revival of self-interest as against social and collective welfare and have served to foster a culture in which 'wealth has been celebrated and rendered apparently free of guilt or responsibilities' (Rustin, 1994, p. 76). The values underpinning such ideas were harnessed to support the new 'individualism' of the enterprise culture of the 1980s (Heelas and Morris, 1992) and have been brought into play to legitimize just about every aspect of educational reform over the last decade or so (Hyland, 1991; Chitty and Simon, 1993).

Russsell (1946, pp. 620ff) traces the growth of individualism in philosophy from the Greek Cynics and Stoics down through the medieval Christian tradition until it finds its fullest expression in the writings of Descartes which provided one of the sources of inspiration for the foundation of English liberalism in the seventeenth and eighteenth centuries. Within the liberal tradition individualistic notions went hand in hand with the growth of mercantilism and, in political theory, the basic ideas date back at least as far as Hobbes and Locke and are encapsulated in the concept of 'possessive individualism' which asserts that the 'individual is essentially the proprietor of his own person and capacities, for which he owes nothing to society' (Macpherson, 1962, p. 263). This theory provides one of the chief philosophical justifications for the market economy and free enterprise system of modern capitalism and, in this respect, the idea of reconstituting education as just another 'positional good' in the market flows directly from the enterprise belief in founding civil society on 'property' rather than 'persons' (Tomlinson, 1993, p. 172).

There is an interpretation of individualism which, as Hemming (1969) observes, regards it as a natural consequence of human evolution and the 'greater individuation of species'. In this sense, there is some justification for the Aristotelian project through which 'individuals have a responsibility to develop their individual capacities' and that we 'should seek to help others to become themselves' (p. 26). It is this sense of individualism which is celebrated in progressive educational theory (Jones, 1983), in the centrality accorded to autonomy within philosophy of education (Callan, 1994) and in the Kantian conception of 'respect for persons' (Korner, 1955).

It is not this autonomous or person-centred notion of individualism, however, which underpins its use in New Right ideology but something closer to the 'possessive individualism' of property ownership and, in its modern reconstruction, the all-powerful conception of the self-interested consumer in a self-regulating market. The attempt to capture the high moral ground for the enterprise culture can be clearly discerned in Douglas Hurd's *New Statesman* article (27 April 1988) in which, after citing Edmund Burke's proposition that 'no cold relation is a zealous citizen', he attempted to argue that the qualities of enterprise and initiative essential to the generation of wealth are also needed to build a family, a neighbourhood and a nation. Mrs Thatcher's avowed disbelief in 'society' – itself based on Bentham's famous dictum that society was but a 'fictitious body' (Kingdom, 1992, p. 1) – only permitted her to offer a rather more oblique message when, addressing the General Assembly of the Church of Scotland in May 1988, she suggested that there was a spiritual dimension to social and economic arrangements founded on the acceptance of individual responsibility. These messages were placed in an educational context by, for example, the National Curriculum Council (NCC) guidance document *Education for Economic and Industrial Understanding* (NCC, 1990) that sought to emphasize the importance of promoting entrepreneurs with social and moral consciences. The *Citizen's Charter* (Great Britain Parliament, 1991) can be regarded as a natural extension of this whole political programme.

None of this, however, has very much to do with autonomy or the Kantian conception of respect for persons. If it can be identified as a morality at all (rather than a political theory based on an ideological commitment to market forces), it owes more to Nietzsche's (1967) conception of 'master morality' than to the mainstream ethical concerns of western society. Indeed, the notion of 'master morality' was devised by Nietszche specifically to oppose and criticize the dominant values of Stoicism, Christianity, Kantianism and universal humanitarianism (which he described as 'slave morality') in the attempt to replace the moral evaluation of judgements and actions with that of persons. The most highly valued persons, according to master morality, are those who, as in the Homeric tradition, are successful in life endeavours. Central virtues are, therefore, a 'matter of actual achievements, actual successes, actual abilities and skills, actual excellences' (Snare, 1992, p. 122). As Kingdom (1992, p. 1) wryly observes, such rampant individualism leads to a form of 'casino capitalism' in which 'people would relate to one another like players at the roulette table; the winners would be applauded while the losers quietly place the loaded pistol in their mouths'.

There is little scope here for a consideration of universal respect for persons regardless of status or achievement, nor are any concessions made to the social and economic inequalities which characterize modern industrial societies. Indeed, there is a distinct anti-social – or perhaps more correctly asocial – assumption underpinning such accounts of individualism which seeks to diminish the role of community in the development of individual citizens. Indeed, as Kingdom (1992, p. 6) observes, by suggesting that persons had an 'identity and character entirely independent of social formations', New Right ideology represented a concerted attack on social democracy and any conception of state welfare policy. As against this, educators from Plato to Dewey have insisted that education is essentially a social activity even though, by definition, it necessarily involves the development of individuals. Hargeaves (1982), for instance, criticizes schools which are 'deeply imbued with a culture of individualism' and which exacerbate social exclusion and injustice by failing to foster 'active community participation' (pp. 87, 145). Similarly, Langford (1985) has attacked the obsession in educational theory 'with the difference which being educated makes to an individual' (p. 3) and argues that 'to become educated is to become a member of society and so to have learnt what it is to be and live as a member of that society' (p. 181).

According to the New Right conception of individualism, rights, citizenship and democracy are all subordinated to the 'vigorous virtues of uprightness, self-sufficiency, energy, independent-mindedness, adventurousness, loyalty and robustness' (Letwin, 1992, p. 35), all the virtues required to enhance Britain's economic prosperity in an era of increasingly global competition. The market reigns supreme and all values are to be constructed in accordance with its dictates. As Carr (1991) observes, there is a world of difference between the 'moral model' of democracy and citizenship which enables people to achieve 'self-development, self-fulfilment and self-determination' through political participation, and a 'market model' which requires an individualistic society with a 'politically passive citizenry and a strong active political leadership . . . circumscribed by the rule of law' (pp. 378–9). On the market model, citizens are empowered only insofar as they are customers and users of services and, as Ranson (1994) points out, the market merely 'confirms and reinforces the pre-existing social class order of wealth and privilege' (p. 96).

Accompanying the economistic and narrowly individualist thrust of recent government policy on education, there has been a 'narrow protectionist view of nationhood' (Esland, 1996b, p. 40). Indeed, there are clear parallels between the restricted individualism of the New Right notions of citizenship and the restricted nationalism characteristic of the current obsession with economic competitiveness reflected in recent government White Papers on education and training (1994, 1995). Indeed, Britain's 'nation-state capitalism' (Esland, 1996b) may be described as a sort of self-interested individualism transferred to the international stage by which, in contrast to other European nation-states (Hutton, 1995), an economic and cultural hostility to 'others' (typified by the ambivalent views on membership of the European Union) comes to dominate domestic and foreign policy.

In the sphere of vocational education and training (VET) the tensions and contradictions between preparing people for a post-Fordist world of global competition and the narrowly pragmatic cultural agenda referred to earlier has tested the system to breaking point. A central paradox arising from the avowed need for high-level, multi-skilled workers for the post-Fordist society as against the actual provision of low-level, competence-based skills of the officially endorsed NCVQ programme for VET has been noted by a number of commentators (Hyland, 1994; Field, 1995). Unlike other European countries such as France and Germany where there has been sustained investment by the state and industry in VET and, more significantly, a partnership between employers, employees and federal government (Green, 1995), Britain has opted for a divisive neo-Fordist rather than a post-Fordist solution to the problems posed by increasing global competition and de-industrialization. Brown and Lauder (1995) remind us that the organizational restructuring, investment in new technologies and flexible accumulation of capital commonly identified with post-Fordist enterprises do not 'necessarily lead to changes in the nature of skills and involvement which are required in order to compete in high value production'. Britain has actually opted for a 'neo-Fordist' solution which may be characterized in terms of a 'shift to flexible accumulation based on the creation of a flexible workforce engaged in low-skill, low-wage, temporary and often part-time employment' (p. 20). The fact that most of the vocational initiatives of the last decade or so have been concerned almost exclusively with lower level skills (NVQ levels 1 and 2) is logically connected with such developments (Hyland, 1994; Field, 1995).

The consequences of such narrow and insular nation-state neo-Fordism have been far-reaching and disastrous for the working population of Britain. The gap between rich and poor is now greater than it has been for decades (Rowntree Trust, 1995; Atkinson, 1996). Structural unemployment is now endemic and, for those still in employment, low pay, insecurity, poorer health and safety and reduced employment rights are facts of life (Kingdom, 1992; Hutton, 1995). Critical commentators now employ the phrase the 'feminisation of poverty' (Hutchinson, 1996) to refer to the preponderance of low-pay, low-skill, temporary and low-status work which women have been coerced into taking over the last two decades or so and, in the sphere of education for children from ethnic minorities and with special needs, there is now ample evidence that the most vulnerable and disadvantaged youngsters in our schools have benefited least and suffered most from the reforms of the last two decades (TES, 1997).

The brave new world of post-Fordism has been characterized essentially by greater inequality and social injustice in all spheres of social life, and New Right rhetoric and apologetics can no longer disguise this (Jenkins, 1995; Hutton, 1995). In terms of education and training policy over the last decade or so, it has been suggested that the 'dedicated authoritarianism and anti-pluralism of the reforms' (Esland, 1996a, p. 39) of recent years can be regarded as an attempt to embed the new enterprise culture through insinuation and subtle indoctrination. Like the 'fake fraternisation' which makes the technicist 'McDonaldisation' (Ritzer, 1993) of more and more aspects of social life seem somehow natural, educational reforms have sought to 'normalize a view of the future of work – based in structural unemployment and underemployment – as not only inevitable but also preferable' (Edwards, 1993, p. 185).

Markets, individualism and nationalism: a moral critique and alternative visions

Having described the key ideological and ethical underpinnings of the New Right agenda for national educational and social policy, I want to offer some critical comments and alternative visions before examining the professional roles of teachers in relation to these issues. In particular, I will seek to point out the ethical shortcomings of markets, individualist philosophies and national parochialism in terms of Britain's educational policy and suggest alternatives in the form of perspectives based on Pring's (1995) idea of a 'community of educated people' and Ranson's (1994) blueprint for a 'learning society'.

Markets, ethics and education

In addition to the many moral, technical and pragmatic objections to what we might call the 'quasi' or 'social' market (Elliott, 1993; Ranson, 1994) in education and the public services, there are of course many similar weaknesses in relation to the 'real' market in capital goods and services. From a moral point of view, for instance, it is very difficult to justify a policy of naked self-interest and rampant individualism for the simple reason that – outside the ethically dubious Nietzschian conception of 'master morality' referred to earlier – most systems of morality regard such character traits as anathema. Indeed, since the broad conception of respect for persons and consideration of the interests of others is a basic feature of moral viewpoints as wide apart

as existentialism, utilitarianism and Marxism (Singer, 1983), it is difficult to see how systems which – celebrating naked self-interest and egoism or, indeed, actually condoning harm to others in the interests of the new individualism (Kingdom, 1992, pp. 8ff) – can in any way escape moral disapprobation.

By way of a supplement to these moral deficiencies of the market, it is worth mentioning the many non-moral, technical shortcomings of the main theories. Since markets are essentially 'irrational' (Smith, 1996, p. 8), the claims about freedom are pure sophistry since, in real as opposed to the ideal markets constructed by academic economists, the key players strive to control the market as far as is humanly possible in order to achieve a competitive advantage (Ormerod, 1994). As Kingdom (1992) explains:

> The real world economy is replete with devices designed to confound the market and reduce its uncertainty, including agreements with suppliers, controlled prices, cartels, monopolies cross-subsidies and much *bogus* competition (as when chocolate bars bearing 'competing' names are disgorged from the intestines of a single giant conglomerate).   (Kingdom, 1992, p. 60)

Moreover, the idea that the market consists of individuals – the rational egoist beloved by classical economists who functions as a sort of 'calculating machine living a cost–benefit–analysis existence' (ibid., p. 10) – is also entirely mythical since the market is actually controlled strictly by large multinationals and corporations.

Indeed, the rational egoist could never be more than a sort of idealist fiction since it is both morally and pragmatically impossible to imagine functioning societies made up of such individuals. As Poole (1990) explains, although markets are theoretically constructed solely on the basis that individuals will maximize their wants and preferences, the 'social relations constituted by the market presuppose a sphere of social life in which the individuals who participate in the market are themselves produced and reproduced'. A market of purely self-interested individuals would not, without the existence of other values and motivations, reproduce itself. Poole argues that for reproduction of the system to occur:

> It would require that purely self-interested individuals enter into relationships with each other in order to produce, nurture and care for other self-

interested individuals like themselves. To make sense of the apparent sacrifices of self-interest involved here we would at the very least have to assume the existence of goods of a quite different kind to those involved in ordinary market transactions. To comprehend the social processes necessary, we also need to suppose that there are human relationships – certainly those between parent and child, probably those between parents – which are conceptually distinct from the contractual and voluntary engagements for mutual benefit typical of the market.   (Poole, 1990, pp. 49–50).

The operation of markets, therefore, is entirely dependent upon the inculcation of values of a non-market, other-regarding kind, namely those values such as respect for persons and general benevolence which educational institutions are typically asked to transmit to future generations. As the Commissioner of Education for New York state explained to delegates at a British conference of educators a few years ago, 'it takes a whole village to raise a child' (TES, 1997, p. 12).

The irony and deep paradox of asking schools and colleges to operate according to a marketized culture characterized by values they are officially meant to be opposed to has not escaped the notice of policy analysts (Heelas and Morris, 1992; Ranson, 1994). Moreover, even the superficial freedom enjoyed by players in the real market disappears in the social market of education. As a public service, education is 'more rigorously regulated than most private sector business markets' (Keep, 1992, p. 115) and it is state rather than self-regulated in the interests of meeting the New Right ideological agenda. In addition to the increasing centralization through the National Curriculum at school level and the Further Education Funding Council (FEFC) control of courses in the post-school sector (Avis *et al.*, 1996), a whole range of quangos – OSFTED, SCAA, NCVQ, HEFC – have been set up to ensure that the market operates in accordance with central government policy which is itself increasingly driven by the ideological objectives referred to earlier (Chitty and Simon, 1993; Avis *et al.*, 1996).

Individuals and communities

In addition to the many practical and moral weaknesses of the market philosophy based on individualism, there is a whole host of positive arguments which claim to show that 'our com-

munal instinct remains part of our primeval inheritance' and that the 'desire for community is not rational but instinctive' and 'fellowship a sublimely good feeling, better than making money' (Kingdom, 1992, p. 88). In a similar vein, Singer (1983) has argued forcefully for the survival value of altruism within natural selection. As Trusted (1987) explains:

> Those individuals that show altruism in respect of their young and near relations . . . will indeed promote the continuance of altruistic characterising genes, because the individuals so favoured will have an advantage over others who are not benefiting from altruism. In time, the 'altruist genes' would spread through the community . . . so the original kin altruism would develop into group altruism, and both can be accounted for by natural selection.   (Trusted, 1987, p. 70)

These arguments move us from instinct and survival to the rationality of theories such as utilitarianism and contract theories of social justice (Rawls, 1972). Modern and post-modern versions of community values (Sayers, 1996) are coming to replace the more extreme versions of liberal individualism as societies, politicians, economists and organizations 'call for a fuller expression of the claims of community and the common good' (Thompson, 1992, p. 269) in order to regulate social relations at all levels. Referring to shifts in economic theory, Ormerod (1994) argues that 'economic success can be achieved, and achieved more successfully' when the power of markets is 'harnessed to the wider benefit of society' (p. 205). Corporations which have adapted most effectively to post-Fordist demands tend to be those which 'encourage a synthesis of members' interests' in order to legitimate the 'organisation as a learning community' (Zuboff, 1988, p. 294).

Educational policy in the form of the recent emphasis on 'family values' reflects such concerns and the overarching principle of 'justice and collective endeavour for the common good of society' (Pyke, 1996, p. 4) was given pride of place in the recent consultation document on shared values issued by the School Curriculum and Assessment Authority (SCAA). It seems that all those criticisms of the enterprise culture by church leaders and public figures throughout the 1980s (Kingdom, 1992) are now being heeded. As the President of the Society of Education Officers noted at a recent conference:

We have reached a point now where there is growing dissatisfaction with the balance we have struck between individual freedom and the shared constraints and commitments needed for the survival of civic society . . . I think there are signs of a shift in emphasis away from individualism and towards a greater investment in social cohesion. (Dean, 1997, p. 14)

Nationalism, globalism and the public good

Just as politicians, educators, economists and, perhaps especially, members of the clergy have started to re-emphasize social and community values against individualism and 'enterprise' goals (Heelas and Morris, 1992) so, on the larger stage, all nations have had to respond to the 'globalization challenge' and acknowledge that as a 'consequence of the deregulated nature of worldwide capital investment, a single nation state has only a tenuous influence over the direction and flow of capital investment' (Esland, 1996b, p. 60). However, as mentioned above, thus far the typical British response has been a retreat to a narrow, parochial, protectionist policy which has failed to meet the new changing conditions. As Avis *et al.* (1996) explain:

> The New Right nation-state has accepted rather than challenged the basis of social and economic inequalities generated by the geopolitical crisis in capital. Overwhelmed by such crisis in the late 1980s and early 1990s the Conservative government retreated into a nationalist bunker while, at the same time, proclaiming the virtues of the enterprise state, vocationalism and the 'skills revolution' as keys to reviving the British economy. (Avis *et al.*, 1996, p. 170)

The disastrous consequences of such policies become morally questionable when contrasted with the very different experiences of countries faced with the same economic facts of life over the last twenty years or so. As Shirley (1991) has argued, countries with 'extensive social policies' such as Denmark, Belgium, the Netherlands, Switzerland and Japan were more successful in maintaining welfare benefits and containing unemployment in the face of global recession than others such as Australia, Canada, Britain and the USA which were 'spectacularly unsuccessful' (p. 150) in these spheres. Moreover, such differences were not merely matters of chance but the result of deliberate policies of 'state intervention geared to productive

investment, both public and private, favoured over boosting consumer demand' and a 'commitment to full employment both as a political priority and as the dominant ethic of economic policy' (Shirley, 1991, p. 152).

The post-modernist fragmentation of values (Perryman, 1994) applies also to capital, and various forms of social, political and economic strategies have been developed to cope with the new challenges. There are radical differences, however, between the two main approaches, described by Albert (1993) as the 'Rhine' model which places importance upon collective success, co-operation and long-term objectives, and the 'neo-American' model which stresses individual success, competition and short-term financial gain. It is just this latter, short-sighted model through which 'human agency is devalued in mechanistic metaphors' (Hutchinson, 1996, p. 4) and which blinds us to alternative possibilities that are less damaging to the environment and social relationships. Avis *et al.* (1996) argue that capital per se is 'no longer the enemy – only those particular forms which are highly exploitative' (p. 169). It is to be regretted that Britain has tended to opt for the morally objectionable, exploitative neo-American model in recent times – typified by our (socially, environmentally and industrially) damaging alienation from the Social Chapter accepted by other European nations – rather than searching for more creative routes to national success and solidarity.

New forms of social solidarity – reflecting the interests of all citizens and not just those minorities favoured by New Right policies – need to be constructed if Britain is to come to terms with changing global economic realities and determine how these should be dealt with at local, national and international levels. Central to this task will be the creation of a 'learning society' which, according to Ranson (1994), must be underpinned by moral values, social justice and democracy so as to bring about the 'creation of a moral and political order that expresses and enables an active citizenship within the public domain' (p. 105). Avis *et al.* (1996) neatly summarize all the key issues when they observe that:

> As the demands of globalization become more pressing, Britain's adherence to an inward looking nation-state view of its role, based on a divided and authoritarian system of education and training, appears increasingly inadequate and inflexible. Serious attention now needs to be given to *educating*

as opposed to training a majority of the population hitherto denied access to further and higher education. (Avis *et al.*, 1996, p. 180, original emphasis)

The globalization of work, capital and communications needs to be matched in education and training practices by 'global and multicultural perspectives' which, following Bennett (1990), stress the democratic values of 'acceptance and appreciation of cultural diversity' in combination with 'respect for human dignity and universal human rights' with 'responsibility to the world community' (p. 281; the World Studies literature emphasizes similar values; see Fisher and Hicks, 1985).

Pring (1995) observed recently that the conception of a 'community of educated people' committed to 'serious reflection' and 'critical scrutiny of others' (p. 126) has proved vulnerable to New Right authoritarianism. The resulting destruction of liberal educational ideals over the last two decades has brought about the 'Orwellian nightmare' (Pring, 1995, p. 142) that now characterizes our national system. It must be a central task of the teaching profession in the years ahead to assist in the reconstruction of the community ideal outlined by Pring so that we may once again enjoy a system underpinned by rational debate, 'corroboration within a tradition of enquiry' and educational aims based on 'moral deliberation and exploration of values and beliefs' (pp. 126, 130).

Professional ethics and national policy

The importance of national policy developments for the nature of education, training, learning and teaching at all levels is self-evident and cannot be avoided by professional educators. Moreover, since, as Carr (1996) argues, 'education and teaching are inherently moral enterprises' (p. 2), it is not possible for teachers to opt out of their responsibility for interrogating policy developments in education (nor to ignore the growing inequalities and social injustice resulting from such policies) in the light of professional and ethical considerations. However, in the face of the widespread 'de-professionalisation' (Barton *et al.*, 1994) of teaching over the last twenty years resulting from the centralized and authoritarian policies already noted, new forms of solidarity and collective awareness will have to be developed before the

reconstructed 'learning society' project outlined earlier can be achieved.

The centralized imposition of curricula and objectives, the highly prescriptive nature of assessment and, most significantly, the introduction of competence-based education and training (CBET) models into professional education (Elliott, 1993; Hyland, 1994; Barnett, 1994) have led to serious deskilling and de-professionalizing within teaching to the extent that 'professional life in Britain has developed a new vocabulary – innovation fatigue, early retirement, stress, overload and breaking point' (Stronach, 1995, p. 9). Moreover, as Elliott (1993) argues, since one of the basic principles of competence approaches is that of 'behaviourism with its implication that the significance of theoretical knowledge in training is a purely technical or instrumental one' (p. 17), this leads to strategies which provide a 'production technology for commodifying professional learning for consumption' and which also operate as an 'ideological device for eliminating value issues from the domains of professional practice and thereby subordinating them to political forms of control' (ibid., pp. 23, 68).

Such technicist approaches to education and training do not acknowledge the extent to which professional knowledge, skills and values are a product of joint social action developed through engagement in a complex set of interwoven social transactions (Wertsch, 1991). Carr (1994) quite rightly points out that most problems in professional spheres such as teaching call for a 'moral rather than a technical response' and that practice needs to be characterized in terms of 'virtues rather than skills' (p. 47). However, the individualistic nature of recent policy affecting the professions – with teachers isolated in opted out schools, nurses in trust hospitals and further education lecturers in corporate institutions (Hyland, 1997) – has reduced the power of professionals to offer a concerted moral critique of policy and legislation.

Professional practice is essentially a social activity concerned with issues which require 'collective, rather than merely individual action' (Barton *et al.*, 1994, p. 540) and this makes it crucial for teachers to maintain collaborative strategies in the face of attempts to fragment solidarity through top-down, non-consultative policy. New work-based models of professional learning modelled on the 'return of the mentor' (Caldwell and Carter, 1993) in education and training have served to re-emphasize the importance of teamwork and collaborative effort which has brought about a 'drive for a stronger culture of service in the public sector' (ibid., p. 208). The attempts to establish a General Teaching Council (GTC) recommended by the National Commission on Education to provide a 'statutory source of advice on issues such as professional training and development, qualification levels of teachers, and changes in curriculum and assessment' (NCE, 1993, p. 233) are to be welcomed in this respect, as is the trend away from damaging competition and 'payment by results' in the post-school sector (Whitehead, 1996).

Perhaps as important as control of internal professional matters, however, is the capacity for teachers, through a democratically controlled collective association, to provide an ethical critique and vision of all aspects of social life to which, in the last analysis, education and training are integrally connected. Rejecting the contemporary technicist role of teachers as no more than 'classroom tutors in the national syllabus', Smith (1994) expounds a conception of teaching as 'one of the three great professions because the triple pillars on which any civilized society is based are the law, health care and education'. He goes on to suggest that:

> In democracies, governments are elected, but they are also transient. The public appreciates the professions have an enduring duty to the community – and so to the state rather than to any particular government. That duty is to sustain and develop services upon which a civilised society depends. The community therefore assumes a compact, an unwritten constitutional bargain, between governments (ephemeral) and professions (permanent). (Smith, 1994, p. 18).

Only through the mechanism of such a powerful mediating agency can teachers – in responding to state policy and legislation on education at all levels – realize and respond to the 'ineliminable moral–educational implications of teaching as a professional occupation' (Carr, 1996, p. 12) and work to construct 'uplifting new visions' and a 'social theory of learning' (Coffield, 1997, p. 20).

Such 'new visions' – particularly since recent changes in government and administration have been marked by a movement away from division and towards consensus (Pyke, 1997) – are leading to new blueprints for education and training such as the recent Kennedy report recommending wider participation in post-school education and student support systems characterized by the 'principles of fairness and transparency' (Baty, 1997, p. 5). If all this really does herald a 'new educational settlement', it must, as Gleeson (1996) rightly observes, be one which 'combines conceptions of social unity and community with competitiveness and productivity', which is firmly established upon the principles of 'participation and distributive justice rather than simple egalitarianism' and which acknowledges 'cultural heterogeneity' (p. 16) in all spheres of educational activity.

References

Albert, M. (1993) *Capitalism against Capitalism*. London: Whurr.

Atkinson, T. (1996) Why do Britain's have-nots have less? *Times Higher Education Supplement* 12 April.

Avis, J. *et al.* (1996) *Knowledge and Nationhood*. London: Cassell.

Avis, J. (1996) The myth of the post-Fordist society. In J. Avis *et al.*, *Knowledge and Nationhood*. London: Cassell.

Ball, S. J. (1990) *Politics and Policy Making in Education*. London: Routledge.

Barber, M. (1996) How to achieve the impossible. *Times Educational Supplement* 13 December.

Barnett, R. (1994) *The Limits of Competence*. Buckingham: Open University Press.

Barton L. *et al.* (1994) Teacher education and professionalism in England: some merging issues. *British Journal of Sociology of Education* 15 (4), 402–7.

Bash, L. and Green, A. (eds) (1995) *Youth, Education and Work*. London: Kegan Page.

Baty, P. (1997) The last shall be first. *Times Higher Education Supplement* 4 July.

Bennett, C. I. (1990) *Comprehensive Multicultural Education*. Boston MA: Allyn and Bacon.

Brown, L. (1985) *Justice, Morality and Education*. London: Macmillan.

Brown, P. and Lauder H. (1995) Post-Fordist possibilities: education, training and national development. In L. Bash and A. Green (eds), *Youth, Education and Work*. London: Kogan Page.

Caldwell, B. J. and Carter, M. E. A. (eds) (1993) *The Return of the Mentor*. London: Falmer.

Callan, E. (1994) Autonomy and alienation. *Journal of Philosophy of Education* 28 (1), 35–53.

Carr, W. (1991) Education for citizenship. *British Journal of Educational Studies* 39 (4), 373–85.

Carr, D. (1994) Educational enquiry and professional knowledge: towards a Copernican revolution: *Educational Studies* 20 (1), 33–52.

Carr, D. (1996) *The Moral Role of the Teacher*. Edinburgh: Scottish Consultative Council on the Curriculum.

Chitty, C. and Simon, B. (eds) (1993) *Education Answers Back*. London: Lawrence and Wishart.

Coffield, F. (1997) The value of one daring question. *Times Educational Supplement* 31 January.

Dean, C. (1997) Breakdown 'threatens education'. *Times Educational Supplement* 17 January.

Dewey, J. (1966) *Democracy and Education*. New York: Free Press.

Edwards, R. (1993) The inevitable future? Post-Fordism in work and learning. In R. Edwards, S. Sieminski and D. Zeldin (eds), *Adult Learners, Education and Training*. London: Routledge/Open University.

Elliott, J. (ed) (1993) *Reconstructing Teacher Education*. London: Falmer.

Esland, G. (1996a) Knowledge and nationhood: the new right, education and the global market. In J. Avis *et al.*, *Knowledge and Nationhood*. London: Cassell.

Esland, G., (1996b) Education, training and nation-state capitalism: Britain's failing strategy. In J. Avis *et al.*, *Knowledge and Nationhood*. London: Cassell.

Evans, B. (1992) *The Politics of the Training Market*. London: Routledge.

Field, J. (1995) Reality testing in the work place: are NVQs employment led? In P. Hodkinson and M. Issitt (eds), *The Challenge of Competence*. London: Cassell.

Fisher, S. and Hicks, D. (1985) *World Studies 8–13*. Edinburgh: Oliver and Boyd.

Gipps, C. (1993) Policy-making and the use and misuse of evidence. In C. Chitty and B. Simon (eds), *Education Answers Back*. London: Lawrence and Wishart.

Gleeson, D. (1996) Continuity and change in post-compulsory education and training. In R. Halsall and M. Cockett (eds), *Education and Training 14–19: Chaos or Coherence?* London: David Fulton.

Gordon, P. and White, J. (1979) *Philosophers as Educational Reformers*. London: Routledge and Kegan Paul.

Great Britain Parliament (1991) *The Citizen's Charter: Raising the Standard*. Cmnd 1599. London: HMSO.

Green, A. (1990) *Education and State Formation*. London: Macmillan.

Green, A. (1995) The role of the state and the social partners in VET systems. In L. Bash and A. Green (eds), (1995).

Halliday, J. (1990) *Markets, Managers and Theory in Education*. Lewes: Falmer.

Halpin, D. and Troyna, B. (eds) (1994) *Researching Educational Policy: Ethical and Methodological Issues*. London: Falmer.

Hargreaves, D. (1982) *The Challenge for the Comprehensive School*. London: Routledge and Kegan Paul.

Heelas, P. and Morris, P. (eds) (1992) *The Values of the Enterprise Culture*. London: Routledge.

Hemming, J. (1969) *Individual Morality*. London: Nelson.

Hodkinson, P. and Sparkes, A. (1995) Markets and vouchers: the inadequacy of individualist policies for vocational education and training in England and Wales. *Journal of Educational Policy* 10 (2), 189–207.

Hutchinson, F. P. (1996) *Educating Beyond Violent Futures*. London: Routledge.

Hutton, W. (1995) *The State We're In*. London: Jonathan Cape.

Hyland, T. (1991) Taking care of business: vocationalism, competence and the enterprise culture. *Educational Studies* 17 (1), 77–87.

Hyland, T. (1994) *Competence, Education and NVQs: Dissenting Perspectives*. London: Cassell.

Hyland, T. (1997) A critique of alternative pathways in vocational and professional education. In A. Morton-Cooper and M. Bamford (eds), *Excellence in Health Care Management*. Oxford: Blackwell.

Jenkins, S. (1995) *Accountable to None: The Tory Nationalisation of Britain*. London: Hamish Hamilton.

Jones, K. (1983) *Beyond Progressive Education*. London: Macmillan.

Keep, E. (1992) Schools in the marketplace? – some problems with private sector models. In G. Wallace (ed.), *Local Management of Schools: Research and Experience*. Clevedon: Multilingual Matters.

Kingdom, J. (1992) *No Such Thing as Society? Individualism and Community*. Buckingham: Open University Press.

Korner, S. (1955) *Kant*. Harmondsworth: Penguin.

Langford, G. (1985) *Education, Persons and Society: A Philosophical Enquiry*. London: Macmillan.

Lawton, D. (1994) *The Tory Mind on Education, 1979–1994*. London: Falmer.

Letwin, S. R. (1992) *The Anatomy of Thatcherism*. London: Fontana.

Maclure, S. (1990) *Education Re-Formed*. London: Hodder and Stoughton.

Macpherson, C. B. (1962) *The Political Theory of Possessive Individualism*. Oxford: Oxford University Press.

Meisner, M. (1986) *Mao's China and After*. New York: Free Press.

NCC (1990) *Education for Economic and Industrial Understanding*. York: National Curriculum Council.

NCE (1993) *Learning To Succeed: Report of the National Commission on Education*. London: Heinemann.

Nietzsche, F. (1967) *On The Genealogy of Morals*. New York: Vintage.

Ormerod P. (1994) *The Death of Economics*. London: Faber and Faber.

Perryman, M. (ed.) (1994) *Altered States: Postmodernism, Politics, Culture*. London: Lawrence and Wishart.

Peters, R. S. (1966) *Ethics and Education*. London: Allen and Unwin.

Poole, R. (1990) Morality, masculinity and the market. In S. Sayers and P. Osborne (eds), *Socialism, Feminism and Philosophy*. London: Routledge.

Pring, R. (1992) Education for a pluralist society. In M. Leicester and M. Taylor (eds), *Ethics, Ethnicity and Education*. London: Kogan Page.

Pring, R. (1995) The community of educated people: the 1994 Lawrence Stenhouse memorial lecture. *British Journal of Educational Studies* 43 (2), 125–45.

Pyke, N. (1996) SCAA shows a way back to goodness. *Times Educational Supplement* 1 November.

Pyke, N. (1997) Blunkett pledges to heal rifts. *Times Educational Supplement* 2 May.

Ranson, S. (1994) *Towards the Learning Society*. London: Cassell.

Rawls, J. (1972) *A Theory of Justice*. Oxford: Oxford University Press.

Ritzer, G. (1993) *The McDonaldisation of Society*. London: Pine Forge Press.

Rowntree, Trust (1995) *Income and Wealth*. Poole: Joseph Rowntree Foundation.

Russell, B. (1946) *History of Western Philosophy*. London: Allen and Unwin.

Rustin, M. (1994) Unfinished business – from Thatcherite modernisation to incomplete modernity. In M. Perryman (ed.) *Altered States: Postmodernism, Politics, Culture*. London: Lawrence and Wishart.

Sayers, S. (1996) The value of community. *Radical Philosophy* **69**, 2–4.

Shirley, I. (1991) State policy and employment. In D. Corson (ed.), *Education for Work*. Clevedon: Multilingual Matters.

Singer, P. (1983) *The Expanding Circle*. Oxford: Oxford University Press.

Skilbeck, M. (1982) Three educational ideologies. In T. Horton and P. Raggatt (eds), *Challenge and Change in the Curriculum*. London: Hodder and Stoughton.

Smith, P (1994) Meet the challenge and raise the standards. *Times Educational Supplement* 6 May.

Smith, D. (1996) Do markets work? *Social Sciences* **30**, 8.

Snare, F. (1992) *The Nature of Moral Thinking*. London: Routledge.

Stronach, I. (1995) Policy hysteria. *Forum* **37** (1), 9–10.

TES (1997) Behind the figures lies a story of deprivation. *Times Educational Supplement* 31 January.

Thompson, K. (1992) Individual and community in religious critiques of the market. In P. Heelas and P. Morris (eds), *The Values of the Enterprise Culture*. London: Routledge.

Tomlinson J. (1993) *The Control of Education*. London: Cassell.

Trusted, J. (1987) *Moral Principles and Social Values*. London: Routledge and Kegan Paul.

Tysome, T. (1992) FE considers three-pronged quality model. *Times Higher Education Supplement* 28 February.

Ward, L. (1996) 'Abolish council', institute advises. *Times Educational Supplement* 15 November.

Wertsch, J. (1991) *Voices of the Mind*. London: Harvester Wheatsheaf.

Whitehead, M. (1996) Payment by results 'carries risks'. *Times Educational Supplement* 25 October.

White Paper (1994) *Competitiveness: Helping Business to Win*. London: HMSO.

White Paper (1995) *Competitiveness: Forging Ahead*. London: HMSO.

Whitty, G. (1990) The new right and the national curriculum; state control or market forces? In B. Moon (ed.), *New Curriculum – National Curriculum*. London: Hodder and Stoughton.

Williams, R. (1961) *The Long Revolution*. Harmondsworth: Penguin.

Zuboff, S. (1988) *In the Age of the Smart Machine: The Future of Work and Power*. New York: Basic Books.

Index